6th EDITION

A Critical Handbook of Children's Literature

Rebecca J. Lukens

Professor Emerita, Miami University
Oxford, Ohio

LONGMAN

An imprint of Addison Wesley Longman, Inc.

New York • Reading, Massachusetts • Menlo Park, California • Harlow, England
Don Mills, Ontario • Sydney • Mexico City • Madrid • Amsterdam

Acquisitions Editor: Ginny Blanford
Associate Editor: Arianne Weber
Marketing Manager: Renee Ortbals
Project Manager: Donna DeBenedictis
Design Manager and Text Designer: Rubina Yeh
Cover Designer: Kay Petronio
Cover Photo: PhotoDisc, Inc.
Prepress Services Supervisor: Valerie Vargas
Electronic Production Specialist: Joanne Del Ben
Print Buyer: Denise Sandler
Electronic Page Makeup: Joanne Del Ben/Sarah Johnson
Printer and Binder: The Maple-Vail Book Manufacturing Group
Cover Printer: Coral Graphic Services, Inc.

For permission to use copyrighted material, grateful acknowledgment is made to the copyright holders on pp. 363–365, which are hereby made part of this copyright page.

Library of Congress Cataloging-in-Publication Data

Lukens, Rebecca J. [date]
    A critical handbook of children's literature / Rebecca J. Lukens.
    —6th ed.
        p. cm.
    Includes bibliographical references and index.
    ISBN 0-321-00361-6 (pbk.)
    1. Children's literature—History and criticism.   I. Title.
PN1009.A1L84   1999
809'.89282—dc21   98-19333
                                                              CIP

Please visit our website at http://longman.awl.com

ISBN 0-321-00361-6

2345678910—MA—010099

Contents

To the Instructor

A *Critical Handbook of Children's Literature,* now in its sixth edition, has grown out of my conviction that literature for children differs from literature for adults in degree, not in kind, and that writing for children should be judged by the same standards as writing for adults. Children, like adults, read to explore the world, to escape the confining present, to discover themselves, to become someone else. Since adults—in the roles of teachers, librarians, or parents—help children choose books, we hope to put into their hands the best literature for these purposes.

What Is *A Critical Handbook of Children's Literature* Designed to Do?

The *Critical Handbook* is directed toward the college classroom audience of mature students who expect to work with children—whether as parents or teachers—but it does not stand alone as a classroom text. Like other handbooks, it accompanies another project, in this case the reading of a great many children's books. Only by reading thoughtfully a variety of stories, poems, biographies, and informational books for children does a student come to be acquainted with children's literature. And by applying critical criteria to these works, the student comes to evaluate them.

Loving children—important, surely—is not enough to make one an effective teacher of children. Being steeped in the literature written for them, however, reminds us of their natures and their concerns, and helps us to direct them toward pleasurable literary experiences, even to make of them lifetime readers. Setting standards for literature addressed to children and applying these standards to each selection sharpens students' critical skills at the same time as it familiarizes them with what's out there.

What Does the *Handbook Not* Do?

This is not a teaching methods book, and it absolutely does *not* recommend this way of "teaching books" to children. It may, however, suggest ways to talk with them about literature.

The *Handbook* does not provide book lists, although recommended titles—not definitive lists—are cited at the ends of chapters. The thoughtful student reads some of these, along with others not listed; determines their quality; and may or may not recommend titles to classmates.

The *Handbook* does not classify books as targeted toward specific age groups, because all of us know something of the infinite variety of interests and reading capabilities of children.

The *Handbook* does not discuss the developmental patterns of the average child.

Nor does it attempt to become an extensive anthology (of poetry, for example), but rather, once again, sets up criteria for readers to judge imaginative poetry and prose, biography, and informational books.

Reading the Classics of Children's Literature

One sure way for you, as an instructor in children's literature, to encourage argument is to tell an adult acquaintance that you teach children's literature, only to hear, "The classics, I hope!" Thinking you have someone interested in your field, you go on to say something like: "Well . . . yes, but sometimes books once called 'classics' don't interest today's children. Not all the books I was told were must-read classics interested me. How about you?" If the reply is honest, it may be, "Well-l-l, no-o-o-o," and conversation may continue, but it often stops at dead silence, or becomes an unwinnable argument.

As Peter Hunt says so well in his article "Passing on the Past: The Problem of Books That Are for Children and That Were for Children" (*Children's Literature Quarterly,* Winter 1996–97), some books *were* for children, and some of them *still are* for children. Yet many of the books we read, books by authors our parents did not know, spoke to us, and if they also speak to a later generation, our own children, they are on the way to becoming new classics. Using as examples the fairy tales, the Little House books, and *The Secret Garden,* Hunt notes that a number of onetime classics have been successfully dramatized, but only by making many significant changes in them. Such changes were essential to make them appeal to today's children whose lives and expectations are so different from those of past generations. Books that speak to children now are many and varied; some will become classics.

Hunt says several other significant things. He suggests, for example, that "in order to survive academically, 'Children's Literature' . . . has played the adult [literature] game, valuing history above the new challenges of literary interaction." Hunt's statement seems valid. College instructors understandably may become engrossed in the goals of academic acceptance, tenure, and promotion. Where pressure is strong for research and publication, instructors may feel that acceptance by their colleagues is possible only through historical or more "scholarly" approaches, or projects in contemporary critical theories. As each new critical theory becomes popular, the understandable pursuit of salary dollars and collegial acceptance prompts instructors to move away from their primary focus: teaching potential teachers and parents to make sound critical judgements about books, and to know and love the literature, old and new, that at this time speaks to children in their classrooms or their homes.

Consider, however, a responsibility to two audiences other than colleagues: college students who are teachers-in-training, and the children *they* will teach: We are teaching college students "Children's Literature" so that they may teach or recommend the best of that literature to children. In the college classroom we help potential teachers learn what makes a children's book good—good enough to read aloud to children in their classrooms, to spend classroom and library dollars on, to encourage reluctant readers to read, and to enlarge children's worlds so they will understand themselves and others. And to enjoy the whole process so that reading becomes a lasting pleasure.

Focusing on History and Critical Theory

Studying literary history and critical theory as they apply to literature for both adults and children belongs in a college classroom, to be sure. But that classroom syllabus is for an audience different from students who have a single classroom experience of children's literature and plan to work with children. The critical approach used in this text—which to some instructors may seem far too simple and intellectually undemanding—is the most basic one of all: formalist criticism, the study of the form literature takes. Furthermore, the text incorporates the techniques of the New Critic, who, in carefully examining literature, believes in its intrinsic worth and thus expands readers' perceptions and appreciation. This approach, too, seems highly relevant. And finally, reader-response theory, with its focus on the implied reader, is relevant here. Although all adults were once children, their responses may be so changed by the years that reading "like a child" is difficult, if not impossible. Observant adults, however, try out books with children and evoke their responses.

Other critical approaches are many. Applying psychological, mythological, and archetypal perspectives or phenomenological, socialist-Marxist, and structuralist approaches are interesting exercises relevant to the study of literary criticism as applied to all of literature. But if we care about the audience that teachers-in-training will face in their careers—including non-reading children—then examining children's stories under these critical approaches is less relevant. These future teachers need to know how to judge a book for children as they keep in mind the responses of their young classroom charges. Including reader-response theory seems the most useful method.

Thinking "Multiculturally"

North America, particularly the United States, nowadays is less frequently called "a melting pot." Perhaps that term was inaccurate even in the late nineteenth and early twentieth centuries, because often immigrant groups did not melt into a great "pot of soup." As each immigrant group arrived, it frequently settled into its own geographic area, urban or rural, and then divided into those who wanted to be assimilated—advocates of a great "soup" of Americans—and a smaller number who wished to maintain their ethnicity through their language, folklore, religious services, and ethnic traditions. Maintenance of group identity has led to what has been called the creation, not of a soup, but of a "salad" of ethnic groups.

The recent focus on multiculturalism seems to me to be part of that "salad" idea. Children of newly arriving immigrants are caught in the ambiguity of their new North American identities. Maintaining the traditions of their origins is important for them and their parents, and reading literature about their origins is thus helpful. At the same time, children whose forebears have long been assimilated may be curious and wish to know about the traditions and beliefs of their new friends and classmates. Since we are now in the midst of great societal change—perhaps moving toward a true melting pot continent—it seems wise that young readers know something of the cultural origins of our many ethnic groups.

New immigrants and those born here have two things in common: their respect for democratic institutions and their common language. Reading about other cultures broadens that common ground. With that in mind, the *Critical Handbook* in its sixth edition includes far more multicultural examples of literature for children than have earlier editions.

Reading Aloud to Children

It is tempting in this sixth edition of the *Handbook* to add a chapter on reading aloud. But in the interest of keeping the book somewhat close to handbook size (it grows longer with each new edition), consider the many books and journal articles on reading aloud. For example, Jim Trelease fostered belief in the importance of reading aloud with his *Read Aloud Handbook. Children's Literature in the Classroom: Weaving Charlotte's Web,* edited by Janet Hickman and Bernice A. Cullinan, includes an article called "'Please Don't Stop There!': The Power of Reading Aloud." Barbara Friedberg and Elizabeth Strong present strong arguments for the cause.

Reading aloud does not stop with elementary-grade children. A substitute teacher, finding that her ninth-grade charges were reading a much truncated version of *A Tale of Two Cities,* decided to show the class what they were missing. She read aloud Dickens's uncut chapter, with its caricatures, its vividly shown actions, its humorous comments on individual behaviors and social mores; the severely cut story was not the story itself, any more than an outline of a history chapter is the chapter itself. That substitute's wish was that a few students would go on to discover the whole of the story.

The benefits of reading aloud begin early and may continue throughout life.

Changes to the Sixth Edition

This edition includes many new titles; it also places the chapter on picture books earlier in the text. A revised chapter on major literary genres delineates the common elements of literature and demonstrates how each genre may emphasize or rely upon one element more than others. Main points are provided in a chart to help readers more easily spot possible shortcomings of a story and pinpoint particularly significant elements. Some readers may find the chart useful; others may find it too simplistic, a common problem when one tries to quantify or make an abstraction concrete. Use the chart with caution.

Other revised chapters focus on the elements common to all imaginative literature—character, plot, theme, setting, point of view, style, and tone. These terms are explained simply and clearly and are illustrated with new or lasting examples from all genres of children's literature. Although these terms are the critical tools and basic vocabulary we use to discuss and evaluate any piece of imaginative literature, writing for children presents some special concerns and problems; chapters that discuss an element of imaginary narrative literature conclude with a discussion of such matters.

The chapter on informational books contains updated examples, but does not deal with periodicals or reference materials. As for reading levels, they are available in the reviewing media. Furthermore, no substitute exists for an awareness of individual differences in the interests and capabilities of children. As any "kidwatcher" knows, children are different, not only at different ages, but also because their consuming interests one month may be succeeded by new fascinations in the next. The bored child considered uneducable by a third-grade teacher may be hiding *Kon Tiki* behind a spelling book. And tales of illiterate high school graduates continue to surface.

The Glossary, of course, defines literary terms. The updated appendixes include lists of award-winning titles, children's magazines, and publications that review children's literature.

Also new to this edition is the following section "To the student." You might want to assign it as an introduction to the course and this book.

Some Final Remarks

During the planning stages of this sixth edition, I have been grateful for numerous comments and suggestions offered by instructors who have used earlier editions. Some have suggested the addition of new chapters, while others have hoped the book would not become forbiddingly long or turn into a teaching methods text. Some have suggested changing and rearranging genre descriptions, while others have hoped that they would stay as they were. Unfortunately but obviously, not all such suggestions can be followed. Including more current titles as examples is important; however, keeping abreast of the very newest is not always possible when a manuscript is due many months before the book is available to instructors. It seems inevitable that changes will please some readers and disappoint others. I can only hope that I have reached a suitable compromise.

One further note: Instructors might wish to assign reading of *Charlotte's Web* early in the term, perhaps even before assigning Chapter 4. Other books frequently mentioned throughout the text as examples might be assigned at appropriate times.

Each time, as I prepare a new edition of the handbook, I immerse myself once again in literature for children and am thrilled and astonished to find that it gets better and better. When I first began working on the *Critical Handbook* twenty years ago, my search for the truly fine was far less rewarding. Now, because this handbook simply cannot mention all of the many works that have pleased and satisfied me, I must confine myself to mentioning just a few of the multitude of fine books published for children. I can only hope that those I have selected are representative of the best. Readers must add their own titles.

One caution as you open this new edition: I make no effort to provide reading lists. My focus is to help readers understand how to make critical judgments; such training will increase the consciousness with which a student-reader employs the techniques of evaluation. Reading lists, furthermore, are available in a number of magazines and journals. Some of the reviewing media and monthly publications that keep abreast of the new are listed in Appendix C.

Acknowledgments

For indefatigable assistance, I thank the librarians of the children's department of the Lane Public Library in Oxford, Ohio, particularly Terry Beck and Patsy Grabach. For reviews and suggestions, I thank the following:

Grace A. Balwit, George Fox University

Fran Bender, University of Tennessee at Chattanooga

Barbara L. Devens, University of Rhode Island

Ellen Jampole, State University of New York College at Cortland

Judith V. Lechner, Auburn University

Mary J. Lickteig, University of Nebraska at Omaha

Amy McClure, Ohio Wesleyan University

R. Craig Roney, Wayne State University

Louise Stearns, Southern Illinois University

Deanna L. Strackbein, University of North Dakota

Virginia A. Walter, University of California, Los Angeles

For their suggestions and frequent letters of support, I am once again grateful to my many colleagues, whom I call friends—those who have used earlier editions of *A Critical Handbook of Children's Literature*.

Rebecca J. Lukens

To the Student

A Critical Handbook of Children's Literature is committed to the idea expressed by the children's poet Walter de la Mare: "Nothing but the best in anything is good enough for the young." Within that guideline, learning to make critical judgements about what constitutes "the best" that is "good enough" is everything. Of the many ways to examine and judge literature, readers' responses to its forms and effects seems the most sensible, simple as it is. Throughout the book, the forms of literature and the elements called character, plot, theme, setting, point of view, style, and tone are explained and exemplified; criteria for judging fiction, poetry, and nonfiction for child readers and listeners are suggested.

The *Handbook* responds to the recent emphasis placed on using children's literature in virtually all areas of the curriculum. This emphasis responds to the "whole language" philosophy, which Ken Goodman describes as freeing "the minds and creative energies of pupils for the greatest gains in their intellectual, physical and social development." Building on Dewey's age-old reminder that we start "where the learner is in time, place, culture, and development," the philosophy suggests that once children are exposed to reading, the decoding process has more meaning for them if they find attractive *what* they read.

Louise Rosenblatt, a pioneer in insisting that the best literature should be the substance of reading, believes that reading is a transaction and that the aesthetic experience (thinking, feeling, and experiencing) of reading literature must be recognized. My own terms for this transaction or aesthetic experience can best be described as the experiences of pleasure and understanding. Thus, Rosenblatt and I agree. To this description of the reading experience, Rosenblatt adds another: "Efferent" refers to the acquisition of information through reading, a concept that reinforces my own thinking, particularly regarding nonfiction.

Despite our differing terms, we agree that reading takes readers where they are with what they have experienced, and thus agree that different readers have different transactions. For example, most students when reading *Charlotte's Web* by E. B. White react pleasurably to the understanding gained about emotions, thoughts, and behavior. Other students—perhaps only a single student—might limit an interpretation of the same story to elucidation of what a general farm is like—even noting the science lesson in how the different parts of a spider's jointed leg enable it to spin a web. In Rosenblatt's terms, the group stresses the private aesthetic experience of understanding, while the single student focuses on the public element, the efferent or informative one. Whatever our terms, I am delighted that elementary teachers are giving children greater pleasure than ever by encouraging them to read literature that involves and pleases them.

But how can we choose "the rarest kind of best" (to quote Walter de la Mare) from the approximately five thousand children's books published each year, as well as from the thousands that remain in print year after year? What are the standards we can confidently apply in evaluating writing for children? We may have felt amused and touched when we read *Charlotte's Web,* but how do we discuss it or decide its literary worth beyond these vague feelings?

Why learn to make critical judgements? Because, although the techniques of judgement may in themselves be ordinary, an increased awareness of them is in itself valuable training. When we say a hearty "I like it!" we may be responding to believable and interesting characters or to something we know is true about people. When we are disappointed in a book—"I don't like it!"—we may be rejecting the story's action as too coincidental or its dialogue as too stilted. Learning to recognize such literary elements as character and plot and theme helps us understand the effects a writer achieves and appreciate the reasons for his or her choices. After all, Peter Rabbit in the Beatrix Potter tale and Rabbit in *Winnie-the-Pooh* are not the same, nor does the setting for *The Wind in the Willows* have the same effect on us as the setting for *Julie of the Wolves.* We could say fairly easily *how* they are different, but we need to go beyond that and say *why* they must be different. Why did the authors make the choices they made, and what are the effects of those choices on us as readers? This knowledge helps us discover the reasons for our emotional responses. It sharpens our perceptions and increases our enjoyment of reading. To use a familiar analogy, do we go to the football game merely to find out who won, or also to enjoy the plays and ploys that determine the winning score? In the same way, do we read only to find out how the story comes out? Or do we also take delight in the people, in the shifts and turns of events along the way, in the words that tingle our spines or quicken our pulses, and in discovering something about ourselves?

Reading the Classics
of Children's Literature

The sacred terms "classic" and "award-winner" frequently get us in trouble. Perhaps it is wise to remember how as children we were sometimes bored by the classics of our parents' generation. I remember my mother steering me toward a classic of her youth, Booth Tarkington's *Seventeen*. As a voracious reader and a dutiful daughter, I read it, but thought to myself, "This is a classic?" It said nothing to me. I loved our beautiful collie, but pulling a milk wagon was not his assignment; *Dog of Flanders* was for children of another era. But when my mother (also my teacher) pointed me toward other books also called classics—*Tom Sawyer, Little Women,* or *Treasure Island*—that was a different matter. My parents' classics came from another day, and some, but not all, met the child I was.

An older student in my children's literature class once proudly told me that her eight-year-old son was in a "high achiever" class and that they were now reading *Moby Dick*. It seemed to me that both she and that classroom teacher were failing to make a distinction between the capacity to decode, sound out, or recognize words and the capacity to understand and take into oneself the significant ideas being "read." *Moby Dick*, a classic, was never for children, but that able eight-year-old, when introduced to books that speak to today's children, might profit in ways other than having his accomplishments become honor badges for his mother. The first profit might even be newfound pleasure in ideas, and in characters who are his contemporaries—rather than merely the pleasure of decoding. Once again, it's a matter of audience. Just as good books of the past, written for children *then*, may say nothing to children *now*, so adult classics may say nothing to children, "readable" though they may be.

Examining Literature Carefully

Why not just read books for children and skip the evaluative process? Because without criteria for excellence, instructors merely turn students training to be teachers loose in the library or bookstore to learn very little beyond "what's out there."

And why the frequent references to *The Tale of Peter Rabbit* and *Charlotte's Web*? Because it is easier to speak about criteria if all students in the classroom have in common at least two books that all have read.

Failing to apply critical standards to children's literature implies that children's literature is inferior to adult literature and that children will not benefit from good literature. But if literature of poor or mediocre quality is all children meet, they may be persuaded that reading is both boring and useless. This handbook takes the other view: With some small differences, literature for children should be judged by the same standards as literature for adults. Children can benefit by becoming lifetime readers when their earliest exposure is to literature of high quality.

Occasionally an instructor whose field is literature or the arts is told that "picking the work apart" destroys both the work and the audience's pleasure in it. The response I once heard from concert pianist Eleanore Vail lecturing about music appreciation seems to apply here: "You and I both love music, but I truly believe that what I know about it vastly increases my appreciation of it." The *Handbook,* as it helps to examine literature, increases appreciation. That appreciation travels from the college classroom to children.

Reading Aloud to Children

The capacity to understand language separates us from other living creatures. That capacity begins in infancy with hearing one's parents converse and continues throughout life. Nothing a parent does for a child's intellectual and social growth is more important than talking to—or by extension, reading aloud to—a small child. Delight in language begins with the repetitions and songs of nursery rhymes and continues with picture books and other stories.

As the child grows, still other rewards of literature continue to accrue. Not only does a child's knowledge of vocabulary and language structure grow through being read to, but also the capacity to be human, to understand others, to satisfy curiosity, to recognize and express compassion, to see cause and effect, to wish for justice and to seek independence, to awaken empathy. All this—and much more—begins with ideas gained through being read to.

A parent who brings a small child to the library is doing a good thing. But telling the child, "You can read now. Choose your own books," shuts off many advantages. Believing that reading aloud is no longer necessary or important when a six-year-old can read is a mistake. New meanings, new relationships, ideas too big or too subtle for words of two syllables but interesting and valuable nonetheless—these are often available only by an adult's reading aloud. In addition, the encircling arm of an older family member presents an opportunity for intimacy that bonds child to adult and adds to pleasurable memories of words and people and family closeness. Furthermore, through reading aloud, strange and larger worlds; new and wonderful people, places, and things; complex emotions and unfamiliar reactions all appear. Together, they constitute intellectual and emotional growth.

Considering Lists of "Children's Favorites"

A final word about children's favorites. It is always useful to learn which books children truly love. Although sometimes stories tied in with the screen dramatizations seem to dominate such lists, we may also be pleased to discover that some favorites are truly fine books. No harm—just delight—in that discovery. The Babysitters and the Goosebumps, like Nancy Drew, the Rover Boys, and Elsie Dinsmore of even earlier days, may have their day, and no doubt similar series will take their places. But meanwhile, learning to judge children's books will increase competence in buying, recommending, and reading aloud literature for children. As children thus discover literature that is even better than some of their current favorites, pleasures of all kinds continue.

When nothing but the best is good enough for the young, everyone wins.

Rebecca J. Lukens

A Critical Handbook of Children's Literature

Charlotte's Web
E. B. White (ill. Garth Williams)

CHAPTER | **1**

Literature:
What Is It?

Any words in printed form—articles, pamphlets, books—are called "literature" by some people. How does the literature we examine and evaluate here differ from all other printed matter?

We pick up *People* magazine at the drug store, *TV Guide* in the supermarket, and *National Geographic* in the doctor's office to give us information and vicarious experience, but they are not literature. Literature *may* give us information and vicarious experience, but it also gives us much more. What sets a chapter in *The Wind in the Willows* apart from a *National Geographic* article on the plant and animal life of the English countryside? Many things, and they are at the heart of our definition of literature. Sometimes called *belles lettres,* literature is traditionally described as the body of writing that exists because of inherent imaginative and artistic qualities. The fine line drawn between literature and writing that is primarily scientific, intellectual, or philosophical—or, in Louise Rosenblatt's terms, aesthetic or efferent—often wavers.

Why do we adults pick up and read a novel or a collection of poetry? For *pleasure*—not to find a lesson in ecology, not to be taught about the natural habitat of the armadillo or about sailing in Colonial America. We choose literature that promises entertainment and, sometimes, escape. If other discoveries come to us too, we are pleased and doubly rewarded. However, our first motive for reading a novel or a poem is personal pleasure. We may lay the book aside with mixed feelings, but if there is no pleasure, we reject it completely or leave it unfinished. For adults who have had a variety of experiences, who have known success and failure, who have had to decide what is "good" and what is "bad," who have had to face their own shaky standards of morality, the nature of pleasure in literature may be different from that for children.

Because we are all different, the pleasures we seek as well as those we may encounter may be very personal. But what is required of us as critical readers is that we examine the pleasure the work aspires to give, the real subject of literary criticism. To paraphrase critic Frank Kermode, it is the function of the writer to make sense out of life, but the function of the critic to evaluate the writer's efforts to make sense out of life. We may restate that argument to say that we as critical readers do not stop with our personal pleasure: "I like it, and that's so personal that it cannot be debated." We go on, instead, to find in the work the sources of that personal enjoyment. To our surprise, they may lie in a painful recognition of ourselves, a satisfying verification of our humanness, or in variations of the great questions of the philosopher Immanuel Kant: What must I know? What should I be? What can I hope? But some kind of pleasure is essential, whether the reader is eight or forty-eight years old.

Literature provides a second reward: *understanding.* This understanding comes from the exploration of the "human condition," the revelation of human nature, the discovery of humankind. It is not explicitly the function of literature, either for children or for adults, to try to reform human beings, or to set up guidelines for behavior; however, it is the province of literature to observe and to comment, to open individuals and their society for our observation and our understanding. If there is any question about what we are to understand, notice that our terms are "human" and "humankind," synonyms for "people."

As for information, it may or may not contribute to understanding. We may know a person's height, weight, hair color, ethnic background, and occupation—this is information. But until we are aware of temperament, anxieties, joys, and ambitions, we do not *know* that person. Information is not a person; spirit is.

Information is part of the story, and when we see it, we expect it to be relevant. The following passage from *Roll of Thunder, Hear My Cry* by Mildred Taylor, for example, contains both summarized and detailed information. Here is Christmas morning:

> In addition to the books there was a sockful of once-a-year store-bought licorice, oranges, and bananas for each of us and from Uncle Hammer a dress and a sweater for me, and a sweater and a pair of pants each for Christopher John and Little Man. But nothing compared to the books. Little Man, who treasured clothes above all else, carefully laid his new pants and sweaters aside and dashed for a clean sheet of brown paper to make a cover for his book, and throughout the day as he lay upon the deerskin rug looking at the bright, shining pictures of faraway places,

Literature is not expected to reform.

turning each page as if it were gold, he would suddenly squint down at his hands, glance at the page he had just turned, then dash into the kitchen to wash again—just to make sure.

The purpose of the paragraph, however, is not merely to tell about the Christmas presents, but to reveal something about the characters and their lives. Here is a family devoted to reading, to education, to learning about the world beyond. Books are precious, so precious that they must be protected, and only clean hands may touch them. The home is simply furnished with a deerskin rug that must have been carefully skinned and cured for use. The family values appearance and takes good care of their and clothing, not taking it for granted; clothes are important as special Christmas gifts, as are fresh fruit and licorice. Information alone without its contributing to understanding is not, by our traditional definition, literature.

Then perhaps a narrative of people acting in a way we can understand is all that is necessary to make literature. No, that is not the case. We may have a short account with understandable action called "Kevin Visits the A&P," and yet it may not qualify as literature. While Kevin's visit might conceivably tell us something about the nature of childhood, it just as easily might not. The grocery store situation provides vivid details about prices and cuts of meat and varieties of vegetables, and the action may be credible because Mother chooses a ripe cantaloupe and pays at the checkout counter. However, the significance of the experience in terms of the characters' lives may be lacking—significance that helps us, whatever our age, to understand a little more about ourselves and others. In the most general terms, then, literature is reading that, by means of imaginative and artistic qualities, provides pleasure and understanding.

To return to the comparison of the *National Geographic* article and *The Wind in the Willows:* We can feel fairly certain that we read the *National Geographic* article primarily for information, and we can also be reasonably sure that we read *The Wind in the Willows* primarily for pleasure; our second reward is understanding.

Literature has many other more specific appeals for us as readers. Literature *shows human motives* for what they are, inviting the reader to identify with or to react to a fictional character. We see into the mind of the character, or into the subconscious that even the character does not know. Through the writer's careful choice of details from the past, the current environment, and the imaginary world of the character, we come to see clearly the character's motivation for action. If in these chosen details we see some similarity to our own lives, we nod our heads and identify with the character, feeling that we understand the motives and can justify the deeds. Or seeing the error in judgment that the character fails to see, we understand. Seeing motives we disapprove of, we condemn, or seeing a reflection of our own mistakes, we are compassionate.

Our *touchstone*[1] book, E. B. White's *Charlotte's Web,* the story that will serve us as a critical standard and a frequent example, shows one character, Wilbur, at one moment crying out: "I don't want to die! Save me, somebody! Save me!" However, months later his motive for action is selfless concern:

> "Templeton . . . I will make you a solemn promise. Get Charlotte's egg sac for me, and from now on I will let you eat first, when Lurvy slops me. I will let you have your choice of everything in the trough and I won't touch a thing until you're through."

On the other hand, Charlotte's motives are born of pure sympathy and a desire to help Wilbur's suffering. She says briskly that Wilbur will not die, and she weaves words into her web until late at night. Our identification with each response to Wilbur's life-and-death crises varies as our experience varies.

Literature may also ***provide form for experience.*** Aside from birth and death, real life has no beginnings or endings, but is instead a series of stories without order, each story merging with all other stories. Fiction, however, makes order of randomness by organizing events and consequences, cause and effect, beginning and ending. When we look back on our lives, we notice the high spots: "the first time we met," or even "the day we sold the Buick station wagon." What once seemed trivial now, with the perspective given by distance in time, seems important. When we look back, we do not look at sequence, since chronology is merely the random succession of life's disordered events. Literature, however, by placing the relevant episodes—"and the next time we met"—into coherent sequence, gives order and form to experience.

In *Charlotte's Web* White selects events that, among other things, demonstrate the purpose in Charlotte's life. When she says, "By helping you, perhaps I was trying to lift up my life a trifle," we see more clearly the pattern of Charlotte's behavior. While she accepts the inevitability of death, she does not accept the prospect of passive waiting. Charlotte chooses instead to fill her days with order and purpose. As White directs our thoughts and alters our feelings in a chosen course, he gives form to the experience of the ongoing cycle of life.

Literature also may ***reveal life's fragmentation.*** Not a day goes by without our being pulled in one direction after another by the demands of friendship—"Please help." Of obligation—"I promised I would." Of pressure—"It's due tomorrow." And of money—"I wish I could afford it." Life is fragmented, and our daily experience proves it. However, literature, while it may remind us of our own and society's fragmentation, does not leave us there. Literature sorts the world into disparate segments we can identify and examine; friendship, greed, family, sacrifice, childhood, love, advice, old age, treasures, snobbery, and compassion are set before us for close observation. Little, if anything, is outside the province of literature.

While literature may be saying or revealing that life is fragmented, it simultaneously *helps us focus on essentials.* May Sarton, a writer of adult fiction, says that her books are born of questions she needs to answer for herself. "Art is order, but it is made out of the chaos of life." This chaos reordered, experience given form, permits us to experience with different intensity but with new understanding the parts of life that we have known: We exclaim, "That's how it happened to me, too!" Or parts we have yet to meet: "Do you suppose I'll ever get my diploma?" Or experiences we may never have: "What must it be like to live in a camp for refugees or in an internment camp?" In the process of giving order to life, the writer sorts out the essential details from the nonessential. Undistracted by irrelevant experiences or minor anxieties, the reader focuses upon the essentials of action, people, events, and stresses. In retrospect, we see that life does not distribute events in order of their mounting intensity or their accumulative effects upon us. Literature, however, because it ignores the irrelevant and focuses on the essentials, makes significance clear. As we read, our detachment helps us to see events and their possible influences. We can know the challenge of making choices, feel the excitement of suspense, and glow with the pride of accomplishment. Literature *says* that life is fragmented. What it *does* is something else: Literature provides a sense of life's unity and meaning.

Literature can *reveal the institutions of society.* Every week we become aware of a new regulation in our personal lives—a higher tax on gasoline, a no-left-turn sign where we have always turned left, or the disappearance of our favorite Tuesday night TV show. A group of people called an institution, something bigger than we are, makes a judgment, and a form of institutional control determines for us something we would like to determine for ourselves. The institutions of society—like government, family, church, and school, as well as forces that shape our jobs—urge and coerce us into conforming to standards. Institutions occasionally seem so threatening, in fact, that we fear they will close in on our lives, restricting us completely. Yet we know that some restrictions establish the order needed for a group to survive. In this way necessary institutions are born and grow. Literature clarifies our reactions to institutions by showing appropriate circumstances where people give in to or struggle against them.

In the institution called farming, for example, it is unprofitable to keep a runt pig, because fattening him will not pay a good return on the dollar. In *Charlotte's Web,* within Wilbur's conflict with an institution, we see what a life-and-death struggle does to an immature innocent. We may not literally identify with Wilbur—since it is highly unlikely we will ever be commodities on an exchange market—but his struggle for life is nonetheless somewhat similar to our own. Wilbur soon discovers who his friends are, how resourceful they can be, how hard they will work for another's safety, and even, in Templeton's case, what a person's price may be. Through Wilbur's struggle with profitable farming we discover in a small way the impersonal nature of society. In other stories we may discover that racism is institutionalized, or that although we individually hate war, it is ordered by a body larger than we are. The variety of such conflicts seems infinite.

Not only do institutions affect our lives, but nature does, too. Some literature *reveals nature as a force* that influences us. Tornadoes on the summer plains, avalanches in the springtime Rockies, hurricanes in the tropical Caribbean, blizzards on the Dakota prairies—we read of them each year, season by season, region by region. Nature constantly reminds us of its effects upon our lives. People's natural environment influences them, whether it be the stress of wind that wearies nerves, intense heat that produces lethargy, or extreme cold and sunlessness that depress spirits. Literature, by presenting human beings involved in conflict with such forces, makes us see their effects upon human life.

Gary Paulsen's *Dogsong* shows Russel running his dogs as he searches for his own song:

> Running in the dark, even in the tight dark of the north where there is no moon, it is possible to see out ahead a great distance. The snow-ice is white-blue in the dark and if there is no wind to blow the snow around, everything shows up against the white. . . . Now, suddenly, there was a dark line ahead of the lead dog. A dark line followed by a black space on the snow, an opening of the ice. A lead of open water, so wide Russel could not see across.

Nature is a force affecting human beings, sometimes demanding that they exert all their powers against it. Although struggling cannot conquer nature, human beings may struggle heroically and yet not be conquered. In such a conflict, the reader can applaud the human will.

Literature provides vicarious experience. It is impossible for us to live any life but our own, in any time but our own life span, or in any space or place but our own. But literature makes it possible for us to live in the time of the French Revolution, in the period of the Vikings, or during the days of the American colonies. Through a good story, we can live in a small river town on the Mississippi, in the hold of a slave ship, in the hills of Appalachia, or even in a castle turret. The possibilities for us to live lives other than our own are infinite, as numerous as the books on the library shelves.

Finally, literature forces us, leads us, entices, or woos us into *meeting a writer-creator* whose medium, words, we know; whose subject, human nature, we live with; whose vision, life's meaning, we hope to understand. We are the student-novice before the artist. In the hands of a gifted writer, we turn from being passive followers into passionate advocates calling new followers. The writer's skill with words gives us a pleasure we want to share, and an understanding we have an urge to spread.

We might say that literature, because it is not an accurate duplicate of life, is lies, all lies. But through "lying," a story may express great truth; through refusing to recount life as it is, the fiction transforms and transcends, adding something to life, remaking, embellishing, or opening it for examination. Events translated into words—life written, not lived—constitute a profound modification, and become a momentary substitute for life, an experience of life different from our own. As novelist Mario Vargas Llosa says, fiction, "by spurring the imagination, both temporarily assuages human dissatisfaction and simultaneously incites it."[2]

Literature for Children

Children are not little adults. They are different from adults in experience, but not in species, or to put it differently, in degree but not in kind. We can say then of literature for young readers that it differs from literature for adults in degree but not in kind. We sometimes forget that literature for children can and should provide the same enjoyment and understanding as does literature for adults. Children, too, seek pleasure from a story, but the sources of their pleasure are more limited. Since their experiences are more limited, children may not understand the same complexity of ideas. Since their understanding is more limited, the expression of ideas must be simpler—both in language and in form. Related to the necessity for simplicity in the expression of ideas are vocabulary and attention span. Stories are more directly told, with fewer digressions and more obvious relationships between characters and actions, or between characters themselves. Children are both more and less literal than adults. They may find discrepancies between two descriptions of a setting and hold the writer accountable for error. On the other hand, children may accept the fantastic more readily than many adults. As long as the world itself is so remarkably complex and incomprehensible, one more fantastic experience in story form presents no impossible hurdle. Often, for example, the personified animals and toys of the child's world, by behaving like human beings, may show what human beings are like. Children are frequently more open to experimenting with a greater variety of literary forms than many adults will accept—from poetry to folktales, from adventure to fantasy.

The many discoveries that children can make through literature might be sought in other ways by adults. Adults might discover human motivation through a study of psychology, or the nature of society and its institutions through a study of sociology, or the impact of nature upon human behavior through a study of anthropology. However, literature can do all of these things for children. Literature is more than a piece of writing that clarifies; it gives the child pleasure as well as understanding. Throughout the pages that follow we will refer to literature as "a significant truth expressed in appropriate elements and memorable language." As we shall discover, the ideas expressed in poetic form, the truths of theme and character explored through the elements of fiction, and the style of the artist with words constitute literature.

Summary

Literature at its best gives both pleasure and understanding. It explores the nature of human beings, the condition of humankind. If these phrases seem too pompous and abstract for children's literature, rephrase them in children's terms:

What are people like?

Why are they like that?

What do they need?

What makes them do what they do?

The answers, or mere glimpses of answers to these questions, are made visible in poetry or in fiction by the elements of plot, character, point of view, setting, tone, and style of an imaginative work; together they constitute literature. Words are merely words, but real literature for any age is words chosen with skill and artistry to give the readers pleasure and to help them understand themselves and others.

Notes

1. A touchstone is a test criterion, or standard; the meaning is derived from the use of a stone as a comparison to detect the purity of silver and gold. Matthew Arnold, using the term in literary criticism, wrote: "There can be no more useful help for discovering what poetry belongs to the class of the truly excellent . . . than to have always in one's mind lines and expressions of the great masters and to apply them as a touchstone to other poetry."

2. Mario Vargas Llosa, "Is Fiction the Art of Lying?" *New York Times Book Review*, October 7, 1984, p. 40.

Recommended Books Cited in This Chapter

GRAHAME, KENNETH. *The Wind in the Willows*. 1908 reprint. New York: Scribners, 1953.

O'DELL, SCOTT. *Island of the Blue Dolphins*. Boston: Houghton Mifflin, 1960.

PAULSEN, GARY. *Dogsong*. New York: Macmillan, 1983.

TAYLOR, MILDRED. *Roll of Thunder, Hear My Cry*. New York: Dial, 1976.

WHITE, E. B. *Charlotte's Web*. New York: Harper, 1952.

Where the Buffaloes Begin
Olaf Baker (ill. Stephen Gammell)

2

Genre in Children's Literature

What does each of the genres contribute to the child reader?

L   ike adult literature, children's literature offers variety. It is not uni-
        form, created with cookie-cutter sameness. We recognize rhymes
        and fairy tales, fantasies and lyrics, and realistic stories about other
countries as well as our own. These and other kinds of literature we sometimes call "genres."

A discussion of genre in literature must begin with an effort to define
the term—not a simple task. A **genre** is a kind or type of literature that has
a common set of characteristics. As soon as we have said this, however, we
face the fact that we can identify as many differences and variations among
examples of a given genre as we can find similarities. Classification is easiest
when each class or group possesses clear-cut, unchanging characteristics.
The chemist's chart of the elements provides a helpful analogy. In fact,
when an element is found that lacks the qualities to fit it precisely into any
category, or that possesses additional qualities, a new class must be added.
While this may work for classification in chemistry, it does not work so
clearly in literature. If, for example, we divide literature into prose and poetry, where do we place rhythmic but nonmetrical writing spaced on the
page in "poetic" line length? Is this kind of work poetic prose because it
lacks meter or regular beat? Or is it prose-poetry because it is filled with
sensory appeals and figurative language? Furthermore, if we decide that a
work is poetry we might go one step further since, for example, both lyric
and sonnet are themselves genres. Yet both are poetry. Must we
subdivide?[1] Genres are not always clear-cut and easily distinguished; the
terms are often used loosely. Today, genre distinctions, although helpful,
are often seen as arbitrary.

Opinions differ about classifications, although each of us may have several reasons for our opinions. Some people may find it unnecessary even to mention genres; others like the sense of order that genre classification provides. For our purposes, the term "genre" can be useful in organizing our discussion of children's literature. First, it helps us to be aware that there is more literature for children than one finds in the familiar genres of stories and nursery rhymes. Second, the literary elements we will be talking about in the following chapters—tone, setting, and others—function differently in different genres. And third, we should be sensitive to the broad and rich variety of literature available to children so that we can help them sample it.

For our purposes we will try to use "genre" in a way that is clear and useful, discussing here the kinds of literature that are most commonly written for or read to children and that are complete art forms when read. Since drama is complete only when staged and viewed, it is not discussed here. In Chapter 11, "From Rhyme to Poetry," we note kinds of poems from folk rhyme to lyric, but in this chapter we look at the kinds, types, or genres of fiction: realistic fiction, with subgenres of animal, historical, and regional realism; fantasy, with subgenres of fantastic stories, high fantasy, and science fiction; and traditional stories, with subgenres of fables, folktales, myths, legends, and folk epics.

All elements of literature are included in each of the major genres of fiction, but within each type one element may be more significant than another. In some cases the genre demands that a particular element be strong or well developed; without that strength, the credibility of the story may be in question. For example, animal realism requires an objective point of view, for we cannot know what an animal—a real animal, not a personified one—is thinking. Historical fiction, to cite another example, relies for credibility upon a clear sense of setting in a past time. And again, since folktales have been told orally from one generation to another, descriptions of setting or details of a character's past or a character's thoughts merely delay the telling. When we listen to a folktale, flat characters seem appropriate, because we recognize them immediately and can move quickly into the action.

The genres, then, are both distinct and overlapping; they contain all elements but in varying combinations and degrees. The chart at the end of this chapter may be a helpful guide, showing how elements relate to the specific genres. Refer to it cautiously, however, knowing that literature is not governed by rigid rules.

Realism

Realism means that a story is possible, although not necessarily probable. Effect follows cause without the intervention of the magical or supernatural. In *Did You Carry the Flag Today, Charley?* by Rebecca Caudill,

---

Genre makes us aware of more literature for children than simple stories and nursery rhymes.

Possible is not the same as probable.

Charley is rewarded because he helped out in the library, not because a fairy godmother intervened. The outcome seems reasonable and plausible; the story is a representation of action that seems truthful. Realistic stories have in common several characteristics: they are fictional narratives with characters who are involved in some kind of action that holds our interest, set in some possible place and time. Once again, keep in mind that if we divide realistic fiction into subgenres the divisions may at times seem to overlap.

Realistic Stories

Problem realism and social issues realism, which are similar in their focus upon problems, were popular twenty years ago; their situations are realistic or possible. The problems are not universal, like searching for friendship, but personal and particular, like being a foster child in *The Great Gilly Hopkins* by Katherine Paterson, or having a retarded sibling as in *Summer of the Swans* by Betsy Byars. Novels about social issues showed the character—usually the **protagonist,** or central character—encountering a kind of problem engendered by society, like discrimination because of race, gender, or social position.

The protagonist's problem is the source of plot and conflict, and that conflict may be with self, society, or another person. In a well-written book, character and conflict are both well developed and interrelated. In a poorly written novel, the character may either be stereotyped or may seem to be made up only of problems so overwhelming that they blot out the credibility of the character as a whole human being made up of a mixture of feelings and thoughts, emotion, and intellect. In poor fiction, the protagonist's problems may be solved in too pat a manner. Such fictional solutions can not only be simplistic and sentimental, but also lack reality and justice. In real life, difficulties are not solved quickly or easily. Readers who identify with the characters may find false hope for their own solutions; readers who observe the problem-ridden character may become condescending. "What's bothering my friend? Look how easy it is in this book!" Such simplistic solutions may then result in false themes or ideas like "Any problem is easily solved" or "Work hard and everything always comes out all right." Difficulty, after all, is natural to a complex problem. *A Hero Ain't Nothin' but a Sandwich* by Alice Childress, in which Benjie struggles with drug addiction, provides an example of a more credible truth: "Despite love and care, a big problem is not easily solved."

Cynthia Voigt's *Dicey's Song,* for example, tells of children whose problems are significant and, in a less well written novel, might seem insurmountable. Dicey has led her four siblings to Maryland from Massachusetts, where they have left their mother in a mental hospital, to seek the grandmother about whom they have just learned. Without money or parents, they settle in with Gram, who reaches out for the help that is available for food, clothing, tutoring, part-time jobs, and even old memories that

In a well-written book, character and conflict are both well developed and interrelated.

become useful rather than bitter. The reality of the family and their friends convinces us of the seriousness of their problems, and the difficulty with which the problems are handled and solutions found convinces the reader. Tough questions have no easy answers.

Tone or attitude are also affected when the novel is poorly written. Works become sensational when, to hold readers' interest, the writer so loads the story with problems that the situation is incredible and the novel becomes sensational and unbelievable.

While all elements are important in realism, we notice particularly the elements of theme, character, and conflict. If such fiction is to help us understand ourselves and others, we must find soundly developed characters and believable conflicts.

Animal Realism

Animal realism remains true to animal nature.

Nonfiction that evokes a thoroughly efferent response should deal accurately with animals, telling the details of their appearances, their habitats, and their life cycles. Animal realism as fiction adds another dimension by giving continuity and conflict or adventure to the story. The setting includes details of the seasons, the geographical regions, and the influence of the elements on the animals. Within the restrictions of scientific accuracy, the fictional portrayal of animals shows them in conflict of some kind. Some are the most important characters in the story, like the three pets of Sheila Burnford's *The Incredible Journey* that determinedly battle with nature to return to their masters through the wilds of Canada. While they may be thought of as characters, they are not given human traits or anthropomorphized. Novels like *The Wind in the Willows* by Kenneth Grahame cannot be considered animal realism, because the animal characters behave, think, and talk, not like animals, but like human beings. Accuracy about animal life requires an objective point of view when the principals are animals, but a human character who is telling the story, like Billy telling about owls in Farley Mowat's *Owls in the Family,* may offer interpretations of the animals' behavior. If the point of view falters and we "get into the mind" of the animal, the story may become not only unrealistic but also sentimental, as is Felix Salten's *Bambi,* where we know not only Bambi's thoughts but even those of the autumn leaves. In the course of an adventure in animal realism, our transaction is also aesthetic; we make some discovery about animals or about their relationships to human beings.

Historical Realism

Historical fiction is placed in the past; details fit the time and place.

Historical fiction is placed in the past, and the time and place in the past determine setting. Details about vehicles, clothing, or food preparation, for example, must fit the time and the place. Sometimes little is known of the period, and at other times much is known; it is possible to write historical fiction about the Vikings, like *Hakon of Rogen's Saga* by Erik Haugaard, as well as about the American colonies, like *The Witch of Blackbird Pond* by Elizabeth Speare. The integral setting demonstrates how the characters live and how families support themselves. Often the setting is a period when living was markedly different, as in the pioneer days of *Caddie Woodlawn* by Carol Brink, or the Revolutionary War era of *Johnny Tremain* by Esther Forbes. Since characters, and particularly the central character, are caught in the events of the time, setting influences plot. When the writer exaggerates the bad or the good of the times, the resulting historical fiction may suffer from sensational or sentimental tone. Although themes are often universal, they may relate clearly to a particular time; a story might easily be united by themes about how in times of civil war brothers fight brothers and families are torn apart, as *Across Five Aprils* by Irene Hunt exemplifies, or how in pioneer days the family unit was important to survival, as it is in the Little House stories of Laura Ingalls Wilder. Style may focus particularly upon descriptions that draw for us time and place: the dress and homes, the work and recreation of the day. Language should be appropriate to the time; obviously our current slang would be out of place in dialogue of Americans during the Revolution.

History presents facts. To turn facts into fiction, the writer must combine imagination with fact, bringing about an integrated story with a fictional protagonist in a suspenseful plot. As the twentieth century draws to a close, matters that not long ago were current events become the materials of a historical period. Today, for example, writers are seeing with increased objectivity the events of World War II, as does Bette Greene in *Summer of My German Soldier,* and of the Great Depression, as does Mildred Taylor in *Roll of Thunder, Hear My Cry.* Such novels show the impact of the times upon the people living in them.

> To turn facts into fiction, the writer must combine them with imagination.

Well-written historical fiction often rouses within the reader a question that begs to be answered: How much of this is true? Such is the case with Lois Lowry's *Number the Stars.* So convinced are we of the truth of the story that we want to know for certain what is truth and what is fiction. In an afterword, Lowry alludes to well-documented evidence of the personal deprivation and sacrifice made by courageous and honest Danish people who helped nearly seven thousand Jewish citizens escape the Nazis by fleeing to neutral Sweden. Events like the destruction of the Danish navy, ordered by King Christian X and carried out by the Danes themselves to keep the ships from the hands of the Nazis, actually did occur.

Sports Stories

Once a kind of formula fiction, sports stories have become increasingly individualized, with well-developed characters struggling with personal issues and discovering the forces and choices they must confront. Characters play, watch, or live on the fringes of all kinds of sports, although team sports such as baseball, football, and basketball are most common. Emphasis on team play and sportsmanship is frequently the theme, but in recent decades, with demand for more stories about integrated schools and non-racist themes, many stories involve acceptance of players of other races. Another shift has occurred with the appearance of sexually integrated sports. Once a genre of undistinguished stories, sports fiction is much improved. Because children take gym classes, watch televised sports, and are involved in organized sports after school, sports are part of their lives; their reading interests may move naturally toward such stories. A sport story of excellent quality is Bruce Brooks's *The Moves Make the Man,* and writers of sport stories whose work is worth noting are Matt Christopher, Scott Corbett, Alfred Slote, R. R. Knudson, and Mel Cebulash, who wrote of Ruth Marini's struggles to become a professional baseball player.

Formula Fiction

Some kinds of stories follow distinct patterns and are therefore called **formula fiction.** Although following a formula does not necessarily eliminate the writer's originality, it may indeed restrict it.

Mysteries and Thrillers

One popular type of formula fiction is the mystery story, in which mystery and often terror play controlling parts. But note that not all mysteries are formulaic. Mystery stories are set in any time, historical or futuristic, as well as the present. They rely for suspense upon unexplained events and actions that are sometimes, by story's end, resolved or explained by reasonable and carefully detected discoveries. Within the genre we include the detective story, as well as novels of crime, suspense, and espionage. The Gothic novel, traditionally filled with magical or mysterious happenings, occasionally with chivalry, and frequently with horror and terror, perhaps rides the borderline between realism and fantasy.

> Mystery stories rely for suspense on unexplained events which must be resolved by reasonable discoveries.

Plot carries most mysteries and thrillers, although those more carefully crafted also show strong characterization. The mood is almost inevitably suspenseful, and setting may include such intriguing places as vacant houses or abandoned buildings. On the other hand, mystery stories may also occur in the most ordinary of everyday settings. One of the traditional qualities of effective mystery stories is the clever planting of foreshadowing; those who read the genre over time acquire skills in putting together the bits of foreshadowing to predict outcome.

Every schoolchild once knew Nancy Drew and the Hardy Boys, the most clearly representative of formula mysteries; currently the Babysitters Club series remain popular, as do the Goosebump stories. A number of qualities make this type of fiction appealing. It is easy to read and understand, it moves quickly with little description and much dialogue, and it comes to satisfying conclusions. Although these novels may present little challenge, their sameness provides comfort and their predictability is reassuring to young readers.[2]

Many mysteries are *not* formula fiction. Many are not only carefully plotted, but also have strong themes, characters we come to know well, and a style that is distinctive to the writer. British writer Philippa Pearce writes such mystery stories; one of her more recent books is *The Way to Sattin Shore*. Kate Tranter fits together, piece by piece, the evidence that leads to her other grandmother—her father's mother—and to the mystery of her missing father. Had he really died on the day of her birth? Why was her mother's mother so grimly secretive? Why was her father never mentioned in the household? Kate puts the puzzle bits together and with her father's return—from Australia, where he had fled under a cloud of false accusation about the mysterious drowning of his brother—the reunited family leaves the vindictive grandmother and begins a new life together. Mystery, a common element in many well-written stories for children, can hold readers in suspense related to character and theme as well as plot. Mystery novels that have been popular for some time include those of Scott Corbett and Robert Newman, and Donald J. Sobol's *Encyclopedia Brown* books. Sobol's *Angie's First Case* began a series about a girl detective.

Romantic Stories

A relatively recent development for young readers has been the burst of popularity of the romantic novel; millions have been sold since the 1960s. They are not a new kind of realism, however, but have been around for generations; heroines in Victorian novels, for example, were often absorbed in them. Under the guise of realism, the romantic story oversimplifies and sentimentalizes male-female relationships, often showing them as the sole focus of young lives. The most thorough study of romances and their market suggests that these "fairy tales of desire" consistently show deeply feminine yet feisty females involved with the male paragon of tender-tough qualities, a combination that both verifies and contradicts the rise of feminism.[3] Romantic stories, since they follow highly similar patterns of plot development and their characters seem to differ merely in hair color or name rather than in personality, lead a perceptive reader to comment, "Read one, you've read them all"—an exaggeration, of course, but containing some degree of truth.

The **romance** differs from formulaic romantic stories. The term is more often used today as describing a story that is freely imaginative, or as

Under the guise of realism, romantic stories oversimplify and sentimentalize male-female relationships.

the *New English Dictionary* defines it, "a fictitious narrative in prose of which the scene and incidents are very remote from those of ordinary life." Under this definition, such stories might include Robert Louis Stevenson's *Treasure Island* or *Kidnapped*.

Series Novels

Many stories are published as parts of a series, some of them with one uniting element and some with others. Gary D. Schmidt mentions several plans of organization, overlapping though they may seem to be.[4] "What ties the novels of a series together . . . is the structure of the novels." The first of these focuses, exemplified by the J. R. R. Tolkien, Ursula Le Guin, and Madeleine L'Engle series, "documents character growth," with plots that are separated though similar in thematic point. The second type is defined by "a strong central character" like Beverly Cleary's Ramona or Lois Lowry's Anastasia. Character focus means that the order of the novels in the series is unimportant, but each one deals with a slight change in the nature of the character.

Characters in a third type of series remain the focus, but here the character is constant and does not change, as in, for example, the Tom Swift and Nancy Drew series, or like Kristy Thomas in the Babysitters Club series. The constancy and predictability of the central characters offer no unsettling changes, but are "as permanent as Egyptian pyramids." Often called formulaic novels and denigrated by critics, these books are, however, reassuring to young readers whose reading speed increases over the series and who finally decide they have had enough and go on to other stories. Perhaps their greatest contribution to literature for children is the way they offer opportunity to share books, and help young readers discover that there is pleasure in reading.

The fourth structure identified by Schmidt is defined by subject and constitutes primarily biography and informational books. The Childhood of Famous Americans series of the 1950s and early 1960s served to cut "the distance between the contemporary reader and the remote figures of the past." The natural history books of Jean Craighead George, "One Day in———," offer another example.

Fantasy

Fantasy, in the phrase of Coleridge, requires "the willing suspension of disbelief." The writer of **fantasy** (sometimes called "literary fantasy" to distinguish it from folk fantasy, which is of unknown authorship) creates another world for characters and readers, asking that readers believe this other world

Fantasy requires the "willing suspension of disbelief," a phrase from Coleridge.

tific laws and technological inventions—like gravity and the speed of light and the contrivances with which to deal with these forces and limitations.

Descriptions and criteria ought to begin with definitions. Robert Heinlein, a well-known author of science fiction, calls it "speculative fictions in which the author takes as his first postulate the real world as we know it, including all established facts and natural laws." Don Moskowitz, a historian of science fiction, says that it utilizes "an atmosphere of scientific credibility for its imaginative speculations in physical science, space, time, social science, and philosophy." Kingsley Amis, critic and author, says that science fiction "is hypothesized on the basis of some innovation in science or technology, or pseudo-science, or pseudo-technology." Unlike fantasy, it must "achieve verisimilitude and win the 'willing suspension of disbelief' through scientific plausibility."

Perhaps the definition that comes closest to our considerations is that proposed by acclaimed writer of science fiction Theodore Sturgeon. He maintains that "a [good] science fiction story is a story built around human beings, with a human problem, and a human solution, which would not have happened at all without its scientific content."[7] In contrast, poor science fiction often shows characters committed to the scientific process of investigation and invention, and may therefore be governed solely by intellect. Their concerns are the products of their minds; they may expend their physical energies and mental powers mainly upon inanimate objects and abstract theories. Intellect may also govern relationships between characters whose source of cooperation seems a union of intellects controlling or using a force either natural or mechanical.

The genre may often rely heavily upon conflict rather than character to hold the reader's interest. Such conflicts are frequently with societies alien to us in form and in values, like the Tripods of John Christopher's *White Mountains* trilogy. When the conflict is person against nature, as it is in *The Time of the Great Freeze* by Robert Silverberg, the battle seems weighted on the side of the natural force. While early science fiction seemed to have few themes, recent work is far more varied and complex. Tone, like tone in any kind of writing, either for children or adults, may be, but is not necessarily, didactic: "If we don't care for our environment . . ." Writers like H. M. Hoover, William Sleator, and Ray Bradbury, however, whose interest in human beings is as keen as their interest in scientific speculation, write with subtlety and understanding of human motives.

Traditionally science fiction has dealt with future worlds, but in one variation on that form, the time-lapse story takes a protagonist either forward into future time or backward into the past. In Susan Beth Pfeffer's *Future Forward,* Scott and Kelly, by traveling back in time, save their neighbor Pop from being injured in a robbery of his store. Happy that their VCR rewind and fast-forward buttons can accomplish such time change—and might even prevent world destruction in World War III—Scott decides to find out the winning lottery numbers in tomorrow's paper. He is tempted to win $42 million for his family, but decides instead to give it to Pop's support group for victims of crime. The altruistic rather than selfish use of the winning sum is compatible with the usual results in time lapse fantasy. The story moves slowly in rather pedestrian language, but intrigues the reader by using everyday equipment to make remarkable time leaps.

It has been suggested that science fiction's mechanical persons or robots may serve as the means by which today's children work out their psychological conflicts and fears, as Bruno Bettelheim believes folk and fairy tales have served for preceding generations.[8] From Frank Baum and his Oz stories on, anthropomorphized machines have explored relationships between persons and twentieth-century inventions, examining such questions as, Which is superior, human or machine? Does it matter how one is created? Are sophisticated robots truly alive? Might the computer, the thinking machine, pose serious threats to human beings and their lives? Who is the smarter chess player—Kasparov or robot Big Blue? Young in comparison to many forms of literature, the best of the genre ultimately asks what it means to be related and connected and responsible for others. Such considerations are the substance and subject of imaginative and artistic writing of any genre.

No other genre or subgenre generates such a sharp division of readers into those who love it and those who do not care for it. Awareness of this division as well as of the evolution of the genre is bringing to readers increasingly complete characters and more varied themes. Science fiction has changed and continues to change, attracting growing numbers of readers.

While, for the most part, British writers with their roots deep in the faerie and folklore of northern Europe have concentrated on fantasy, American writers have created their specialty—fiction that depicts the conflicts between technology and the laws of nature and, increasingly, the moral laws of human relationships. Such generalizations may no longer hold as American writers like Robin McKinley create high fantasy and British writers move into science fiction, long thought to be an American domain.

Traditional Literature

The term "traditional" (or "folk" literature) implies that the form comes to us from the ordinary person, an anonymous storyteller, and exists orally rather than in writing—at least until some collector finds, records, and publishes the stories or rhymes, thus setting them into temporary form. There is, then, no final and definitive version of a piece of folk literature.

Folktales have been called the "spiritual history" of humankind, the "cement of society," binding a culture together. They seem to express the universality of human wishes and needs. Hundreds of versions of the same story, such as "Cinderella," occur in countless cultures and show almost infinite variations, but are similar in their focus on human yearning for social acceptance and material comfort. We are now fortunate that because of scholarly collecting, folktales that once flourished only in communities where people did not read or write have become the property of all people.

Folktales that once flourished only where people did not read or write have become the property of all.

Fables

The **fable** is a very brief story, usually with animal characters, that points clearly to a moral or lesson. The moral, an explicit and didactic or preachy theme, is usually given at the end of the story and is the reason for the existence of the fable. The fable makes visible and objective some lesson like that we see in "The Tortoise and the Hare": "Slow but steady wins the race." Brevity dictates that one or two characters each have a single trait. It also dictates that conflict be sharp and clear—as it is in "The Dog in the Manger." The setting is a backdrop for the action, and the action has no interpretive narrator telling extra details of characters' thoughts or feelings. Style is crisp and straightforward. Everything in the fable exists to make an abstract point, to make a lesson clear—as clear as the moral in the story of the milkmaid who dreamily drops her basket of eggs on the way to market: "Don't count your chickens before they hatch." As more and more fables from cultures other than Europe appear, it seems that most contain morals.

Folktales

In form the **folktale** relies on flat characters, bad ones and good ones, easily recognized. Since folktales were heard by the teller and then retold in the teller's own words, there was hardly time for subtle character development. A brief phrase, which may be repeated often, serves to draw character, since the teller cannot risk losing the audience by departing from the fast-paced narration of action to describe thoughts and feelings.

Stock characters, like the fairy godmother and the wicked stepmother in "Cinderella," frequently appear. Conflicts are often between people or personified animals in person-versus-person conflict, like Jack and the ogre in "Jack and the Beanstalk." Plots are progressive, with the climax coming at the very end and the closing as brief as "They lived happily ever after." Action, fast and lively, is at the heart of the folktale. In European tales, incidents can occur singly, in threes as they do in "The Billy-Goats Gruff," or occasionally in more repetitions; in stories from Native American and other traditions, the numbers vary. The setting is usually a backdrop for the action, a background that creates universality by its vaguely recognizable appeal. Point of view is rarely first person, since the tales are told about flat characters in fantastic situations. Tone varies; it may be sentimental, as in "Beauty and the Beast," objective, as in "The Little Red Hen," or humorous, as in "The Squire's Bride." Themes also vary, but comment on human needs and wishes, like the theme in "The Fisherman's Wife": "People are never satisfied."

For years Americans read and heard few tales other than those from Europe, although some read the Uncle Remus stories or saw them dramatized in animation. Now, with the collection, retelling, and publication of African tales by Harold Courlander, Ashley Bryan, and Verna Aardema, all children may meet them. Virginia Hamilton and Julius Lester effectively retell black American folk literature. Many of these stories are animal tales, showing how the weak defeat the strong, as does Br'er Rabbit, for example. A particularly attractive edition in very readable language is Hamilton's *The People Could Fly: American Black Folktales*. Native American tales are also published in collections and as single tales, like, for example. *Arrow to the Sun* by Gerald McDermott, who has published tales from several countries. As people from Asia, Africa, and Latin America join us in the West, their tales are added to enrich ours. Now children can read Eric Kimmel's *Baba Yaga*, a Russian tale; Celia Barker Lottridge's *The Name of the Tree,* an African tale; or Susan Roth's *pourquoi*—tales that respond to the questions "why"—*Fire Comes to the Earth People.*

Folk literature throughout the world is often quite similar. European tales and Asian tales may have identical themes, reenforcing what might be regarded as universal law. For example, the tales from ancient China retold by Linda Fang in *The Ch'i-lin Purse* sometimes conclude with morals stated as flatly as they are in Aesop's western fables: "If you have a chance to do something good, be sure to do it. Happiness will come back to you. . . . Everyone has a talent that will prove useful one time or another."

The style of the folktale relies upon recurring images like "no bigger than my thumb" and often includes short rhymes like those in "Snow White": "Mirror, mirror, on the wall/Who is fairest of us all?" The cadenced prose fits the rhythm of oral telling. We recall "No, by the hair of my chinny chin chin/I will not let you in." From the South American collection *Tales from Silver Lands* comes "A Tale of Three Tails," where we find "They sing and they play/For half of the day," and "I must do what I can/Is the thought of a man." From "The Calabash Man" comes "From forest to hill/We come at your will./Call, Aura, call."

Sometimes folktales[9] are subdivided into tales of magic, romance, *pourquois,* cumulation, religion, sillies, talking beasts, tall tales, and realistic situations. These categories often overlap; the subgroups only emphasize the richness and variety of the genre,[10] all of them ideal media for the picture book. In *Why Mosquitoes Buzz in People's Ears,* for example, Verna Aardema boldly tells a **cumulative tale**—*Mosquitoes* reverses the cumulation (usually a series of additions like those in "The House That Jack Built")—to unravel the question of how the owlet was killed.

Myths

Myths are stories that originate in the beliefs of nations and races and present episodes in which supernatural forces operate. Because they, too, are handed down by word of mouth, they have no right or wrong form. Myths, like that of the god Thor and his hammer of thunder, are stories that interpret natural phenomena. Some myths try to make visible and concrete the ways that human beings see nature, like the division of the year into seasons: In the story of Ceres and her daughter Proserpine, the girl is abducted and kept for part of the year in the underworld of Pluto, an explanation for the disappearance of summer's warmth and growth. Myths may show people's relationships with each other, like the generosity demonstrated in the myth of Baucis and Philemon, in which hospitality is rewarded by an eternally filled oil cruse and an endless supply of meal. Myths show the ways that human beings see the forces that control them, like the separation of day and night caused by Apollo's crossing the sky in his sun chariot. Myths explain creation, religion, and divinities; they guess at the meaning of life and death, or at the cause for good and evil, as made clear in the myth of Pandora's box. As Virginia Hamilton says in an introductory note to *In the Beginning: Creation Stories from Around the World,* although "fairy tales take place *within* the time of human experience . . . myths . . . take place before the 'once upon a time' . . . [and] go *back beyond anything that ever was,* and begin *before* anything has happened."

Past generations have had experience primarily with myths of western European origin, but in today's multicultural society, we should ideally meet myths from many lands. One of the benefits to readers of myths is the reinforcement of the truth that all peoples value similar human traits, and furthermore, that faraway countries can be warmly affectionate about human foolishness, as *Once the Hodja* by Alice Geer Kelsey shows in the stories about the simple country man who constantly gets in and out of trouble.

Each mythical character represents one or a very few qualities—for example, fertility—and therefore the supernatural or unexplainable issues of seasons and growth. Plots are often single incidents or a few incidents linked by characters. An opening phrase like "Long ago in ancient China" is sufficient for setting. Since the abstract issues or themes that myths explore are broad and universal, their tone is dignified and somewhat mystical. The effective telling of a myth has dignity and simplicity, for it tries to recreate the spirit and intention of the original. When myths are poorly

Myths originate in the beliefs of nations or races and present episodes where supernatural forces operate.

told, as they are by Nathaniel Hawthorne in *A Wonder Book,* they condescend to or even insult the efforts of earlier societies to find meaning in life. When myths are well told, they appeal to something deep within us.

Legends and Hero Tales

Legends are similar to myths because both are traditional narratives of a people; sometimes the two subgenres are interwoven. Legends, however, often have more historical truth and less reliance upon the supernatural. When, for example, we read the legends of the Trojan War, we are aware of the actual siege of the city as well as of legendary heroes and actions. Although there was a King Arthur, most stories about him are not historical truth but legend. The grandeur of the legend is maintained in *The Legend of King Arthur* as it is retold by Robin Lister, beginning with Arthur's pulling the sword from the stone and setting up the Round Table, to his love and loss of Guinevere and his final departure for the magic isle of Avalon. Such figures as Abraham Lincoln, a national hero, accumulate legends rooted in the authenticity of the character but fictional in detail.

Folk Epics

A hero is larger than life, superhuman in physical and moral qualities.

The **folk epic** is a long narrative poem of unknown authorship about an outstanding or royal character in a series of adventures related to that heroic central figure. This character or hero is, like Beowulf, larger than life, grand in all proportions, and superhuman in physical and moral qualities. The action may involve journeys and quests, and it may show deeds of great courage and valor coupled with superhuman strength; the forces of the supernatural intervene from time to time. The setting is vast, including a nation, a continent, or even the universe. Point of view is objective, for the story is so grand that a protagonist of such remarkable accomplishments seems to need no interpretive narrator. The tone is dignified, and the style is therefore elevated. Often the story, which begins in the middle of things, includes long lists or catalogs of warriors, treasures, gifts, or ships. Extended comparisons called "epic similes" frequently occur. Like the best retellings of myth, those of epic do not condescend in any way; they show the values of the society and awe the reader with the possibility of great courage and moral strength. Few retellers are so masterful as Rosemary Sutcliff, who tells of Finn MacCool and of the Hound of Ulster.

Poetry

Poetry, a kind of imaginative and artistic writing, can also be called a genre of literature. And, as with many genres, there are subgenres. For the sake of simplicity, we might identify them here as ballads, narrative poetry, and lyric poetry, acknowledging, however, that these categories are not absolute any more than the genres of fiction are absolute. A lyric, or "personal poem" as some might call them, may have balladlike qualities—a refrain, for example—and a narrative may have lyric or songlike passages. Compactness is essential to poetry to make words say much more than literal or denotative meaning. Ballads, too, rely upon compactness; they are elliptical in their phrasing, often forcing the reader or listener to leap from inference to inference. Perhaps the narrative poem at first glance does not seem to demand compactness. In all probability, however, the account of action and tension in a narrative poem uses far fewer words than a prose account of the same action and tension.

In poetry words say more than their literal meaning.

We often make the mistake of calling any writing that has rhythm, rhyme, or short lines "poetry." Much of it, however, is rhyme or verse. Steeped as we are in the Mother Goose nursery rhymes, we identify them easily, and do not call the rhymes poetry. But when short lines are written in rhythm, or address a subject that lacks the familiarity of nursery rhymes, we think they might be poetry. A trace of uncertainty, however, may linger: Where does verse end and poetry begin? To answer that question we enter into one of the age-old literary controversies; we will not try to answer it here, although some effort to address the issue is made in Chapter 11.

Nonfiction

Purists might find the title of this volume inaccurate, perhaps even blasphemous, because within a handbook of children's literature we have the temerity to include nonfiction. What is the rationale? Some nonfiction is written with high artistry; we think of Jean George's descriptions of the working of the natural world, or of the philosophical discourses of Plato's *Republic*—to juxtapose modern and ancient writings. Where to draw the line? Rather than draw any line whatsoever, we might instead express the wish that all nonfiction, informational books as well as biography, could be written with high artistry. Nonfiction is included here because it is written and read by children for their pleasure and understanding, evoking both aesthetic—or emotional and intellectual effects—and efferent transactions (to use Louise Rosenblatt's terms). We hope to discover how to recognize the best available.

Both efferent and aesthetic transactions, as well as pleasure, occur with nonfiction.

Nonfiction, too, can be subdivided, but with little likelihood of satisfying all readers. We might look at the librarian's classifications and decide that we must address each of the categories, from natural and physical sciences, social sciences, and history (if it is not seen as part of the social sciences) through the arts, then subdivide even further. In fact, we might go on and on with genres and subgenres. Once again, we must be practical.

For that reason, we might subdivide nonfiction into informational books and biography, knowing full well that some would like finer distinctions. The standards for informational books of all kinds, however, are similar. And standards for biography, the account of the life of an individual, can be set with some degree of common sense.

Across Genre Lines

What is there left to consider?

There are some books we cannot put neatly into categories because, although they have qualities in common, they cross genre lines. Some books we group together, not because of subject matter, but because they rely upon pictures to extend the story—picture books, of course. (For a full discussion of picture books, see Chapter 3.) Other books are singled out for another reason; they are placed in a loose and overlapping group called "classics." These works come from all genres and are works that have lasted for some time.

Classics

Classics are books that have worn well, attracting readers from one generation to the next. They cross all genre lines; they are historical fiction, regional literature, and high fantasy. Although picture books have a short history, they too have classics among them: books like *Madeline* and *Goodnight, Moon* have survived. Literature written for children has a brief history; books that interest two or three generations can be called classics, and we may thus regard the Little House and Pooh books as classics, for example. Some books have had a strong impact on generations of writers and readers; the recent arrival of many stories about early America may result from the popularity of Laura Ingalls Wilder's writing, as well as the TV series. Others, like *The Secret Garden* by Frances Hodgson Burnett, after a generation of being little read have returned to become regarded as classics. What seems to keep classics in continuous circulation may be the significance of theme, the credibility of character, the continuing reality of the conflict, or the engaging quality of style. Furthermore, they often serve as models; the success of the mischievous Tom Sawyer, for example, has resulted in periodic spates of books about mischievous boys.[11] What seems important, however, is that mischief is not what keeps *Tom Sawyer* alive. Instead it is far more complex and universal matters like Twain's perceptive portrayal of the adults in the community; his mixture of the experiences, emotions, rites, and yearnings of childhood; the significance of ideas like courage and sacrifice for the sake of other people; and Twain's lively variety of tones and the aptness of his language.

Classics last because of significant themes, credible character, real conflicts, or engaging style.

GENRE IN CHILDREN'S LITERATURE

REALISM

Genre	Character	Plot	Setting	Theme	Point of View	Style	Tone
REALISM EXAMPLES: *Roll of Thunder, Hear My Cry*; *The Wild Children*	Best novels have round central characters. Poor ones load protagonist with problems, or have flat or stereotyped characters[a]	Any kind of conflict. If problem is solved too easily, story is flawed	Any	Any. Sentimentality, sensationalism, didacticism are flaws[a]	Any	Uses all devices	Any, but sentimentality or sensationalism are flaws[a]
ANIMAL REALISM EXAMPLES: *Incredible Journey*; *Owls in the Family*	Realistic portrayal of animals, without animal personification	Conflict is usually versus nature	Usually integral[a]	Usually related to some discovery about animals or their relationships to human beings	Objective in respect to the animal character; human characters may be shown in other points of view[a]	Uses all devices	Any, but if point of view falters, tone may become sentimental[a]
HISTORICAL FICTION EXAMPLES: *The Witch of Blackbird Pond*; *Summer of My German Soldier*	Protagonist has universal human traits, but is a product of the time and place[a]	Any, but conflict more often person versus society or self, as well as another person	Integral setting with focus on particular time and place, usually time of stress or crisis, or of social change	Any universal theme	Any	Uses all devices. Relies for credibility on accurate descriptions of place—costumes, activities, etc.	Any, but flawed if past is recreated sentimentally or sensationally[a]
REGIONAL REALISM AND STORIES OF OTHER COUNTRIES EXAMPLE: *Where the Lilies Bloom*	Protagonist has universal human traits, but is a product of the time and place	Conflict often related to the region, whether topography, livelihood or mores of area[a]	Integral and essentially so[a]	Any universal theme	Any	Uses all devices	Any
MYSTERIES EXAMPLE: *The Way to Sattin Shore*	Well developed	Usually carries story; some coincidence	Any; often spooky	Any	Any	Uses all devices	Mysterious

[a]Represents elements that have special importance in a genre, or elements that are frequent sources of inadequacy in a work.

(continued)

Genre	Character	Plot	Setting	Theme	Point of View	Style	Tone
SPORTS STORIES EXAMPLES: *The Moves Make the Man; The Baseball Bargain*	Realistic	Involves sports	Any	Often personal growth	Any	Uses all devices	Any
FORMULA FICTION Romantic Stories: EXAMPLES: Sweetheart novels	Flat, stereotyped	Boy-meets-girl	Any, often exaggerated wealth	Often "Love conquers all"	Any	Trite[a]	Sentimental[a]
Formula Mysteries: EXAMPLE: Nancy Drew; Hardy Boys	Flat, Stereotyped	Suspenseful	Any	Unimportant	Any	Often vernacular	Factual, or mysterious

FANTASY

Genre	Character	Plot	Setting	Theme	Point of View	Style	Tone
FANTASTIC STORIES EXAMPLES: *The Borrowers; Charlotte's Web; Winnie the Pooh; "The Fir Tree"*	Like or unlike human beings; magical qualities; personified toys, animals, objects	Any kind of conflict	Often realistic world with some fantastic qualities	Any	Any	Any	Any; often humorous
HIGH FANTASY EXAMPLES: *The Hero and the Crown; The Rats of NIMH; The Mermaid Summer*	Realistically portrayed	Any, but underlying conflict is good vs. evil	Often special world, an integral setting where time and place have special qualities of expansion or limitation	Universal, important themes of good/evil in conflict	Any	Usually highly sensory	Serious, awed
SCIENCE FICTION EXAMPLES: *The House of Stairs; The Lost Star*	Flawed stories often have inadequately developed central characters[a]	Any kind of conflict; often mechanical or natural forces are antagonists. Plots usually progressive and suspenseful	Often distinguishes one story from another; set in future time sometimes on unexplored planets	May be subtle, implicit, but flawed stories have didactic theme[a]	Any	All devices; often much description in concrete forms	Often objective, factual, but flawed story may be heavily didactic

[a]Represents elements that have special importance in a genre, or elements that are frequent sources of inadequacy in a work.

TRADITIONAL TALES

Genre	Character	Plot	Setting	Theme	Point of View	Style	Tone
FABLE EXAMPLES: "The Boy Who Cried Wolf"; "The Fox and the Crow"	Flat and stock; often personified animals with single traits	Person-versus-person conflict; extremely brief; usually a single incident[a]	Backdrop	Explicit and didactic	Objective or dramatic	Terse, lacking imagery or connotative language	Straightforward, didactic, and moralizing
FOLKTALE EXAMPLES: "Cinderella"; "Jack and the Beanstalk"; A Story A Story	Flat, even the protagonist; bad and good characters easily identified; stock characters like the wicked stepmother and the fairy godmother	Person-versus-person or person-versus-personified-nature conflicts. Action moves rapidly to a climax and stock closing	Backdrop setting: "Long ago and far away . . ."	Either implicit or explicit. Often strongly focused on justice	Usually omniscient or limited omniscient	A few recurring images; often short verses; cadenced prose[a]	Varied. May be sentimental, humorous, objective, but is not often didactic
MYTH EXAMPLES: "Apollo's Sun Chariot"; "How Fire Came to Earth People"	Gods and heroes with traits linked to supernatural powers	An incident or incidents linked by character	Backdrop: "Long ago in ancient China . . ."	Explanations of natural phenomena or human relationships	Usually objective	Significant symbols, abstract terms, little or no dialogue; brief descriptions of action	Dignified, perhaps mystical. Sentimentality is flaw
LEGEND OR HERO TALE EXAMPLES: "King Arthur"; "Robin Hood"	Historical figures with fictional traits and situations	Any conflict featuring protagonists	Backdrop: "When Arthur was king . . ."	Fictional glorification of historical figures	Usually objective	Significant symbols, abstract terms, little or no dialogue; brief descriptions of action	Often objective. Sentimentality is flaw
FOLK EPIC EXAMPLES: Beowulf; Finn MacCool; Gilgamesh	Protagonist is heroic, superhuman	Begins in middle of things (in medias res); conflict is person versus person, society, or nature. Often three incidents showing hero victorious against supreme odds[a]	Undefined long-ago, but set in the vast world or the universe	Good can be victorious over evil, but only after great struggle against superhuman odds and with assistance of gods[a]	Objective or dramatic	Long, cadenced lines of oral language; symbols and images; grandeur and simplicity; epic similes and elaborate comparisons; extended formal speeches	Dignified; grand; awesome

[a]Represents elements that have special importance in a genre, or elements that are frequent sources of inadequacy in a work.

(continued)

RHYME TO POETRY

Genre	Form or Focus	Rhythm	Rhyme	Devices
Nursery Rhymes	Topics open to young children; usually brief; any tone; folk in origin	Regular	Regular	Personification, simile, metaphor, and others
Verse	Easily understood; for specific purpose; meaning less important than form; often trite, banal in form, subject, or phrasing[a]	Highly rhythmic; rhythm often more important than meaning	Usually regular in scheme; often forced, or more important than meaning	Often ordinary images, predictable; less emotion, imagination, intensity than poetry
Narrative Poetry Examples: "The Highwayman"; "The Worm"	Storytelling, long or short	Suited to story	Any form	Any, though fewer than in lyrics
Ballad Folk Ballad: (author unknown) Example: "John Henry" Art Ballad: (author known) Example: "Rime of the Ancient Mariner"	Narrative of physical courage; incidents in lives of common people; supernatural; largely dialogue, little characterization; great simplicity; refrains, often incremental; abrupt transitions; single dramatic episode	Great variation, but usually lines 1 & 3 having four accented syllables, lines 2 & 4, three unaccented syllables; variations in number of unstressed syllables	Refrain often used; usually *abcb* rhyme; approximate rhyme very common	Any (See "Form or Focus")
Lyric or Personal Poetry	Brief, subjective; personal emotional response; single unified impression; "An end in itself"; intense, compact	Suited to topic and emotion evoked	Rhymed or unrhymed	All figurative and sound devices used to produce compactness

[a]Represents elements that have special importance in a genre, or elements that are frequent sources of inadequacy in a work.

NONFICTION

Genre	Essential Qualities	Organization and Scope	Style	Tone	Illustrations
INFORMATIONAL BOOKS	Gives information and facts; relates facts to concept; stimulates curiosity; "starter," not "stopper"	From simplest to most complex; from known to unknown; from familiar to unfamiliar; from early developments to later; chronological; may have slight narrative for younger reader	Imagery, figurative language, all devices; comparisons extremely useful; flawed if style is monotonous, repetitious, fragmented in statements[a]	Wonder, not mystery; respect; objectivity, occasional humor; fostering scientific attitude of inquiry. Flaws: condescension, anthropomorphism, oversimplification; facts not separated from opinions[a]	Diagrams and drawings often clearer than photographs
BIOGRAPHY	Gives accurate, verifiable facts and authentic picture of period; subject worthy of attention	Assumes no omniscience; shows individual, not stereotype; does not ignore negative qualities of subject; focuses not only on events, but also on nature of person	Storytelling permissible for youngest readers; too much invention destroys credibility	Interest; enthusiasm; objectivity; didacticism and preaching to be avoided	Authentic

[a]Represents elements that have special importance in a genre, or elements that are frequent sources of inadequacy in a work.

A work may be popular for a time and then fade, as was the case with *A Dog of Flanders* and *Seventeen*. What seemed the height of ingenious word-play at one time may at another time seem dull and trite; the wit in the once-popular *The Peterkin Papers,* for example, now seems heavy-handed. *Alice's Adventures in Wonderland,* on the other hand, remains an incomparable work of nonsense; readers have never outgrown Carroll's wit, and his playful inventiveness remains unsurpassed. Similarly, even if the diversified family farm becomes extinct, E. B. White's finest novel, *Charlotte's Web,* will last. White's thorough portrayal of character and his choice of life-and-death conflict, his affectionately humorous tone, and his universal themes about friendship, satisfaction, and death are elements that identify classics. The classics of one generation may be supplanted by later works, but the appeal of other books may remain for a surprisingly long time. To paraphrase Ezra Pound, a classic is "news that stays news." It is not the Classics List graven in stone, but time, that will tell.

Summary

Awareness of the similarities and differences in the genres of children's literature may or may not be useful. Perhaps the most obvious and most important thing to realize is that not all books or all genres appeal to all children. However, a child hooked on one genre—science fiction, for example—may find the craving for adventure is further satisfied through sports or other realistic stories. Curiosity about imaginatively created worlds may lead the reader to find pleasure in another closely related genre—high fantasy, for example. Expansion of the young reader's world results as the reader finds new styles of writing, broader themes, and other motivations in characters with varied experiences. Greater appreciation of self and of other human beings and their societies results as such vicarious experiences grow in numbers.

The charts in this chapter summarize similarities and differences in the genres. They may prove helpful, but only if we keep in mind the dangers of generalizing. Literature, since it is not so easily classified as the chemical elements, will often be elusive, refusing to fit neatly into a genre. The charts may, however, keep us aware of the tremendous breadth of literature available to children for their great pleasure and increased understanding.

Notes

1. In Shakespeare's *Hamlet,* Polonius's speech praising the actors (Act II, Scene 2) makes fun of the genres of drama in such phrases as "pastoral-comical" and "tragical-comical-historical-pastoral."

2. Barbara Moran and Susan Steinfirst, "Why Johnny (and Jane) Read Whodunits in Series," *School Library Journal,* March 1985, p. 113.

3. Janice Radway, *Reading the Romance* (Chapel Hill: University of North Carolina Press, 1984).

4. Gary D. Schmidt, "'So here, my dears, is a new Oz story': The Deep Structure of a Series," *Children's Literature Association Quarterly* 14 (Winter 1989): 163–165.

5. For an enlightening discussion of the narrator and the reader-audience in fantasy, see "Some Presumptions About Fantasy" by Perry Nodelman, in *Children's Literature Quarterly,* Summer 1979.

6. Eleanor Cameron, *The Green and Burning Tree* (Boston: Little, Brown, 1969), p. 72.

7. These definitions come from *Alternate Worlds: The Illustrated History of Science Fiction* by James Gunn (Englewood Cliffs, NJ.: Prentice-Hall/A&W Visual Library, 1975).

8. Margaret Esmonde, "From Little Buddy to Big Brother: The Icon of the Robot in Children's Science Fiction," in *The Mechanical God,* ed. Thomas P. Dunn and Richard D. Erlich (Westport, Conn.: Greenwood, 1982).

9. In an observation about folk tales, Jack Zipes responds to Bruno Bettelheim's optimism regarding folktales, saying that "such focus on resolution and happiness only points to our tenacious capacity to avoid unpleasant insights into childhood experiences. . . . Perhaps the most therapeutic aspect of these stories is the reassurance they give *parents* that children survive the horrors they impose on them." "Child Abuse and Happy Endings," *New York Times Book Review,* November 13, 1988, pp. 39, 60.

10. Claire L. Malarte-Feldman, in her review of *Beauty, Beasts and Enchantment* by Jack Zipes, and *Beauty and the Beasts: Visions and Revisions of an Old Tale* by Betsy Hearne, says that fairy tales indicate "their strong vitality . . . as a genre that has survived because of its extraordinary ability to adapt to new forms of expression. This is the power of fairy tales: narratives without fixed texts, stories without authors, their origins are impossible to trace with precision. Their sources can be found in our strongest emotions: love and hate, violence and jealousy, fear and courage . . . a symbolic expression of our need for love and of our belief in the power of love." *Children's Literature* vol. 20 (New Haven: Yale University Press, 1992), p. 240.

11. While critics call *Huckleberry Finn* the better novel, *Tom Sawyer* seems more clearly a book for children.

Recommended Books Cited in This Chapter

AARDEMA, VERNA. *Why Mosquitoes Buzz in People's Ears.* Illustrated by Leo and Diane Dillon. New York: Dial, 1975.

AESOP. *Fables.* New York: Dutton, 1963.

ANDERSEN, HANS CHRISTIAN. *The Ugly Duckling; The Little Fir Tree; The Little Tin Soldier.* New York: Macmillan, 1963.

BRINK, CAROL. *Caddie Woodlawn*. New York: Macmillan, 1946.

BROOKS, BRUCE. *The Moves Make the Man*. New York: Harper & Row, 1984.

BURNETT, FRANCES HODGSON. *The Secret Garden*. 1911. Reprint. New York: Viking, 1989.

BURNFORD, SHEILA. *The Incredible Journey*. Boston: Little, Brown, 1961.

CARROLL, LEWIS. *Alice's Adventures in Wonderland*. 1865. Reprint. New York: Dutton, 1954.

CAUDILL, REBECCA. *Did You Carry the Flag Today, Charley?* New York: Holt, 1966.

CHILDRESS, ALICE. *A Hero Ain't Nothin' but a Sandwich*. New York: Coward, 1973.

CHRISTOPHER, JOHN. *White Mountains*. New York: Macmillan, 1970.

FANG, LINDA. *The Chi-lin Purse*. New York: Farrar, Straus & Giroux, 1995.

FORBES, ESTHER. *Johnny Tremain*. New York: Dell, 1969.

GRAHAME, KENNETH. *The Wind in the Willows*. 1908. Reprint. New York: Scribner's, 1953.

GREENE, BETTE. *Summer of My German Soldier*. New York: Dial, 1973.

GRIMM, JACOB AND WILHELM. *Grimm's Fairy Tales*. New York: Grosset, 1962.

HAMILTON, VIRGINIA. *The People Could Fly: American Black Folktales*. New York: Knopf, 1985.

————. *Sweet Whispers, Brother Rush*. New York: Putnam, 1982.

HAUGAARD, ERIK. *Hakon of Rogen's Saga*. Boston: Houghton Mifflin, 1963.

HUNT, IRENE. *Across Five Aprils*. New York: Follett, 1964.

JACOBS, JOSEPH. *English Fairy Tales*. New York: Dover, 1898.

KELSEY, ALICE GEER. *Once the Hodja*. New York: Longman's, Green, 1943.

KIMMEL, ERIC. *Baba Yaga*. New York: Holiday House, 1991.

L'ENGLE, MADELEINE. *A Wrinkle in Time*. New York: Farrar, 1962.

LEWIS, C. S. The Chronicles of Narnia. New York: Macmillan, 1951.

LISTER, ROBIN. *The Legend of King Arthur*. New York: Doubleday, 1988.

LOWRY, LOIS. *Number the Stars*. Boston: Houghton Mifflin, 1989.

McDERMOTT, GERALD. *Arrow to the Sun*. New York: Viking, 1974.

McKINLEY, ROBIN. *The Hero and the Crown*. New York: Greenwillow, 1981.

MOWAT, FARLEY. *Owls in the Family*. Boston: Little, Brown, 1961.

NORTON, MARY. *The Borrowers*. New York: Harcourt, 1965.

ORWELL, GEORGE. *Animal Farm*. First published 1945. New York: Harcourt Brace, 1995.

PARK, RUTH. *Things in Corners*. New York: Viking, 1989.

PATERSON, KATHERINE. *The Great Gilly Hopkins*. New York: Crowell, 1978.

PEARCE, PHILIPPA. *The Way to Sattin Shore*. New York: Greenwillow, 1983.

PFEFFER, SUSAN. *Future Forward*. New York: Delacorte, 1989.

ROTH, SUSAN. *Fire Comes to the Earth People*. New York: St. Martins, 1988.

SALTEN, FELIX. *Bambi*. New York: Grosset & Dunlap, 1929.

SILVERBERG, ROBERT. *Time of the Great Freeze*. New York: Harper, 1964.

SOBOL, DONALD. *Angie's First Case*. New York: Four Winds, 1984.

————. *Encyclopedia Brown*. New York: Nelson, 1970.

SPEARE, ELIZABETH. *The Witch of Blackbird Pond*. Boston: Houghton Mifflin, 1958.

STEVENSON, ROBERT LOUIS. *Kidnapped*. 1886. Reprint. New York: Scribner's, 1913.

————. *Treasure Island*. 1883. Reprint. Scribners, 1911.

SUTCLIFF, ROSEMARY. *The High Deeds of Finn MacCool*. New York: Dutton, 1967.

————. *The Hound of Ulster*. New York: Dutton, 1963.

TAYLOR, MILDRED. *Roll of Thunder, Hear My Cry.* New York: Dial, 1976.

TOLKIEN, J. R. R. *The Lord of the Rings.* Boston: Houghton Mifflin, 1974.

TWAIN, MARK. *The Adventures of Tom Sawyer.* 1866. Reprint. New York: Macmillan, 1966.

VAN ALLSBURG, CHRIS. *The Widow's Broom.* Boston: Houghton Mifflin, 1992.

VOIGT, CYNTHIA. *Dicey's Song.* New York: Random House, 1982.

WHITE, E. B. *Charlotte's Web.* New York: Harper, 1952.

WILDER, LAURA INGALLS. The Little House Books. 1932–43. Reprint. New York: Harper, 1953.

The Girl Who Loved Wild Horses
Paul Goble

3

Picture Books

Words or pictures: Which are more important?

Over 50,000 books for children are currently in print, Bowker statisticians assert, and a quick glance at the many on library shelves shows clearly that illustration is growing in importance. We might call a book illustrated when it includes merely a pictorial dust jacket, a cover picture, a frontispiece, or three or four pictures throughout, but the profusely illustrated picture book is the genre most clearly dependent upon illustration. Thanks to a more affluent society, to increased awareness of the importance of childhood, to courses in children's literature and its critical evaluation, and very importantly to the growing significance of awards given to children's books, as well as to publishers' profits accompanying such winning books and to the attractive packaging of many more, we seem to be continuously blessed with well-illustrated children's literature. This is not to say, of course, that poorly illustrated books do not abound, but instead that artistic excellence is increasingly apparent and appreciated.

Perhaps because illustration has historically been tied to text, it has often in the past been regarded as a lesser art. Although at one time Degas, Daumier, and Roualt all illustrated for the public, they are more appreciated now for their other art. Howard Pyle and N. C. Wyeth, who spent their professional lives making books beautiful, were not taken as seriously as other artists, but as printing processes improved and publishers employed art editors, successful artists like Leo and Diane Dillon, Chris Van Allsburg, Maurice Sendak, and a multitude of others were attracted to illustrating children's books and collaborating on them.

Because illustration has the characteristics of an art form, however, it should be regarded as art. Illustrators use the techniques of representation, expressionism, impressionism, and surrealism, of cubism and pointillism, of naive, folk, and collage styles as well as photography. Like other art forms, illustration uses symbolic language for communication. It has both meaning and content created from visual and usually verbal symbols as well. It creates its own illusions of reality often dissimilar to those of the practical world, and by use of figurative devices of all kinds, it opens for us an imaginary vision. Successful art takes us away from our current world to a level of understanding deeper and wider than our limited lives, maybe to a world more ugly or more beautiful, more humorous or more somber, more simple or more complex. And like the best of any art form, it forces us to confront the depths of our secret selves.[1] Unlike looking at the natural world to take it in and to appreciate it, looking at a picture book involves associational meaning, connecting picture with text, or in the wordless book relating what we see through the whole of the story.[2]

It is sometimes said that picture books for the younger child require simpler composition than those for older readers. But real artistry means that complexity may be appropriate for any age, as it is, for example, in *Anno's Journey* by Mitsumasa Anno or in any of Errol LeCain's or Susan Jeffers's pictures.

In any composite of verbal and pictorial storytelling, we see the picture's contents all at once, but are exposed to the verbal story a little at a time in linear progression. Joseph Schwarcz comments that we remember, assemble, and associate the elements of the verbal story, keeping them in mind as we simultaneously acquire new information. In a similar but reverse way, we look at a picture to see it as a whole, then absorb the details little by little, noting how they compose the whole. We may wander over the picture, lingering here and skipping there, absorbing, assimilating, connecting details, colors, and shapes, until we have observed all of the picture. As Schwarcz says, "Following an illustrated text is, then, a complex activity." Despite complexities, however, and more likely because of them, children never weary of the intimately interwoven visual and verbal arts, demanding to see and hear new illustrated stories as well as being excited by continuing discoveries in the familiar ones.

Since finding the earliest records of pictorial art in cave drawings, we have assumed drawings were made to accompany verbal storytelling, that one complements the other. "Associates in a partnership" is one term used to describe the relationship of the writer and illustrator of a picture book. No matter what terms we use, it is clear that if two artists work separately and in differing media, together they create a whole. Pictures make the verbal visible and extend the textual meaning; they permit the artist to add personal interpretation while staying within the story, but they do not overwhelm the text. "Their responsibility is to reflect truly the imaginative tenor of the text (or, in the case of books without text, of the subject) and to create a sequence or group of pictures which add up to a consistent whole,"as B. W. Alderson says. Alderson says further:

> Among the virtues of the traditional approach to book illustration is its care for the details of a picture's narrative content and design. This is not

to say that there is always necessarily something going on in the illustrations, but that there is nearly always a nuance of detail for the eye to feed upon and one which in the best work will be in complete harmony (and may even be visually integrated) with the printed text.[3]

Decrying both artwork that is trite and artwork that distracts and seems to exist for the sake of showing off the artist's skill, Alderson reminds us of the technique, artistry, and versatility that have existed throughout the history of illustration, from Howard Pyle to present-day illustrators.

We note such partnership somewhat differently when we examine pictures made of dolls and puppets in a photograph. There is an interdependence of several artists: the writer, the doll or puppet creator, the designer of the stage, and the director of the whole. Although one person may act in two or more capacities, the result is a compiled effort. Despite photographic techniques of long shots and close-ups, these illustrations convey a sense of still life and seem to be a moment from a play captured by the photographer.

The Illustrative Elements of the Picture Book

Designing the Book

Although illustration and other two-dimensional art have much in common, designing an entire picture book is not like designing other works. Publication requires that the illustrator's work be reproducible in mass, and that requirement determines the whole book design, including size, shape, single- or double-page pictures and the placement of the gutter, endpapers, title page, cover, and dust jacket (whether it uses a wraparound illustration or separate pictures for front and back). Some pages call for decoration, some are best left "silent"; other illustrations may be framed or unframed or may fill the page, edge to edge. All this requires decisions about placement of pictures and text, to create formality or informality, to suit the tone or pace of the story or poem.

Perry Nodelman, who has written extensively about picture books, believes that children who come to understand their conventions and structures can enjoy them with great vitality and conscious appreciation, discovering how pictures and words work together.[4] He suggests that the two kinds of texts are read at different speeds, and that one of their pleasures lies in grasping an element in one narrative that the other does not treat, and that furthermore these details are presented at the proper time. "Reading its short text is a relatively speedy process, whereas reading the series of pictures that accompany the words is a lengthy one that involves the need for close attention, the search for clues, the putting together of apparently disparate pieces of information, the scanning, the remembering, projecting, predicting, discriminating."[5]

The illustrator puts into visual form what the words say, or sometimes what they merely suggest. In *The Snowy Day,* Ezra Jack Keats needs many words to describe Peter's trek through the fresh snow, "with his toes pointing out, like this," dragging "his feet s-l-o-w-l-y" or dragging the "something" and making a third track. In *Fish Is Fish,* Leo Lionni, who like Keats is both author and illustrator, tells in pictures what would take a page of verbal description. When the frog returns to tell the fish of the wonders on land, they can picture only fish bodies: birds as fish with wings, people as fish in clothes, and fish-cows with horns, four legs, and "pink bags for milk." The illustrator has not only put into visual form what the words say, but he has successfully added to the text, creating incongruous humor and commenting on how we see others in terms of ourselves.

Occasionally an illustrator will use *continuous narrative,* the technique seen frequently in comics, in which action is depicted through the repeated picturing of the character in different places or motions all within the same illustration. Using this technique in *A Whistle for Willie,* Keats shows two separate actions in one illustration. Willie, disappointed that he cannot whistle for his dog, tries to distract himself from his feeling of discouragement, first by walking the sidewalk cracks, then by trying to run away from his shadow.

Look next at a longtime favorite, Wanda Gág's *Millions of Cats,* first published in 1928. Gág is steeped in European folktales, and this original fantasy has the traits of such stories. Thumbnail characters (a very old woman and a very old man), the long cadenced lines of oral tradition, and a repeated rhythmic refrain—"Hundreds of cats, thousands of cats, millions and billions and trillions of cats"—are some of the folktale elements. The fantasy that all of these cats could eat each other up and leave only one survivor is revealed at the brisk climax, and the refrain concludes with a happily-ever-after variation: "And not one was as pretty as this one."

The illustrations in sharp black-and-white lithographs are as straightforward and unadorned as the text; the design of each page produces emphatic rounded shapes and patterns that move the eye left to right across the spread. Shading and texture create three-dimensional hills, clouds, fields, trees—and cats, trillions of cats. Cats seen close up are individuals; the anonymous crowd stretches over the infinite hills.

On every page the illustration is adjacent to the substance of the relevant text. As the very old man chooses the first cat for his wife, the spread is balanced with a segment of tree branch over his shoulder on the left margin and a similar picture on the far right. Centered beside the book's gutter and below the text are two views of him choosing cats, each one with a semicircular tree curving protectively around him and the chosen ones. The picture illustrating "And they began to quarrel" is chaotically filled with

Pictures show what the words tell—and more.

cats in all positions and contortions; it seems they may indeed eat each other up. In the final spread Gág utilizes continuous narrative illustration, beginning top left with the skinny survivor cat, picturing it greedily eating in eight additional poses that carry diagonally to the lower gutter and then move to the top right where the plump and contented cat sits. The little figures divide each page into two triangles; within the two upper triangles of each spread is the brief text. Of particular note is the way in which Gág has placed her hand-lettered text, often in centered lines, as part of the overall page design. Nothing is placed casually on the page. When we examine *Millions of Cats,* we understand the concept of *designing* a book.

A particularly satisfying marriage of text and pictures occurs in the more recent *The Name of the Tree,* a Bantu folktale retold by Celia Barker Lottridge and illustrated by Ian Wallace. Illustrations have a misty look that sharpens the feeling that this is a faraway land and a long-ago time when the jungle, the riverbank, and the parched plains yielded no food for starving animals, the lion was king of the jungle, and all the animals lived comfortably together. In quiet neutrals, the title and first pages show the vastness of the arid land and on the horizon silhouettes of the various animals trekking off in search of food. On the edge of the land is a bump that becomes a miraculously tall umbrellalike tree laden with every kind and color of fruit, but all so far up it can be reached by none. The tree itself, described in minimal words, is a colorful spread from margin to margin, with spidery branches topped by a mass of colorful fruit and foliage. The next page is particularly effective—an aerial view of the tree and its much larger shadow of fruited top and tracery branches. Next, a sober group of tearful animals confers with the central figure, a huge tortoise who tells them that to gain the fruit they must learn the name of the tree from the jungle king. The gazelle, fastest of all animals, offers to make the trip to ask the question; Wallace shows the confident gazelle leaping off, close to flight, knowing he will learn the name and return so quickly he cannot possibly forget it.

Now we encounter the lion, a drowsy-looking king roused from sleep on a jungle branch, who kindly says that Ungalli is the fruit tree's name but cautions that he will not tell it again. Bounding along now on the pride of his accomplishment, the gazelle carelessly steps in a rabbit hole and goes "head over hoofs over head over hoofs" and forgets the name. Wallace next shows only heads of eager waiting animals, mouths open in anxious questioning, and includes only part of an elephant trunk, foreshadowing that that beast, known for its memory, may be the next messenger. We move to another misty page where the questing elephant seems small compared to the vast land. His interview with the lion is quite different; the king's eyes blaze, and teeth show in a snarl as he angrily names Ungalli a second time. As the prideful elephant returns to the hungry animals, knowing she cannot forget, she cockily recites the names of all the trees in the jungle and in the rest of the world, but in her arrogance steps in the rabbit hole, and in

The intimate relationship between words and pictures can be called a marriage.

her struggle forgets the name. Now, as Wallace shows her return, we see animal bodies showing despondency, heads down in discouragement, among them a monkey cradling her hungry infant. A small and lowly young tortoise, taught by his great-great-great-grandmother how to remember, next offers to save the starving group, and plods, plods endlessly, "one short leg ahead of the other," across the cracked plains to the jungle, there to encounter a furious king crouched in snarling attack position and nose-to-nose with the humble tortoise. The polite tortoise recites the name over and over, and inches back across the land, creeping over rough rocks but faithfully remembering. As he says the name Ungalli, the tree branches, so spidery before, now bend to allow the animals to reach the luscious fruit. No longer hungry, they encircle the tree as they chant its name, and in their gratitude elevate the very young tortoise. The final page shows an empty tree as an umbrella once again, silhouetted against the misty sky with the contented animals beneath it. The animals, once again silhouetted against the vast sky, provide a frame for the story and a sense of contented closure for the reader.

Illustrations can create a frame for a picture book.

Picturing Figurative Language

Figurative language is inherent in human speech. As children add new experiences and experiment with language, they speak figuratively, exploring how this and that are surprisingly like or unlike. Perhaps one of the most interesting ways in which an illustrator enlivens and complements the text is by picturing figurative language. The most common is the personification of animals, as in Robert McCloskey's *Make Way for Ducklings,* or of inanimate objects, as in Virginia Lee Burton's *The Little House.* Sometimes, however, the illustrator may try a literal picturing of a metaphor, and the mood changes. For example, the moon's kiss on the face of a drowsy child awakens our sense of wonder at the luminous moon. But literally picturing the moon descending into the bedroom to touch the child's face would totally destroy the mood. In her illustrated version of Rudyard Kipling's tale *The Elephant's Child,* Lorinda Bryan Cauley avoids showing the elephant's nose as "no bigger than a boot"; the comparison is convincing as she pictures it but would be distracting if illustrated literally.

Amplifying the Text

The illustrator clarifies and amplifies text, extending it beyond the words or the reader's imagination. "Form," said Ben Shahn in a lecture at Harvard thirty years ago, "is the visible shape of content."[6] Even in books for older children, where illustrations are not as frequent as in picture books, the visual images enhance the text. In Robert McCloskey's *Homer Price,* for example, Uncle Telly's ball of string, "six feet across . . . biggest ball of string in the world," is funny to read about, but vastly more humorous when we see Homer sprawled across the top, trying to add another yard of string. Pooh, tracking the Heffalump, is alarmed at the third set of tracks going round the tree; Ernest Shepard has made us laugh as the illustration solves Pooh's mystery. It is far easier to see the relative size of the Borrowers when Beth and Jo Krush picture them in their home beneath the floor, where postage stamps are hung as pictures, spools are used as stools, and stacked matchboxes serve as chests. The illustration creates a recognizable world and compels us to believe that Borrowers do indeed exist.

In another example, Keats uses somber tones for a picture book when he paints with a dark palette the shadowy tenement of *Apt. 3*. Splotches of dark color give the impression of dinginess, dirty walls, lack of light, and a sense of mystery—what goes on behind these closed doors? This is not physical detail added to text but the mood of the whole. When Sam and Ben invite the blind man to take a walk next day, his harmonica music changes to become quiet and soft, and the double-page spreads change to happier, lighter tones of the earlier colors. The final, lighter-colored spread says nothing about a walk, but silhouetted television aerials and a sky, smoky but blue, answer that question. Here illustrations do not merely extend the text, but the two present a complete and inextricable combination, the creation of a new world. This is what Maurice Sendak, creator of *Where the Wild Things Are,* calls "seamlessness," or the perfect joining of text and pictures.

Sendak calls a perfect joining of words and text "seamlessness."

Arrow to the Sun by Gerald McDermott deserves its Caldecott Award status. Not only are the sun and Southwest colors striking as they range from gold and rust to brown and black—punctuated by occasional spots of green, blue, or rose—striking, but the brief story maintains a folktale economy of language. The few characters of the Pueblo story are identified simply as the Lord of the Sun, a young maiden, the Boy, and the Pot Maker. The angular and vivid illustrations placed at the point of the text force the reader to search for additional meaning. Each of the kivas or ceremonies demanded by the Sun Father is distinctively pictured. Mountain lions, drawn in acute bright angles, are followed by a page of quiet. Being attacked by bees and surrounded by lightning are further tests of the Boy's sonship. Glorious color attends his return to earth to bring his father's spirit, and the lively Dance of Life begins. The book is a perfect marriage of text and picture.

The Legend of the Bluebonnet, retold by Tomie dePaola, is another picture book illustrated with flat and static Indians. Color is more interesting than form in this early dePaola book about a Comanche child who gives her most cherished doll as an offering to the gods so that they will send rain to the village. Everyone in She-Who-Is-Alone's life has died of the famine, but the little girl's sacrificial gift of her only possession, a doll, causes bluebonnets to grow upon the arid earth, and all begins to thrive.

Contrast is provided in *The Story of Jumping Mouse.* a Native American legend of the Northern Plains retold and illustrated by John Steptoe. The effective black-and-white illustrations are proof that picture books do not need bright color. The moral tale, however, is far more wordy than most traditional legends. Keeping hope alive within carries Jumping Mouse along on his journey to a far-off land he longs to see. As he gives to wolf and bison his own senses of smell and sight, he never loses the vision of his goal; his compassion transforms him into an eagle.

An examination of *The Girl Who Loved Wild Horses,* written and illustrated by Paul Goble, can be nearly endless. Each page is wealthy with interesting form and color. Stones, birds, yucca lilies, horses, butterflies, and the Girl are meticulously shown in all shapes and sizes. Plunging immediately into story, the first page tells readers that the people move from place to place following the buffalo. The Girl, who loves her people, understands and protects all horses, burden carriers, and buffalo hunters. She awakens to hear the horses stampeded by crashes of thunder and lightning, and among them finds a beautiful spotted stallion with whom she and the lost horses live in freedom and happiness. The richness in the pictures holds attention throughout.

Changing the Story

The illustrator influences, and in some cases changes, the story—not the text, but the story. The greater the proportion of illustrations to text, the greater the influence the illustrations have in the creation of the composite. In some cases text and pictures seem to provide two stories; the impact of Pat Hutchins's *Rosie's Walk,* for example, is dependent upon recognizing this duality. The text tells us that Rosie walks innocently across the farm; the pictures tell us her life is threatened by the menacing fox. Holding these two stories in mind simultaneously constitutes the delight of the whole. In another example, objective narration combined with humorous illustration creates a two-dimensional story as pictures provide plot that is unspoken in words. This double story occurs in Nancy Tafuri's *Have You Seen My Duckling?* We see the absent duckling, although the searching mother cannot.

Illustration may also give more exact information, create a mood and atmosphere by depiction of a setting or action, or make us care about a character because the pictured dress and countenance reveal more of a person than does the text. Thus illustration not only clarifies and amplifies text, but extends it beyond our own imaginations. In A. A. Milne's *Winnie-the-Pooh,* Pooh's gluttony as he sits surrounded by water "on his branch, dangling his legs . . . beside him . . . ten pots of honey" is made vivid by Shepard's illustration. By contrast, notice how Gustav Tenngren's illustrations for *Snow White and the Seven Dwarfs* change the story. We assume from the title that this is Snow White's story, but that is not the case.

Illustrations may also distort a story.

Because the bland beauty of Tenngren's Snow White is no match for the personalities we read on the faces of the seven dwarfs and the wicked witch, this has become *their* story: *The Seven Dwarfs, the Witch (and Snow White)*. The story has changed, and we do not face so clearly one of its major themes, that the forbidden is tempting.

When illustrated by different artists, a story becomes many quite different tales, each influenced by the vision of the artist, the episodes selected for picturing, the chosen palette, the rhythm and movement of line, the meticulous detail or the bold sweep of pen or brush. Look, for example, at different versions of the Cinderella story, of which new editions continue to appear. Despite knowing well the texts of Charles Perrault and others, the reader still gains very different impressions from the various versions. In Shirley Hughes's retelling with 25 pictures, Cinderella herself, whose story this is, appears 18 times, often in less than central focus, while her wicked stepsisters appear 11 times, and often as the major focus. We see Cinderella being scorned by her stepmother, dressing her stepsisters' hair, scrubbing the floor while the sisters preen, watching wistfully in the doorway while in the foreground they dress for the ball, abjectly weeping while we focus on the fairy godmother, and, in a rear view, watching as the splendid coach appears. Then, at long last, on a full page, we see her dressed in her magical finery. In the next picture, she does not appear at all, and in still others, she shares equal billing with the prince, the townspeople, the fairy godmother, the chamberlain. In ratio of two pictures of the stepsisters for every three of Cinderella, we meet stepsisters echoing their mother's sneer on the frontispiece, and kneeling in supplication for mercy in the twenty-fourth picture. Because of the strong focus on the stepsisters, the impact of the story is that Cinderella is the victim of their envy but is magically saved.

In Paul Galdone's version, Cinderella appears not as beautiful and good, but as pathetic, as Goldone seizes the opportunity to paint wonderful lizards, mice, horses, town criers, coach, and cartoonlike stepsisters. Plot details seem to carry illustrations; Cinderella herself, though important, still does not illuminate the theme of the good person who yearns for and receives acceptance and appreciation.

In still another version. Errol LeCain's highly stylized illustrations distance us from all the characters. In a palette of low color intensity and in pictures swirling with stylized motion, all characters are strictly fairy-tale-never-happened figures. The illustrator seems to have been carried away with the infinite possibilities for creating elaborate coaches, footmen, ball guests, and an evil-looking witch never mentioned in the text. Since in this book pictures are often unrelated to the accompanying text, they serve more as decorations than as illustrations for the story.

The way in which the pictures portray or add to the textual information creates the information itself, as we might note from Nonny Hogro-

Illustrations which subordinate the major character may affect the theme of the story.

gian's version of Cinderella. She uses soft pastels in illustrations bathed in a mist of fantasy that enhance the fairy-tale qualities. Cinderella, herself a lovely girl not unlike lovely girls we might know, convinces us by her humility and devotion that she is indeed as good as she is beautiful and deserves therefore to be rich and to live happily ever after.

Look next at another contrast. Two picture-book versions of Hiawatha's childhood provide an interesting comparison. Both books record the Longfellow text about the legendary Native American, but the two are very different. As Errol LeCain often does, here he creates a sense of mystery with his dark colors and intricately framed action. Young Hiawatha is a wide-eyed child who resembles the long-ago Campbell's Soup Kid with his round face and round eyes. This is Hiawatha's story, but the double-spread title page features in tiny profile his ancient and wrinkled grandmother Nokomis. Hiawatha's bent knee, normally indicative of running movement, does little to animate a picture, nor do the animals from whom he learns have any but stationary form. LeCain's illustrations have a static quality, as though a camera had taken pictures. No one and nothing is animated. On the other hand, Susan Jeffers's title page pictures the forest environment, and opens the story by showing Nokomis grieving for her dying daughter Wenonah as Wenonah lies beside her newborn infant Hiawatha. The story has already begun. Using a subdued palette, Jeffers depicts in heavenly shadow the warrior ghosts as Nokomis teaches Hiawatha the lore known to Native Americans. Wide-eyed Hiawatha grows older from page to page as he learns more and still more of human relationships with the natural world of animals, flowers, sun, and moon. By the endpaper, the boy is close to manhood, a young brave at home in the forest and carrying bow and quiver. LeCain's book is a group of pictures; Jeffers's is a story with illustrations that extend the text.

The most effective illustrations extend the text.

The Literary Elements of the Picture Book

We are often deceived into thinking that because the text for picture books is brief, the writer of the text need not be judged by the standards of literary excellence. When we see, however, that it is possible to develop surprisingly full characters, like Beatrix Potter's Peter Rabbit, to create an engaging plot, as Maurice Sendak so skillfully does in *Where the Wild Things Are,* to show with words as well as pictures an integral setting like that in *Just a Dream* by Chris Van Allsburg—when we see all this, we realize that a good picture book is not as simple as it looks. Our appreciation grows when we notice that words make comparisons and sound resembles meaning—that style is important. As Perry Nodelman comments: "The excitement of a good picture book is the constant tension between the moments isolated by the pictures and the flow of words that join these moments together. The jumpy rhythm of picture books is quite different from the gradually intensifying flow of stories told by words themselves."[7]

Thus, words as well as pictures—fresh comparisons, vivid sensory appeals, and the writer's intelligence and wit—make the most successful story. Some slight tension holds our interest, and the simplest of thematic ideas, such as "We need food for the spirit as well as for the body" from *Frederick* by Leo Lionni, ties it all together. The elements of literature, then, are important here too, just as they are in other genres. By pinning pictures to words and words to ideas, the best text can enlarge the child's world in ways that even the most careful observation of pictures cannot do.

How Raven Brought Light to People, retold by Ann Dixon in the long phrasing of an oral *pourquoi* tale, begins traditionally—"Long ago when the earth was new" and there was no light, the Raven used his magical powers to become first a pine needle, then a willful child beloved by his adoring grandfather, who gives the crying child the boxes that hold sun, moon, and stars. The familiar threes—doting grandparent, mischievous child, magical changeling raven—and traditional ending implying that now the world will be blessed with light, constitute a familiar form for a tale of southeastern Alaska. Illustrations are as convincing as text. The Chief's age and power, the Native American dress and totem poles all convince the reader that this is a true tale.

By contrast, *Dreamplace* is a place for tourists to speculate about the Pueblos. Tourists and Native Americans appear in the same pictures, as travelers attempt to picture the life lived by the former dwellers. Text and pictures do little but confuse rather than clarify.

Character

One of the surprising discoveries about **character** in fiction is that a round character can emerge from a brief story for a small child. Contrast *Peter Rabbit* with *Cowboy Small* by Lois Lenski. What does any child remember from *Cowboy Small?* It might be called "a ho-hum book—soonest read, soonest forgotten."[8]

Cowboy Small saddles, mounts, rides, dismounts, cooks, eats, sleeps under the stars, rides again, rounds up cattle, eats again, ropes a calf, helps in branding, plays a guitar and sings, sleeps, rides a bronco, falls off, and rides again. Cowboy Small is just his name, and even that is no name. Such a story has been written with a message in mind, namely to acquaint a child with the job description of the mythical American cowboy.

Would Cowboy Small have stuffed himself as Peter Rabbit did? We know Peter Rabbit and the Ugly Duckling; from their actions we know a

Even the briefest of picture book texts can show fully developed character.

great deal about their feelings and thoughts. We understand and come to care about them; we remember them. In a text shorter than that about *Cowboy Small*, Ezra Jack Keats shows another Peter in *The Snowy Day* as a real boy who is delighted at the snowfall, happy with his angel making, sad at his snowball's melting, and wistful about joining the snowball fight; in short, Keats's Peter is a character we know and like.

Perhaps at this point it is necessary to disgress, since in Potter's *Peter Rabbit* some adults may find rabbits and people difficult to interchange. What matters here is not that Peter, like a rabbit, moves on four legs and lives in a sandbank under the roots of a fir tree, nor for that matter that, like a child, he wears a little blue jacket with gold buttons. What makes Peter a little boy is his childlike personality and behavior.

While adults may find it difficult to attribute to animals the traits of human beings, this is not difficult for most children. The child listening to *Peter Rabbit* has no difficulty seeing Peter as a child, because he is a developed, or round, character. When an animal in a children's story is a believable human being, the **anthropomorphism** creates fantasy. If the fantastic but believable character is involved in action related to character, children feel very much at home with the whole idea.

Character and incident in *Peter Rabbit* are so closely tied to one another that we can see no separation. Peter is mischievous from the start; throughout the story he believes he knows better than he actually does. He is adventuresome, since he crawls under the gate, despite his father's accident, which resulted in his being eaten in a rabbit pie. He is greedy: he gorges himself on lettuces, French beans, and radishes. He is frightened and frantic in his flight and, woebegone, he cries. As we hear that this is the second lost jacket and shoes in a fortnight, we know Peter's behavior is consistent. Uncomplaining, Peter accepts the kind nursing of his loving mother; he is a secure child. Peter is no cardboard, two-dimensional rabbit. He is instead a round and believable central character.

Maria of *Too Many Tamales* by Gary Soto yields to temptation while kneading tamale dough and tries on her mother's diamond ring. The whole extended family enjoys the tamales, but Maria suddenly discovers she has lost the ring in the dough, and her cousins must join her in eating them all—to find the ring. Here, illustrations by Ed Martinez serve to demolish stereotypes of Mexican-Americans as poor, dependent migrants.

In *Armien's Fishing Trip* by Catherine Stock, a truly multicultural society lives peacefully on the southern tip of Africa. Filipinos, Europeans, and freed slaves from Malaya and Java are all part of the fishing enterprise. The story follows a boy who is taunted for having lost his skills once he moved to the city. To prove himself, he stows away on his uncle's boat, sees an old sailor swept into the sea, and becomes a hero through his cries and quick thinking. The issue is not that many cultures can live peacefully; Armien's challenge and response show him as a strong character, whom we know well.

Children have no problem with talking animals or objects.

In *The Patchwork Quilt,* Valerie Flournoy and illustrator Jerry Pinkney show character clearly as they tell of Tanya's beloved grandmother in the midst of making her masterpiece quilt, one that includes, among many others, scraps from a brother's old jeans and her mother's holiday dress. Tanya's diligence in finishing the quilt entices her family into joining in the project, and its completion coincides with the grandmother's recovery.

Can we say that children want to hear their favorites again and again because of curiosity about the outcome of the story? Hardly, since the first reading satisfies both parents and children on that score. There must be other considerations. While Beatrix Potter's detailed, delicately colored illustrations as well as suspenseful action give pleasure to the reader and the listener, the character of Peter Rabbit as the universal child is the magnet that pulls us back to read and reread the book. Peter's actions are inherent in his personality, or as F. Scott Fitzgerald says, "Action is character." The one produces the other, true to Henry James's views on the interrelatedness of character and action.

Plot

The brevity of text in picture books does not eliminate the necessity for some kind of **plot,** some action or tension, the quality most likely to keep us reading. Peter Rabbit's curiosity and waywardness create the tension in his story; Max's wild behavior in *Wild Things* opens the action, and the exciting roars and threats followed by his taming them all continue the tension. Even the story *The Snowy Day* has its quiet surprises, the simplest kind of plot.

In *The Bravest Flute: A Story of Courage in the Mayan Tradition* by Ann Grifalconi, a small boy chosen to play his flute and lead the procession on New Year's Day barely has the strength to walk the long way to the assembled elders and shamans at the cathedral. He must also carry the big drum strapped to his back while the bigger drummer bangs away on it. Fortified by a rainbow and a glass of water, he bravely makes the long walk and is rewarded by the recent widow of the former flutist. The boy finishes the walk with new energy and the silver-and-black gift of the flutist's instrument. His courage is rewarded by the elders; his family will have food and seed corn for the next year. The handsome child and the gentle, peace-loving Mayans are vividly pictured as they celebrate.

Another bilingual picture book, *Calling the Doves*—by Mexican poet Juan Felipe Herrera—shows what life must be for a migrant worker. Juan was born on the road, his mother tells him. The narrator recalls in simple but evocative language the pleasures of sitting under the starry night sky; hearing his father's stories of his immigration from Chihuahua and his imitated bird calls; eating his breakfast in the open air; and the moving from farm to farm while laborers pick broccoli, melons, and lettuce and leave the grapes to dry in the sun to make raisins. Juan's memories are all pleasant—

of his father playing his harmonica and his mother healing migrants' painful legs and feet. Finally, when it is time for Juan to stay in one place and go to school, the family lives in a little house his father has made on the chassis of an abandoned car. Now the father works as a gardener. Despite their itinerant lifestyle, the family is stable and happy. The quiet title about doves, symbol of peace, reflects the story's tone—quietly appreciative of family, of the wonders of nature, and of growing and working. Illustrations in bright colors, "happy colors," show stylized fabric design, rolling hills, brightly colored birds, and contented families.

Occasionally we find a picture book with an **open ending,** such as *The Garden of Abdul Gasazi* by Chris Van Allsburg, which leaves us wondering if Fritz the dog has actually been turned into a duck—temporarily.

Picture books without tension or conflict are less successful. There are many examples. Look at *Hold My Hand*, described on the jacket as "a moment of intensity," yet there is no tension, no intensity. For a specific example, consider *Willie Goes to the Seashore,* a picture-story book with little excitement. The family has a small cottage at the beach. In a total of 75 printed lines, they unpack, roll in the sand, swim, hunt shells, build a sand castle, rebuild the sand castle, and splash in the water. They hang seaweed around their necks and go to bed. Next day Willie finds an old boat, explores the rocks, sees a crab dart off, collects firewood, and puts weiners on roasting sticks. Willie "never had such fun." Willie does everything—and nothing.

Suppose, instead, that Willie had built an elaborate sand castle, planning it, admiring it, embellishing it, and patting it into shape. Then, during the weiner roast, the waves in their regular tidal shifts destroy the castle! Result: tension. Or suppose Willie had explored the old boat, found it had oarlocks and a hollow bow, and made an imaginary fishing expedition beyond the point. Now the seashore truly becomes a place to have fun, and some tension or conflict is the cause. Look at *Margaret's Birthday* and note the similarities to the random activity of Willie's seashore experience.

Even in a simple plot each character has a part to play; in fact, the simpler the story, the more confusing it is to have irrelevant characters. In *The Tub People* we meet seven small wooden dolls lined up on the edge of the tub: father, mother, child, grandmother, doctor, policeman, and dog. The child disappears down the drain, the drain slows, the plumber pulls him out, and he is reunited with his father and mother. Now they all stand on the bedroom windowsill. At no time are the grandmother, the doctor, the policeman, or the dog part of the plot; they are merely pictured. The author chose to write about seven specific toys, known to the writer, and although there was no point in including them all, no adjustment was made in plotting; this is therefore not a well-planned story.

Straightforward chronology is easily understood in two picture books that trace a family through generations of change. In *Island Boy* by Barbara Cooney, a father buys an island, builds a house, raises a family, and sees

Some kind of tension is needed to hold a reader's interest.

twelve children leave; one returns, cares for the father's grandchild there, and is finally lost at sea. In a second, by Patricia Polacco, *The Keeping Quilt,* a quilt made of scraps from family life left behind in Russia provides for generations a tablecloth for festivities, a huppa (tent) for weddings, a tent for play, and a blanket for newborns.

By contrast, *Soon-Hee in America* lacks any organization and is merely a collection of photographs of a Korean child in school, at the zoo, in New York or Washington. There is no recognizable logic for the sequence, and the static pictures seem the sole reason for the book.

Look, too, at *Nessa's Fish,* a story of Arctic dwellers identified only by their depiction in clothing of the Far North. Nessa and her grandmother ice-fish, "jigging" all day. But what is that? Grandmother falls sick, and Nessa protects her from freezing, as well as from foxes, wolves, and bears. How does Nessa know what to do? Are there traditions, legends, charms that help? Are intergenerational fishing trips common? The disappointing story lacks suspense or action, and just stops as Nessa walks home with her parents and her grandmother.

Plenty of excitement accompanies the fanciful (and bilingual) *My Aunt Otilia's Spirits* by Richard Garcia as Aunt Otilia's visit brings mysterious wall knocking, kitchen crashes, and shaking beds. But when Aunt Otilia's bones leave her body and fly out the closed window, that's truly remarkable. Demonio puts the body parts back together all wrong, suspenseful action that Robin Cherin and Roger L. Reyes picture wonderfully. Garcia says in an afterword that Latin Americans often believe in the supernatural.

Birthday parties are favorites for children. In Valiska Gregory's *Happy Burpday, Maggie McDougal,* Maggie, who has spent all her money, cannot buy a gift for her best friend, Bonkers. But Grandma turns up the first Green Lizardman comic book ever printed, Bonkers's absolute favorite of all time. Problem solved. Meanwhile, in the classroom, a frustrated teacher tries to explain a "family tree" with its branches, which do *not* include puppies and goldfish; she has no better luck with heirlooms that have been "handed down"—through a group of relatives, each one taller than the last. Families and friendships are the substance of the story, which is interspersed with "the grosses," like big burping binges and jealousy. Plot moves as casually as life itself.

The brief text and plot of Sherry Garland's *The Lotus Seed* tell the story of a seed taken from the garden of the Vietnamese emperor, who is forced by war to leave his throne. To the grandmother, the lotus seed represents her country and its traditions. When a child steals the seed and plants it, the blooming lotus brings joy: its seeds will preserve the immigrants' culture in their new homeland.

Yang the Youngest and His Terrible Ear by Lensey Namioka is another story of integration into the American way of life. In a progressive plot, Chinese Yang loves baseball, and his friend Matt loves the violin. At the obligatory music recital, Yang bow-syncs while from behind the screen Matt plays the violin for the Yang family's quartet. Matt's huge success leads Matt's surprised father to allow him to take violin lessons and Yang's father to let Yang forget the violin and learn to play baseball. To the boys, customs and language are baffling. Matt, staying for dinner at Yang's house, asks to go to the bathroom, wanting to wash his hands; he finds live carp in the bathtub because Chinese never buy dead fish. When Matt's father is "laid off," Yang wonders whether he fell and got hurt. Furthermore, how does one sit a baby?

In *The Drinking Gourd* by F. N. Monjo, the handle of the Big Dipper, the gourd of the title, points toward the North Star. Slaves, working and singing, refer to the "Drinking Gourd" as the way to freedom on the Underground Railroad. Tommy discovers that his father is a conductor who hides slaves in his barn, and guides them to the next station. When Tommy finds a hiding slave family of four, he fakes a story for the marshall about his own flight from punishment by driving off in the sanctuary hay wagon. Bond between father and son is strengthened as they assist families in defying the unjust Fugitive Slave Act. Plot is revealed in chronological order.

Quiet suspense is carried throughout *The Wednesday Surprise* by Eve Bunting, illustrated by Donald Carrick, as we wonder about the birthday gift being prepared for Papa. Only at the end do we realize that the narrator, seven-year-old Anna, has secretly taught Grandma to read. The story concludes with a **closed ending.** A similar triumph occurs in *The Day of Ahmed's Secret,* as told by Florence Parry Heide and Judith Heide Gilliland. Ahmed—who, judging from the lush and detailed illustrations by Ted Lewin, seems to live in the Middle East—is proud that he can contribute to his family by earning money delivering bottles of fuel to city dwellers, always holding his secret close until he is at home in the evening: He has learned to write his name.

Even the simplest stories for children can have conflict or tension. Will Goldilocks be caught? Will the Three Little Pigs survive by the hair of their chinny-chin-chins? Will the troll who lives under the bridge get the Billy-Goats Gruff? Suspense builds in each of these stories as a threat is repeated three times, and conflict is climaxed by defeat of the threatener. Goldilocks gets away, the wolf falls into boiling water, and the troll is crushed to bits, body and bones.

Theme

Some stories for young children are both humor-filled and rich with a variety of **themes,** but check the shelf of children's fare in any bookstore and notice how often action or situation humor is its only element. The popularity of books like Hans Rey's *Curious George,* with its exciting action and variety—the monkey's balloon flight, which coincidentally ends on top of the traffic light, and his play with the telephone, which calls in a fire alarm—seems to suggest that a child can appreciate only coincidence and situation humor. But children love George for a different reason: his curiosity matches theirs.

There is additional satisfaction in a story with a theme. The South African children of Rachel Isadora's book *At the Crossroads* greet the reader with great smiles. They are gathered to await the return of their fathers, who work for ten months at a stretch in the mines. In the heat, the families sing and dance as they await the trucks bringing fathers and husbands. One by one, family by family, they leave until only six children are left at the crossroads in the moonlight. The final picture shows the children, hugging their fathers and marching home in joyful song. As the fathers carry little ones on their shoulders, they demonstrate the theme: Families are loving units in all cultures.

The simplest story can illustrate a significant point. The jacket blurb of *Billy the Great* by Rosa Guy, illustrated by Caroline Binchy, says that parents cannot determine a child's future, but its implied theme is that racial prejudice may work in both directions. Billy's best friend is white and the son of a tattooed truck driver, not good enough for Billy's black parents, who want him to grow up to be a doctor. Billy just wants to play baseball with Rod. Fun is fun.

> Even a simple story can make a significant point.

From the first words in *Mama, Do You Love Me?* by Barbara Joosse, the theme is apparent. As the little girl who lives in the Arctic repeats her question, she posits several scenarios: Even if I break ptarmigan eggs, or turn into a musk-ox or moose, will you love me? Nothing, not even misbehavior or transformation, limits a mother's love.

In Maurice Sendak's *Where the Wild Things Are,* we have a character, Max, whom we care about, acting out a conflict that interests us—and all united by an implicit theme that can be stated in several ways. The story is more than a situation with wonderfully effective illustrations, more than the pleasure of its rhythmic style. The story also has a strong theme.

Many kinds of stories have their place for small children: some offer the listening child laughter from a narrative with physical or situation humor, or the reassurance found in pure, day-to-day routine, the unexciting commonplace. Other stories, like Miska Miles's *Annie and the Old One,* combine freshness in language, imagination in plot, and significance in theme, as well as distinctive illustrations.

Once again we refer to *The Tale of Peter Rabbit,* which has its own implicit theme. Action and suspense race to the point of Peter's flopping down on the sandy floor of the rabbit home, where he shuts his eyes. Mother, who is busy cooking, wonders what he has done with his new clothes, but she does not lecture, or spank, or compare naughty Peter to good Flopsy, Mopsy, and Cotton-tail. Although Peter didn't feel very well that evening, there is no hint of "It serves him right. He was naughty."

Peter's mother puts him to bed and gives him a dose of camomile tea. Potter does not call the tea punitive medicine, nor does she describe it as tasting bad. Nor does she call Flopsy, Mopsy, and Cotton-tail's bread, milk, and blackberries reward for goodness.

Is the story didactic? Although we adults see clearly that disobedience and curiosity can get you into trouble, *Peter Rabbit* is, after all, for a small child. The theme is implied, but not didactic. *Peter Rabbit* becomes didactic, however, if a reteller adds a single phrase to Potter's final paragraph, saying that Flopsy, Mopsy, and Cotton-tail, "who were good little bunnies," ate bread and milk and blackberries at suppertime. Or when we see another illustrator's picture showing an admonitory plaque hanging on the kitchen wall, saying, "Good bunnies obey," or preaching a more positive lesson, "Obedience is rewarded." It seems likely that an implied theme—"Even when you're naughty, mother loves and accepts you"—has kept *Peter Rabbit* a much-loved story.

Lucille Clifton writes picture book texts clearly focused on theme. Her book *My Brother Fine with Me* is a simple story of Baggy, the little brother who wants to leave home with his minibike cards and a toothbrush to be independent, to be a black warrior without parents to make rules. Johnetta, who says she likes it fine at home except for him, doesn't wish to join him. But Johnny finds it lonely without Baggy to bother her, to watch over at the park, to eat the peanut butter and jelly sandwiches she fixes. Thus the theme: My brother's fine with me.

When Africa Was Home by Karen Lynn Williams portrays an interracial friendship; this one blooms when Peter lives in Africa and plays with Yekha, eating balls of corn paste from the same bowl and dipping them in the African sauce. When Peter's father must leave for another job in the United States, Peter is afraid he won't know what to do. He knows no other way of eating or playing, or of being mannerly. When the family's stay in the United States is over, Peter is delighted to return to Africa and his friends. The theme is that acceptance is easy in childhood.

A controversial picture book published in 1990 is Michael Willhoite's *Daddy's Roommate,* a matter-of-fact picture of gay family life in which Daddy's friend comes to live with him. The speaker is a boy who tells us that Daddy and his friend work, and eat, and shave, and fight and make up, and sleep together. They also read to him, catch bugs, play ball, picnic, and shop with him. The boy's mother explains that this is one more kind of love and that love is a good thing. The boy is happy, and that is that.[9]

An increasing number of books for all ages explore the theme of conservation and the restoration of the earth. Two such picture books are *The Land of Gray Wolf* by Thomas Locker and the wordless *Window* written and illustrated in collage by Jeannie Baker. In the first, land taken from Indians is cleared and farmed until the soil is exhausted and returns to wilderness. In the second, the family sees their country lot gradually surrounded by development and tract housing, and the next generation moves to the country, looking for the landscape of childhood. Chris Van Allsburg, frequent prizewinner for his picture books, has produced another beauty with *Just a Dream*. Unenlightened Walter is too lazy to recycle—until his dream takes him into a future time when trash submerges homes, neon-lit hotels rest on mountaintops, fishermen finally celebrate the first fish of the week, and forests become factory land. Walter thus realizes that protecting the environment is important.

Themes of all kinds occur in picture books. Names are our identity, and Kevin Henkes's *Chrysanthemum* explores the idea that having one's name ridiculed makes one miserable, but approval can change self-image. *The Big Orange Splot* by Daniel Manus Pinkwater explores the idea that being identical to other people is far less fun than acting on a dream. When a seagull drops orange paint on the roof of Mr. Plumbeam's house, he doesn't paint it over so he'll again fit into the "neat street" of identical houses; instead he jazzes up his house with all kinds of vivid color, plants palm trees, hangs a hammock, and has an alligator for a pet. Before long, owners of every house on the street have painted their dream homes: a ship, a balloon, a castle, and a pillared porch.

In Margaree King Mitchell's picture book *Uncle Jed's Barber Shop,* the implicit theme is "despite setbacks, hold on to your dream." Uncle Jed, too poor to open his own shop, walks across the county cutting hair. Sarah Jean's operation and the Great Depression took his savings, but Uncle Jed manages to save enough so that at the age of 79, he can open his own shop complete with four chairs, a shining floor, and a barber pole. Throughout the story, the reader glimpses discrimination against African Americans, who must wait in separate rooms to see a doctor when they are sick, are not called until all white patients have been seen, and must pay before treatment; separate water fountains, restrooms, and schools are also mentioned. The strong theme, however, depicts pride and determination rather than self-pity.

Readers discover similar values in quite different cultures.

Or look at a more traditional tale. By tradition, Native American women trade with humility and gratitude. *Heetunka's Harvest* by Jennifer Berry Jones, illustrated by Shannon Keegan, is filled with naturalistic drawings of the tiny mouse and her environment, fitted into framed pages. The moral tale of greed is about a woman who fails to trade her own corn for the white beans she discovers and steals from a mouse's shallow nest; greed is rewarded with disaster.

Setting

Picture books can and often must be extremely effective in depicting **setting**. The brief text of Cynthia Rylant's *When I Was Young in the Mountains* describes primarily the actions of the child narrator, but the pictured swimming hole, the cabin kitchen, the general store, the backyard pump, and the porch swing are all extensions of the text. We see from pictured setting more than from the words why the child never wanted to go anywhere else.

Contemporary society, as we are reminded by the battering of advertisements, is relying less on words for communication and more upon pictures. The trend toward nonverbal communication is reflected in contemporary picture-story books that often depend entirely upon illustration to create setting. All we know of setting in *Ming Lo Moves the Mountain,* for example, is the mountain. Arnold Lobel's pictures do the rest to show the Oriental setting. In literature for children, however, word pictures give the child an opportunity to create setting in his or her own mind, a special kind of experience that is one of the delights of literature. Similarly, in an effective and seamless joining, words and pictures unite to show setting in *Where the Buffaloes Begin* by Olaf Baker.

The Tale of Peter Rabbit is a classic example of **integral setting.** As both author and illustrator, Potter integrates visual and word pictures; setting is so closely interwoven with character, action, and theme that we are never aware of description as such. On the first page, the family home appears with its soft, sandy floor—the bank under the roots of a large fir tree. Soon we are under the gate and can see the cucumber frame. In this garden, cabbages and potatoes as well as French beans and lettuces grow not far from the net-covered gooseberry bush and the toolshed, with its watering can and its three flower pots on the windowsill. The stone wall has a gate and a stone step; close by are a pond and a wheelbarrow. We even hear the garden sound of the "scritching, scratching" hoe. This setting is not a suburban front yard. What happens to Peter is influenced by elements in the garden: the gate, the cucumber frame, the gooseberry bush, the pond, and the toolshed with its three flowerpots. Although she mentions each item in the setting, nowhere does Potter stop the action to describe it, and yet at no point is setting unimportant. In this perfectly integrated picture book, illustration and text work together to create setting.

Point of View

Point of view, or the mind through which the writer chooses to tell the story, also varies in picture books, as it does in all literature. Beatrix Potter wishes to tell a story about a rabbit whose mischievous nature gets him into trouble in a vegetable garden. How should she tell the story? Potter has several choices of point of view. She can be objective, telling just what happens and saying nothing about the effect of events upon Peter's feelings. If Mother Rabbit tells Peter's story, she might be weary of Peter's regular disobedience and of buying new jackets and shoes, but loves Peter just the same. If Flopsy, one of the good little bunnies, tells the story, we might see a prim little sister who, because she is always good, thinks Peter really ought to know better. Cotton-tail might tell the story enviously: "If I had

We "see" setting through words as well as pictures.

any courage, I'd have some excitement, too." But Potter chooses to tell her tale from a point inside Peter's feelings and thoughts. We know Peter's curiosity, his appetite as he munches on, his worry as he asks directions, and his panic as he upsets the flower pots. We are as relieved as Peter when he finds his way home and is not scolded for his adventure. Every element in the story has been affected by Potter's choice of point of view. Peter is the protagonist and Mr. McGregor the antagonist. We know the character of Peter; his conflict is determined by the setting. Because of Peter's adventure and his mother's kind care, we understand the thematic point—that although a child is naughty, he or she is still loved.

There are first-person stories among picture books for the smallest child, such as Dr. Seuss's *If I Ran the Zoo.* The "I" narrator of these stories, however, is of minor significance, since the focus is on the sheer nonsense of the doggerel and the pleasure of the sounds and rhythms, to say nothing of the stories' greatest assets, the inventive illustrations. *And to Think That I Saw It on Mulberry Street* uses first-person point of view effectively; it is not only skillful nonsense, but it also shows a child's imagination creating a fantastic parade. In writer Diane Siebert and illustrator Wendell Minor's collaborative *Heartland,* the heartland of America is the speaker. The heartland speaks of all it sees and is, what it grows, the blessings of nature and the trials it endures, and how it changes with the seasons. A serious book, it praises the farms, the farmer, and all that the heartland contributes.

The Polar Express by Chris Van Allsburg, although published in 1985, is fast taking its place as a Christmas classic. It, too, is written in first-person point of view, one that perfectly fits the story itself. The boy did not wish to believe there was no Santa Claus, and his experience disproves his friends' skepticism. He boards the Polar Express train when it stops in his front yard at midnight to take him and the trainload of children to the North Pole to meet Santa and his elves. Given a single sleighbell by Santa, he is delighted—but loses it through the hole in his pajama pocket. Yet under the tree next morning is the bell, wrapped and accompanied by Santa's note. No one can hear the bell but the boy and his sister Sarah—because no one else believes. This story we must hear from the believer himself; it requires the first-person narrator.

We see some successful objective point-of-view narration at picture-book level, like, for example, Ludwig Bemelmans's *Madeline,* in which minimal omniscience is present. Ezra Jack Keats's *The Snowy Day* seems at first glance to be objective. We know that Peter has a happy time in the snow because we see all his fun, and we remember our own similar pleasures. But an omniscient writer also comments that Peter thinks it might be fun to play with the big boys, and he knows he isn't old enough. When Peter cannot find the vanished snowball he had tucked into his jacket pocket the night before, he feels sad. Even this simple and short story makes brief use of an interpretive omniscience. Perhaps, by the process of elimination, we can conclude that either of the omniscient points of view may be successful in stories for the young child.

Style

Picture books, too, need style that awakens the interest of the young child in the nuances of possible meaning and the pleasures of language. The Blackfoot Indians of the plains have a traditional belief that the buffalo herd springs from a misty lake in the west. *Where the Buffaloes Begin* by Olaf Baker is a beautiful book in black and white, impressive in its evocation of the infinite plains and their awesome buffaloes. Little Wolf is caught in a stampeding herd: A "heaving mass of buffaloes billowed like the sea." His "blood stirs along his scalp," and to his cry the animals reply, "bellowing a wild answer that rolls" above the plains like thunder. Contrast these phrases with the halting style of *Mika's Apple Tree:* "They dressed and went into the house. Supper was ready. They had cabbage soup with rye bread and butter. They had pancakes with jam." Even combining short sentences would create more vitality in style, and yet, if the early reader were reading alone, it would add no more difficulty to the language.

Look again at *Peter Rabbit,* the imagery describing setting, the blue jacket with brass buttons, the five currant buns. Notice the understatement of Father's getting into trouble there, the mock-serious tone of "implored him to exert himself," the onomatopoeia of "scritch-scratch" and "lippety, lippety," the assonance and consonance of "Flopsy, Mopsy, Cotton-tail," and the surprise of the name "Peter." *Peter Rabbit* has style.

One of the pleasures of Jamake Highwater's *Moonsong Lullaby* is the figurative language. The moon sings a sweet lullaby to the people beside the campfire, while the rabbit and the fox dream, the hawk praises the moonlight, and the roots burrow into the depths of the earth. The night is a shelter for troubled souls, and the moon caresses them. All of nature is personified, and each image connotes contentment and security.

Owl Moon, Jane Yolen's very successful picture book, achieves a soft silence by her phrasing. Stillness pervades the snowy landscapes painted by John Schoenherr, and stillness is everywhere in the text. The woods are "quiet as a dream," the snow more white "than the milk in a cereal bowl." The child narrator is going owling with Pa. "But I never said a word./If you go owling/you have to be quiet/and make your own heat." When they do sight an owl, they watch silently "with heat in our mouths,/the heat of all those words/we had not spoken." The text and pictures are in quiet, beautiful synchrony.

A very different style is apparent in Judith Viorst's *Alexander, Who Used to Be Rich Last Sunday,* illustrated by Ray Cruz. Alexander is the first-person narrator, telling in a child's diction how little by little, four cents by thirteen, he has spent his grandparents' gift dollar. "Anthony told me to use the dollar to go downtown to a store and buy a new face. Anthony stinks."

A successful style may use many devices.

But instead, Alexander buys fifteen cents' worth of gum, bets away another fifteen, rents a snake for twelve, and is fined ten for "certain words" a boy can't ever say, "no matter how ratty and mean his brothers are being."

Rhythm often appears in picture book narration, as in a story about a boy whose name is too long, *Tikki-Tikki-Tembo* by Arlene Mosel, illustrated by Blair Lent. Recite the name "Rikki-Tikki-Tembo-no sa rembo-chari bari rucki-pip peeri pembo" and the pleasure begins. And in Maurice Sendak's *Where the Wild Things Are* as well: "And when he came to the place where the wild things are they roared their terrible roars and gnashed their terrible teeth and rolled their terrible eyes and showed their terrible claws."

Tone

Tone may vary in picture books, just as it does in books of other genres. The thoughtful tone of Norma Farber's *How Does It Feel to Be Old?* or the serious tone of Virginia Lee Burton's *The Little House* is as appropriate as the mock-serious tone of *The Elephant's Child* or the joyous one of *Frog Went A-Courtin'*. Like character and point of view, tone too is the choice of the author or author-illustrator. Humor—that important quality that helps us develop a perspective on life's ups and downs and keeps us sane— seems essential in the life of a small child. Many writers and illustrators respond to that need, or perhaps they respond to their own need to see things through the sound of laughter.

The train ride from New Jersey to Cottondale to spend the summer with the narrator's grandmother opens *Big Mama's* by Donald Crews. Unlike the urban coast, Big Mama's country has bumpy, narrow roads leading to the big house and farmyard, where the children fill the bucket at the well and drink from a dipper. They wash up on the back porch, hunt for eggs under the tractor, and marvel at the big pot for making cane syrup. The final page shows the grown-up narrator hoping to wake up and find himself down on Big Mama's farm. The simple story shows the historical change in the move from rural to urban living, and despite its nostalgic tone—which does not always appeal to children— it is an interesting return to other days.

A nostalgic tone may not appeal to children

By helping to carry a book's text, illustrations become a large part of the book's humor. John Langstaff's *Frog Went A-Courtin'* is filled with personification, cover to cover. Feodor Rojankovsky, whose drawings are convincingly both animal and human, increases the humor by dressing them in suitable garb for their roles in the verses. Beetles of different kinds wearing aprons and chef's caps and carrying spoons and forks, a table-setting moth sporting a fuzzy domestic hairpiece, an insect trio performing atop the wedding cake, a bonneted snake who looks benign rather than fearsome—all of these are part of the pictured humor.

Humor comes from pictures as well as wordplay.

Ray Cruz, who illustrated Judith Viorst's *Alexander, Who Used to Be Rich Last Sunday,* chooses to amplify the humor of Alexander's frittering away his dollar by showing the gleeful antics of his two older brothers. The text itself is effectively understated ("And even when I told my friend Donald I'd sell him all the gum in my mouth for a nickel, he still wouldn't buy it."), while Alexander's cheeks bulge with three packs of gum. The final two illustrations show Alexander, his hand on his chin, squashing his face, contemplating what he has to show for his ventures; on the last page, he is alone and looking away, holding two bus tokens, back where he started.

The mock-serious tone of Rudyard Kipling's *The Elephant's Child* is humor of its own delicious kind, and Lorinda Bryan Cauley's black-and-white illustrations add to it in a harmonious way. Seeing a family of four elephants marching across the title spread, each one with a nose no bigger than a boot, is a startling verification of Kipling's *pourquoi* tale: This is the way it was—before. Off goes the Elephant's Child to find out what the crocodile has for dinner, wearing big pouchy saddlebags filled with long purple sugar cane, short red bananas, and green crackly melons. His tracks are littered with rind, "because he could not pick it up." When we come to the crocodile who "winked one eye—like this" and "wept crocodile tears" to show his sincerity, we are delighted with his deceptiveness. The breathless Elephant's Child, kneeling on the bank, his round eyes and open mouth eager for the answer to his question, is truly innocent. Each page has its own textual humor; humorous illustration contributes to an inspired story.

Humor is common in picture books. Ogden Nash, long known for nonsense verse, is author of the picture-book text for *The Adventures of Isabel* illustrated by James Marshall; in the brief story Isabel banishes every known bugaboo, and the cartoonlike hyperbole of her successes rouses our laughter. Vyanne Samuels and Jennifer Northway's collaboration on the picture book *Carry Go Bring Come* is also laughable as Leon is helpful on his sister's wedding day by fetching and toting the elaborate bridal accoutrements and wearing them. A tone of high gaiety runs all through Grandpa's reenactment of his old role as *Song and Dance Man* by Karen Ackerman, illustrated by Stephen Gammell. A satisfying combination of humor and tenderness characterizes Mem Fox and Julie Vivas's efforts in *Wilfred Gordon McDonald Partridge*. Old Miss Nancy, Wilfred hears, has lost her memory. In his search for the word's meaning, he is told that memory is sad, funny, and precious, then finds things that are dear to him, and gives them to Miss Nancy. Each one awakens a memory for her.

We may all dream of turning the tables on one who has exploited us, but the mother of *The Boy of the Three-Year Nap* by Dianne Snyder accomplishes this. Her lazy son Taro plots to marry the daughter of the wealthy rice merchant next door, and Taro's mother tells the merchant that his daughter cannot live simply—their house must be enlarged and improved, and Taro must find a job to support the girl. Lazy Taro goes to work at the merchant's storehouse manager. Humor makes the point for the story.

Exaggeration is part of childhood play as well as adult humor. Patricia C. McKissack has written a story filled with hyperbole, *A Million Fish . . . More or Less.* Hugh Thomas has heard the tall tales of Papa-Daddy and Elder Abbajon, but in his own tale he has caught a million fish in the bayou, then has had to forfeit them to the talking alligator, raccoons, crows, and Chantilly the talking cat, leaving him with just three tiny fish. Dena Schutzer's pictures are as filled with hyperbole as brilliantly colored as the tale. In order for Pauline of *The Easter Egg Farm* by Mary Jane Auch to lay eggs, she has to concentrate; then whatever she sees is reflected in the colored egg she lays—the sky or Mona Lisa's smile, for example. Of course, Easter eggs are the result. Although the imaginative text has humor, Auch's vivid pictures double our amusement.

The quiet verbal humor of Russell Hoban's picture books has merit, too, and yet it is quite unlike the vividly phrased ironic humor of Isaac Bashevis Singer—in *The Fools of Chelm and Their History,* for example—who also refuses to give children only slapstick. The humor of Maurice Sendak's *Pierre, a Cautionary Tale* is, in fact, a spoof of didacticism. Arnold Lobel's *Frog and Toad Together* is funny not only because of situation—they are odd animals for stepladder climbing—but also because of understated verbal humor, a surprise in basic vocabulary. Lobel uses a series of limericks for *The Book of Pigericks,* which is illustrated with pigs in all positions. Whenever his rhythms falter, departing from the required meters of the limerick, the humor stalls. When his rhythms work, his humor works. In Eric Kimmel's *Hershel and the Hanukkah Goblins*—illustrated by Trina Schart Hyman in her usual rich and imaginative manner—the humor results from Hershel's tricky defeat of the goblins, who don't want the candles lit for the festival. One is frightened away by Hershel's ability to break a stone in his hands (really a boiled egg); another gets his hand stuck in the pickle jar and cannot snuff out the candle; another loses his gold in the dreidel game; and the biggest of all is just not visible to Hershel, who insists that the goblin light all the candles so that he can be seen. When the goblin lights the Hanukkah candles himself, they will never again be snuffed out by goblms at festival time. The lowly outwit the powerful once again.

Lasting Favorites

We cannot speak of picture books without looking to Maurice Sendak, his view of the illustrator's function, and his best-known and most-loved book, *Where the Wild Things Are,* the book that Selma Lanes calls "the most suspenseful and satisfying nursery tale of our time."[10] In describing the role of the illustrator, Sendak speaks of the "seamlessness" of the perfectly integrated picture book, distinguishing between the direct approach that puts the facts of the story into clear and simple images and the "illumination" of a text, in which just as the musical composer interprets the words of a poem, the pictures interpret the text, "serving the words" by enlarging and interpreting. He goes on to say that the illustrator does not picture exactly the words that are written, but he or she finds a space where pictures can go further than words. In fact, "they each tell two stories at the same time. . . . Words are left out and the picture says it. Pictures are left out and the words say it." Pictures "quicken" text; they are "not something just glued onto the page" beside the words. Liveliness, conviction, vitality, "the touch and smell and *hold* of a book," the "zing" and the animation of the whole—these are Sendak's descriptive terms. As he praises Randolph Caldecott's illustrations, Sendak says that words take "on unobvious meanings, colors, and dramatic qualities. He *reads* into things, and this, of course, is what the illustrator's job is really all about," interpreting text as a conductor interprets a musical score.[11]

Sendak's *Wild Things* was published in 1963. For many adults, it focused their difficulty in acknowledging the anxieties and preoccupations of childhood, wanting children to be happy-happy-happy, to deny all unpleasantness and uncertainty. In addressing this issue, Sendak takes a different view. He marvels "that children manage to grow up," to get through childhood, defeating "boredom, fear, pain, and anxiety." He says that he remembers "sounds, feelings, and images" or the emotional quality of significant childhood moments. He successfully pictures many of these feelings and images in his books.

Great variety in feeling can be found in picture books, as Sendak demonstrates.

Maurice Sendak's Caldecott Award–winning *Wild Things* exemplifies a perfect marriage of text and pictures. The first pictures show Max as angry and naughty as he pounds a huge nail into the wall for a clothesline made of knotted clothing. He bounds down the steps, jabbing at his dog with an enormous fork, making "mischief of one kind or another," and threatens in boldface capitals to eat his mother up as he stands scowling, defiant, a wolf claw on his hip. The text tells us that a forest grew inside his room, and now Max is content, giggling, even smug, about the new turn of events, exotic foliage the setting for his dancing. As the first six pictures grow from $4 \times 5\frac{1}{2}$ inches to a full 9×10-inch page, the story's suspenseful pace accelerates. In his private boat named Max, his body is confident, then uncertain before the wild things, then more assertive as he waves his arms like a magician and with a stare tames the ferocious creatures, so that in fear they soon cover their faces and ears. "The most wild thing of all" has tamed them, and they line up to give obeisance to the crowned "king of all wild things." In total command, Max orders the rumpus to start and for three double-page spreads they rampage—until he sends them off to bed. Now Max is lonely for those who love him "best of all," and departs in his boat while the wild things roar, roll their eyes, show their claws, and reach out to him. Quietly pleased with himself, Max returns through time and space to his room, no longer a wild thing but a boy in his loving home. Sendak's ideal of seamlessness in words and pictures is perfectly realized.

Another favorite is *The Tale of Peter Rabbit*, Beatrix Potter's classic story for young children, first published in 1902. Its popularity endures among children all over the world. Potter once said that many stories for children are "condescending, self-conscious inventions," but Potter herself was never condescending or self-conscious in either pictures or text. First, Potter insisted on the $4 \times 5\frac{1}{2}$-inch illustrations, reminding us of Sendak's comment on the importance of "the touch and *hold*" in a picture book. Pictures alternate with text and are consistently in vignette form, irregular ovals surrounded by white space. But perhaps the little gem has had enough examination here. Each rereading may uncover new pleasure.

"It's a good feeling to be able to put down a line and know it is right," Robert McCloskey has said, the reason *Make Way for Ducklings* is still a great favorite with children, and one adults seem not to weary of either. The pages can be examined again and again, each time yielding new details. In a perfect union of text and pictures, the uniqueness of the ducklings and their parents, realistic yet individualized, is never lost. The pictures give excitement and vitality to the text, resulting in a new composite whole.

Aside from accuracy in picturing the mallard family, the book has a number of assets, including humor. The balanced first pages are an effective bird's-eye view of the world as with Mr. and Mrs. Mallard we look down in perfect perspective for the right spot to build a nest. Size, placement on the page, depth of tone, and force of line show that this is the mallards' story. Below, in distant and softly shaded areas and incomplete lines, are houses, water, and woods. Turn the page, and we are still in the air with the ducks, but now the scene below is clearer, more particular; obviously we are coming closer to the earth and perhaps to the perfect homesite. Now the page is balanced by the two mallards and a tree strikingly bare in early spring on the left, opposite the diagonal bridge and the little island in the Public Garden on the right side. Noting tiny details, we can count eight children walking with parents along the water's edge, and when we turn the page to see the swan boat's passengers, we count again: seven children and their parents. Along the water's edge five more children play, an emphasis that carries throughout: This is a family story.

As we turn to the spread of the bicyclist speeding past the ducks, tie and shirttail flying behind him and his action filling the whole right-hand page, Mr. and Mrs. Mallard's fear and shock are apparent. Mr. Mallard is knocked off his feet and Mrs. Mallard is tilted off-balance with one foot raised. Placing the text at the top of the left-hand page and using a large triangle of white space to duplicate the triangle formed by the startled birds gives emphasis to their terror. Shadowing horizontal lines show the bicycle's rapid movement, and diagonals echo the sudden movement of the startled ducks. The gutter dividing the pages is the right division for the action. Three more spreads show from the air the mallards' search until at ground view, children's height, we look at stones and weeds and bushes and nest, a domestic scene in a quiet island setting. A new figure now enters in the person of Michael the policeman, benign, hospitable, his kindness and roundness reassuring us about safety. Next page, the balance is reversed: the focus at left in "power position" is Mrs. Mallard counting her eggs—and we must count them too. The following page is filled with parental pride revealed on the left by the imposingly dark and vertical father, and on the right by the horizontal line of Mrs. Mallard's back echoing the quiet horizontal of the text block. If there is any disappointment, it is the hiding of one duckling in the gutter of the spread. Here, as in all other pictures, the parents are confident, dignified adults. Like children, each duckling is different from the others; the identical puffball ducklings of mass-produced picture books are boring by comparison.

In a "perfect marriage," effectively designed pictures enhance text. Each spread is different; each page is an addition to the text; each one begs us to count the ducklings, to notice their differences. Within each picture one or two are mavericks, watching a butterfly, hurrying to catch up, following in proper single file but looking the other way. As they approach the traffic, McCloskey incorporates into the pictures the raucous sounds of cars, ducks, and a police whistle. When we reach the point of Michael's run to save the mallard family, he again dominates the picture. His heavy dark boots, and the diagonal of his outstretched leg continued in the diagonal of his meaty hand raised to stop the traffic, are the focus, yet we never lose track of the mallard family. For the next pages the city takes over, but the ducklings are always there, strutting down the walk as mere dots in one picture, tiny individuals noticed and marveled at by passersby in another. Finally they are isolated in a big empty space in the midst of traffic stopped in four directions. The ducklings might easily have been lost in the city fray, but McCloskey keeps focus on them through skillful composition using white space; dark and light tones; and thin, fat, or shaded lines for solid forms—and of course through the placement of pictures close to relevant text. The last few spreads, devoted again to family and security, show the setting in detail, with the family all settling into a serene routine, following the swan boats and the peanut-throwing passengers and returning at night to their island home.

Virginia Lee Burton's *The Little House* has been a favorite since it won the Caldecott Award in 1943. The frontispiece condenses and simplifies the story, the title page is illustrated, the dedication is encircled by a wreath of daisies, and even the page numbers are carefully placed for the sake of design. Text is placed rather consistently on the left-hand page, with pictures on the right. Clouds circle across the first page, the sun, with varying expressions, arches across the next spread, while stars light a swirl of navy blue sky in a third. As seasons change, the hills take on different colors, moving from light to deep green to autumn rust to winter white. In spring

Color, white space, dark and light tones, thin or fat lines, placement of text and pictures all contribute to a successful picture book.

a group of robins flies from top left around the shaped text to lower center; in summer daisies follow a similar pattern; in fall leaves drift from top left to lower right; and winter snowflakes follow a similar route.

As the little house is slowly surrounded by encroaching roads, then by other houses, and then by apartment and tenement houses, the colors become somber browns and grays, on to deep charcoal gray lit by inadequate circles of city street lamps. Cars, trucks, buses, trolleys, and subway and elevated trains surround the drab little house, and by now the rolling, tranquil country landscape has changed into a series of dark and darker buildings surrounded by a frenetic visual clamor. Here Burton's pictures are drab grays of all shades, the only color that of the trucks and train cars, the tiny hurrying pedestrians, and a faded little house. Once the little house begins the move back to the country, the colors become lively again; the sun, moon, stars, leaves, daisies, and snowflakes reappear, and the expression on the face of the house is again cheerful. Throughout the book, the cyclical history of the little house has been illustrated with the circular flow of seasonal images and the swirling lines of the pictured settings.

Perhaps the final picture of the house at night, placed on the left facing a blank page, is unnecessary. As we have just read, "Once again she was lived in and taken care of," and that seems sufficient; we need not hear the "never agains" to know that the little house will thrive and be happy. All in all, this is a most satisfactory picture book. The change in time of day, in seasons, in the takeover by city life, and in the little house that remains the same yet changes with its changing surroundings—all these elements are there for endless detailed examination.

Wordless Picture Books

Like works in any genre or subgenre, wordless picture books vary in quality. What seems important is that they have a focus and a unity created by the pictures themselves and by the format in which they are presented. When pictures tell it all, words are unnecessary. Unlike wordless object and number books, picture books have some thread of story, but because pictures tell it all, words are unnecessary.

> When pictures tell it all, words are unnecessary.

Wordless books provide complexity and detail, as well as continuity and consistency. For example, look at the many qualities in Mitsumasa Anno's book *Anno's Journey*. The intricacy of the pictures offers enduring pleasure, each complex double-page spread filled with detail shown from above. The shore, woods, farm, village, town, park, city, cathedral square, and festival all show people in characteristic actions. Hours of looking could occupy a child: taking in each of the people, each of their varied actions, the architecture, the foliage, the vehicles—it goes on and on. In addition to the consistency of aerial views, as the journey moves from simple country life to complex city and back to country life, all pictures are spreads; tiny Anno returns to the shore to complete the circle of his journey. The result is a totally successful wordless book.

Similar continuity and consistency characterize *The Secret in the Dungeon* by Fernando Krahn, in which each picture is framed with white space and shows a separate action. Marked by her red dress, a spot of color in the shaded line drawings of the castle, the pony-tailed little girl is always the focus. Lost from the tour group, she wanders through the castle, falls down the water chute, and lands on top of a sleeping dragon whose smoky breath next catapults her through the chimney flue back into the midst of the group. The adults, who of course know better be cause they have listened to the guide, laugh and won't believe her story about the dragon in the dungeon. The final left-hand picture shows her gazing sadly out the back window of the car as the family leaves the castle. The story is successful in the clarity of its thematic content: Though it is common for adults not to believe children, children find it hard to accept. The story line is clear, the humorous tone is consistent, and even without verbal description or comment, the protagonist is still a believable little girl.

In another successful wordless picture book, *Sunshine* by Jan Ormerod, sunshine awakens a little girl, who then awakens her father. They breakfast together, prepare a tray for her mother, and linger in bed for a while. The little girl then gets up to dress for school, leaving her parents to drop back to sleep. When she is dressed and ready to go, she appears in her parents' room with the alarm clock. The ensuing pictures show the parents in various actions—hasty dressing, showering, father leaving—and then the little girl is off to school. Here the pictures vary in size, but with reason and continuity. A series of twelve narrow pictures in one spread, for example, shows the girl removing her nightclothes and putting on one item of clothing after another. The story is simply about getting up and getting out in the morning, but the additional interest lies in the child's relationship with her father, and in her taking responsibility not only for her own readiness but also for that of her parents.

"Tuesday evening, around eight," "11:21 p.m.," "4:38 a.m.," and "Next Tuesday, 7:58 p.m." is the only text in David Weisner's *Tuesday,* the story of delighted frogs whose lily pads sail off into the night, through windows, into the clothesline, and back to the pond, leaving puzzled police to wonder about the abundance of lily pads found on the busy street; behind them the clouds resemble frogs.

In *First Snow* Emily Arnold McCully also tells a simple story without words. None of the mouse characters has a name, but we easily single out the one with the pink scarf (obviously a girl from the color she wears) who is afraid to slide down the hills on her sled. Support from her grandparents (the ones with the glasses who drive the truck) and the fun she has with her

Even without words, a protagonist and the action can be believable.

friends (cousins, perhaps) are not sufficient encouragement. But when she discovers the great fun for herself, she cannot be stopped. She's off, her sled tracks running up and down the hill, and everyone must wait for her when they reload the truck. The action for the most part is clear, although one of the last pictures shows her seemingly terrified, flying downhill on the overturned sled, while the connecting page shows her delighted with her success. The illustrations, which are usually double-page spreads, are somewhat humorous. Having developed that expectation that these illustrations are spreads, we are mildly puzzled when two pictures that each bleed into the gutter occasionally show two different actions.

Like all books in a given category, variety in subject matter as well as in quality is infinite. A wordless picture book with little significance, *Time Flies*, is built around a natural history museum as setting. A bird enters, and flies as time is supposed to do, going in and out among the skeletal reconstructions of dinosaurs, and is surprised by a skeleton that snaps. The bird flies on, however, in and out of jaws and rib cages. A more intriguing wordless book is Istvan Banyai's *Zoom*, which reverses the device of accumulation. Beginning a closeup of a rooster's comb, zoom camera action then reverses, taking the reader back and back as the pictures include more and more information. Children watch the rooster through the window; next one sees the whole house, a toy town, a child building the town, that picture on the cover of a toy catalog held by a boy, the boy sleeping by a pool, and so on until the pilot of a plane looks down at the town, then the country, and then flies off into the atmosphere, the world revolving in space, a speck in the universe. Each provocative picture shows proportion and position in space.

A book with far more story is Jeannie Baker's *Window*, a story illustrated in collage pictures that is easily followed as the pictures grow increasingly complex. At the window is a mother with an infant boy looking out at the wooded lot in the country. As the child grows, the view from the window changes, first to show a single house in the distance, then a small town, and finally a city. Now grown to manhood, the child sees through the window the too-close houses, billboards, traffic, litter, and stores; he loads a van with his possessions and moves away to a country lot, where he finds a country house and plans to raise his family in an environment like that of his own childhood. But as he stands in the window with his own infant, he sees the city in the distance, and the river before him—but beyond is the sign advertising lots for sale. And we know that the cycle will repeat itself. The story makes a point about the changing country as urbanization takes over, and about what seems the inevitability of such change. The story moves and has a point, its increasingly intricate pictures a source of both curiosity and familiarity. The tone is regret that this is what happens, and the theme hints at the sad truth of the loss of country and a simple bucolic life.

Not all wordless picture books are successful. The Waldo books, for example, are closer to puzzles than picture books. Others seem to have little reason to exist, and may be merely a way of getting a series of pictures published. There is little story to hold our interest in *Oink,* for example. A sow with eight piglets naps, feeds her young, walks across the field to a puddle, and there they all get in and get wet. They nap, she sleeps, but the piglets awaken and wander off, find an apple tree, and throw themselves at the tree, where they get stuck in the branches searching for apples. The sow's loud "Oink" brings them down, and they march off behind her. In *The Birthday Trombone,* the arrangement of pictures presents a major problem. Most pictures are a single page, but they are without frames of any kind around the separate actions. Once we are accustomed to the lack of white space—even in the gutter, which might tell us that each page is separate—we are surprised to find a full spread. Now we must count the tigers, hippos, rhinos, giraffes, lions, and monkeys before deciding that this double page represents one action, one picture. The monkey's birthday trombone startles each of the animals: the zebra hanging up striped socks and shirts, the rhinoceros riding a bicycle, the giraffe rocking her small giraffe, and the lion doing a jigsaw puzzle. When a huge snake suddenly appears, threatening to surround all of these large animals, the monkey uses his trombone for snake-charming, and all is well. The story lacks a point; instead, it seems to be an opportunity for the artist to draw animal pictures.

Wordless picture books, like those with text, require consistency. While the conventional "art" of the mass-produced book does not hold our interest, a personal vision can. Mere cleverness and facility are not sufficient here, any more than in other children's books.[12]

A highly imaginative wordless picture book is Molly Bang's vividly colorful *The Grey Lady and the Strawberry Snatcher.* Silently pursued by the blue-skinned Snatcher, the Grey Lady evades him through town, into the country, and through the woods, until, distracted by blackberries, the Snatcher gives up. The last spread shows the Grey Lady sharing berries with a happy family in a colorful house complete with baby, cat, and parrot. The story rests on the suspense of pursuit and the intriguing way in which the Grey Lady disappears into the background.

Ed Young's two books—*Up a Tree* about a cat, and *The Other Bone* about a dog—have more to interest us. In shadowy black and white, the cat plays, leaping at a butterfly, its body in typically beautiful cat configurations. When it is chased by a dog, it climbs a tree, and there we see its many expressions. When a group of turbaned men try to rescue it with a ladder, the cat resists with fearful grimaces. Only when it smells a fish does it decide to climb down on its own, and cocky and secure it walks away. *The Other Bone* shows a napping dog dreaming of a bone, stretching, wriggling, lying on its back pawing the air, and generally relishing its possession. When it awakens, it knows the bone to have been a dream. Its disappointment is soon over when it smells a bone in the garbage can. Attacking, then dumping the can to retrieve the bone, the dog once again is happy as it prances off. Walking beside the pond, it sees the bone reflected. Like Aesop's dog, greedy for another bone, it drops the bone for the reflected one, then unsuccessfully dives in after it. The dog shakes vigorously, looks puzzled, and again daydreams about the bone. In both brief stories the animals are distinctive and yet characteristic in their poses. Pages are uncluttered so that focus is strong and the story clear. Both amuse, and allow the reader to speculate.

Summary

Picture books are dependent upon illustration; some contain text and others are wordless. The design of the whole—the entire book, including size, shape, whether there are single pictures or double-page spreads, endpapers, title page, cover, dust jacket, and the placement of the gutter—all are important. The illustrator puts into visual form what the words say, and yet, in amplifying the text, conveys more than what the words say. When put into pictures, figurative language can be enhanced. By picturing one element or incident rather than another, illustrations can also change the story so that identical text—a folktale, for example—with different pictures creates different stories. Like other stories for children, the text of a picture book is judged by standards of literary excellence in plot, character, theme, setting, point of view, style, and tone. Wordless picture books require focus and unity, created by pictures and the format of presentation. Complexity and detail may accompany continuity, consistency, and a unique personal vision.

Children's taste, like that of most adults, is dependent largely upon exposure. While it is important to learn what children like or dislike, we remember that children have had only limited exposure to literature and art. Their taste cannot be the most important criterion for judging which illustrations are acceptable, suitable, or desirable. As more than one critic has said, the popular taste is not untrained, but wrongly trained. The training is the responsibility of parents and educators in the arts as well as in literature. Exposure to trite, cliché-ridden illustration, like exposure to trite cliché-ridden language, does little to move the child along.[13] As we contemplate illustration in leisurely enjoyment, as children do, we attend to it as an extension of experience, an additional source of pleasure.

Notes

1. Joseph H. Schwarcz, *Ways of the Illustrator: Visual Communication in Children's Literature* (Chicago: American Library Association, 1982), p. 169.

2. Donald Weisman, *The Visual Arts as Human Experience* (Englewood Cliffs, N.J.: Prentice-Hall, n. d.), pp. 18–21.

3. B. W. Alderson, *Looking at Picture Books* (New York: Children's Book Council, 1973), p. 6.

4. Perry Nodelman, *Words About Pictures: The Narrative Art of Children's Picture Books* (Athens: University of Georgia, 1988). Nodelman refers to Rudolf Arnheim, Norman Bryson, and E. H. Gombrich on visual perception, sources well worth study.

5. See the excellent review of Nodelman's book by Jane Doonan in *Children's Literature,* vol. 20 (New Haven: Yale University Press, 1992), pp. 204–210.

6. Ben Shahn, *The Shape of Contents* (New York: Vintage Books, 1957), p. 124.

7. See Perry Nodelman, "How a Picture Books Works," in *Image and Maker,* ed. Harold Darling and Peter Neumeyer (New York: Greenwillow, 1984).

8. See Sheila Egoff, *The Republic of Childhood* (New York: Oxford University Press, 1967).

9. Perry Nodelman in "The Other: Orientalism, Colonialism, and Children's Literature" (*Children's Literature Association Quarterly* 17 [Spring 1992]: 29–35) suggests that childhood may never have been "as innocent, as creative, as spontaneous as adults like to imagine. Perhaps children are always more like adults than adults are ever able to see." Addressing innocence, he maintains that by literature's silence on sexuality, we suggest their lives are devoid of sexuality and "make it difficult for children to speak to us about their sexual concerns: Our silence on the subject clearly asserts that we have no wish to hear about it, that we think children with such concerns are abnormal." And we become "unable to hear what children are saying even if they do attempt to speak about such matters," a convincing argument for openness on all issues concerning sexuality.

10. Selma G. Lanes, *The Art of Maurice Sendak* (New York: Harry N. Abrams, 1980), p. 87. Much has been written about Sendak's work; this is just one of many sources.

11. See the interview with Maurice Sendak in *Victorian Color Picture Books,* ed. Jonathan Cott (New York: Chelsea House, 1983).

12. Pop-up books and other novelties are regarded by many as toys masquerading as books, but they have their place. Although Selma Lanes suggests that it "is wise to look with suspicion on books . . . that can be scratched and sniffed, that float in bathtubs or burst into song . . . an evanescent genre," some author-illustrators are creating them.

13. The move to simplify language recurs although we know how language skills decline for lack of stimulation. A recent horror in this movement is the version of *Peter Rabbit* (London: Ladybird Press) in which "It would have been a beautiful thing to hide in, if it hadn't had so much water in it" becomes "Peter hid in the watering can but the watering can had water in it, and suddenly Peter felt a sneeze coming on." The humor of the understated punchline is gone. Illustrations are now stuffed animals with plastic eyes. See also Susan Ohanian, "Ruffles and Flourishes," *Atlantic Monthly,* September 1987, pp. 20–22.

Recommended Books Cited in This Chapter

ACKERMAN, KAREN. *Song and Dance Man.* Illustrated by Stephen Gammell. New York: Macmillan, 1989.

ANNO, MITSUMASA, *Anno's Journey*. New York: Putnam, 1977.

AUCH, MARY JANE. *The Easter Egg Farm*. New York: Holliday House, 1992.

BAKER, JEANNIE. *Window*. New York: Greenwillow, 1991.

BAKER, OLAF. *Where the Buffaloes Begin*. New York: Warne, 1981.

BANG, MOLLY. *The Grey Lady and the Strawberry Snatcher*. New York: Four Winds, 1980.

BANYAL, ISTVAN. *Zoom*. New York: Viking, 1995.

BEMELMANS, LUDWIG. *Madeline*. New York: Dutton, 1937.

BUNTING, EVE. *The Wednesday Surprise*. New York: Clarion, 1989.

BURTON, VIRGINIA LEE. *The Little House*. Boston: Houghton Mifflin, 1942.

CLIFTON, LUCILLE. *My Brother Fine with Me*. New York: Holt Rinehart and Winston, 1975.

COONEY, BARBARA. *Island Boy*. New York: Viking Kestrel, 1988.

CREWS, DONALD. *Big Mama's*. New York: Morrow, 1991.

dePAOLA, TOMIE. *The Legend of the Bluebonnet*. New York: Putnam, 1983.

DIXON, ANN. *How Raven Brought Light to People*. Illustrated by James Watts. New York: Macmillan, 1992.

FARBER, NORMA. *How Does It Feel to Be Old?* New York: Dutton, 1988.

FLOURNOY, VALERIE. *The Patchwork Quilt*. Illustrated by Jerry Pinckney. New York: Little Brown, 1992.

FOX, MEM. *Wilfrid Gordon McDonald Partridge*. Illustrated by Julie Vivas. New York: Kane/Miller, 1989.

GÁG, WANDA. *Millions of Cats*. New York: Coward McCann, 1928.

GALDONE, PAUL, *Cinderella*. New York: McGraw-Hill, 1978.

GARCIA, RICHARD. *My Aunt Otilia's Spirits*. Illustrated by Robin Cherin and Roger Reyes. New York: Children's Book Press: n.d.

GARLAND, SHERRY, *The Lotus Seed*. San Diego: Harcourt Brace Jovanovich, 1993.

GOBLE, PAUL. *The Girl Who Loved Wild Horses*. New York: Bradbury, 1978.

GREGORY, VALISKA. *Happy Burpday, Maggie McDougal*. Illustrated by Pat Porter. Boston: Little Brown, 1992.

GRIFALCONI, ANN. *The Bravest Flute*. Boston: Little Brown, 1994.

GUY, ROSA. *Billy the Great*. Illustrated by Caroline Binch. New York: DelaCorte, 1991.

HEIDE, FLORENCE PARRY, and JUDITH HEIDE GILILLAND. *The Day of Ahmed's Secret*. Illustrated by Ted Lewin. New York: Lothrop, Lee & Shepard, 1990.

HENKES, KEVIN. *Chrysanthemum*. New York: Greenwillow, 1991.

HERRERA, JUAN FELIPE. *Calling the Doves*. Illustrated by Elly Simmons. New York: Children's Book Press, 1995.

HIGHWATER, JAMAKE. *Moonsong Lullaby*. New York: Lothrop, Lee & Shepard, 1981.

HOGROGIAN, NONNY. *Cinderella*. New York: Greenwillow, 1981.

HUTCHINS, PAT. *Rosie's Walk*. New York: Macmillan, 1968.

ISADORA, RACHEL. *At the Crossroads*. New York: Greenwillow, 1991.

———. *Ben's Trumpet*. New York: Greenwillow, 1979.

JONES, JENNIFER BARRY. *Heetunka's Harvest*. Council on Indian Education, 1994.

JOOSSE, BARBARA. *Mama, Do You Love Me?* Illustrated by Barbara Lavallee. New York: Chronicle, 1991.

KEATS, EZRA JACK. *Apt. 3*. New York: Macmillan, 1971.

———. *A Whistle for Willie*. New York: Viking, 1962.

————. *The Snowy Day*. New York: Viking, 1962.

KIMMEL, ERIC. *Herschel and the Hanukkah Goblins*. Illustrated by Trina Shart Hyman. New York: Holiday House, 1989.

KIPLING, RUDYARD. *The Elephant's Child*. Illustrated by Lorinda Bryan Cauley. New York: Harcourt Brace Jovanovich, 1983.

KRAHN, FERNANDO. *The Secret in the Dungeon*. Boston: Houghton Mifflin, 1983.

LANGSTAFF, JOHN. *Frog Went A-Courtin'*. Illustrated by Feodor Rojankovsky. New York: Harcourt, Brace & World, 1955.

LIONNI, LEO. *Fish Is Fish*. New York: Random House, 1970.

————. *Frederick*. New York: Pantheon, 1966.

LOBEL, ARNOLD. *Frog and Toad Together*. New York: Harper & Row, 1972.

————. *Ming Lo Moves the Mountain*. New York: Greenwillow, 1982.

————. *The Book of Pigericks*. New York: Harper & Row, 1983.

LOCKER, THOMAS. *The Land of Gray Wolf*. New York: Dial, 1991.

LONGFELLOW, HENRY WADSWORTH. *Hiawatha*. Illustrated by Susan Jeffers. New York: Dial, 1983.

————. *Hiawatha's Childhood*. Illustrated by Errol LeCain. New York: Farrar Straus & Giroux, 1984.

LOTTRIDGE, CELIA BARKER. *The Name of the Tree*. Illustrated by Ian Wallace. New York: Macmillan, 1990.

MACAULAY, DAVID. *Black and White*. Boston: Houghton Mifflin, 1990.

McCLOSKEY, ROBERT. *Homer Price*. New York: Viking, 1943.

————. *Make Way for Ducklings*. New York: Viking, 1969.

McCULLY, EMILY ARNOLD. *First Snow*. New York: Harper & Row, 1985.

McDERMOTT, GERALD. *Arrow to the Sun*. New York: Viking, 1974.

McKISSACK, PATRICIA. *A Million Fish . . . More or Less*. Illustrated by Dena Schutzer. New York: Knopf, 1992.

MILES, MISKA. *Annie and the Old One*. Boston: Little, Brown, 1971.

MILNE, A. A. *Winnie-the-Pooh*. New York: Dutton, 1926.

MITCHELL, MARGAREE KING. *Uncle Jed's Barber Shop*. New York: Simon & Schuster, 1993.

MONJO, F. N. *The Drinking Gourd*. Illustrated by Fred Brenner. New York: Harper Trophy, 1993.

MOSEL, ARLENE. *Tikki-Tikki Tembo*. Illustrated by Blair Lent. New York: Holt, 1968.

NAMIOKA, LENSEY. *Yang the Youngest and His Terrible Ear*. Canada: Little, Brown, 1992.

NASH, OGDEN. *The Adventures of Isabel*. Illustrated by James Marshall. Boston: Little, Brown, 1991.

ORMEROD, JAN. *Sunshine*. New York: Lothrop, Shepard & Lee, 1981.

PARISH, PEGGY. *Amelia Bedelia*. New York: Harper & Row, 1963.

PINKWATER, DANIEL MANUS. *The Big Orange Splot*. New York: Hastings House, 1977.

POLACCO, PATRICIA. *The Keeping Quilt*. New York: Simon & Schuster, 1988.

POTTER, BEATRIX. *The Tale of Peter Rabbit*. New York: Warne, 1902.

RYLANT, CYNTHIA. *When I Was Young in the Mountains*. Illustrated by Diane Goode. New York: Dutton, 1982.

SAMUELS, VYANNE. *Carry Go Bring Come.* Illustrated by Jennifer Northway. New York: Four Winds, 1988.

SENDAK, MAURICE. *Pierre, a Cautionary Tale.* New York: Knopf, 1962.

———. *Where the Wild Things Are.* New York: Harper & Row, 1963.

SEUSS, DR. *And to Think That I Saw It on Mulberry Street.* New York: Hale, 1937.

———. *If I Ran the Zoo.* New York: Random House, 1950.

SIEBERT, DIANE. *Heartland.* Illustrated by Wendell Minor. New York: Crowell, 1989.

SINGER, ISAAC BASHEVIS. *The Fools of Chelm and Their History.* Illustrated by Uri Shulevitz. New York: Farrar Straus & Giroux, 1973.

SOTO, GARY. *Too Many Tamales.* Bilingual book. Illustrated by Ed Martinez. New York: Putnam, 1993.

STEPTOE, JOHN. *The Story of Jumping Mouse.* New York: Lothrop, Lee & Shepard, 1984.

STOCK, CATHERINE. *Armien's Fishing Trip.* New York: Morrow, 1990.

TAFURI, NANCY. *Have You Seen My Duckling?* New York: Greenwillow, 1984.

VAN ALLSBURG, CHRIS. *The Garden of Abdul Gasazi.* Boston: Houghton Mifflin, 1979.

———. *Just a Dream.* Boston: Houghton Mifflin, 1990.

———. *The Widow's Broom.* Boston: Houghton Mifflin, 1992.

VIORST, JUDITH. *Alexander, Who Used to Be Rich Last Sunday.* Illustrated by Ray Cruz. New York: Atheneum, 1978.

WEISNER, DAVID. *Tuesday.* New York: Clarion, 1991.

WILLHOITE, MICHAEL. *Daddy's Roommate.* Boston: Alyson, 1990.

WILLIAMS, KAREN LYNN. *When Africa Was Home.* Illustrated by Floyd Cooper. New York: Orchard Books, 1991.

YOLEN, JANE. *Owl Moon.* Illustrated by John Schoenherr. New York: Philomel, 1987.

YOUNG, ED. *The Other Bone.* New York: HarperCollins, 1984.

———. *Up a Tree.* New York: HarperCollins, 1983.

The Boy of the Three-Year Nap
Diane Snyder (ill. Allen Say)

CHAPTER **4**

Character

Why begin with character?

Children sometimes say: "I like stories where the people are one way at the beginning of the book, and different at the end."

We often have the superior notion that children are too immature to recognize what makes a whole human being, or to see how people can be one thing at one time and become something else with the passage of time or events. We also falsely assume that children have neither the experience nor the training to relate to fictional people and their differences. As a result of our assumptions, we may cheat children by choosing for them stories that merely recite daily routine, like *About a Bicycle for Linda,* or that rely for interest almost entirely on excitement and suspense, like the Goosebumps or Nancy Drew, or on the very familiar, like the Babysitter Club series.

Children can catch many of human nature's subtleties. They care about human beings and are sensitive to them. Even an infant responds to differences in people, hiding in a protective shoulder to avoid a noisy stranger, leaning out of a crib to be snuggled by a familiar friend. The smallest child, furthermore, knows and expects consistency in people. Try to persuade a child that the usually brusque and irritable Aunt Amy is—this time— friendly and kind. By turning away from what he or she regards as Aunt Amy's fakery, the child clearly demonstrates not only sensitivity to personality but also an expectation of consistency.

It seems to follow that if even the smallest children are aware of personality in the people around them and can detect their differences, children are able then to recognize personality in stories they read. It also seems natural that the child who responds to real people will respond to people in a story and will be sensitive to consistency in their actions. If the functions of literature include the giving of pleasure and the discovery and

The child who responds to real people will respond to characters in fiction.

understanding of ideas and of other human beings, then character development in literature makes its own contribution to these ends.

Character as the term is generally used means the aggregate of mental, emotional, and social qualities that distinguish a person. In literature, however, the term **character** is used to mean a person, or in the case of children's literature, sometimes a personified animal or object. Each of the living beings in a story, play, or poem is a character.

When we add the word *development* we have a literary term, **character development,** which also has a special meaning. In life the development of a person's character or personality is a matter of growth and change. In literature, however, character development means showing the character—whether a person or animal or object—with the complexity of a human being. Each of us in real life is three-dimensional; that is, we are a mixture of qualities. None of us is completely generous; we have our limits. None of us is completely selfish; we have other traits. In the full development of character in the literary sense, the writer shows the whole, composed of a variety of traits like those of real human beings.

The importance of a character in a story determines how fully the character is developed and understood.

The writer has both privileges and responsibilities in this matter of character development. Since we are following a central character in a story, it is the writer's obligation to make this person's thoughts and actions believable. On the other hand, if the character is less important, the writer has the privilege of making the character two-dimensional or even representative of a class—for example, the bossy older brother or the impish little sister. The importance of a character in a story—primary, secondary, minor, or background importance—determines how fully the character is developed and understood. The closer the character comes to the center of the conflict—and therefore the more important the character is—the greater is our need to know the complexity of the character's personality. Conversely, the more the character functions merely as background, the less likelihood that the character needs to be developed.

Revelation of Character

In life we become acquainted with people in many ways. We see our new neighbors from a distance and draw tentative conclusions about age, occupation, and social status. We hear the accent of the Cockney, the twang of the Texan; even the precision or the explosiveness of short sentences indicates something about temperament. From their public actions we decide that the neighbors seem to be neighborhood assets, since they prune their shrubs and walk their dog in the proper places. Finally, if the new neighbors are known to our friends, we listen to their opinions. We have come to know these neighbors by how they look, what and how they speak, how they act, and what others say about them.

In literature the process of coming to know a character is comparable. In literature, however, the writer has an additional alternative: the author may choose to tell what the characters are thinking. In this case, the writer may fill in details about the characters' innermost anxieties and dreams, the patterns of childhood behavior, and early home life.

By Actions

Templeton in *Charlotte's Web* is an example of a character whose actions help to define his nature. After Wilbur moves to the barn, we meet Templeton, who creeps up cautiously to the goslings, keeping close to the wall. Templeton's furtive manner arouses our curiosity; we are as suspicious as the barn animals. Twice in the story Templeton grins, first when Wilbur lands with a thud, hurt, crushed, and tearful after his unsuccessful web-spinning efforts. Templeton grins a second time as he takes Wilbur's tail and bites it as hard as he possibly can. Gleefully savage, Templeton delights in slinking about and nipping at his friend; he is surly, sneaky, and ill-tempered, pleased at others' discomfort. He is self-centered and gluttonous, going to the Fair only to scavenge in the garbage and litter. Templeton's actions create a picture of Templeton's character.

By Speech

Accompanying Templeton's actions are his predictable sarcasm and ill-tempered outbursts as he gripes to Wilbur in sneering tones. He crawls into Wilbur's crate as a stowaway and grumbles:

> "Kindly remember that I am hiding down here in this crate and I don't want to be stepped on, or kicked in the face, or pummeled, or crushed in any way, or squashed, or buffeted about, or bruised, or lacerated, or scarred, or biffed. Just watch what you're doing, Mr. Radiant."

At the Fair, when Wilbur is optimistic that he may avoid becoming bacon, Templeton cannot resist commenting that when Zuckerman hankers for smoked ham, he will take the butcher knife to Wilbur. Templeton boasts about every grudging action and every carefully bought favor; he even pretends his motives are kind when he bites Wilbur's tail or saves the rotten egg. Complaining, "What do you think I am, anyway, a rat-of-all-work?" Templeton resentfully orders the directors' meeting to break up because meetings bore him. He grumbles at his commission, finding words for the web; he is not spending all his time rushing over to the dump after "advertising material." Templeton characterizes himself by what he says, showing himself to be cynical and selfish, resenting any intrusion on his own pursuits.

By Appearance

Gluttony is one of Templeton's most obvious traits, and his appearance shows it. He returns after his night of gorging at the fair, swollen to double his usual size. Only an appeal to appetite will tempt Templeton to fetch the egg sac, and as he eats first at Wilbur's trough every day, he grows fatter and bigger than any other known rat. Templeton's appearance verifies and supplements what we know of his character: gluttony and self-interest are the essence of Templeton.

By Others' Comments

Templeton is characterized by what he does, what he says, and by the way he looks. However, there is more to be learned from the comments of others about him. The animals carefully watch his furtive actions, since they neither like nor trust Templeton. The old sheep enlists Templeton's help in finding words, saying that the rat can be persuaded only by appeals to "his baser instincts, of which he has plenty." Since the sheep is on our side, the side of saving Wilbur, we trust his judgments. And we distrust those characters who are on the wrong side of our sympathies. We are less accepting of their judgments, just as we would doubt Templeton's opinions on any character because we know how deceitful he is. The comments of the other characters, like the comment of the old sheep, help to show character.

By Author's Comments

White's comments also add to the picture we have of Templeton's character. He calls Templeton a crafty rat who does as he pleases; even his tunnel shows his cunning. White's thoroughly negative description of Templeton verifies the goose's and gander's feelings about the rat who "had no morals, no conscience, no scruples, no consideration, no decency, no milk of rodent kindness, no compunctions, no higher feeling, no friendliness, no anything. He would kill a gosling if he could get away with it." Templeton becomes a character we know so well that we know what to expect of him in almost any situation; he is consistent.

Unity of Character and Action

The writer creates the whole cast of characters for the story—some important, some minor, some complex, some relatively simple—through the use of these techniques. As we come to know these characters, we respond to them.

Most of us respond to other human beings as we see similarity to ourselves, or if not similarity, recognizable traits and responses. We may say we "identify with" someone. Reading a story, we make the same demands of character—not that every character be exactly like ourselves, but that a character be credible.

In real life we know that change occurs in ourselves and in those we know well. We recognize that change only if we see a person before and after. We say that a child has grown, but even that statement implies a comparison between what *was* his or her height and what is *now* that height. If we must know both the *was* and the *is* to see growth, so it is with a character's change. If the impact of the events shapes or reshapes the personality of the character, the author is obligated to show how that change has come about.

Implicit within the acceptance of change is, of course, the idea of cause, and cause involves the story—its action. Given this complex character and adding these events, the combination may result in change. In life we say "Just what you'd expect of her" or "It could only happen to him," and by these words we admit that character and action are inseparable. The phrase "unity of character and action" may not mean much to you at first glance, but it expresses an important idea, one of the most important in understanding any fiction. In the best fiction, according to Henry James, "What is character but the determination of incident? What is incident but the illustration of character?"[1] *This character* because of *this personality* provokes *this action:* this action by its nature demonstrates this character. In literature the skillful writer shows characters by means of actions and speeches so that character, incident, and outcome seem interwoven—and, at the end, inevitable. Think of Brian Robeson in Gary Paulsen's *Hatchet* or *The River,* or Laura from the Little House books. Can you think of these characters apart from the actions they take part in? (When we say "actions," we are also talking about plot, of course, the subject of the following chapter.)

Look at Hans Christian Andersen's "The Ugly Duckling" as an example of James's view on the unity of character and action. Notice how we come to know the central character. The Duckling's *appearance* seems of primary importance, since that is the basis for his being excluded. He is big and ugly, clumsy and grayish black throughout the story. However, at the end of the story his strong wings, white ruffled feathers, and slender neck

> "What is character but the determination of incident? What is incident but the illustration of character." —Henry James

have replaced his earlier awkwardness with beauty and grace. As for the dejected Duckling's *actions,* he does not look up when he is bitten and ridiculed in the duckyard. In the old woman's cottage, his panic sends him into the milk dish, the butter trough, and the flour barrel. But at the end of the story he floats gracefully upon the water, his head tucked modestly under his wing. What the Duckling *says* is equally revealing of his character; several times he says sadly, "I'm so ugly," or "Even the dogs won't bite me." The Duckling is sure that he is an inferior nothing, and he never resists his enemies. At the end of the story, the Duckling shows by his speech that he is still modest when he says joyously, "I never dreamed of so much happiness when I was the ugly duckling."

As for what *others say* about the Ugly Duckling, his mother says he is not pretty, his brothers and sisters that they will not put up with him, for he is too big, and some wish that the cat would get him. The old woman's hen calls him a fool and finds him no fun. However, at the end of the story, the children call him the prettiest, "so young and lovely!" Finally, Andersen the *writer* has kept us informed about the Duckling not only by describing appearance and actions and reporting speeches, but also by his writer's comments, the result of his knowing everything. Andersen calls him a poor duckling and tells us he is miserable, exhausted, unhappy, terrified, a laughingstock. He calls the Duckling "poor thing!" and informs us of the Duckling's strange desire to float on the water, of his mysterious yearning to join the migrating swans. Finally, at the end of the story, Andersen tells us of the Ugly Duckling's beauty, which combines with his shyness, his happiness without pride as the Duckling speaks "from the depths of his heart."

Through all the means at his disposal, Andersen has shown us the character of the Ugly Duckling. The result is that we know this character well, and know that the story is the result of the character's traits combined with the actions that occur. The two are inextricably intertwined; together they demonstrate the unity of character and action. The character of the Ugly Duckling lives because the trials and harassments he goes through in the course of growing up determine his personal change and are his character; the story identifies the reality of maturing. Family rivalry, rejection, fear of failure, inability to find friends or to relate to others, even the feelings of ugliness and wishing one were dead are included in Andersen's story of the self-doubt of childhood.

At the beginning of Beverly Cleary's *Strider,* Leigh Botts is feeling sorry for himself. His parents have split up, he has moved with his mother to a "shack" of a house, he rarely sees or hears from his father, and he cannot have a pet. When he finds the dog Strider, he is forced to share him with his only friend, Barry, and must run the dog regularly. In the process of such exercising, he finds that he enjoys running, that he meets more friends, and that he is good enough for the track team. Over time these events change Leigh from a quiet stay-at-home to a more extroverted boy who not only gets praise for schoolwork but makes a name for himself and is open to many new friendships. Leigh—who says himself that he has changed—exemplifies the unity of character and action.

In the early chapters of *The Watsons Go to Birmingham* by Christopher Paul Curtis, Byron is a troublesome boy who grows steadily more defiant of parents and teachers. His parents, thinking he needs to see what may be ahead for an African-American in this country, take him to Birmingham, Alabama. There younger brother Kenny takes a risk and is almost drowned in a whirlpool. To Kenny's surprise, Byron rescues him, but is angry that Kenny has been so foolish. Little by little, By pays more attention to his family, and when someone sets fire to the church where little sister Joetta is attending Sunday School, he, like Kenny, is deeply concerned. By's next behavior is significant evidence of change: persuading Kenny—depressed at such acts of hatred—that he has not been negligent. By manages to bring Kenny out of his deep depression and help him to see his strengths. Byron has changed from a self-destructive adolescent to a caring brother. This change develops slowly, just as people change slowly.

In *The Thief,* which might be called high fantasy, Megan Turner writes of rude, impudent Gen, who brags that he "can steal anything" and is "a lot more important than anyone else" in prison. Bitter and rebellious, Gen angers everyone. His captor, Sophos the magus, who has saved Gen from a prisoner's death, is an admirable character, and his example has impact on Gen. By the end of the suspenseful search for an engraved ruby, Gen is thoughtul and honest, his cockiness turned to concern for the royal family—who, he finds, are his own family.

On the other hand, not all writers are successful in integrating or unifying character and action. Perhaps one of the biggest disappointments to a perceptive reader of Judy Blume's novels is the inadequate portrayal of characters: even the main characters in such novels as *Then Again, Maybe I Won't* seem shallow and unbelievable. Speaking in clichés, possessing little self-understanding, and acting in stereotypical fashion, the young people and the adults contribute little to our understanding of human motivation or to the integral nature of human beings and their actions. Judy Blume's popularity seems to lie in her selection of situations common to children rather than in portrayal of believable characters.

> Perhaps one of the biggest disappointments for a perceptive reader is inadequate character portrayal.

A contrast to the work of Judy Blume is the writing of Norma Fox Mazer, whose stories also address issues common to children. In *Babyface,* for example, Julie and Toni begin as best friends, but experience a separation as their experiences differ—a situation that frequently occurs in real life. Toni's relationship with her older sister is far from close, as such sister relationships often are, and their rapprochement is neither simple nor instantaneous. But by building full characters for whom miracles in relationships do not occur, Mazer manages to keep the reader interested and the conflict both believable and interesting.

Types of Characters

There are certain terms that describe the degree of character development and that refer to change or lack of it in a character in the course of a story. Briefly, a **round character** is one that we know well, who has a variety of traits that make him or her believable. A **flat character** is less well developed and has fewer traits. A **dynamic character** is a round character who changes, while a **static character,** despite credibility, does not change in the course of the story.

Flat Characters

Let us begin with the less important characters. They are essential to the action, but since they are not fully developed, we call them **flat.** In most stories, we must have these flat characters to help carry the action, to show how the central character behaves or relates to others, to make the setting a believable place because in this setting live these people. Flat characters are quickly made known to the reader, and they quickly assume their necessary places in the narrative so that the story can then focus on the central characters.

For example, in *Charlotte's Web,* Fern is a relatively flat character, a child with an intense interest that absorbs her for a time. She treats Wilbur like a doll, and listens to the animals' conversations and reports them to her incredulous parents. She plays and quarrels, and she loves the Ferris wheel and the freedom of the Fair. However, Fern has few traits that distinguish her from other little girls; she remains a believable little girl but not a special one. Wilbur's relationships and worries are the focus of the story, and the conflict goes on without Fern's being totally aware of all that spiders and pigs mean to each other. Because this is Wilbur's story, not Fern's, she needs no greater development. Dr. Dorian and Mr. Arable are more obviously flat characters.

When a character has very few individual traits, the character does not seem to exist as an individual human being. When the character seems only to have the few traits of a class or of a group of people, the character is called a **stereotype.** Each of us has a few mental stereotypes—of politicians, mothers, athletes, or poets. When we examine these mental pictures and compare them to individuals we know well, we find that each stereotype is inaccurate and unjust. In literature, however, the stereotype, like the stock character who appears in many stories, is useful, since he or she quickly settles into a background position and performs there in an easily understood role.

In *Charlotte's Web,* Lurvy is an example of a stereotype—in this case of a hired man. Lurvy has only the expected traits and does only the expected things. He nails down the loose board on Wilbur's pen, he slops Wilbur, he discovers the exploded dud. Lurvy is neither eloquent nor imaginative:

> "You notice how solid he is around the shoulders, Lurvy?" "Sure. Sure I do," said Lurvy. "I've always noticed that pig. He's quite a pig." "He's long, and he's smooth," said Zuckerman. "That's right," agreed Lurvy. "He's as smooth as they come. He's some pig."

As Lurvy's speech shows, stereotypes describe themselves by what they say as well as how they say it.

Occasionally the writer may use a **foil,** a minor character whose traits are in direct contrast to those of a principal character, and thus highlight the principal. The snobbish lamb is as young and naive as Wilbur, but she is smug instead of humble. Pigs are little or nothing to her. Since the lamb is consistently disdainful, her behavior contrasts sharply with Wilbur's humility, and in this way she acts as a foil.

Stereotyping, or compressing people into flat caricatures that eliminate individual differences, is useful in literature for particular background figures that fill narrow roles. Flat and stereotyped characters, however, are not suitable protagonists; we should be particularly watchful for stereotypes of people from cultures other than the dominant ones, because they do great injustice. (We will discuss the flat characters of folk literature shortly.) We have noted the necessity for character and action to be unified. However, flat and stereotyped characters do not truly grow out of action, and action cannot grow out of their less-than-full human natures. It seems more descriptive of flat characters and action to say that they coexist; flat characters and stereotypes move over the surface of the action, rather than being integrated with the action. Flat characters, furthermore, make little contribution to our understanding of human nature. In fact, if we read only about stereotypes, our perceptions about people may be narrowed rather than expanded. While stories for adults do occasionally make their points by careful stereotyping, these protagonists are reaching a more sophisticated readership, one that is capable of seeing a point by contrast to what is already known of the complexity of human nature.

Stereotypes in literature about cultures other than the dominant one are unfair and misleading.

Stereotypes of Chinese-Americans do not occur in Laurence Yep's *Child of the Owl.* Casey, the protagonist, struggles to find a connection between her footloose life with her father and her new life, living first with her wealthy Uncle Phil, then with her grandmother in Chinatown. As she lives the ways of the transplanted Chinese society, she is aware of her failure to understand them or to speak their language, and struggles to discover who and what she is.

Round Characters

A **round character** is one that is fully developed; we know this character well, because the many traits are demonstrated in the action of the story. We know appearance and actions, speeches and opinions, what others say and think about the character, and oftentimes what the writer thinks about him or her. The character is so fully developed that we may even be able to predict actions and reactions. Yet, like a real person, the character may surprise us or respond impetuously on occasion. It is as though we know the character so well that the character has become a real person, one we wish we could meet or might enjoy knowing.

In children's literature there are a great many round characters that we may feel we know. However, in order to help us see clearly what is meant by a round character, compare the many traits of Wilbur, for example, to the few traits of Mr. Arable, or the stereotype Lurvy. From the first words of the first page, when Fern asks where her father is going with the ax, we are anxious about Wilbur's fate. We soon discover that Wilbur's struggle is the conflict, and that he is therefore the **protagonist,** or central character. Tiny, dependent Wilbur has almost no life of his own at the opening of the story, except to amuse himself like a toddler, finding the mud moist and warm and pleasantly oozy. When he goes to live in the barn, he is bored, unable to dream up anything exciting to do. Friends must introduce themselves to him. When he squeezes through the fence and is pursued, he has no idea what to do with freedom, and his constant appetite makes him captive again. Since Lurvy's pail of slops is irresistible, Wilbur plans his day around his body: sleeping, eating, scratching, digging, eating, watching flies, eating, napping, standing still, eating. On the day that Wilbur wants love more than comfort and food, he has grown. But now he wonders uncertainly about friendship, which seems such a gamble. After Wilbur makes a friend, life becomes more exciting and he becomes confident enough to try spinning a web. Cheerfully, he tries and fails; humbly he admits that Charlotte is brighter and more clever. Wilbur's innocence and dependence are clear when he pleads for a story or a song, for a last bedtime bite, a last drink of milk, and calls out the series of quiet good-nights to Charlotte. Panic is Wilbur's reaction to news of his destiny—the Arables' dinner table. But once he is assured that Charlotte can perform miracles, he calms down to be patient, trusting, and humble. The congratulatory words in Charlotte's web make Wilbur an exemplary pig; he decides that if he is called "radiant," he must act radiant, and in his way he becomes radiant. Despite all the admiration Wilbur attracts, he remains modest. Happy and confident, he honestly admires Charlotte's peach-colored egg sac and gazes lovingly into the faces of the crowd. He looks both grateful and humble. Wilbur has enough traits to classify him as a round character.

Change in Character

If there is a unity of character and action such as James speaks of, then the character is not only affected by events, but his or her nature may bring about various events. Frequently, the events of the story may change a character.

> A character is not only affected by events, but a character's nature may bring about certain events.

When the word *dynamic* is used in ordinary conversation, it may mean forceful, or perhaps exciting. However, in the context of literature, the word has special meaning, since a **dynamic character** is one who changes in the course of the action. He or she may change from being shy to being poised or even domineering; or from cowardly to brave, from selfless to selfish. The character may demonstrate a new realization about himself or herself, or about his or her personal values. He may show that he is now able to take care of himself, or she may show that she has become able to care for others as well as herself. Somehow, the events of the story and qualities of the character have effected some basic character change. The variety of possibilities for change is huge.

The character, of course, may grow older by an hour or by a decade in the course of the novel's action. However, the mere passage of time is not sufficient evidence of character change. Some people are as immature at thirty-five as they were at seventeen. On the other hand, we know some people who have been changed by a single event—a traumatic experience or a simple and joyous one that has brought a realization of some kind. It is not then the passage of time that is important in character change, but the impact of events on the character—the unity of character and action—creating new traits to supplant or alter the old. The character may not necessarily be aware of his or her own change, just as in looking back we may see that we are different from what we once were, but cannot necessarily account for the *where* or *when* of our change. The essential matter is that we are different.

Wilbur changes. He is a believable character early in the story, although he is young and immature. The experience of receiving selfless friendship makes him able to give selfless friendship. Slowly, as we watch this change occurring, Wilbur is altered by his part in the action, by his receiving so much. Now he is the same Wilbur, and yet not the same. To his early qualities of humility and naiveté are added dependability and steadfastness, sacrifice and purpose. Even Wilbur's vocabulary matures. When first he hears the bad news, he is a panicky child:

> "I can't be quiet," screamed Wilbur, racing up and down. "I don't want to die. Is it true . . . Charlotte? Is it true they are going to kill me when the cold weather comes?"

By the end of a summer of maturing, Wilbur responds to news that his dearest friend will die, and he knows that he must save the egg sac. Notice how his vocabulary has changed to adult words, and his tone has changed to reasonable persuasion:

> "Listen to me! . . . Charlotte . . . has only a short time to live. She cannot accompany us home, because of her condition. Therefore, it is absolutely necessary that I take her egg sac with me. I can't reach it, and I can't climb. You are the only one that can get it. There's not a second to be lost. . . . Please, please, please, Templeton, climb up and get the egg sac."

Wilbur does not scream; he uses "please" liberally. His desperation does not arise from his own need, but from the need of another. Charlotte had once said to the screaming Wilbur that he was carrying on childishly; the new Wilbur tells Templeton to "stop acting like a spoiled child." Wilbur—who once planned his day around his slops—can now, out of deep concern for Charlotte, promise solemnly that Templeton may eat first and take his choice of all the goodies in the trough.

During winter Wilbur warms the egg sac with his breath in the cold barn. By the end of the story, it is Wilbur who offers the first mature greeting, a cheerful Hello! for the baby spiders. The change is significant, and it occurs slowly. It is convincing. Little by little events have molded a self-centered child into responsible maturity; we believe in Wilbur's maturity just as we believed in his childishness.

The historical novel *Lyddie*—written with Katherine Paterson's usual skill—follows Lyddie, who leaves a poor life in Vermont to work in the weaving mills of Lowell, Massachusetts. There she and the many other young women work unconscionably long hours in freezing cold or boiling heat. Bent upon earning the money to repay a loan on the Vermont family home, Lyddie refuses to join union protests about pay and working conditions. As the young women grow sick from inhaling the pervasive cotton lint 18 hours a day, and exhausted almost to death, Lyddie loses production time and wages to take on the training of younger girls. As she watches the struggles of those she has come to care about, Lyddie shifts her goals. When she signs the union peitition, Lyddie is no longer focused on toughing it out, on "staring down the bear," as she once had in Vermont; she now cares for a two-year-old orphaned sister and thinks about others. Change in the way she sees herself results in new behaviors.

For still another example of a dynamic character, look next at *A Girl Named Disaster*, Nancy Farmer's story of an African girl from Mozambique. An old man's fourth wife at the age of 11, docile Nhamo is a drudge, a virtual slave to her new mother-in-law, who treats her brutally and accuses her of bringing the disaster of cholera to the village. Her resig-nation and passivity change when her grandmother advises her to flee to her father's people. With new physical strength and determination she sur-vives wild animals and wilderness travel, struggles on, and then finds herself in a research community where she is appreciated. Physical stress might have left her spirit cowed; that is not the case. Each period of difficulty has brought change, and Nhamo is now an independent young woman in both body and mind.

Since less important characters are not so closely focused upon, and may even remain on the fringes of the action, their change is unlikely to be important or to grow out of the events of the plot. Furthermore, their changing could even be distracting.

A **static character** is one who does not change in the course of the story. The conflict does not influence the character to make any impact upon personality or outlook. Flat characters—including stereotypes and foils—will not change; they are not known well enough for us to recog-nize changes or to care. A round character, too, may be unchanged by the conflict, and, in fact, even the protagonist may be unchanged by the action.

Although Charlotte is not the center of Wilbur's story, we know her consistent nature very well. Charlotte is not only motherly, but hardwork-ing as well, and her web words prove it. She is the same wise and selfless character at the end of the story that she was at the beginning, and we therefore call her a static character.

It is not necessary that a story have a dynamic or changing character. In one story the round central character may change, and in another the round central character may not. The change or lack of it does not consti-tute a judgment about the quality of characterization. However, the static or dynamic nature of the protagonist does help the reader to see the action and to understand the idea behind it.

In life a person rarely changes overnight, and in literature we find such a change unbelievable. In Victor Barnouw's *Dream of the Blue Heron,* Wabus, a Native American boy, must choose between his own culture and the white man's. Wabus sees brutality, rigidity, depersonalization, and the substitution of material goals for spiritual ones, all epitomized in the char-acter of Mr. Wickham, the disciplinarian in the government school, who hustles Wabus roughly, rips and tears his clothing, seizes him by the hair, and jams a hat on his cropped skull. When he finds the tribe ceremonially burying Wabus's grandfather, however, at the end of the story, Mr. Wick-ham changes. In minutes he flashes a smile, makes an offering, reassures Wabus, springs to carry the body, seizes a shovel, and leaps into the grave to dig furiously. Then, although he is convinced of the innocence of Wabus's father, he turns him in to the law. In the final pages of the story, he offers books to the father in prison and promises to help Wabus become a lawyer. Wabus's choice to follow the culture of the white man is unbelievable and insufficiently motivated. Nothing in the white society he has experienced is appealing. The source of *our* dissatisfaction is the sudden change in Mr. Wickham's character.

In another story contrasting Native American and white cultures, note the experience of Matt in Elizabeth Speare's *The Sign of the Beaver* compared to that of Wabus. Left to keep the new cabin in Maine when his father leaves to bring the family north, Matt must survive by means of fishing line, rifle, and garden, experience enriched by his friendship with the Native American boy, Attean. During the seven months of waiting, Matt matures, learning to live in solitude, to find his way through the forest, to adapt to the Native American culture, and to triumph in his independence.

The character Suds in *Fourth Grade Rats* by Jerry Spinelli changes during the course of even a slight story. Joey Peterson insists that the time for being "third grade angels" is over, and it's time to become fourth grade rats. Don't be afraid of bees or spiders; eat meat—baloney—not peanut butter and jelly; push the first grade babies and second grade cats off the swings; refuse to bathe; defy your mother; make a mess of your room, and you'll be a rat, the first step to being a man. Suds tries to conform, but it's just not him; he's too nice for that behavior. But when Judy Spalding coos at Joey, it's too much. So Suds becomes a rat. The mothers become firm, and Suds confesses that it really wasn't fun. He gives up being a rat and returns to his old agreeable self. Given this brief story, we cannot expect a profound character change, but we have seen the artificiality of Suds's behavior and are prepared for his return to his old self.

Or look at the changes in Alex, the central character in Felice Holman's historical novel about the starved and homeless children after the Russian Revolution, *The Wild Children*. Alex returns from school to find his home empty and in disarray. In panic, he turns to his teacher with the "enormous, black, onimous" truth that his family has been taken. At twelve, he does exactly as his teacher tells him. Alex is taken in by a band of homeless Moscow children who follow the leader Peter and scavenge, beg, and steal to stay alive. Months later, at the end of the novel, kind Peter is temporarily demoralized by his own brutality, and Alex fills the leadership void that takes them to Leningrad and to freedom in Finland. "All these children would go because he had thought of it. It amazed him that he might be affecting someone else's actions, someone's choices, when he had scarcely ever been asked to make one for himself."

Trauma may cause sudden character change.

A totally credible character change occurs almost overnight for Harriet Hemings in the historical novel *Wolf by the Ears* by Ann Rinaldi. Secure Harriet, daughter of Thomas Jefferson and his slave Sally Hemings, is the victim of an attempted rape by Jefferson's son-in-law. So shattered is she by the experience that she sleeps for two full days, until her mother insists that she rise and dress.

> Get up, she says. I told her I didn't want to get up. Want to stay here, I told her. The days, they just bleed right into each other, and that suits me just fine.
>
> Then she tells me I have to get up. . . . She's purring it, the way she does when she wants something out of me. So I said I would. I ought to know better than to trust Mama when she purrs like that, but somehow I just never learn.

A few pages later, Jefferson tells Harriet that she should leave Monticello at 21 and from then on "pass for white." Now, in the language of a grown woman, she says,

> I was a child no longer. What had happened the other night had ended my childhood forever. It had put me face to face with a brick wall and nowhere to go. And this dear, kind, misunderstood man [Jefferson] was forging a hole in that wall for me and attempting to lead me through it.

The number of round characters depends upon the complexity of the plot, and thus there can hardly be a firm rule about number. Katherine Paterson, for example, draws a variety of characters, many of whom we know rather well, considering their places in the story *Jacob Have I Loved*. Best of all, of course, we know the narrator, jealous Wheeze, but we also see quite clearly her irrascible grandmother, the elderly retired Captain, dull and honest Call, and secure Caroline who knows she is loved. Certainly it is not feasible that every character be round. It seems evident, furthermore, that a large number of fully developed characters becomes highly distracting in a story for children. Even *Charlotte's Web*, which has three round characters, focuses more fully on Charlotte and Wilbur than on Templeton, important as he is. Some writers, in speaking of the writing process, say that a too fully developed minor character can get out of hand and become so round as to lose his or her place as subordinate and take over, thus changing the plot. For the sake of unity in the story, it then becomes the writer's choice between flattening out the character once again, or giving him or her new importance in what must now be an altered plot.

Special Issues of Character in Children's Literature

While character study alone may be enough for some adults, it is not enough for most children, and for several reasons. First, the younger the

Study of character alone is not enough for most children.

child, the more limited his or her awareness of alternatives. Young children are often prevented by their elders from making discoveries about "what happens if"; they often hear instead "Do this, so that may happen," or "Don't do this, or that might happen." Chances for exploring outcomes and discovering alternatives on their own are often denied them. A related problem for the young reader is a limited understanding of motivation. Children rarely see motives for behavior beyond what they would like to see happen. Furthermore, to the young, choices are black and white, yes and no; unaware of their own mixed motives, they rarely see those of others. With maturity—which the experience of literature increases—children become aware of unselfish motives like Wilbur's, or of subtle and self-serving motives disguised as unselfish, like Templeton's.

Although children may have keen interest in character, they want character involved in action and making decisions. Children, like adults, are intent on the peace or uproar that results from the characters' decisions. Children, too, like to follow characters and their motives through their emotions and their reasoning as they face decisions and make choices. Children are also excited by the possibility of the accidental, and perhaps even more by the inevitable. The likelihood of success or the chance of defeat keeps readers of any age involved in a story's action. While character, then, is essential, there are other considerations.

A discussion of character in children's literature is incomplete without reference to various kinds of protagonists, since characters are not only people or animals, but may also be inanimate objects. Winnie-the-Pooh and Piglet may once have been stuffed toys, but now they are believable characters. Hans Christian Andersen shows skill in characterizing the inanimate—from tiny toy soldiers to willow trees, from shirts to darning needles—endowing them with few or many traits, depending upon the length of his story and the theme he is exploring. He can give to the old lantern will-power and intelligence, to the starched collar pride, to the teapot arrogance, and to the silver shilling imagination. In the many tales that Andersen has told and that are still frequently read, it is the unity of character and action that makes each story live. The Steadfast Tin Soldier, although an inanimate object, is a convincing character.

We cannot ignore the characterization provided by picture-book illustrations. The limited text of *Wilfrid Gordon McDonald Partridge* by Mem Fox is enhanced by Julie Vivas's pictured portrayal of the little boy: a child in constant motion on skateboard, trapeze bar, and blocks, upside down on the floor, feet up the back of the sofa, collecting his possessions, looking eye to eye with the hen, sharing his personal finds with Miss Nancy. This is one busy, happy child at home with the old people in the house next door. And no Grandpa was ever more delighted to be back in the past than the one in Karen Ackerman's *Song and Dance Man,* who gleefully dons his hat and grabs his cane to be the vaudeville dancer he once was. Stephen Gammell's illustrations show a loving and demonstrative older man who might look a bit out of shape, but who surely can dance and still loves to.

Traditional Literature

Traditional literature has been handed down orally from generation to generation and finally been set into print. Perhaps because of the necessity to keep the spoken story moving with suspense, the folktale relies upon stock characters. The jealous fairy, the foolish youngest son, and the girl as good as she is beautiful are all useful stock characters. "A beautiful daughter" calls from the listener of any culture the same set of responses each time the phrase is used. Since suspense and action carry the folktales and the usually optimistic ending makes its comment upon life, characters need only be mentioned by a class name to be known. In a sense, this is one of the pleasures of traditional literature; we enjoy meeting characters we have met before, and whose actions are thoroughly predictable. We are free then to concentrate on action and idea as it all moves along quickly. Our discovery of the nature of human beings comes, then, from the relationship of theme to action, often a discovery about universal human yearnings.

Stock characters or character types like the wicked stepmother or the charming prince often appear in folk literature. Baba Yaga the Russian witch, for example, is capable of acts of both cruelty and kindness, both of which she performs in *Baba Yaga* as retold by Eric Kimmel. The trickster is another such character; in stories from the Plains Indians, Iktomi the trickster is often tricked himself, as in Paul Goble's *Iktomi and the Ducks*. Br'er Rabbit tricks the Fox, who is the trickster in the Uncle Remus tales.

It is interesting to note that stories from many cultures focus on the lazy but tricky person, usually a boy or man. Not only do Andersen, the Grimms, and Perrault have such stock characters, but we find them in stories from other countries as well. Dianne Snyder's retelling of the traditional Japanese tale *The Boy of the Three-Year Nap* uses as the central character the clever but lazy boy who nonetheless marries the wealthy merchant's daughter and settles into a job. *The Magic Leaf,* a Chinese story retold in folktale tradition by Winifred Morris, is about Lee Foo, who believes himself highly intelligent because he reads big books. One of these books tells him that hiding behind the leaf under which the praying mantis hides before attacking the cicadae will make him invisible. Arrested when he believes himself invisible, he hoodwinks the judge with that same leaf. The Irish tale *Jamie O'Rourke and the Big Potato,* retold and illustrated by

Folk literature of many cultures shows a lazy but tricky person.

Tomie DePaola, is about the husband who will starve when his wife is sick unless he gets out of bed and works. He, too, comes out on top as he manages to make the whole village his food suppliers.

Animal Realism

In fantasy like *Charlotte's Web* and *The Wind in the Willows,* the animals are people, but in a realistic story we expect animal characters to behave like real animals, to be true to their natures. Sheila Burnford, in her award-winning novel *The Incredible Journey,* knows the qualities of her animal characters and depicts them as true to family and breed. In a story filled with suspense and conflict, she has made us care what happens to her three central characters as they struggle for survival against the Canadian wilderness.

First, there is Luath the Labrador retriever, a one-man dog who is slow to warm up to anyone but his first master. A hunting dog, Luath is at home in the wilderness. Though his soft, protective mouth is not good for fighting, he can ford a river and encourage the cat and the terrier to swim.

The two followers are the Siamese cat and the English bull terrier, an independent loner and a sociable clown. The feline aristocrat is also true to family and breed: she races straight at her friends and then darts away, opens doors with a leaping twist. The English bull, always the pet, seeks out people along the way; he smiles at the hermit, expecting like any pet that his dinner time is his own. While shy Luath seeks the trail, the bull terrier seeks human habitation along the way.

As we shall note in a later chapter (Chapter 8, "Point of View"), animal realism is at its best when the animals act only like animals. The temptation for the writer is to guess and to report what thoughts and feelings the animals are having. However, the writer, who does not really know what animals think or feel, must draw conclusions from observing appearance and behavior. And, of course, when the writer permits the animals to talk with one another in human speech, realism is destroyed and fantasy created. Burnford, however, has developed the characters of her animals primarily through observation, and we therefore believe in their reality.

Writers of realism about animals may be tempted to guess their thoughts and feelings.

Science Fiction

Examining literature by genre sets up a collective set of expectations derived from our experiences with the particular genre. Science fiction has been called the fiction of change, "future history." Although some historians of the genre credit Heraclitus and Aristophanes with the seeds of it all, others credit H. G. Wells and Jules Verne with its beginnings. Wells and Verne are still much read, but more frequently readers use the term *science fiction* to cover the work of more recent authors. Historian James Gunn notes that it springs from naturalism, or the view of humankind as animal, but a dominant animal that must be tough and aggressive while using innate human qualities to temper animal qualities with love, self-sacrifice, and creativity, combined with a concern for the race. In the changing of science fiction from naturalism toward more mainstream contemporary literature, science fiction now has greater concern for character, for a subjective reality, and for subtlety in language; it is now reaching a larger audience. As critic Kingsley Amis says in verse, "These cardboard spacemen aren't enough,/ Nor alien monsters, sketched in rough,/ Character's the essential stuff." Although such broadening of concern to encompass character may extend science fiction's audience, it also causes regret among some writers and critics because they see science fiction as growing virtually indistinguishable from mainstream fiction.

Note, for example, the stereotyped scientists in Ben Bova's *The Flight of Exiles.* By page 45 we have met thirteen characters of almost equal development, names rather than people. Unable to identify the protagonist, we can scarcely be expected to identify the murderer. Specialists—psychotechs, cryogenists, molecular geneticists, and one astronaut—are all known only by their technical jobs. In Henry James's terms, characters and action are not fused but described only from the outside.

A more satisfying work is William Sleator's *Interstellar Pig,* the account of Barney's involvement with three mysterious neighbors who draw him into a new board game in which a player draws pieces and instruction cards that change the player into the monster described: lichen, giant spider, or gill-breathing waterman, for example. The goal of the game is to find The Piggy, the source of power. Through fearful transformations of nightmare proportions, Barney battles the three stranger/monsters and finds that The Piggy, the prize, is really powerless. The novel abounds in themes, the most significant being that power merely for its own sake corrupts. If we did not become caught up in caring for a very real Barney, it would not matter. Another of Sleator's novels. *The House of Stairs,* in which the power of human love conquers the inhuman machine (as it does in Madeline L'Engle's *A Wrinkle in Time*), carries our concern for the outcome because the believable human qualities of the characters give the action significance.

The characters of *The Ear, the Eye, and the Arm* by Nancy Farmer are futuristic fantasies themselves. The title lists names of characters in a detective agency, men who grew up near a nuclear reactor: Arm can outreach anyone, Ear can fold his ears in "like morning glories," and Eyes has no whites, only pupils. By the year 2194, toxic waste threatens the "family," many species are extinct, and most characters are mutants of some kind: gardener robots, house robots, an automatic Doberman, and a walking communicator whose feelings can be hurt, for example. Praise from the Mellower makes everyone feel good, and the three children respond. Even Father, who is harshly military, relaxes under the Mellower's praises. Children who are trapped in the house for security reasons even "go to Scouts" by holophone, although they'd like to attend a Scout meeting without bodyguards. The frightening world outside the house is filled with genetically engineered monkeys and rats—Fist, Knife, and the Sea Elephant, for example. Even mounds of trash stand up and approach the three children. Characters in this society are strange to us and seem to have few recognizable qualities; perhaps that is what makes the book lack appeal to many readers.

If we apply the axioms of character development, we realize that believing in the reality of character makes us believe in the experience. If the experience is fantastic, as it is in science fiction, a believable character can make us feel that the discoveries within the story have significance. Shallow character delineation limits our discovery about ourselves. When action does not grow out of the nature of character, the plot seems contrived and unimportant. The failure of such a story is often one of failure in character development.

Clearly some science fiction suffers from inadequate character development, but such inadequacy is not inevitable in this genre and is becoming less frequent.

Classics

A **classic** is not enshrined but must continue to appeal to readers.

A **classic** is a book that lasts, not because it is continually enshrined on lists, but because it continues to be read. The most memorable stories—those that, like *Peter Rabbit,* we take with us from childhood to adulthood—are those that create solid and believable characters. Frequently, what characters did—or what the plot was—has faded from memory, but we recall with vividness the characters themselves.

Look at two classics of what we now classify as historical fiction, read perhaps by more girls and boys than any other two. They are two very different novels. Louisa May Alcott's *Little Women,* which has very little action or plot, is primarily a story of daily activity, even routine, and the thinking and doing of five females. Mark Twain's *The Adventures of Tom Sawyer* has many chapters of seemingly unrelated episodes, but it still has action and suspense leading to an exciting climax and discovery.

The character of Jo March carries *Little Women* and has made it one of girlhood's favorites.[2] In her family, composed of vain Amy, saintly Beth, proper Meg, and worn but cheerful Marmee, Jo is the center. Jo is alive— aggressive and tomboyish, awkward and clumsy. She invents, acts, directs, complains and teases, sings off-key, and resents any restriction that would turn her into a stereotyped girl. She makes up games, dreams of heroism in active roles, and without guilt or gloom drops her bread on the carpet, butter side down.

Tom Sawyer is a second classic example of memorable character—as innumerable imitators tend to prove. Tom, seeking freedom, goes off pirating; fear-stricken, observes a murder; ingeniously hunts treasure; smugly attends his own funeral; levelheadedly finds the way out of the cave; contritely does favors for Muff Potter; and courageously gives evidence in court. We remember Tom for the variety of character traits, each demonstrated in episodes of action throughout a long and absorbing story.

Not all characters are as memorable as Tom Sawyer or Jo March, but there are others. The Ugly Duckling and Peter Rabbit have been tested and have endured. Perhaps Wilbur will live as long as Tom and Jo. However, other characters are so real to us that we feel we would recognize them on the street—characters like Laura of the Little House books. Our pleasure in our earliest introduction to the characters is renewed each time we recall an event from the plots involving them. Because we have known these characters, we have not only experienced vicariously their exciting adventures, but we have come to understand something about ourselves and others. Furthermore, one generation is pleased to find that the next enjoys the same stories but is disappointed to learn that a favorite does not speak with the significance it once did. In a sense, the characters of true classics are a social cement, joining one generation to another by common exploration of human beings.

Summary

In life and in books, children can sense differences in human beings and are capable of recognizing and responding to well-developed characters. Even in the simplest stories it is possible to find characters that verify truths about human nature. We meet these characters in action that seems part of their natures. We learn to know them—whether they be personified objects, real or personified animals, or human beings—by their appearance, words, actions, and thoughts, and the opinions of others about them. Round characters have many traits, while flat characters have limited development. Two kinds of characters that serve as background figures or contrasts are stereotypes and foils. Central characters in the action are round, so that by believing in their reality we are led to discover something about humanity, and we are thereby convinced that the conflict in the story, like conflict in life, is significant. The round characters may or may not change, but if they do, we expect such change to be convincing.

We find great pleasure in reading about people like ourselves or people we know, beings both wise and foolish, brave and cowardly, frightened and confident, lonely and secure. It is this pleasure of recognition that leads to understanding. Children, as much as adults—or perhaps even more than adults—need the discovery of themselves as part of humanity. Conversely, they need the pleasure of discovering that humanity exists in themselves. If literature is to help children understand the nature of human beings, we need reality in the portrayal of character. Nothing—not style, nor conflict, nor adventure, nor suspense, nor vivid setting, nor laughter, nor tears— nothing can substitute for solid character development in creating a pleasurable and lasting literature for children as well as adults.

Notes

1. Henry James, *The Art of Fiction* (New York: Oxford University Press, 1948), p. 13.
2. As we will note in the chapter on theme, the strengths of *Little Women* lie in theme as well as character.

Recommended Books Cited in This Chapter

ACKERMAN, KAREN. *Song and Dance Man*. Illustrated by Stephen Gammell. New York: Knopf, 1988.

ALCOTT, LOUISA MAY. *Little Women*. 1868–69. Reprint. New York: Dutton, 1948.

ANDERSEN, HANS CHRISTIAN. *The Steadfast Tin Soldier*. New York: Atheneum, 1971.

———. *The Ugly Duckling*. New York: Macmillan, 1967.

BURNFORD, SHEILA. *The Incredible Journey*. Boston: Little, Brown, 1961.

CLEARY, BEVERLY. *Strider*. New York: Morrow, 1991.

CURTIS, CHRISTOPHER PAUL. *The Watsons Go to Birmingham*. New York: Delacorte, 1963.

DEPAOLA, TOMIE. *Jamie O'Rourke and the Big Potato*. New York: Putnam, 1992.

FARMER, NANCY. *A Girl Named Disaster*. New York: Orchard Books, 1996.

———. *The Ear, the Eye and the Arm*. New York: Orchard Books, 1994.

FOX, MEM. *Wilfrid Gordon McDonald Partridge*. Illustrated by Julie Vivas. New York: Kane/Miller, 1990.

GOBLE, PAUL. *Iktomi and the Ducks*. New York: Orchard Books, 1990.

GRAHAME, KENNETH. *The Wind in the Willows*. 1908. Reprint. New York: Scribner's, 1953.

HOLMAN, FELICE. *The Wild Children*. New York: Scribner's, 1983.

KIMMEL, ERIC. *Baba Yaga*. Illustrated by Megan Lloyd. New York: Holiday House, 1991.

L'ENGLE, MADELEINE. *A Wrinkle in Time*. New York: Farrar, Straus & Giroux, 1962.

MAZER, NORMA FOX. *Babyface*. New York: William Morrow, 1990.

MORRIS, WINNIFRED. *The Magic Leaf*. New York: Atheneum, 1987.

PATERSON, KATHERINE. *Jacob Have I Loved*. New York: Crowell, 1980.

———. *Lyddie*. New York: Penguin, 1992.

PAULSEN, GARY. *Dogsong*. New York: Macmillan, 1983.

RINALDI, ANN. *Wolf by the Ears*. New York: Scholastic Hardcover, 1991.

SAMUELS, VYANNE. *Carry Go Bring Come*. New York: Macmillan, 1989.

SLEATOR, WILLIAM. *The House of Stairs*. New York: Dutton, 1974.

———. *Interstellar Pig*. New York: Dutton, 1984.

SNYDER, DIANNE. *The Boy of the Three-Year Nap*. Boston: Houghton Mifflin, 1988.

SPEARE, ELIZABETH. *The Sign of the Beaver*. Boston: Houghton Mifflin, 1983.

SPINELLI, JERRY. *Fourth Grade Rats*. New York: Scholastic, 1991.

TURNER, MEGAN WHALEN. *The Thief*. New York: Greenwillow, 1996

TWAIN, MARK. *The Adventures of Tom Sawyer*. 1876. Reprint. New York: Macmillan, 1966.

WHITE, E. B. *Charlotte's Web*. Illustrated by Garth Williams. New York: Harper & Row, 1952.

WILDER, LAURA INGALLS. The Little House Books. 1932–43. Reprint. New York: Harper, 1953.

YEP, LAURENCE. *Child of the Owl*. New York: Harper & Row, 1977.

The Trees of the Dancing Goats
Patricia Polacco

5

Plot

Without some plot in a story, what may happen to the reader?

While some adult readers may be more interested in character than in any other element in the story, most of us—and most children—cannot get involved with stories that are only character studies. We want things to move and things to happen; we call this order **plot**. Plot is the sequence of events showing characters in action. This sequence is not accidental but is chosen by the author as the best way of telling his or her story. If the writer has chosen well, the plot will produce conflict, tension, and action that will arouse and hold our interest.

The child wants what most adults want in literature: action, happenings, questions that need answers, answers that fit questions, glimpses of happy and unhappy outcomes, discovery of how events grow and turn. For the very small child there is pleasure in finding recognition of daily routine within the pages of a book, but many people think that *all* a child needs in a narrative is the recognition in printed words of an everyday happening they call action—an action as prosaic as going to bed at night or waking up in the morning. It is surprising that adults who would never find pleasure in a literal, hour-by-hour account of their own daily routines expect such accounts of children's daily lives to satisfy them. No matter how content the young are with daily order, children very soon expect that they should find life more exciting in a story than in their own experience. Here, in a book, children and adults alike can lose themselves in possibility as they pose the big question of all literature: What if? This element of possibility, of possible action and reaction that confronts character, builds the plot.

Types of Narrative Order

One of the writer's privileges is to reorder existence, to rearrange events, or in other words, to create plot. The writer may focus on one moment of a day and ignore all others, or he or she may charge one hour with significance and portent that influence months or years of a life. The writer may either ignore the segments of time that have little significance or simply summarize those moments. The writer makes alterations and deletions that our memories are unable to make for us in our own lives. The writer's selectivity and purposeful reordering and highlighting create plot.

Children learn about narrative order very early in their lives, as C. W. Sullivan III reminds us.[1] Earliest play with babies in "This Little Piggy" and "Patty Cake" follows simple narrative form; nursery rhymes use narrative a bit more complex in "Mary Had a Little Lamb" and "Jack and Jill." Soon children hear "Little Red Riding Hood" and "The Three Little Pigs." As they listen to and tell for themselves the ghost stories, folk jokes, and jump rope rhymes, they learn about situation and sequence and come to expect the "beginning, middle, and end" of Aristotle's "Poetics." **Narrative order** in fiction, the order in which events are related, may follow several patterns, but the most common pattern in young children's literature is the chronological arrangement.

Chronological Order

As we all know, our lives are one 24-hour period followed by another. This time order is simple chronology. If a story relates events in the order of their happening, the story is in **chronological order,** perhaps moving with the characters from one place of action to another and yet chronological. The writer may make the story line more complex by showing action that occurs with one character in one place, then turning to action that occurs to another simultaneously, but in another place: "Meanwhile, back at the ranch . . ." The accounts of simultaneous action follow one another in the story, but the events have occupied the same point in time; therefore, the action is still chronological.

The short novel *Dagmar Shultz and the Green-Eyed Monster* by Lynn Hall, for example, is chronological. The first time Dagmar meets her new eighth-grade classmate, she knows it's trouble: Ashley is far too beautiful. The Green-Eyed Monster of jealousy begins to mutter away in Dagmar's head that Sunday, and cannot be squelched during the school week when Dagmar's boyfriend, Aron—who had kissed her in the third-floor boys' bathroom while she had one foot stuck in the toilet (*Dagmar and the Angel Edna*)—falls madly in love with Ashley. Feeling like a leftover, Dagmar shops for Christmas dance dresses with Shelly (her used-to-be best friend) and Shelly's new best friend, Ashley. At the dance, Dagmar tries to get even by untying Ashley's spaghetti straps. Ashley's dress falls to the floor and leaves her standing there "in nothing but a head of hair and white pantyhose." But instead of the humiliation she had planned. Dagmar admits that now Ashley "could sell raffle tickets just for a chance to walk her to class. . . . The dropping of the dress was a pure act of God. A blessing from the patron saint of teenage boys."

Flashbacks

In fiction for mature readers, narrative order may involve a **flashback.** Many readers can recall their first experience with a flashback: it was puzzling. "What happened? How come?" The writer disrupts normal time sequence to recount some episode out of the character's past, showing how that event influences the character's response to an event in the present. Or the writer shows in flashback a past event that has brought on the present one. In either case, the writer chooses to juggle time to make a point about the character and the character's story. The small child, however, may find it difficult to follow such movement back and forth in time.[2]

The child relies on his or her own experience of time to understand when and how events occur. Since the child knows from experience, for instance, that one falls asleep and dreams, he or she understands Maurice Sendak's *Where the Wild Things Are*. The child knows that such a marvelous adventure could happen to Max while he sleeps or daydreams, since the child has had similar dreams. As the child grows in sophistication, he or she comes to comprehend the possibility in literature of mixing memory, imagination, dream, daydream, and flashback. As the child matures, the experience of literature provides growing recognition of time in its infinite variations. Television probably increases children's exposure to flashback and dream techniques, and this experience could help them to recognize the techniques in literature. Jean George, for example, uses flashback effectively in *Julie of the Wolves*. She plunges into the story of Miyax's or Julie's dependence upon the wolves for survival on the Arctic tundra; then, in a flashback (Part II), "Miyax, the girl" tells us of her early life. Finally, Part III returns us to Miyax's struggle and safe arrival at her father's house.

> As children mature, they begin to understand time in its infinite variations.

Types of Conflict

Plot is a more inclusive concept than narrative order or its synonym, story line, since it involves not only sequence of events, but also **conflict.** In this discussion of books for the young, tension, friction, force, alternatives, excitement, suspense, discovery, and resolution are parts of conflict. Conflict occurs when the protagonist struggles against an **antagonist,** or opposing force. In short, it is conflict that, added to narrative order, makes plot.

In the following subsections we will discuss four kinds of conflict in literature: person-against-self, person-against-person, person-against-society, and person-against-nature.

Person-Against-Self

Consider, for example, the classic *Tom Sawyer*—not Twain's best, but his most popular work for children—which has a plot of such complexity that we can discover several types of conflict. Mark Twain shows Tom as he faces an internal conflict, a tension within Tom that pulls him toward either of two courses of action. Tom happens to see Injun Joe—a pejorative name that would be unacceptable today—murder the doctor. He makes a pact with Huck not to reveal what he has seen, and signs it with his blood, but Tom cannot forget that the town has condemned innocent Muff Potter while Joe goes free. Tom takes tobacco and matches to Muff in jail. He often speculates about how to free him. Afraid of Joe's revenge, but guilty about keeping Muff's innocence secret, Tom cannot sleep. When he does, he talks in his sleep. Fearful lest he tell what troubles him, Tom ties his mouth shut. Such an internal struggle is between Tom's fear and his conscience, and there is no mistaking its intensity. When Tom's conscience—his keen awareness of his moral responsibility even in the face of danger—wins the battle, he goes to the judge to tell the truth about the murder. Such an internal conflict of feelings within the protagonist is called **person-against-self.** This kind of conflict also exists for the narrator in James Lincoln Collier and Christopher Collier's *My Brother Sam Is Dead* as he struggles with his anger and bewilderment—to be a Tory, or to be a Rebel like his brother.

A particularly good example of internal conflict occurs in the high fantasy *A Wizard of Earthsea* by Ursula K. Le Guin, written for an older reader. In the struggle between good and evil within himself, Ged must first recognize his own flawed nature, represented by the shadow:

> Aloud and clearly, breaking that old silence, Ged spoke the shadow's name, and in the same moment the shadow spoke without lips or tongue, saying the same word: "Ged." And the two voices were one voice.
>
> Ged reached out his hands, dropping his staff, and took hold of his shadow, of the black self that reached out to him. Light and darkness met, and joined, and were one.

Ged neither wins nor loses the battle, but by seeing that the shadow and he are one, he makes himself whole: "a man: who, knowing his whole true self cannot be used or possessed by any power other than himself." He will from now on live his life for its own sake, not for hatred, pain, ruin, or the darkness of evil.

Internal conflict is the core of Katherine Paterson's *Lyddie,* a story set in New England in the mid-nineteenth century. When a bear enters the family's tiny house, Lyddie, determined to save her family, stares him down, and he turns tail and runs. Although Lyddie would like to go on to college, she leaves for Lowell, Massachusetts, to earn money working 18-

hour days at the cotton mills to pay off a loan made to the family earlier. Ignoring the recruiting union members pushing for shorter work days, and better pay and working conditions, she suffers instead with the long hours and constant air-borne lint with its inevitable effect on health. Only when a young woman she has coached and guided is victimized by the supervisor does Lyddie confront him—just as she had confronted the bear. She will sign the petition and take charge of her life. "'I'm off . . . .' she said, and knew as she spoke what it was she was off to. To stare down the bear! The bear she had thought all these years was outside herself, but now, truly, knew was in her own narrow spirit. She would stare down all the bears." And she goes off to Ohio to be a student at the only college that admitted women. Lyddie's conflict is internal, person-against-self.

Many other examples exist. In *On My Honor* by Marion Dane Bauer, Joel's internal conflict arises from his guilt. He is afraid to tell anyone that he has disobeyed and gone into the polluted and dangerous river, and he is afraid to admit that after he dared Tony to swim to the sandbar, Tony drowned. The guilt is so strong that he wishes he could sleep, run away, or even die. Only when his father understands Joel's anguish is Joel in any way able to deal with his internal conflict. In *Shadow in Hawthorn Bay* by Janet Lunn, Scottish Mary, immigrant to the Canadian wilderness, has second sight and can predict what is to happen. Mary must struggle to be true to her "gifts" and to rid herself of the malevolent call of her cousin Duncan, who had emigrated to Canada before her and who had drowned himself in the Bay. Her growing love for Luke and for the new land conflicts with old loyalties, but she is finally free of the old to embrace the new.

Internal conflict may mistakenly be called "idea against idea," but such a term omits the protagonist who is the one "of two minds." Tensions and conflicts in stories vary; some seem more likely to occur in the lives of children and may, therefore, seem more real, but others may give readers glimpses of important moral issues.

Person-Against-Person

Tom Sawyer must face an additional conflict. Muff Potter is freed only because Tom has the courage to testify—in court and in Joe's presence—that Joe is the murderer. From the moment of his testimony, Tom's life is in danger. Joe disappears, and then, disguised as a deaf-and-dumb Spaniard, he comes back to prey upon the town and to steal the buried treasure. Once again Joe is a very real threat to Tom's life. As the boys hide breathlessly in the haunted house, they know that Joe will turn on them viciously if he finds them there. Later, lost in the cave with Becky, Tom catches a glimpse of Joe and knows that his murderous enemy is close by, hiding from the law. Here we have a **person-against-person** conflict.

The terms in which we describe the conflict are not so important. What does matter is that we see clearly the protagonist and the antagonist. The strain between the two forces is what holds our continuing interest and our intense curiosity about the outcome. Tom's internal conflict, his growing awareness of justice opposing his fear for his life, forces him to take action in a person-versus-person conflict, causing him to face the vengeance of a villainous man. Children's literature is filled with suspenseful examples of person-against-person conflict. In *Peter Rabbit*, Peter evades Mr. McGregor; in *The Hundred Penny Box* by Sharon Bell Mathis, Michael and his mother conflict about letting his grandmother keep her precious box; and in Madeleine L'Engle's *A Wrinkle in Time*, Meg defeats IT, the disembodied brain.

In folktales, where protagonists are stereotypes or stock characters, person-against-person conflict is very common. Jack climbs the beanstalk and defeats the giant. Hansel and Gretel shove the wicked witch into the oven and all is well. Both Red Riding Hood and the Three Little Pigs face wolves. In some folktales, the person-against-person conflict moves quickly and vigorously to conclusion, and in others conflict travels with gentle humor to an equally satisfactory resolution, as it does in "The Squire's Bride," or "The Old Woman and Her Pig." Virginia Hamilton's stories *The Time Ago Tales of Jahdu* and *Time Ago Lost: More Tales of Jahdu*, with their traditional motifs of African and African-American folklore, show Jahdu running, in conflict with Trouble as he helps Trouble's victims and shows the creatures how to manage against adversity and puzzlement.

Television cartoons, too, are filled with examples, as Coyote frantically battles to overcome Roadrunner and Popeye is in perpetual conflict with Bluto.

Person-Against-Society

Conflict and an unknown outcome keep us reading *Charlotte's Web*. Wilbur's struggle is serious: life and death. Although we may define the struggle as a **person-against-society** conflict, the child knows it simply as "Will Wilbur live? Will Charlotte save him from being made into bacon?" In this case we may regard society as the farming business, which, after all, is based on profit. A runt pig is not worth keeping. Although the child reading *Charlotte's Web* gets involved in the conflict of Wilbur-versus-dinner-table, the conflict is actually Wilbur against good business. The conflict begins immediately, page one, line one: "Where's Papa going with the ax?" Whether or not Wilbur will be saved from death commands our interest. This conflict of Wilbur against the business of farming keeps our interest from start to finish.

Person-against-society conflict is much more easily understood by adults than by children. When we read, for example, of Hester Prynne's conflict with the Puritan society in *The Scarlet Letter,* we see society's instrument of degradation—the stocks. We know the society by bits of dialogue as the crowd shouts its taunts at Hester's back, or plots to take Pearl from Hester. To children, however, society as antagonist is clearer if a person is representative of society.

Southern society of the 1960s is the antagonist in *The Watsons Go to Birmingham* by Christopher Curtis. Chicagoans Kenny and Byron find that to them as Northerners, Birmingham seems another world. They are surprised at segregated facilities, violence against blacks ignored by authorities, vicious comments overheard, and lawless actions barely concealed. At the burning of the black church, they see clearly the nature of the powerful antagonist—Southern society.

Person-Against-Nature

Julie in Jean George's novel *Julie of the Wolves* experiences **person-against-nature** conflict. Having run away from her village to the wild, frozen Arctic lands, Julie faces possible death by freezing and starvation. The wolves who befriend her save her life, leaving her to continue her search for her father.

In *The Talking Earth,* another book by Jean George, young Billie Wind, a Seminole alone in the Everglades who wants to learn the Indian lore of reliance upon nature, is trapped in a cave by a raging fire. George describes a cave at the bottom of a sinkhole, Billie's refuge as the fire roars and crackles:

> Yellow and red fireballs shot through the trees. A live oak burst into flame; a mahogany tree shimmered in the heat, then exploded in fire. . . . Creeping deep into the cave, she hugged her calves and dropped her head onto her knees.
>
> After a long while she looked up. The island was a firebox. Green limbs came to a boil and exploded like bullets. Flames ran up and around the trees like slithering serpents: millions and millions of them. A burning limb fell into the pit, struck the water, hissed like a snake and went out.

Lizards fall from trees. Creeping into the pool of cool water, turtles and snakes die or survive, while Billie Wind realizes that she will be confined to her cave for a long time—until rain has cooled the earth sufficiently for her to walk on it.

Master of suspense Gary Paulsen has written several books with a conflict of person-against-nature, *Hatchet* and its sequel, *The River,* among them. Brian Robeson, whose plane goes down in the northern wilderness while he is on his way to see his father, struggles and survives for 54 days because he has one tool—a small hatchet. Breathlessly we follow his defeat of the natural forces that seem insurmountable. When in *The River* the

government wants him to repeat the survival task so that a watchful representative can follow and record Brian's experiences and thus be able to
train others, he reluctantly agrees. His mother agrees only because Brian
sees that he can be helpful, and because she is assured that there will be all
kinds of life-sustaining equipment available so that Brian's life will not be
endangered. Once in the wilds, however, Brian sees that provided with life-
sustaining supplies, this trip will not be a true test—that having no real
struggle will not only prove nothing about how to survive but will also dull
his senses to what must be done in crisis after crisis. Therefore he sends the
plane back with its entire load of equipment, leaving him and the government agent Derek with only a radio. A true test comes when lightning
strikes Derek, leaving him unconscious and destroying their radio. Brian
has nothing but his own wits; this experience is totally different because
now he has nothing and is not only responsible for his own survival but
also for getting the unconscious Derek to civilization. We read of Brian's
falling down a crumbling cliff, but in the process finding flint to strike fire.

Without tools, Brian must build a raft, move Derek and tie him to it,
maneuver the unwieldy raft down the winding river, survive the rapids, and
when thrown into the turbulent water, must swim until he finds the rapids-
tossed raft with its inert body. Once again he must manipulate the raft farther down the river to the trading post—a single dwelling where help can
be found. At no point are we certain of the outcome: can Brian's strength
last? Even when Brian is tempted to lose Derek's body in the wild river so
that he can move more easily, we wonder if he has the courage to continue
in his rescue. Person-against-nature tension holds us to the final page.

A variety of conflicts may exist in a single story.

A story may involve a combination of conflicts, as does Avi's *The True
Confessions of Charlotte Doyle*. In a keenly suspenseful historical novel,
Charlotte tells of her 1832 Atlantic crossing as the only passenger on a
trading ship commanded by a cruel captain, who on the surface seems to be
as kind and genteel as her own father, the shipowner. Charlotte, a well-
brought-up 13-year-old, knows she must obey, and yet cannot do as she is
told and accept the Captain's vicious and vengeful behavior. Her conflict
between accepting her father's instructions to place herself in the captain's
care and her rejection of his immorality provokes internal struggle. But to
free herself from his power, she must defy the captain himself; in a person-
against-person conflict she aligns herself with the rebellious crew and works
as hard as any sailor, dressing as a boy and climbing 130 feet of mast to the
main royal yard. The story causes us to pay breathless attention to what
happens: Whom can Charlotte trust? What were the murderer's motives?
Who is the murderer? Does the crew think Charlotte guilty? How can she
prove her innocence?

Conflict of any kind grows out of character. Peter Rabbit's character—
his mischievous nature, combining curiosity with greed—brings him to Mr.
McGregor's garden and keeps him eating long enough to be discovered. In

Scott O'Dell's *Island of the Blue Dolphins,* Karana's womanhood and the traits it implies in her culture make suspenseful her struggle against nature. Tom Sawyer's inner conflict of conscience results from his sense of loyalty and justice.

In some stories with minimally developed characters conflict carries all of the reader's interest; some are mysteries like the Nancy Drew series or depict everyday events like the Babysitters Club. Plots are so predictable or coincidental that children are finally bored. On the other hand, the traditional stories from folk origins do not depict fully developed protagonists or lack conflict but rely upon universal human traits and dreams expressed in their themes. These themes seem to take the place of character as the origin for conflict.

Intent upon conflict, television often neglects to create a fully drawn protagonist; as a result children do not learn to see the relationship between conflict and character. Plot incidents seem merely to happen *to* protagonists, rather than to be brought about by the protagonist's personal traits; the result is a dramatic story that makes little contribution to the viewer's understanding of human beings.

Patterns of Action

Plot is more than the sequence of actions or conflict. It is also the pattern of those actions. If we oversimplify plot patterns by diagrams, we might describe them as a line slanting upward, a straight horizontal line, or line with a peak and a downward slide.

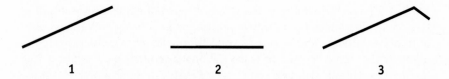

1   2   3

The first of these patterns moves from one incident to another related incident, building upon discoveries, and changes toward a final climax that brings the action to its peak and ends there! Such a pattern is clearly demonstrated in Mary Norton's *The Borrowers,* a story with a **frame,** since it begins and ends with Mrs. May relating the events to Kate. Within the frame enclosing the developing plot occur the events that involve the Clock family. The borrowers change from people with simple needs to a family ruled by their possessions. Homily's materialistic grab for more and more leads to discovery, to the rat-catchers, the fumigators, and the high suspense surrounding the family's escape. In the final chapter, a return of focus to Mrs. May and Kate, we know only that the borrowers might have established a new home by the hawthorne hedge, or perhaps that the family might have been a figment of a small boy's imagination. The plot line of development has moved steadily upward to leave us in uncertainty.

The second of these patterns of action, a straight line, can be demonstrated by Sharon Creech's story *Walk Two Moons.* Tension does not mount to a breaking point, but keeps us interested in the friendship between Phoebe and Salamanca—misnamed for the Seneca tribe of her ancestry. Despite minimal suspense, there is a conflict consisting of concern, curiosity, and pleasure in knowing narrator Sal and in watching her unravel the story of the disappearance of her own mother, as well as that of Phoebe. In *Little House in the Big Woods,* Laura Ingalls Wilder shows Laura's life as eventful and filled with pleasure; the security of Laura's home keeps the reader interested in day-to-day happenings, but without building anxiety.

The third pattern of action is more complex. The story rises to a peak or climax and then clearly concludes. **Rising action** begins with a situation that must be shown and explained; we must know what has happened before the story opens, what has created the current situation. This explanation of the situation and the characters' condition is called **exposition.** In most stories for children, it is woven into early action so that attention is caught immediately and held. When, for example, on page 8 of Mildred Taylor's *Roll of Thunder, Hear My Cry,* Little Man is nearly run down by the school bus loaded with white children, we are aware of the situation, of the feelings between blacks and whites.

In the historical novel *The True Confessions of Charlotte Doyle,* exposition is essential even to the earliest action, and writer Avi fills the reader in. The first page begins: "Just before dusk on the late afternoon of June 16, 1832, I found myself walking along the crowded docks of Liverpool, England, following a man by the name of Grummage. Though a business associate of my father, Mr. Grummage was, like my father, a gentleman. It was he my father had delegated to make the final arrangements for my passage to America. He was also to meet me when I came down from school on the coach, then see me safely stowed aboard the ship that my father had previously selected."

Writers of series books may write each one independent of the other except for the characters, or may build upon events in preceding novels with the same characters. Phyllis Reynolds Naylor, in her five books about Lynn, Mouse, and Mrs. Toggle the witch, chooses to connect them by tying the events of a previous story to those of the new one. *Witch's Sister, Witch Water, The Witch Herself,* and *The Witch's Eye* are followed by *Witch Weed.* Now, as the story opens, through Lynn's responses to the questions of the psychologist, Naylor gives us exposition or background that will make the new story understandable. The school psychologist is seeing

Exposition tells what has happened before the story opens.

Lynn about her "fantastic, imaginary" stories about Mrs. Toggle. We are reminded of the nine crows who followed Lynn, of Mrs. Toggle's eye with mysterious powers, of the control she had had over Lynn's mother, sister, and little brother, and of how Mouse saved Lynn by throwing the glass eye into Cowden's Creek. When in *Weed*'s first few chapters we read of the flock of crows and of the strange smell that makes them feel "woozy," we have enough information to move into the story, and can see that we are back in the realm of Mrs. Toggle's influence.

A great deal of background can be given in brief lines of exposition, as it is in *Shades of Gray* by Carolyn Reeder. Following the North's victory in the Civil War, Will is going to live with his Uncle Jed, who, as Doc Martin says, "didn't help the Yankees, he just refused to help them." Will is furious. In order to follow the story we must know Will's reasons for fierce resentment of his uncle, and for his having to live with his family. On the buggy ride from the Shenandoah Valley to the Virginia Piedmont, Will hears from Doc Martin that it is time to forget the bitterness.

> Forget? . . . It was fine for Doc Martin to talk. The war hadn't ruined *his* life. *His* father and brother hadn't been killed by the Yankees. *His* little sisters hadn't died in one of the epidemics that had spread from the encampments into the city. And *his* mother hadn't turned her face to the wall and slowly died of grief.

Since children's stories are usually short and must move quickly, **complications** begin very soon. The elements of a story that deal with rising action are suspense, the cliff-hanger, foreshadowing, sensationalism, the climax, denouement, and inevitability. Each of these terms will be treated separately in the following subsections.

Suspense

From the first line in the first chapter of *Charlotte's Web*—"Where's Papa going with the ax?"—we know that Wilbur's fate is uncertain, and from that initial moment White holds us in **suspense,** a state that makes us read on. By tears, sobs, cries, and yells, Fern wins temporary reprieve for Wilbur, who becomes Fern's baby. Wilbur's brothers and sisters are all sold, and it is Wilbur's turn. There goes Wilbur. But see if Uncle Homer Zuckerman will buy Wilbur so Fern can visit him at the nearby farm. Wilbur is lonely, finding his life boring without Fern as constant companion. When he finds a friend, loneliness vanishes. Then, electrifying news comes: An old sheep spitefully tells Wilbur he is being fattened for Christmas slaughter. Charlotte to the rescue. She weaves the words "Some Pig" into her web; people

Suspense is the emotional pull that keeps us reading.

come from miles around to see Wilbur. Mr. Zuckerman now admires him, and no celebrity has ever been made into sausage.

As the excitement wears off, our worries revive. Charlotte, however, sends Templeton to the dump for more words. When each of the woven words miraculously appears, we have new hope. Then Wilbur's protector announces regretfully that she cannot accompany Wilbur to the Fair. Catastrophe looms again, but a ray of hope glimmers: "We'll leave it this way: I'll come to the Fair if I possibly can." Our security lasts only until we overhear Arable and Zuckerman talking about the fine ham and bacon he'll make. A huge pig called Uncle is stiff competition: "He's going to be a hard pig to beat." Wilbur's doom is sealed. Suddenly, an unprecedented award, but Wilbur faints and "We can't give a prize to a *dead* pig. . . . It's never been done before." No prize. Then Templeton bites Wilbur's tail, and Wilbur revives and wins the prize.

But Charlotte is languishing. Can Wilbur survive without Charlotte? Charlotte spins her final magnum opus and dies, and Wilbur, now mature, takes responsibility for Charlotte's egg sac. When spring comes, Wilbur is still alive and hearty, and life continues.

Suspense, the emotional pull that keeps us wanting to read on, involves us in conflict up to the climax in the final pages. These moments of suspense, however, are not panic points in the story, nor at any time do we know the outcome with certainty. White controls the suspense to keep it peaking and leveling, and at every point we remain not only curious but concerned for the outcome, because either success or failure looms and we cannot be completely certain which will prevail.

Suspense has kept us reading, but White has carefully led us with optimism, never despair. The author skillfully builds the story so that nowhere is the ending too predictable, lest we lose interest, or too frightful, lest we give up. At the end of the book, the reader feels that the ups and downs of "perhaps he'll win, perhaps he'll lose" are finally settled. Suspense does not go beyond the story's ending. White, as he pulls us to the satisfactory end of the story, makes us heave a final, relieved sigh. The feeling that all will be well, even after the final page, results from White's skill in handling suspense. Our optimism has been justified.

To cite another example, the authors of *Where the Lilies Bloom,* Vera and Joe Cleaver, keep readers in suspense by implied questions: Will Roy Luther die? Will his death be discovered? Will the children be sent to the county home? Will Kiser honor his bargain about the house? Will they have to move into a cave? Such suspense keeps us reading. Betsy Byars in *A Blossom Promise* sustains this question of what will happen next by means of short sentences repeating the same grammatical form:

> He threw back his head, opened his eyes, and looked at the blinding blue sky. He was now gasping for breath. Each breath seemed his last . . .

Interest flags if the ending is too apparent.

He started to run. He ran up the hill, blindly, his arms flailing the air.
At the top of the hill, he stopped. He twisted from one side to the other.
His eyes were wild.

Number the Stars by Lois Lowry moves from one suspenseful time to
another. Annemarie, a Danish schoolgirl who lives in German-occupied
Copenhagen, does not see herself as courageous, although she protects her
Jewish friend from embarrassment and arrest by the Nazi soldiers. The
family, part of the underground movement that spirits away Jewish families
to neutral Sweden, hides Annemarie's friend Ellen until Nazi searches become too thorough to evade. Then the two girls go to a fishing village,
where mysterious events occur, including the funeral of a never-known
aunt, a walk through the forest in the depth of night, a dropped package
supposed to keep them safe from the soldiers who search the fishing boat,
and finally the discovery of a tiny hidden compartment in the fishing boat
that transports the Jewish family of four to Sweden. Friendships are strong
and vital even through the most painful times.

Both realism and fantasy by Avi establish and maintain strong suspense. *Bright Shadow,* for example, the story of a 13-year-old girl who has
unwilling control over just five wishes, catches her breath and ours with her
struggle to hang on to them. Knowing that she must "use them well, waste
them not," Morwenna also knows that when her five are gone, she will be
gone as well. But struggle with prudence as she may, she cannot resist the
wish to save her friend Swen when on four occasions his life is threatened.
She struggles with her effort to remain outside Swen's crises, but as each
wish to preserve him is instantaneously granted, she feels herself enveloped
more fully by the shadow. Suspense is even more gripping in Avi's realistic
novel *Shadrach's Crossing.* Shadrach knows that the small populace of his
tiny island is thoroughly intimidated by the smugglers, enslaved by their
fear of the operation; they dare not mention it to the Coast Guard. One of
Avi's successful devices to maintain suspense is the kindness done by the
mysterious Mr. Nevill, who seems allied with the lawbreakers, and the U.S.
government worker who is actually a fraud. As we follow Shadrach's uncertainty, the threats to his safety, his perilous and defiant scouting, his life-
threatening effort to cross the marshes to the mainland and give warning,
his confusion about who are the bad guys and the good guys, we are as
breathless as he. Using an occasional chapter cliff-hanger, Avi ably maintains the suspense.

Another example of the increasing numbers of stories about slavery is
the Colliers' *Jump Ship to Freedom,* fairly throbbing with suspense. The
first line is: "I crept up the cellar stairs in the dark, with the bundle of hay
in my arms, going as quiet as I could." The slave Daniel Arabus has a plan
to recover payment from his master's wife for his father's service in the
Civil War, money that she has taken "for safekeeping," money to buy

Daniel and his mother's freedom. Daniel hides the bank notes, is accused of theft, and is shipped off to be sold in the West Indies. Perilous work in the ship's rigging, near death in a hurricane, a desperate swim to land in the New York Harbor, hiding again, then flight with a Quaker and more—all just ahead of the ship's captain and his handbills describing the fugitive slave. The central facts of the story are established in a final Author's Note.

The most interesting books for early readers also have suspenseful plots, and their mystery format seems most intriguing. For example, Marjorie Weinman Sharmat's *Nate the Great and the Fishy Prize* tells, in simple vocabulary, how Nate's dog Sludge solves the puzzle of the missing prize. Nate checks out all the possibilities, going from one master and pet to the next, all of them entering the Smartest Pet Contest. The thread line of Nate's biking to the store for ingredients to make pancakes, his stop at each entrant's house, and Sludge's curious sniffs at the grocery bag lead to the missing trophy, a tuna fish can lettered "Smartest" in gold. Of course, Sludge is the winner. The brief story has all of the elements of a progressive plot, from exposition to final climax and denouement. *Sebastian (Super Sleuth) and the Bone to Pick Mystery* by Mary Blount Christian and *Judge Benjamin: Superdog* by Judith Whitelock McInerney also have detective dogs as protagonists. These dogs solve mysteries successfully.

There is no shortage of suspense in Gary Paulsen's *Hatchet* as Brian, the protagonist, withstands a black bear, an attacking moose, and invasion by a porcupine.

> . . . slithering. A brushing sound, a slithering brushing sound near his feet—and he kicked out as hard as he could, kicked out and threw the hatchet at the sound, a noise coming from his throat. But the hatchet missed . . . and his leg was instantly torn with pain, as if a hundred needles had been driven into it.
>
> Now he screamed, with the pain and fear, and skittered on his backside up into the corner of the shelter, breathing through his mouth, straining to see, to hear.
>
> The slithering moved again, he thought toward him at first, and terror took him, stopping his breath. He felt he could see a low dark form, a bulk in the darkness, a shadow that lived, but now it moved away, slithering and scraping it moved away and he saw . . .

The Cliff-hanger

A form of suspense that White does not use is the **cliff-hanger,** the exciting chapter ending that makes it hard to lay the book aside. Unlike the chapters in *Charlotte's Web,* wherein each contributes to the central conflict in the total plot, each moving to its own peak and yet managing to end quietly, the cliff-hanging chapter ends with such suspense that a listening child's plea, "Please, just one more chapter!" is irresistible. The cliff-hanger is most obvious in the old series novels like Nancy Drew and The Hardy Boys, and in today's soap operas, as well as in newspaper, magazine, and Saturday movie serials of the past. Each child left the darkened theater for the afternoon sunlight, worried about the hero, left, perhaps literally, hanging by the fingernails from a sheer cliff. The hero was in mortal danger and might not survive until the following Saturday matinee.

In old movie serials, the protagonist might be left hanging. Would he survive till next Saturday?

The cliff-hanger is also used by John Bellairs in his time-lapse novel *The Trolley to Yesterday,* a story in which Fergie and Johnny travel by decrepit trolley back to A.D. 1453, when the Turks seized Constantinople. Chapters 1 through 5, for example, end in these words: "I should have *known.* You're going to ruin everything!" "This was not a movie set or a dream or a Viewmaster slide. It was real, and he was there." "Happy about the wild experience they had had, and anxious to try it again sometime soon. But Johnny was still worried about the professor."

Highly effective use of cliff-hangers to create suspense operates throughout *The Philadelphia Adventure* by Lloyd Alexander. The plot is essentially a chase as Vesper, the Weed, and the narrator seek the kidnapped children of the Brazilian president, who is in Philadelphia to open the Exposition of 1876. The chase is not simple; all kinds of misadventures and surprises keep it going. Cliff-hangers conclude the chapters. After the middle of the novel, the rescuers catch up with the children, only to have the three-year-old turn on him: "She kicked me in the shins." The group seeks haven in a quiet, friendly town, only to hear, "Everybody in Kellytown's looking for us." After the group ends a long chase, which includes commandeering a Quaker carriage, they return eagerly to the narrator's home. There they find their enemy, the villainous Dr. Helvitius, waiting for them: "'Welcome home,' said Dr. Helvitius." Another chapter ends with "I know how he'll do it [kill the whole group of Brazilians], and I know where he'll do it. . . . Little Januaria told us." The next chapter concludes with the appearance of Dr. Helvitius's accomplice: "I flung open the doors of the carriage house and stared into the grinning face of Sergeant Shote."

Foreshadowing

The writer for children must decide how much suspense the child can sustain and how much reassurance is needed to balance suspense. To relieve the reader's anxiety and to produce a satisfying sense of the inevitable, the writer must drop clues about the outcome—without destroying suspense. These clues are called **foreshadowing.** Such clues must be planted artfully and unobtrusively within the action. Not all readers will be alert to all dropped hints, it is true, but White in *Charlotte's Web* uses them to hint at

Stories for young children balance suspense and reassurance.

Wilbur's ultimate safety and Charlotte's death, and to reassure us that finally all will be well.

In Wilbur's first conversation with Charlotte, we learn that gentle Charlotte lives by eating living things, and friendship looks questionable. Seeing a need to reassure, White adds that "she had a kind heart, and she was to prove loyal and true to the very end." The first clue suggests friendship; the second, "to the very end," has a prophetic ring.

Foreshadowing and suspense balance throughout the narrative. When in "Bad News" Wilbur hears he is being fattened for slaughter, he wails. However, his safety is foreshadowed when Charlotte says calmly, "I am going to save you."

Another event for which we must be prepared is Charlotte's death. If her death had been unforeseen, we might accuse White of playing with our emotions. But Charlotte's acceptance of her life span foreshadows her approaching death and prepares Wilbur and the readers. The song of the crickets foreshadows death of all kinds. "Summer is over and gone. . . . Over and gone. . . . Summer is dying, dying," they sing. Charlotte, whose life, like the crickets and the seasons, has a predictable cycle, "heard it and knew that she hadn't much time left." Of the word "humble," she says, "It is the last word I shall ever write." When she says that she is "languishing," she is peaceful and contented, and we are as resigned as she. *Charlotte's Web* concludes with a sense of inevitability, and, because of the 514 baby spiders, with optimism.

Clear examples of foreshadowing occur throughout good children's stories. For example, in William Armstrong's *Sounder,* the father has been sent to prison for stealing food for his family. When at long last a figure appears in the red dust of the road, Sounder the coonhound revives. Once near death from the sheriff's gunshots, now, before the approaching figure is identifiable, Sounder pants, whines, wags his tail, and paces the dooryard. His agitation foreshadows the father's limping return. In *Dicey's Song* very early on we see Jeff hanging around after school with his guitar. When he stops Dicey to talk with her, their eventual friendship is foreshadowed.

Foreshadowing is clear in Marion Dane Bauer's *On My Honor*. Tony wants to swim, and although Joel has promised his father not to, Joel, goaded by Tony, finally challenges Tony to swim out to the sandbar. As the boys walk into the dangerously fast Vermillion River, Joel calls out, "Watch out for the current." Tony grabs his throat with both hands: "The current! It's got me. It's going to suck me under . . . swallow me up!" When Tony jumps into the water, he thrashes about, and Joel mutters, "Doesn't look like he even knows how." As he fights the current, Joel sees similar significance in Tony's earlier false claims about his hang-gliding experience. Good swimmer that he is, Joel remarks that the current frightens him. When he calls back without looking, his voice bounces off the bluffs.

In *The Mermaid Summer*, Mollie Hunter uses the Howdy, or wise woman of the Scottish fishing village, as the chief source of foreshadowing. Eric Anderson—who has ridiculed the mermaid and fears that his ridicule will bring disaster on the community—on advice from the Howdy leaves to go to sea intending never to return. But as gifts arrive for Eric's children, the Howdy hints that three will be important to the village, to the family, to Eric, and to the mermaid's threat: The conch shell, the sharp fishing knife, and the crownlike comb of jade. With the help of these gifts and the Howdy's advice, Eric's children Anna and Jon defeat the mermaid and extract from her three promises that bring safety and good fortune to the fishing fleet, and Eric home to his family. Each confrontation with the mermaid has high suspense and threat of failure, but in each instance the love of Anna for her Granda keeps them secure.

Even in a suspenseful story with a well-developed protagonist, however, plotting problems can occur. In *Jasmin* by Jan Truss, for example, we miss adequate foreshadowing of events, like a violent storm and the arrival of the social workers to take retarded Leroy away to a special home and school. Without foreshadowing, we are surprised at the outcome.

Inadequate foreshadowing leaves the reader surprised or even shocked.

Sensationalism

If the reader is to feel satisfaction as the story unfolds, the author must drop reassuring hints about what is ahead. In the strong life-and-death conflict of *Charlotte's Web,* unrelieved suspense might be too much for the small child. The skill of the writer lies in balancing two elements—suspense over the action and hints at the outcome.

Unrelieved suspense, however, makes a story *sensational;* it plays us like instruments, keeping us holding our breaths in crescendoes of anxiety. The writer for adults has greater latitude in the creation of anxiety, since adults can tolerate it; with persistent enthusiasm, some adults read **sensationalism:** mystery stories, murder thrillers, and survival adventures. The suspense absorbs them; they breathe horror and terror with the protagonist. However, they are never deceived, since they never forget that it's just a story. Other adults are bored with the unrelieved suspense because they, too, know that it's just a story, and wanting more than sensationalism, they seek some discovery of real people in suspenseful action. They demand the significance of well-developed character in a conflict that reveals something about human beings.

A situation of unrelieved suspense, on the other hand, may be more than a child can bear. Take, for example, the folktale "Snow White and the Seven Dwarfs." The storyteller, watching the expressive faces of the listeners, relieves the suspense with reassuring hints about outcome. In making the movie, however, Walt Disney turned suspense to sensationalism, and

many children were upset by it. The ugly witch with clawlike hands and viciously evil features roused sheer terror. Many children hid their faces and
suffered nightmares long after they had seen—as the ad described it—"the
great children's story come alive on the screen."

Any action may be made sensational, but important and even violent
events can be described with accuracy and sensitivity, yet without sensationalism. Sensationalism results when the writer focuses on the thrilling or
startling at the expense of character and idea. For example, the Colliers's
description of Sam's execution before a firing squad at the end of *My
Brother Sam Is Dead* is not sensational.

The Climax

The peak and turning point of the conflict, the point at which we know the
outcome of the action, is called the **climax.** Throughout the development
of plot, from initial recognition of the conflict through the critical turns
and irregular progress, past reversals and discoveries, up to the point where
we know who wins the conflict, we follow the plot to the climax. While we
speak of the climax as the turning point in the conflict, children call it "the
most exciting part," or "where I knew how it would end." No matter
which term is used, the climax is inextricably related to conflict.

A Day at the Beach and *Willie Goes to the Seashore* lack climaxes because
they lack conflict. Instead of plot being resolved, it merely peters out. Instead of coming to a decisive conclusion, the narrative just quits. The result
is disappointment.

Climax of some kind exists in any story with conflict (Hooray! Peter
Rabbit made it through the gate!), although the climax may come with
varying degrees of intensity or varying closeness to the end of the story. For
example, in the three parts of *Beowulf,* there are dramatic confrontations
and triumphant battles between Beowulf and Grendel, Beowulf and Grendel's mother, and finally, between Beowulf and the dragon.

However, look at the quiet climax of *Charlotte's Web.* Here, in the
conflict of person-against-society, Wilbur is in a life-and-death struggle.
The climax logically comes when we know that he will live. Checking on
suspense, we find that the high point, brought on by frequent minor crises
and excitement peaks, finally comes when Wilbur revives and wins the
prize—the handsome bronze medal for "attracting so many visitors to our
great County Fair." The runt pig has defeated good business, since Wilbur
has taken the final round of the contest. By his additional award—the special prize of twenty-five dollars—Zuckerman is rewarded with money and
Wilbur is a good business investment after all; this is the climax. From here
on Wilbur has nothing to worry about; the conflict is resolved.

In *The Borrowers,* where the conflict pits the family of tiny people
against Mrs. Driver the housekeeper, the climax comes within a few excit-

Intense or quiet, the climax
comes when we know the
outcome of conflict: protagonist
vs. antagonist.

ing pages of the end. Mrs. Driver's discovery of "the little varmints," living amidst their borrowed luxuries below the floorboards, brings on the rat-catchers. They board up the gratings and seal the space below the floor. Then they start the gas and the fumigating bellows, hoping to kill the creatures, whatever they are. But the Borrowers, whom we have worried about since Chapter 1, have a friend in the Boy, who sets out to give them ventilation:

> Pick-ax in hand [he] ran out of the door. . . . Already, when he reached it, a thin filament of smoke was eddying out of the grating . . . a flicker of movement against the darkness between the bars . . . behind him the crunch of wheels on the gravel and the sound of horse's hoofs. . . . [W]ith two great blows on the brickwork, he dislodged . . . the grating. It fell . . . .

Although we do not see the Borrowers fleeing from the gas, we think they may have escaped. With the airtight grating gone, their path to fresh air and freedom is open.

Sid Fleischman brings his story *Jim Ugly* to a strong climax when Jake's dog, inherited from his father, finds evidence of murder in the place where an accident was assumed to have taken the father's life. Jim Ugly's finding the evidence means that the mystery of an accident now opens a just search for murderers.

The Witch of Blackbird Pond poses a conflict for a young woman who emigrates from Barbados to the witch-hunting Puritan society of New England. Elizabeth Speare shows us how Kit's independence, her compassion, her defiance of ridiculous rules, even her luxurious wardrobe and her swimming ability, work against her to prove to the Puritans that she is a witch. Accusation and trial bring us to the climax. The accuser, faced with evidence that Kit has not bewitched his child but has taught her to read, drops charges, and Kit is now free and innocent. Throughout the story Kit has been different: she is different, willful, and she will not conform. We have seen the frowning and suspicious community and concluded that witchcraft charges will be brought. But it has not all been so pat. Will Prudence be brave enough to prove that Kit was teaching and not bewitching her? Will Nat's ship be in port? Will he be able to help Kit? He has been forbidden to enter the town; how can he help? Will he be able to convince the villagers of the truth? When all these questions have been answered, the climax is reached.

The final chapter of *A Wrinkle in Time* is filled with Meg's thoughts, and yet Madeleine L'Engle maintains suspense to the climax. When Meg, the protagonist, finally gathers her courage to return to Camazotz and to confront the monster brain that holds her brother prisoner, we know that the climax approaches. Meg discovers that she has love and IT has not; she adds all the love of those who surround her with all she feels for them, and love and will together defeat evil and bring joy. Only when Meg's battle with IT frees the last hostage are we satisfied about the final outcome. Conflict and suspense have been intense until the last two pages. For one final example, look at the keen suspense built into the conclusion of H. M. Hoover's *The Shepherd Moon,* where the struggle between two dying cultures comes to its climax when the alien Mikel dies and the great house that represents Merry's corrupt culture collapses.

In looking back over these examples of climax, we note that each involves the final battle of the protagonist with an antagonist. Each results in victory for the protagonist, and this victory seems right in children's literature. Antiheroes, or badly flawed protagonists, and defeated protagonists are for adults only, or more accurately, for some adults only. The child has been involved in the life of a protagonist and wanted the protagonist to win. However, the winning has not happened without a struggle. There is a difference between the climax that says with sticky sweetness, "The world is good, since right always wins," and one that says, "The forces of evil are powerful, but courage and justice together can defeat them." A conflict brought to a climax makes the idea of the story clear through plot that has tension and resolution.

Denouement

Children who are following an exciting story may have trouble pinning down what for them is the climax. Agreeing on that, however, is not as important to the success of the story as agreeing that the story ends with a sense of completeness, or **resolution.**

The **denouement** begins at the climax, at the point where we feel that the protagonist's fate is known. From here the action of the plot is also called the **falling action.** In the denouement of *Charlotte's Web,* Templeton and Wilbur, the two survivors of the original trio, reach a bargain about who eats first at Wilbur's trough. Wilbur returns the egg sac to the barn, and its presence sustains the feeling that Charlotte is still there. Finally, warmed and protected by Wilbur's breath, the eggs hatch. Joy, Aranea, and Nellie, three of Charlotte's tiny progeny, stay on in the barn to keep Wilbur company, and to learn from him the ways of barn life. The seasonal cycle continues; everything is resolved. There is no question left unanswered. We say there is a resolution.

The unknotting of the plot is highly satisfactory in Janet Lunn's *The Shadow in Hawthorn Bay.* In the final pages Mary rids herself of the ghost of her cousin Duncan (to whom she has felt tied since birth), fearlessly walks into the alien forest, and claims it as her new land, acknowledging both her love for Luke and her wish to mother his little brother Henry. She takes responsibility for making her own decisions.

When the reader is assured that all is well and will continue to be, we say that the denouement is closed, or that the plot has a **closed ending.** In this case, the tying of the loose ends is thoroughly optimistic and satisfac-

> Denouement is called either the unknotting of ends or the tying up of loose ends.

tory, a good conclusion for a small child's story. There is no anxiety for reader or listener on the last page of *Charlotte's Web*. The sigh is not a breath of anxiety, but one of regret that so good a story is over.

In an **open ending,** an occasional thing in adult fiction, we are left to draw our own conclusions about final plot resolution. Among enduring examples of children's literature, there seem to be few with open endings, although stories do appear from time to time. The realistic stories of the 1970s, particularly those for the older child, occasionally leave the end open. At the end of Alice Childress's *A Hero Ain't Nothin' but a Sandwich,* for example, we are left with an urgent question: Will Benjie show up for the drug counseling session?

Although some adult readers are intrigued by such inconclusive mystery, others find such endings frustrating. Just as some adults find the open-ended story unsatisfactory, many more children are left dissatisfied and uncertain by unsolved mystery. Depending upon the gravity of the conflict and the maturity of the readers, they may even be left frightened. Without the experience and perspective needed to supply their own endings, some children may turn away from the story with a disturbing sense of anxiety. If tension has been high and the possible outcome serious, the unresolved plot and the open ending seem far less suitable for a children's story.

Inevitability

Through White's use of the device called foreshadowing, we are well prepared for Wilbur's salvation and Charlotte's death. Her life is complete, and her mission accomplished. She has saved her dearest friend and produced her egg sac to carry on another spider generation. There is no other way for the story to end. Although there may be a shadow of sadness, there is a more profound sense of the quality called **inevitability,** or "it had to be." "It was inevitable" is high praise for a writer's skill in bringing plot to conclusion.

Properly motivated action that grows out of character provides inevitability, just as Peter Rabbit's curiosity and greed bring about his inevitable squeezing into Mr. McGregor's garden, his flight, and his stomach ache. At the other end of the literary spectrum, Beowulf, "mightiest yet mildest of men," is the organizer and leader of the band who sail to Hrothgar's country to liberate it from Grendel's scourge. Since Beowulf is pure valor, unsullied by any past defeat or any selfish motive, and since his motive is love for his fellow beings, he cannot lose his battle with personified evil. Despite the suspense of the epic story, we are sure that such goodness will conquer evil. The battle must be to the death, since too easy a victory demeans the godlike hero. The struggle is satisfying in its intensity, but the outcome is inevitable.

The plot that depends for resolution of conflict upon sudden and incredible changes in character fails because it lacks inevitability. In *Dream of*

Small children seem to prefer the reassurance of closed endings.

Open endings force readers to consider the options.

"It was inevitable" means the reader has been prepared for outcome by foreshadowing.

the Blue Heron, Mr. Wickham, the cruel disciplinarian, without foreshadowing becomes kind and sympathetic to Wabus, who will someday be a lawyer because he can count on the assistance of the unbelievably reformed Wickham. Since the resolution of the conflict depends upon unbelievable character change, the plot lacks inevitability.

Types of Plots

Progressive plots come to a climax and conclude with a denouement.

The plots of *Charlotte's Web* and *A Wrinkle in Time,* with their central climaxes followed quickly by denouement, are called **progressive plots.** Apparently people have always liked suspense and climax because the progressive plot is common in traditional European tales. In "The Shoemaker and the Elves," for example, we move directly into the action from a few short phrases—"once upon a time," and "the couple was very poor." The first short paragraph also includes the elves' first visit and the work they leave behind. By the end of the second paragraph, the shoemaker is rich and we are halfway through the story. The couple hides to watch; their grateful gift of clothes for the elves brings on the climax—the dance of the delighted elves, who then disappear. In "The Wolf and the Kids" the climax comes three lines from the end; filled with stones, the wolf falls into the well and drowns. The Bremen Town Musicians raise a furor that frightens the robbers away; the musicians stay forever. When the Fisherman tells the fish that his greedy wife wishes to be God, they are returned to their vinegar jug. The teller of oral tales knows that once the climax comes, he may lose his audience; he must finish the story quickly and conclusively.

It is natural that as groups of people arrive in the Western world from around the globe, their tales should be added to the wealth of folk literature available to us. Because these tales speak of countries and ways of life different from the new land, the folk stories may vary in many ways. We know the Uncle Remus tales brought here by the black slaves, stories in which the underdogs outwit their masters, a theme also common to the folk literature of some Western European groups. Elsewhere social structures may vary, and stock characters may be different. Victims and perpetrators come from anywhere in the social structure. Form, too, may differ from the traditional European tales of the Brothers Grimm or Hans Christian Andersen, which usually follow a progressive plot.

Despite cultural differences in form, "traditional Western values" are often found in tales from all cultures.

The Chinese tales so ably retold by Laurence Yep seem to meander, ignoring what by the Grimms' standards might seem discursive. They comment, nonetheless, on human behavior and values, as do the tales of other ethnic groups. Yep says in the introduction to *The Rainbow People* that "trying to understand Chinese-Americans from these tales is like trying to comprehend Mississippian ancestors by reading a collection of Vermont folktales. Some tales come from a common heritage; but others are specific to the region." One thinks of the Captain Stormalong tales of New England and those of Big John from the mining regions, as well as Pecos Bill from the Southwest. Just as the people enrich our society, all of these stories enrich their readers.

Some book-length stories for children have another type of plot, an **episodic plot** in which one incident or short episode is linked to another by common characters or by a unified theme. A clear contrast to the progressive plot of *Charlotte's Web,* already discussed in some detail, is the episodic one of *The Wind in the Willows.* Like White, Kenneth Grahame uses personified animals as characters in his fantasy. In the twelve short chapters, each a separate story and each a part of the whole, Mole meets Rat, they picnic, and they meet Toad, who can think only of motor cars; Mole, lost in the Wild Wood, is found by Rat and they visit Mole's home. Toad "borrows" a car and is jailed, but he escapes and returns to Toad Hall. The events of *The Wind in the Willows* are quiet in total effect, although some chapters have their own suspense. Each is an episode in the life of an idyllic community of kindly animals whose lives are intertwined by loyalty and mutual concern. Any suspense in a chapter is usually resolved within it. Although there are twelve chapters, only the last two contribute to the conquest of Toad Hall. Instead of a central conflict, what holds our interest are the relationships of the group of developed characters. Rat is consistently kind and reliable; Toad is consistently inconsistent, but Mole, as his self-confidence increases, changes from follower to leader. The idyllic community life of these diverse beings, living their leisurely and unselfish lives, is the discovery of *The Wind in the Willows.* We are further warmed by discovering among other things that one loves one's home where one's belongings are, and that even the most contented find faraway places alluring.

Winnie-the-Pooh supplies another example of episodic plot, and its form is well suited to its young listeners. One episode follows another, each with its own high point and resolution, and with a natural stopping place at the end of chapter and episode. To keep readers reading and listeners listening, the episodic plot relies upon characters, theme, and tension within each chapter, rather than upon suspenseful progress to the climax. Books with episodic plots make excellent bedtime stories.

In Eloise Greenfield's *Sister,* an episodic plot allows glimpses of Doretha's life with her family. Each chapter has a different focus: teen infatuation with a singer, a father's death, sister Alberta's rebellion, a friend's sudden moving away. Each seems a separate memory.

Robert McCloskey's *Homer Price* amuses children with the story of the runaway doughnut machine, or Miss Terwilliger's huge ball of string that she unwinds in county fair competition. Each chapter is a story, and many of the same characters appear throughout—Uncle Ulysses and the Sheriff, for example. Other books, like Beverly Cleary's *Henry Huggins,* show a

> Episodic plots may consist of a series of incidents related by central character.

> Books with episodic plots make excellent bedtime stories.

boy's mischief in a series of episodes. New stories in episodic form, both fantasy and realism, are continually written for children, stories that rely upon character, theme, humor, or nonsense to sustain the reader's interest.

There is great possibility for variation and combination in plot structure. *Alice in Wonderland* combines progressive with episodic plot. The underground setting, Alice's growing and shrinking, and her increasing self-confidence provide unity and progress. We recall the many ingenuities—the pool of tears, the caucus race, the caterpillar's advice, the mad tea party, and the croquet game—without being sure of their order. However, the story concludes in a flurry of excitement and a whirl of angry cards as Alice sees the ineffectual adults at the trial and finally asserts herself. *Tom Sawyer*, too, combines elements of episodic structure with progressive plot and climactic focus. Although there are a strong conflict and a final climax, there are also many chapters that are merely episodes in the life of a small-town boy and those, though enjoyable in themselves, make little contribution to the central conflict.

Special Issues of Plot in Children's Literature

Most of what we have said about plot up to this point applies to plot in adult literature as well as in children's literature. For the remainder of the chapter we will discuss some of the special problems in stories for children.

In our earlier discussion of patterns of action, we mentioned the dangers of sensationalism. While adults may choose such stories, children may find sensationalism is more than they can bear. Sensational suspense, furthermore, places the focus upon tension rather than upon human beings and ideas. If the functions of literature are pleasure and understanding, the latter is slighted by sensationalism.

Coincidence

Action happening by mere chance is coincidence.

The concurrence of events apparently by mere chance is **coincidence**. In real life, we well know that coincidence does occur. In literature, however, where the truths of human nature and human existence are explored, reliance on coincidence to resolve conflict weakens plot. One example in which excellence is flawed by coincidence is *The Incredible Journey*. As the three pets find their way through the Canadian wilderness, three chance happenings without foreshadowing leave readers puzzled, perhaps doubting the larger plot. A handwritten note blows into the fireplace and leaves the housekeeper baffled. Later, by a "twist of fate," a crumbling beaver dam gives way at just the right moment to sweep the frightened cat downstream. Third, a boy, hunting for the first time with his own rifle, saves the Siamese cat from a lynx by one remarkably accurate shot. Fortunately, however, the story of the pets' struggle against the wilderness is so strong in many other ways, from character to style, that perhaps the coincidence can be overlooked.

Such fictional strength is not always the case, however, since inadequate foreshadowing leads the reader to doubt the credibility of an event. The test of coincidence, therefore, is foreshadowing. We are prepared to accept the concurrence of events if the incident does not seem to be mere chance, but a previously threatened or foreseen possibility.

Coincidence is tested by foreshadowing.

White might easily have fallen into the coincidence trap in *Charlotte's Web*. If, for example, the enormous and healthy Uncle, the obvious choice for first prize, had happened to take sick at the fair, that would have been coincidence. However, had Wilbur won the blue ribbon by mere default, our pleasure in the outcome would then have been a mixed pleasure over a far less satisfying victory. Furthermore, if Charlotte had by incredible coincidence eventually lived as long as Wilbur, she would have defied the natural laws of a spider's life cycle. Charlotte may talk and write words in her web, but she is a spider leading a spider life. White, by using foreshadowing and by rejecting coincidence, has given *Charlotte's Web* an inevitable, satisfying conclusion.

Sentimentality

Nor should another negative element, called **sentimentality,** mar a well-constructed plot. We term **sentiment** a natural concern or emotion for another person. When, for instance, our parents are hurt in a painful accident, our natural sentiment, called love, causes an emotional response. We are hurt with those we love. However, when our sentiments are used, or played upon as they are in soap opera, we have what we call a tear-jerker situation, or sentimentality.

Sentimentality evokes disproportionate emotional response.

We have all at some time left a movie theater surreptitiously wiping our eyes, knowing the movie wasn't worth tears. At other times we have been unashamed of our tears, perhaps even proud. It is the legitimacy of our emotional reaction that makes us feel honest. When we are honestly moved by art, we may weep because we suffer with the character empathically, taking his or her sorrow upon ourselves. But sometimes the writer may cause us to weep or to exult and we are uncomfortable because we are asked for an emotional response in excess of what the situation requires.

Sentimentality takes varied forms. Character may be sentimentally drawn. For instance, a saintly, sweet woman who never raises her voice, who is patient, kind, loyal, and true; and who keeps a full cookie jar and a spotless kitchen is no reality. She is a cardboard, two-dimensional figure, a highly sentimentalized picture of Mother. Sentimentality may also occur in a plot. Sydney Taylor's *All-of-a-Kind Family* pictures growing up poor in an Orthodox Jewish family. However, the writer not only creates a sentimental picture of Mother, but sees family life as a continually joyful chain of events, or perhaps nonevents. Five identically dressed little girls going happily to the library in a group, living frictionless lives in a large family, accepting and making the happy best of poverty, inviting the librarian to dinner and causing a loving marriage to result from her meeting with another guest—these sentimentalized pictures challenge our knowledge of the reality of family life. Because we reject, or are dubious of, Taylor's sentimentalized view of family life, we may, unfortunately, reject the far more important discoveries about the practice of Jewish orthodoxy.

A typical story and a great favorite among children of the late nineteenth century was a supposedly realistic horse story called *Black Beauty,* Anna Sewell's novel told in first person by Black Beauty himself. The book made an influential appeal to Victorian society about cruelty to animals, but as we look at it now, it strikes us with heavy sentimentality. The pathos of Beauty's own life is comparable to that of "Poor Ginger," as one chapter is entitled. Ginger tells Black Beauty her story, and the short chapter concludes with Black Beauty's observations:

> A short time after this a cart with a dead horse in it passed our cabstand. The head hung out of the cart-tail, the lifeless tongue was slowly dropping with blood; and the sunken eyes! but I can't speak of them, the sight was too dreadful. It was a chestnut horse with a long, thin neck. . . . I believe it was Ginger; I hoped it was, for then her troubles would be over. O! if men were more merciful they would shoot us before we came to such misery.

While none of us would argue that people have a right to be cruel to any animal, Sewell's sentimentality is apparent. The graphic description of a lolling, bloody tongue, the frequent exclamation points, and even the basic idea of a realistic story of a horse being told in first person by the horse—all are tear-jerkers. Because of the sentimentality, the reader may sob more soulfully over Ginger's death than over that of a human being—although there is little confusion in our minds as to which misused creature is more deserving of grief.[3]

A steady diet of sentimentality may cause emotional shallowness.

Rarely do we have sensationalism in folktales, and rarely does the storyteller stop to rouse our tears by false sentiment. The wicked wolf whose stomach is full of rocks falls into the well and is drowned; we waste no sighs. The unkind girl whose punishment is to spout toads creeps into the corner and dies. The rapid pace of the folktale plot seems to prohibit pauses for tears. We appreciate the celebration of a marriage "the very next day," and we are not anguished over the fate of Rumpelstiltskin, who stamped his feet so hard that he split in two and "that was an end of him." Instead of being sentimental, the tale-teller resorts to humor. Some of Hans Christian Andersen's stories, however, are sentimental, including one of his personal favorites, "The Little Match Girl." Those of his tales told in the folktale manner do not lapse into sentimentality.

Charlotte's Web does not resort to sentimentality. Lingering sobs and whimpers from Charlotte at her own death would have destroyed credibility. Charlotte is a spider and knows it. Her spider-defined life prepares us, Wilbur and the readers, for her dignified and inevitable death. Or again, Wilbur's fainting might easily have become sentimental panic, but is instead humorous. Or Templeton might have broken down, become a reformed rat, and committed some unselfish or heroic act. Such an incredible change would have been sentimentality. Our every response to each situation in White's story is legitimately roused, never exaggerated or superficial, and therefore unsentimental.

What is wrong with sentimentality? A good cry never hurt anyone. Perhaps not. However, there are dangers inherent in a steady diet of forced emotion. We have all had our turns at sneering at soap opera, but perhaps we have not really considered why we sneer. One after the other, one dramatic occurrence, one crisis, and one tragedy pushes another out of our memories. We are like pumps primed to spout tears and then, just as we have settled down, primed again.

The most destructive element in the overuse of sentiment is not boredom, but the fact that the young reader, faced with continual sentimentality, will not develop the sensitivity essential to recognize what is truly moving and what is merely a play on feelings. The use of judgment and the sense of proportion grow and mature when we see honest emotion, whether it be joy or sorrow. If, after all, we regard the death of a pet mouse with the same degree of emotional intensity as the death of a brother, we have no sense of emotional proportion.

By contrast to *Black Beauty*, notice in Katherine Paterson's story *Bridge to Terabithia* the wide range of emotions that readers wrestle with. They follow Jess from his shyness with other children to his rivalry with his sister Brenda, from pleasure over the secret bridge to the hideaway island, to numbness and grief at his friend Leslie's drowning. Or chart the genuine sentiment that a small child, reading or being read to, experiences over the relationship with Charlotte and Wilbur. Here he or she comes to know loneliness, friendship, sacrifice, tact, patience, loyalty, and maternity—as well as death and continuity; the child meets such negative human traits as selfishness, avarice, and gluttony. Furthermore, among the more surprising

Sentiment, yes. But sentimentality inhibits the growth of emotional honesty.

discoveries is the way in which such significant human traits and experiences are explored in both books—not with bathos or sentimentality, but with seriousness and deft humor. The total impact of White's book embodies respect for animals, yes, but more importantly, respect for people, as Wilbur and Charlotte personify human beings.

The child fed only on such surface sentimentality as soap opera and Walt Disney—with their sterile and stereotyped pictures of human beings and their distorted sensationalism with simplistic solutions—this child risks developing emotional shallowness.[4] The child nourished through real literature in the breadth and depth and range of true emotion grows in understanding of human nature.

Lack of Conflict

Many of today's mass-produced storybooks, like those often found on racks in supermarkets and drugstores, lack conflict. Events follow one another in chronological narrative. Without any struggle, the story lacks suspense, any hint of alternative outcomes, a sense that it had to happen, and therefore satisfaction. All that the reader can say at the conclusion of such a story is, "So what does that prove?" Conflict, the tension that keeps a story interesting, has never appeared.

Inadequately developed conflict, like flat characterization, leaves us unconcerned about the outcome of a story. Conflict holds our attention if it presents some semblance of a fair fight, and if the question of outcome is open. In poor science fiction, too, the protagonist combats an irresistible natural force, or in person-against-person conflict, the ingenuity of the two intellects without emotions becomes a dry, academic struggle. When pure intellect does battle with itself in person-against-self conflict, the struggle is merely a problem with a rational answer. The reader who is uninvolved in either characters or conflict becomes apathetic; "I cannot conceive of it; I therefore cannot care."

Once again, however, take the example of *A Wrinkle in Time*, where conflict is person-against-person. Meg battles against a disembodied brain that controls the citizens of Camazotz, whose people are programmed to be identical. Meg and Calvin struggle against "IT"'s magnetic persuasion, but Charles Wallace, whose allegiance to mind is stronger than it is to spirit, arrogantly gives in. Pure mind, however, cannot conquer stubborn Meg, whose believable flaws make her human enough for us to care about her. When Meg sees that her strength lies in her power to love, she overcomes IT and frees Charles Wallace. These human responses of will, dependence, and love oppose the antagonist IT. We are concerned about the

Without conflict, the reader may shrug and say, "Who cares?"

outcome, yearning to help Meg in a fantastic plot based upon the possible reality of opposing forces in conflict.

Summary

Character study alone rarely carries the child's interest, but character becomes inextricably woven into plot by the very nature of the protagonist as well as the antagonist in the conflict. Order is easier for the child to follow if it is within his or her experience; chronological order is therefore more frequent, while flashback is more common in stories for older children. In a progressive plot, suspense pulls the reader through the rising action to the central climax, where conflict is resolved in a manner foreshadowed and thus inevitable; the last questions are usually answered in a denouement, with its closed ending.

By contrast, each chapter in an episodic plot may have its own small tensions and be joined to the others by theme and character. Finally, a well-plotted story relies on neither sentimentality nor coincidence for action and resolution.

There is no right plot structure in a story for children. There are only variations of the two principal forms. The understanding of the child—reader or listener—may determine the length or structure of the story, whether that story be a single progressively arranged unit or an episode in a longer work. However, what does matter is that the piece of literature sustain interest and give pleasure as it is read.

In considering the plot development, we are most aware that without sufficient conflict or tension, accompanied by suspense, foreshadowing, and inevitability, a story is just plain dull. Few adults want to read a dull story, and certainly no children will.

Notes

1. C. W. Sullivan III, "Narrative Expectations: The Folklore Connection," *Children's Literature Quarterly 15* (Summer 1990): 52–55.

2. For a discussion of time in time fantasy, a subject in itself, see Eleanor Cameron, "The Green and Burning Tree," in *The Green and Burning Tree* (Boston: Atlantic Monthly Press, 1969), pp. 71–134.

3. Readers take opposite views on *Black Beauty*. Perhaps it is not the personification in a realistic story, but the injustice of the horse's treatment and the justice of his feelings that prompts their responses.

4. For a discussion of Walt Disney's work, see Frances Clarke Sayers, "Walt Disney Accused," in *Children and Literature: Views and Reviews,* edited by Virginia Haviland (Glenview, Ill.: Scott, Foresman, 1973), pp. 116–125.

Recommended Books Cited in This Chapter

ALEXANDER, LLOYD. *The Philadelphia Adventure.* New York: Dutton, 1990.

ARMSTRONG, WILLIAM. *Sounder.* New York: Harper & Row, 1969.

AVI. *Bright Shadow.* New York: Bradbury, 1985.

———. *Shadrach's Crossing* New York: Random House, 1984.

———. *The True Confessions of Charlotte Doyle.* New York: Orchard Books, 1990.

BAUER, MARION DANE. *On My Honor.* Boston: Houghton Mifflin, 1986.

BELLAIRS, JOHN. *The Trolley to Yesterday.* New York: Dial, 1989.

BURNFORD, SHEILA. *The Incredible Journey.* Boston: Little, Brown, 1961.

BYARS, BETSY. *A Blossom Promise.* New York: Delacorte, 1987.

CARROLL, LEWIS. *Alice's Adventures in Wonderland.* 1865. Reprint. New York: Dutton, 1954.

CHILDRESS, ALICE. *A Hero Ain't Nothin' but a Sandwich.* New York: Coward, 1973.

CHRISTIAN, MARY BLOUNT. *Sebastian (Super Sleuth) and the Bone to Pick Mystery.* New York: Macmillan, 1983.

CLEARY, BEVERLY. *Henry Huggins.* New York: Morrow, 1950.

COLLIER, JAMES LINCOLN, AND CHRISTOPHER COLLIER. *Jump Ship to Freedom.* New York: Doubleday, 1981.

———. *My Brother Sam Is Dead.* New York: Four Winds, 1974.

CREECH, SHARON. *Walk Two Moons.* New York: Harper, 1992.

CURTIS, CHRISTOPHER. *The Watsons Go to Birmingham.* New York: Delacorte, 1995.

FLEISCHMAN, SID. *Jim Ugly.* New York: Green Willow, 1992.

GEORGE, JEAN. *Julie of the Wolves.* New York: Harper & Row, 1972.

———. *The Talking Earth.* New York: Harper & Row, 1983.

GRAHAME, KENNETH. *The Wind in the Willows.* 1908. Reprint. New York: Scribner's, 1953.

GREENFIELD, ELOISE. *Sister.* Toronto: Fitzhenry and Whiteside, 1974.

HALL, LYNN. *Dagmar and the Angel Edna.* New York: Scribner's, 1989.

———. *Dagmar Shultz and the Green-Eyed Monster.* New York: Scribner's, 1991.

HAMILTON, VIRGINIA. *Time Ago Lost: More Tales of Jahdu.* New York: Macmillan, 1973.

———. *The Time Ago Tales of Jahdu.* New York: Macmillan, 1962.

HOOVER, H. M. *The Shepherd Moon.* New York: Viking, 1984.

HUNTER, MOLLIE. *The Mermaid Summer.* New York: Harper & Row, 1988.

L'ENGLE, MADELEINE. *A Wrinkle in Time.* New York: Farrar, Straus, & Giroux, 1962.

LE GUIN, URSULA K. *A Wizard of Earthsea.* Berkeley: Parnassus, 1968.

LOWRY, LOIS. *Number the Stars.* New York: Houghton Mifflin, 1989.

6

Theme

"What happens" and "Whom it happens to"—is that all there is?

We each have at least one friend who tells a story by linking one anecdote to another, using slender threads of association as continuity: "And the next night . . ." or "And then we . . ." We have heard a more artful storyteller whose stories are involved and who keeps us in suspense: "You'll never believe what she said then," or "And what do you think should happen next but . . . !" The first of these narrators can bore us quickly; the second can hold our interest longer. However, the storyteller we especially value is someone whose stories awaken us to awareness of new meaning—of the inconsistency of people, or the mixed joys of family living, or the pain of social exclusion, for example. This storyteller is aware of meaning and has reached for idea, or theme.

In storytelling "What happened next?" is a question about chronology and narrative order. "Why did it happen?" is a question about conflict and plot. But when we ask, "What does it all mean?" we begin to discover theme.

Theme or Unifying Truth

Theme in literature is the idea that holds the story together, such as a comment about society, human nature, or the human condition. It is the main idea or central meaning of a piece of writing.

Ask a woman about the plot of *Little Women,* the story she loved as a child, and she looks baffled and perhaps chagrined that she cannot remember it. Setting, too, has faded from memory to become merely "in the past." Character, however, is still with her, because restless Jo, who has difficulty fitting into traditional female roles, seems to be Every-woman—or at least Manywomen. And chances are the adult's memory of the idea or theme of the novel is still strong; she can confidently say, "It's about a loving family of varied but accepting people." The characters of Louisa May Alcott's story convince us of one of its themes—the love of family members for each other is real and enduring.[1] Theme comes alive and becomes memorable as the characters act out the plot.

Our definition of literature, you will recall, is "a significant truth expressed in appropriate elements and memorable language." The "significant truth" is an essential element to turn a simple narrative into literature. This truth goes beyond the story and comments on human beings. The discovery holds the story together so that long after details of plot are forgotten, the theme remains.

This significant truth unifies and illuminates a story, giving the reader pleasure. The reader gains one pleasure from the discovery of the simplest of truths, and another from the discovery that truth is not simple.[2] Theme provides this discovery, this understanding, this pleasure in recognizing "Yes, that's the way it is!"

Types of Themes

Explicit Theme

Stating theme in a sentence clarifies its focus.

Sometimes the writer states theme openly and clearly—an **explicit theme.** Once again we turn to *Charlotte's Web* for examples. The devotion between Charlotte and Wilbur suggests many ideas that make the reader say, "It's true"; their relationship reveals and defines friendship and suggests other themes.

Charlotte has encouraged, protected, and mothered Wilbur, bargained and sacrificed for him, and Wilbur, the grateful receiver, realizes that "friendship is one of the most satisfying things in the world." And Charlotte says later, "By helping you perhaps I was trying to lift my life a little. Anyone's life can stand a little of that." Because these quoted sentences are exact statements from the text, they are called explicit themes.

Notice the explicit statement "Love is just the beginning" and the implied "Caring must follow and continue," the theme of Cynthia Rylant's *A Fine White Dust* as stated in its closing pages. Pete has worked through his disillusionment with The Man, the revival preacher who had left him, but remains forgiving. "It's a world where good guys . . . are happy atheists, and nice folks . . . don't care much about church and spiritual people like me wander around the earth wishing it was heaven."

As immigration and population numbers alter the makeup of American and Canadian society, the trend toward multicultural stories is justifiably common in today's books for children. In *Class President* Johanna Hurwitz states an explicit point about ethnic pride when the new teacher, Mr. Flores, gives Julio's name its proper Spanish pronunciation: *Hulio.* "It's a good Spanish name and you should be proud of it. . . . Your name is a very important part of you." He tells the class that when they elect a president, it should not just be a popularity contest. "A good leader is . . . fair and . . . stands up for what he or she thinks is right." Julio begins to stand up for what he believes in, first of all his ethnic heritage.

Like Mildred Taylor's *Roll of Thunder, Circle of Fire* shows the impact of the Ku Klux Klan on society. In an explicit thematic statement, author William H. Hooks replies to Harrison's question. "Why?" by having Pa say:

> "Your Grandma would tell you that they're just poor white trash and that quality folks would never resort to such meanness. . . . But there's more to it than that. There's something in all of us that wants to be top dog, that wants to keep *our kind* in control. Human decency doesn't seem to be a God-given gift. It's a precious thing you have to learn early and keep working at."

Hooks does not leave it at that, but in a concluding author's note reminds us of the KKK's prevalence everywhere and warns, "These same events could happen today." Such explicit themes are common in children's literature because the writer may wish to be sure the reader finds the unifying truth.

Sometimes a theme is flatly stated, as it is in *The Year of the Boar and Jackie Robinson* by Bette Bao Lord: 'In the life of our nation, each man is a citizen of the United States, but he has the right to pursue his own happiness. For no matter what his race, religion or creed, be he pauper or president, he has the right to speak his mind, to live as he wishes within the law. . . . To make a difference." Readers may react differently as they consider the effect of such a straightforward—even preachy—statement.

Throughout Karen Cushman's *The Midwife's Apprentice,* Alyce's life changes from having to sleep in a warm dung heap to being praised for delivering twin calves, and then delivering a healthy infant for the bailiff's wife. Failure later sends her away to become an "inn girl" and there her curiosity about the Magister's writing helps her learn to read. A "miraculous" birth of the young squire's infant follows. With successes behind her and a strong will to learn all she can, Alyce returns to become the midwife's apprentice. In the last lines of the book, Alyce states an explicit theme: "I know how to try and risk and fail and try again and not give up," the real source of success.

Implicit Theme

Underlying *Charlotte's Web* are certain implied or **implicit themes,** as important and almost as apparent as explicit themes. If two such different characters as a runt pig and a carnivorous spider can find friendship, others can; even a self-centered rat can be a friend of sorts. White thereby implies that friendship can be found in unexpected places.

Charlotte's selflessness—working late at night to finish a new word, expending her last energies for her friend—is evidence that friendship is giving of oneself. Wilbur's protection of Charlotte's egg sac, his sacrifice of first turn at the slops, and his devotion to Charlotte's babies—giving without any need to stay even or to pay back—leads us to another theme: True friendship is naturally reciprocal. As the two become fond of each other, still another theme emerges: One's best friend can do no wrong. In fact, a best friend is sensational! Both Charlotte and Wilbur believe in these ideas; their experiences verify them. These themes are all developed through the characters, their action, and their thoughts as we see them throughout the story's conflict.

Throughout the realistic *Jacob Have I Loved* runs the implicit theme that one is not deprived of love but finds what one is open for. Not only does Wheeze feel that Caroline has cheated her out of the family's love and the community's favor, but that she has also taken from her what she was not even sure she wanted—Call's love. Grandmother, too, in her aged fantasies, feels that her daughter-in-law has stolen her son from her, as in her youth another had stolen from her the Captain's love. And yet, no one steals love from anyone. H. M. Hoover's fantasy *The Shepherd Moon* is the story of a cold and privileged society attended by vast numbers of slaves. One implicit theme is that freedom is so important that it is worth even the threat of annihilation.

When we think of theme as "a moral" or "a lesson," or even as "a message," we are repelled by the idea that we must learn how or how not to behave. But a good story is not meant to instruct us. Its purpose is to entertain us by its action and characters; at the same time, it gives us insight into people and how they think and feel, and enlarges our understanding. However, when we think of theme as the unifying idea that holds the other elements of a good story together, we are pleased to find that we have not only been entertained, received pleasure, but that we have made a discovery of some kind.

The theme of Ruth White's novel *Belle Pater's Boy* is that appearances are less important than what one is inside. Arbutus, called Beauty by her father, dislikes the focus on her appearance, and calls herself Gypsy instead. When Cousin Woodrow, who hates his crossed eyes, moves in next door, Gypsy comes to love him dearly. She learns that his mother was a loving but unattractive woman, and that her own gentle father killed himself because, following his heroic rescue of a child in a fire, he could not accept his disfigurement. Gypsy's mother says that "appearances were too important to your father" and he became deeply depressed. The outside doesn't matter; inside, each was worthy of love.

Virginia Hamilton's *Cousins* is a story in which the protagonist dreads the death of her aged Gram Tut and is haunted by the memory of seeing her cousin Patty Ann drown. Absorbed in both her grief at Patty's death and her own guilt at being jealous of her pretty cousin, Cammy cannot face death but buries it, then chews it over and over until she is helped by Gram Tut to recognize that death happens to us all. Some wait for it, like Tut; for others it comes too soon, as it does for Patty. Because the theme of the novel is suggested by such statements as that cited above and not stated precisely at any point, it is implicit.

Implicit themes also underlie *Circle of Fire* by William H. Hooks: "Friendship knows no ethnic barriers." Harrison values his black friends and adds another, Liam Cafferty, among the migrant Irish gypsies traveling the eastern seaboard. Harrison's fear that his father might be a Klan member dissolves when Pa is responsible for the eviction of the Klan from the area, but the implicit theme remains: "When we don't know the facts, we may doubt even those we love."

It may seem unnecessary or even unwise to state theme in sentence form. Why not say, "The theme of *Charlotte's Web* is friendship"? Notice what happens if we do state the theme this simply. *Friendship* is too broad a term. "Friendship is fraudulent" or "Friendship is a useless luxury" or "Friendship is all giving and no receiving"—any of these statements concerns friendship and might reasonably be explored and proven in literature, but none is the truth of E. B. White's story. When we force ourselves to make a specific statement based upon the facts of the story, we define the theme more carefully.

Multiple and Secondary Themes

Each reader brings to a story a personal past, a present, and plans for the future. These elements shape our *responses* to the story. It seems absurd, then, to expect that diverse human beings must agree upon exactly the same ideas as being the most important, and must take from the story exactly the same themes, since the story speaks to us out of our own individual and varying experiences. It speaks a universal truth to us, but our own universal truth, a personal transaction.

Although complexity and variety in themes may be one of the strongest proofs of a work's excellence, most literature for children seems to center upon a **primary theme.** When a story contains a variety of themes, they are often linked.

Consistent with high fantasy's focus upon good-evil conflict, Ursula K. Le Guin's *A Wizard of Earthsea* explores the greatest of all struggles: that within one's self. Ged, in his flight from the shadow, heeds the advice of his mentor: "You must choose. You must seek what seeks you. You must hunt the hunter." When, after sailing for days, Ged confronts the thing that has sloughed off all human form, and recognizes it as the evil within himself, he is strong enough to win the battle. Internal conflict has illuminated theme. Other less personal themes abound. "Need alone is not enough to set power free: there must be knowledge." "To hear, one must be silent." "Danger must surround power." "As a man's real power grows and his knowledge widens . . . he chooses nothing, but does only and wholly what he must do." "The wise man is one who never sets himself apart from other living things." The novel is rich in thematic ideas.

If a story has multiple themes, some seem less important than the primary one. These we call **secondary themes.**

In *Charlotte's Web,* almost as important as the themes about the nature of friendship is a secondary one about death. It is the possibility of Wilbur's death that disturbs us; we would feel different if he were an old boar who had lived long and well. We recognize, just the same, that "death is inevitable and not to be feared." Charlotte, knowing her life cycle, foresees her own death, but neither dreads it nor asks for pity. Others accept death too. Seasons die when they have run their terms. Maple trees, crickets, lilacs, baby spiders, and the Harvest Fair all celebrate the inevitable cycle of birth, life, and death. There is no grief, only acceptance.

A wealth of minor themes also emerges in *Charlotte's Web:* "People are gullible"; "People don't give credit where credit is due"; "The meek may inherit the earth"; "Youth and innocence have unique value." Each character accepts and maintains the simplicity of his or her own particular style of living, so "Be what you are." As for nature, "There are beauty and wonder in all things, even the simplest," "Life in nature is constant and continuous," and finally, "Nature is a miracle," from the silver forest of asparagus to the waterproof egg sac.

In *Cousins* the return of Cammy's divorced father when she is suffering with grief and shock suggests an optimistic secondary theme about change, implying that even in difficult times, things may change and good things happen. In her brief novel *Journey* Patricia MacLachlan suggests related themes. Journey and Cat are left to live with their grandparents when their mother, grieving over a husband lost when he abandoned the family, in turn abandons her two children. "Try though we may, we cannot always understand the behavior of others" comes through to us. "A family need not be the traditional parents and-children, but may be a different form" is a second theme.

A story should have a thematic idea or point.

In one story, value lies in the explicit yet nondidactic statement of theme. In another, the fact that the theme is implied and must be stated by the reader for himself or herself is value of another kind. The only general rule that can be made is that a theme should be there. On first reading a good story, we usually see one or a few thematic ideas, both explicit and implicit. We see more perhaps on second reading. However, thematic wealth in a book for children often lies in the continuous discoveries.

James Lincoln Collier and Christopher Collier, writers of *Jump Ship to Freedom,* show how Daniel Arabus grows in character and strength by confronting crises and solving problems. Early in the story he calls himself a "nigger," a "stupid darky," "not as smart as white folks." "I knew that black folks were supposed to be more stupid than white folks; that was God's way, the minister said. . . . If God had made black folks smart, they'd have got restless about doing the hard work." But by the time he has saved himself from apprehension under the Fugitive Slave Act, worked like a seasoned seaman in the rigging of the square-rigger, and managed to save his father's Civil War soldier pay, he is told that he is a smart and resourceful young man. But Daniel disagrees. "If I'd been really smart I'd have figured out a way to get those soldiers' notes [long ago]." By the story's end, he calls himself by his given name, thinking to himself, "When you figured you was one kind of person all your life, it's hard to start thinking of yourself as another kind." Once we accept a negative view of ourselves, accepting another is not easy.

Children differ, and the variety of their capacities for discovery as well as for phrasing that discovery is almost infinite. The smaller the child, the less likelihood of a coherent statement. We realize, however, that although a small child cannot define "home" or "mother," even the youngest knows what each concept is. Security and love, comfort and constancy, warmth and protection are abstractions they know, but abstractions beyond articulation. For children, knowing and saying need not be—and rarely are—the same.

Special Issues of Theme in Children's Literature
Traditional Literature

Folktales have similar themes even though they originate in different cultures. Their presence in traditional literature passed on from one generation to another seems to be evidence that people create and respond to similar ideas about life and human nature. By noting just a few of these themes, we become aware that a simple, optimistic core of truth like "Good can conquer evil" is explored in a great many of the tales, Asian and South American as well as European. Some leave the theme as simple as that, but others explore ideas a bit more complex, clarifying the kind of good or the kind of evil. "The Goosegirl," a German tale, explicitly identifies the conquered evil as deception: the servant girl who threatens and impersonates the princess is punished. "Snow White," another German tale, defines the defeated evil more clearly as jealousy; the witch-queen tries ceaselessly to kill the one more beautiful than she. "Drakestail," from the French, identifies the particular good as humility; the modest hero calls upon the Fox, the Ladder, and the River to save him from a tyrant king.

Other folktales, like the Norwegian "The Three Billy-Goats Gruff," prove that keeping your wits about you can save you from danger. In the German tale "The Twelve Dancing Princesses," the soldier outwits the princesses and wins one for his bride. The Scandinavian "Boots and His

Brothers" shows that if you have the wit to see its potential, curiosity can pay off. Both the Russian "The Little Humpbacked Horse" and the Norse "The Princess on the Glass Hill" praise the capacity of cleverness to bring success. Both "The Bremen-Town Musicians" from Germany and "The Ram and the Pig Who Went into the Woods" from Scandinavia offer proof that each creature can use its gifts to contribute to common success. Tales told over and over, tales told in one land or another, tales complex in structure for older readers or simple in outline for younger readers—most have themes that state a universal truth.

Similar themes from all cultures seem to surface.

Folktales about outwitting the powerful, for example, occur in many cultures. In *Fire Came to Earth People,* a West African tale from Dahomey retold and illustrated by Susan L. Roth, earth people had no fire because Mawu the selfish Moon-god kept it all to himself. Even the strongest could not steal fire, but returned saying, "Fire is not meant for earth people." The chameleon and the tortoise became sacred to the people because only these lowly ones had the wit to steal coals, set fire to straw, and hide the fire beneath the shell of the tortoise. The story has the familiar form of the *pourquoi* or "how/why?" tale. The three tasks set for Ananse the Spider Man by the Sky God of Gail Haley's Caribbean-African *A Story, A Story* are completed by a simple man who ties the leopard in a net of vines, catches the hornets in a calabash, and captures the fairy-whom-no-man-sees by means of a latex-covered wooden doll reminiscent of Joel Chandler Harris's Tar Baby. Now the Spider Man carries the Sky God's stories to the world. In the Native American story "How the Bear Got His Stumpy Tail," the bear is outwitted by the fox, who tells him he can catch fish by leaving his tail in the ice. And in *The Name of the Tree,* a Bantu tale retold by Celia Barker Lottridge, neither the fleet gazelle nor the elephant with the long memory can remember the name of the tree; only the youngest tortoise manages.

Like the conflicts in folk literature that so obviously set protagonist against antagonist, the themes are straightforward and easily seen. Although themes are often implicit, the conflict and the characters make them so evident that explicit statements are unnecessary. Hard work can bring success; intelligence is more valuable than physical strength; kindness brings rewards—these are basic issues that the vigorous action of the folktale makes clear. The prominence of them in traditional stories seems to verify the human wish to know not only what happened, and how it happened, but also why it happened and what it means. According to Wayne Booth, one of the strongest of human interests is the "desire for causal completion." "Not only do we believe that certain causes do in life produce certain effects; in literature we believe that they should." This interest is distinct from the "pleasure of learning, of satisfaction of intellectual curiosity."[3]

One of the strongest of human interests is "the desire for causal conpletion."   —Wayne Booth

The Myths of the Orient, retold and illustrated by Barbara Chestesen, are perhaps as old as any told. In each of them, virtuous behavior is rewarded. The son's wish to pay for his father's funeral is so strong that he sells himself as a slave. The daughter whose royal father cannot have the right combination of metals for a beautiful bell throws herself into the boiling metal; her death melds the metals into a perfect, sweet-toned bell. The kind-hearted Ming Li, who cannot kill the tortoise for food, finds that wealth and a king's daughter are his.

Not all folktale themes are optimistic. *Heetunka's Harvest,* a picture book by Jennifer Berry Jones, illustrates how greed is rewarded by disaster in Indian society. Among the tribes, women trade with humility and gratitude, but Heetunka, who takes white beans from the mouse's nest, fails to trade and is punished.

Human beings are not totally good or completely successful; good does not always conquer evil. Hans Christian Andersen, although he uses the traditional forms of folktales, makes no effort either to be constantly optimistic or to preach about what people ought to be. He is too busy showing what people are. Many of his stories of humble people, animals, and inanimate objects demonstrate one of his most personal and optimistic themes, that of the Ugly Duckling: "Humble beginnings and painful trials can end in happiness." But Andersen's themes also frequently remind us that people are foolish; they value the artificial and the trivial more than the real, as "The Swineherd," "The Nightingale," and "The Princess and the Pea" tell us. People will do anything for vanity, as we see in "The Emperor's New Clothes." Whether we like it or not, the rogue sometimes wins the prize, as he does in "The Tinder Box." Andersen[4] honestly admits that death is sometimes sudden and may leave children bereft; he explores serious themes and develops them into individualized and realistic comments on humankind. His stories prove that literature for children as well as for adults can make sad or even negative comments and still give both pleasure and discovery.

Didacticism

We often wish to help children by telling them what they ought or ought not to do. We give them little mottoes and short, preachy verses to hang on their bedroom walls. From our own past experience we tell them stories which really are instruction disguised as reminiscence. The result may be the child's comment, "I'm sick of hearing how my dad *loved* to walk to school every day. And according to him, it was uphill both ways." No one is fooled.

Or we admire the welcome hyacinths in the springtime flower bed, but instead of comparing their varied colors, smelling their fragrance, or touching their curled, waxy petals, we turn our admiration into a botany lesson on stamen, pistil, and corolla. The science lesson has its place, of course, but not every flower bed must stimulate it. A growing awareness of startling beauty and perfection in nature may sometimes be stifled by a lesson from Botany 101.

Didacticism, or instruction, is the function of textbooks. Some literature gives a great deal of information without letting it take over from suspenseful and exciting plot, or from well-developed characters. Other narratives are so filled with teaching details about a historical period, a geographical area, a social inequity, or a physical disability that conflict, character, and theme are lost in "what the reader ought to know." If the information displaces the understanding, then didacticism has won out. Literature, on the other hand, does not teach; it helps us understand.

Nor does literature preach. "Eat it; it's good for you" never persuaded anyone. Adults who choose stories for children that force a moral upon them think that a story is good only if it contains obvious lessons. However, knowing our own adult dislike for "do this, but don't do that," we can scarcely expect children to enjoy such preaching, and we may be preventing the child from making discoveries personally. We may be impeding growth rather than fostering it. Furthermore, sugar-coating a moral by surrounding it with a shallow story deficient in plot, character portrayal, and style does injustice to children. They come to a story excited by the promise of pleasure only to discover they have been tricked into a sermon. The preached-at child may come to reject all reading and thus close off the vast discoveries about human beings and society available in literature.

The obvious purpose of some narratives, like *I Want to Be a Homemaker,* shows little imagination on the part of the writer and awakens little response from the reader; it may even stimulate resistance.[5] Because everything in this narrative is commonplace, the narrative itself is commonplace. We have a sexist view of what a homemaker does: She bakes and sews and tends the baby. Why? Because that is her job. But there is no word of what a mother *is.* A real mother loves her children and finds satisfaction in providing for them—like the mothers of Peter Rabbit and the Moffats, or the mother of the troubled children in *Roll of Thunder, Hear My Cry.* In a story exploring motivation in a real parent, we might come to see the dimensions of such love.

A selfish, tit-for-tat approach to friendship that says "Be nice to your friends and they will be nice to you" or "Make everyday occurrences into fun" would be preachy. Throughout a story, understanding of friendship may grow and ordinary experience may be joyful, but the stories need not be reduced to neat little mottoes suitable for framing.

Although the setting of science fiction is commonly future time and alternative worlds, science fiction of the past often seemed to have a "missionary" bent; it often urged upon readers a new set of morals and ethics, of religious views, of thinking patterns, a new way of living life, in fact. It has been called "the last refuge of the morality tale." In the changes over the years, we see a movement from exploration to colonization of the solar system. In order to colonize successfully, however, human beings must learn

Didacticism is the function of textbooks; pleasure and understanding those of literature.

Early science fiction was intent upon reform

to conquer war, pollution, and overpopulation, and to conserve natural resources. If our children are to inherit a world worth anything, we must be careful conservators. To accomplish these goals, human beings must learn to control themselves. And to achieve such overwhelmingly difficult transformations, writers often take their characters to new and alien worlds. Moving from concern for survival of humankind to a sense of futility about changing human behavior, writers create successors to human beings, new species that are less corrupt. Given missionary concerns, science fiction writers may be dedicated to proving that prejudice and sentimental or romantic views of reality make no sense; the universe is indifferent and has concern for neither human life nor death. It is this indifference that in the past distanced many readers from the genre. Some advocates of distance and objectivity regret the movement away from the common sense of logical outcome toward regarding human emotions as more "real."[6] Didacticism in science fiction seems, if not inevitable, at least difficult to avoid.

Going backward and forward in time is a variation on science fiction themes. Time travel is the fantasy element in Jane Fresh Thomas's *The Princess in the Pigpen*. Arriving in the twentieth century from her life in the seventeenth, Elizabeth marvels at disease cured by pills, at electricity, clothing, women doctors, horseless carriages, and gasoline power. The point of the story seems to be that inventions cannot take the place of family; Elizabeth longs to return to her own.

Even the slightest stories in the I Can Read series may have themes. Katherine Paterson in her first book for new readers, *The Smallest Cow in the World,* suggests that an active imagination is a good thing to have. Marvin misses Rosie, the cow that has been sold: in her place an imaginary Rosie lives in Marvin's little bottle. Ridiculed in school, he is saved by Jenny, who proclaims loudly that the other kids have no imagination, but Marvin does! *Harry's Mom* by Barbara Ann Porte manages, despite the narrative simplicity, to convey an important idea. Harry learns that "orphan" means someone who has lost father or mother and tells his father, who lovingly sends him to Aunt Rose and his own dog Girl; there he hears stories about his mother. Then he talks with his grandparents about her. Memories can help to complete a family. *Blackberries in the Dark* by Mavis Jukes is a short story about a boy's visit to his grandmother's ranch; both are grieving the loss of grandfather, and to their mutual solace, they relive his favorite activities, especially trout fishing: sharing grief helps.

Nonsense

Such nonsense-fantasy stories as Kipling's *Just So Stories* or *Pippi Longstocking,* and even *Alice in Wonderland,* seem to lack theme, but each has as its core the idea of wonder and delight at the order and disorder of life.

Even nonsense may have a theme.

We marvel as the *Just So Stories* tell why whales have tiny throats and leopards have spots; *Winnie-the-Pooh* seems to say that people do strange and exciting things—and with such solemnity. Although adults find satire and social comment in *Alice,* Carroll in his opening poem speaks of:

> The dream-child moving through a land
> Of wonders wild and new . . .
> And half believe it true.

Nonsense as a whole seems to say, "The world and all its inhabitants—thank heaven—are illogical and inconsistent." Nonsense, in its own way, may develop such a theme as "Life is easier and more enjoyable if we don't take ourselves too seriously." If it doesn't, it finally palls.

Mature Themes in Children's Stories

As we look back on our own lives, themes occasionally emerge. In literature, however, the writer can look at and recount the events of a life and show that they add up to a pattern that becomes a theme. Such is the case in Ann Rinaldi's historical novel set during the American Revolution, *A Ride into Morning: The Story of Tempe Wick.* In a single paragraph Rinaldi says explicitly and in several different ways that "everyone . . . is just part and parcel of the whole of their life experiences. Everything we do in life, every transaction we have with another human being, is overshadowed by the events that make us what we are. We carry with us always the burdens and joys of the past, like so much baggage." The central characters of her novel demonstrate this theme. Tempe, a young woman of twenty-two, is left to care for a sick and aged mother. She also has the farm to run, a farm on which her father before his death permitted the Rebels to camp. Her unfamiliar management role and other responsibilities beyond her experience temper her behavior; she is always willing to compromise for safety's sake. Mary, sent to join her Rebel cousin Tempe, refuses to give in to demands other than those of the Rebels; her life with her Tory family has convinced her that the Rebel cause must go forward—without compromise. Tempe's brother Henry feels he has been a coward, and to avoid ridicule feigns madness while he acts as a spy for the Rebels. Sergeant Bowzer, British turncoat, chooses duplicity once again when he organizes a Rebel mutiny against General Wayne. Each has been influenced by the differing burdens and joys of a different past. A secondary theme emerges as Mary, the narrator, finds that, after all, people are not perfect. *"And if this is what growing up means . . . then I don't like it."* "We all live with the choices we make," says Tempe to her brother Henry, still another secondary theme. In keeping with what we noted earlier about reader response, one theme may speak especially to one reader, and another to a second.

Stories like those from Hans Christian Andersen may introduce children to ideas far more mature than we would expect them to grasp, ideas we find difficult to explain in other ways. Fear, for example, is very much a part of childhood. However, what one is afraid *of* is often hard to pin down. Child psychologist Bruno Bettelheim writes of the capacity of folk and fairy tales to help the child "externalize" the fears that go on in the child's mind. Folktales confront and thus legitimize universal fears like that of the death of a parent in "Hansel and Gretel," the attractiveness of evil in "Snow White and the Seven Dwarfs," and the fear of going out into the world in "Dick Whittington and His Cat."

The Borrowers can carry the child through a variety of fears that may haunt the reader in real life and yet are rarely clarified. We fear the unknown: Homily fears what will happen to Pod on his cup-borrowing expedition. Both parents keep Arrietty at home lest she be seen by a human being. They fear the fate of Uncle Hendreary, and what the Boy will do; they fear Mrs. Driver, her friend Mr. Crampfurl, and the exterminators. Most of all, Homily fears moving, emigration to the unknown world beyond the floorboards. Moreover, there is in *The Borrowers* another idea that adults find easy to understand but hard to put into words for children: Materialism is a destructive force. Homily admits, "My mother's family never had nothing but a little bone thimble which they shared around. But it's once you've *had* a tea cup . . ." Homily nags Pod for new blotting-paper carpet, and sends him off for things to store away. Even when she is screaming with fright at the Boy's appearance, she wants more possessions. Homily's materialism sends Pod to his "club" upstairs, and brings on the exterminators. Materialism has disrupted the family and brought it to disaster—a big discovery for readers too young to know the word "materialism."

Such adult themes as the reasons for divorce can also be handled with sympathy by the skillful writer, as Beverly Cleary does in *Dear Mr. Henshaw*. Romantic love alone cannot hold a marriage together; two adults also need to be able to rely on each other.

In recent years, situations and themes in stories for older readers have been changing. With society today more open in its discussion of the many problems of growing up, recent novels have confronted subjects that were once taboo. Although there are boy-meets-girl romances, novels now explore the growth of sexuality and its effects. Stories for older children deal with impotence, premarital sex, pregnancy, forced marriage, and abortion. What has been called the perfect-parent syndrome has been broken. Books for young people show parents as imperfect and human—unreliable, perhaps, or alcoholic, or simply shallow. Other stories deal with such problems as death, divorce, drugs, and disease. These subjects attract readers partly

Stories can clarify where explanations fail.

Topics once taboo are now a part of children's literature.

because of their former taboo status, but also because these matters do concern today's youth.

Often these stories seem to have been written for the vast market that the pulp magazines once appealed to; often the quality of the writing seems comparable. Sometimes the young reader is carried along by sentimentality and coincidence; writing is drab in style and shallow in characterization; themes are didactic and oversimplified. On the other hand, some writers are dealing with the issues of today with sensitivity and skill, writing about the problems that confront the young in ways that create suspenseful stories and make the reader care about the protagonist's problem. Style and characterization show skill and perception, while the themes show the universal truths that arise from the conflicts.

Take, for example, the following stories about young people, each with a problem. First there is *Deenie* by Judy Blume. Deenie has scoliosis and wears a back brace. While we do feel sorry for Deenie, she is so close to being a stereotyped adolescent—interested only in boys and beauty—that we soon find her uninteresting. One theme of the book, that even girls with back braces can find friends, seems didactic and unconvincing because we have little interest in or understanding of the flat protagonist.

Although two readers may have essentially the same experience of theme, their choices of words to state the theme may be somewhat different. Examples of another reader's themes might read somewhat differently from those that follow. Looking back again at *The Watsons Go to Birmingham,* the theme might be stated as "Life can be unjustly difficult for African-Americans, but personal strength can remain and grow." William Dean Myers's story of the integration of an orphaned white girl into an all-black baseball team might suggest a theme for *Me, Mop and the Moondance Kid:* "There are no easy victories, but a strong ego can mask failures." The title of *Beware of Kissing Lizard Lips* by Phyllis Shalant may suggest humor only, but there is more. Too-tall Lizard Lips hates being ignored by the boys, Zach hates being small, and Nikki's Korean immigrant English arouses jeers: "Growing up is not easy." Natalie Babbitt's lasting favorite *Tuck Everlasting* explores the idea of living forever and concludes: "Being forever young is not totally desirable." Bruce Brooks's story *What Hearts* explores the idea of faking feelings, his own about his pushy stepfather and his mother's about her second marriage. "It's best to be honest with oneself."

In keeping with our contemporary interest in the vast varieties of human lifestyles, mores, and traditions, many recent books are broadening our understanding to encompass life in other lands. An engrossing example is *Shabanu* by Suzanne Fisher Staples, who writes of a 12-year-old girl living a nomadic life on the desert of Cholistan, Pakistan, in a culture far different from our own. With Shabanu we see what it is to herd camels, to survive extreme drought and deadly sand storms, to live in a close family structure knowing that at the age of 13 a girl leaves her home and moves to the household of her husband, there very soon to produce sons. The father of girls struggles to accumulate sufficient wealth to provide the dowry necessary for a daughter's good marriage to an adolescent boy. Carefully breeding camels for their strength and ability to dance, moving from dry water hole to small stream, avoiding marauding clans, caring for the infirm elderly, and finding an appropriate burial spot are just part of what Shabanu's story reveals to us. We follow the growth of her pet, an orphaned camel, and note that the animal's difficulty in fitting into a new life is similar to what faces Shabanu. Although in our own society one is still a child at the age of 12, in Shabanu's culture one must struggle at a tender age to be grown, to leave home and family for a new identity.

Today's themes often involve cross-cultural change. Gary Soto's story *The Skirt* is about a Mexican girl who, on moving to the States, wants to retain the tradition of Mexican dances, *folklorico,* for the school recital. She is given a new and vivid skirt to replace her mother's old and now drab one, but the dance must still be traditional. "Moving to another country does not necessitate leaving all tradition behind." But when she proudly takes the skirt to school, she forgets it on the bus. Her adventures in recovering it from the bus are the story, but the theme concerns the pride one feels in one's heritage.

Current stories often deal with realistic problems. They can show us real characters; they can explore the problems of today's youth. However, what is true for other literature seems to be true here, as well: When we believe in the character, we believe in the experience, and are then prepared to accept the theme. When, on the other hand, theme seems to have been the first motive for writing—"Now I'll write a story about the evils of smoking pot"—the stories may become didactic, as does *The Grass Pipe*. If we look beneath the surface of many realistic stories for young people, we find didacticism and sentimentality; such stories are likely to be a fad. The well-written stories, however, will convince us of the truth of the theme and thus contribute to the readers' growth and discovery. Mature themes can be explored in children's literature; they contribute to understanding when they meet the requirements of excellence.

> When we believe in the character, we believe in the experience, and can accept the theme.

Summary

Theme, stated explicitly or implicitly, is essential to a children's story if it is to merit the name of literature. A narrative with action and people but without theme is a story without meaning that leaves the reader wondering at the close, "So what?" A piece of writing—a collection of words with plot, character, setting, style, and meaning (without preaching)—is literature for children just as it is for adults. The theme we take to become part of ourselves is the one that enlarges our understanding and the one we ourselves discover, not the one delivered didactically by the author.

Notes

1. Social historian Stephanie Coontz comments on such themes in *The Way We Never Were: American Families and the Nostalgia Trip* (New York: Basic Books, 1992).

2. Wayne Booth makes this comment in *The Rhetoric of Fiction* (Chicago: University of Chicago Press, 1961), p. 136.

3. Booth, *The Rhetoric of Fiction*, p. 126. The satisfaction of knowing causality in children's literature is most obviously demonstrated in cumulative tales like the humorous "Old Woman and the Pig" or the verse story "This is the House That Jack Built."

4. Jack Zipes, in *Fairy Tales and the Art of Subversion* (London: Heineman Educational Books, 1983), discusses the tales of Grimm and Andersen. The former seeks to show girls and women their subordinate roles; the latter, though commonly thought to show a triumph over misfortune by the poor and lowly, actually admires the hierarchy.

5. *I Want to Be a Homemaker* by Carla Greene (New York: Children's Press, 1961) is shelved in many libraries among the picture books as JE or Juvenile. Commenting on the book here reminds us of the difference between real stories and instructive narrative. Others in the series of 54 books describe jobs; *Homemaker* seems to be describing a role.

6. See "The Shape of Things to Come" in James Gunn's *Alternate Worlds: The Illustrated History of Science Fiction* (Englewood Cliffs, N.J.: Prentice-Hall, 1975), pp. 225–239.

Recommended Books Cited in This Chapter

ALCOTT, LOUISA MAY. *Little Women*. New York: Dutton, 1948 (first published, 1868–69).

ANDERSEN, HANS CHRISTIAN. "The Ugly Duckling," "The Swineherd," "The Nightingale," "The Princess and the Pea," and "The Tinderbox." In *The Twelve Dancing Princesses*, ed. Alfred David and Mary Elizabeth Meek. Bloomington: Indiana University Press, 1974.

BABBITT, NATALIE. *Tuck Everlasting*. New York: Farrar, Straus, & Giroux, 1975.

BROOKS, BRUCE. *What Hearts*. New York: HarperCollins, 1992.

CARROLL, LEWIS. *Alice's Adventures in Wonderland*. 1865. Reprint. New York: Macmillan, 1963.

CHESTESEN, BARBARA. *The Myths of the Orient*. Shaker Heights, Ohio: Raintree, 1977.

CLEARY, BEVERLY. *Dear Mr. Henshaw*. New York: Morrow, 1983.

COLLIER, JAMES LINCOLN, AND CHRISTOPHER COLLIER. *Jump Ship to Freedom*. New York: Delacorte, 1981.

CURTIS, CHRISTOPHER. *The Watsons Go to Birmingham*. New York: Delacorte, 1963.

CUSHMAN, KAREN. *The Midwife's Apprentice*. New York: Houghton Mifflin, 1995.

HALEY, GAIL. *A Story, A Story*. New York: Atheneum, 1970.

HAMILTON, VIRGINIA. *Cousins*. New York: Putnam, 1990.

HOOKS, WILLIAM H. *Circle of Fire*. New York: Macmillan, 1982.

HOOVER, H. M. *The Shepherd Moon*. New York: Viking, 1984.

HURWITZ, JOHANNA. *Class President*. New York: Morrow, 1990.

JONES, JENNIFER BERRY. *Heetunka's Harvest*. Niwot, CO.: Roberts Rinehart, 1994.

JUKES, MAVIS. *Blackberries in the Dark*. New York: Knopf, 1985.

KIPLING, RUDYARD. *The Just So Stories*. 1902. Reprint. Garden City, N.Y.: Doubleday, 1986.

LE GUIN, URSULA K. *A Wizard of Earthsea*. Berkeley: Parnassus, 1968.

LINDGREN, ASTRID. *Pippi Longstocking*. New York: Viking, 1950.

LORD, BETTE BAO. *The Year of the Boar and Jackie Robinson*. New York: Holt Rinehart, 1984.

LOTTRIDGE, CELIA BARKER. *The Name of the Tree*. New York: Macmillan, 1990.

MACLACHLAN, PATRICIA. *Journey*. New York: Doubleday, 1991.

MILNE, A. A. *Winnie-the-Pooh*. New York: Dutton, 1926.

MYERS, WALTER DEAN. *Me, Mop and the Moondance Kid*. New York: Doubleday, 1988.

NORTON, MARY. *The Borrowers*. New York: Harcourt, 1965.

PATERSON, KATHERINE. *The Great Gilly Hopkins*. New York: Crowell, 1978.

———. *Jacob Have I Loved*. New York: Harper & Row, 1980.

———. *The Smallest Cow in the World*. New York: HarperCollins, 1991.

PORTE, BARBARA ANN. *Harry's Mom*. New York: Greenwillow, 1985.

POTTER, BEATRIX. *The Tale of Peter Rabbit*. London: Warne, 1902.

RINALDI, ANN. *A Ride into Morning: The Story of Tempe Wick*. New York: Harbrace, 1991.

ROTH, SUSAN L. *Fire Came to Earth People*. New York: St. Martin's, 1982.

RYLANT, CYNTHIA. *A Fine White Dust*. New York: Bradbury, 1986.

SHALANT, PHYLLIS. *Beware of Kissing Lizard Lips*. New York: Dutton, 1995.

SOTO, GARY. *The Skirt*. Illustrated by Eric Velasquez. New York: Delacorte, 1992.

STAPLES, SUZANNE FISHER. *Shabanu*. New York: Knopf, 1989.

TAYLOR, MILDRED. *Roll of Thunder, Hear My Cry*. New York: Dial, 1976.

THOMAS, JANE FRESH. *The Princess in the Pigpen*. Boston: Houghton Mifflin, 1989.

WHITE, E. B. *Charlotte's Web*. New York: Harper, 1952.

WHITE, RUTH. *Belle Pater's Boy*. Putney, VT: Threshold Books, 1996.

At the Crossroads
Rachel Isadora Turner

7

Setting

Does setting have to be important? Change the setting and see.

B oth depiction of character and working out of plot and theme occur, of course, in time and place. These latter elements we call **setting.** In an adult novel, action may occur anywhere, even in the
mind of the protagonist, and may need little delineation of place or time.
However, the story for children almost always occurs in a time and place
described in some detail.

The possibilities for setting are endless. It is possible to write of a time
when human beings lived in caves, or of a time when they may live on a
space station. As for settings in place, from cave to space station, the spread
is equally broad. When we consider all of the times and places known to us,
and add to them all those we are capable of imagining, there is no limit to
possibilities. Sometimes the writer wishes to make setting very clear, because the story depends upon our understanding and envisioning the particular setting. At other times, the writer deliberately refrains from closely
examining and describing setting. Making the setting a specific time and
place might for a particular story limit the universality of conflict, characters, or ideas the writer wishes to explore. It is the writer who determines
the nature of the story, and thereby determines the setting.

Sometimes we must know the physical description of the setting, the
details of what is present, how it all looks, smells, feels, and sounds. These
are the relevant details that will directly influence character, conflict, and
theme. Such details at other times—kinds of sounds and smells, kinds of
buildings, quality of light and climate—may create the mood of the time
and place and so create the atmosphere for the characters and the conflict.

In our discussion of character and plot we found those two elements
influencing and reflecting each other. This interdependence with other elements is true of setting, too. If, for example, *The Why's and Wherefore's of
Littabelle Lee* by Vera and Bill Cleaver were to take place not among the

rivers and valleys and cliffs of the Ozarks, but on the plains of North Dakota or in glittering Miami Beach, the story would be very different. Aunt Sorrow's fall over the cliff on her burro, for example, could not have happened; Littabelle's wonder about what to do with her life would have included options other than teaching or woods doctoring. Such settings would create totally different novels. The Cleavers did not hit upon their choice of setting accidentally; it was *the* setting for *this* story. In evaluating a piece of literature, we should be aware of the basic kind of setting, and then decide how it functions in the story. As we analyze this relationship, we evaluate the effectiveness of the author's selection.

Types of Settings

In any piece of literature, whether for child or adult, there are essentially two types of setting: (1) the **backdrop,** or relatively unimportant setting and (2) the **integral,** or essential setting.

The importance of setting—whether it is integral or backdrop—depends upon the writer's purpose. For example, in a story of internal conflict, the first-person narrator may tell the progress of the plot in narrative, dialogue, action, or diary form. The reader may not need to know where or when the character lives, since understanding depends upon interest in character and in the character's internal conflict as the narrator reveals the inner tension. Time and place are merely a backdrop. This kind of setting contrasts sharply with the significant integral setting in a nonfiction book such as *Anne Frank: The Diary of a Young Girl*. Although this autobiographical account, too, has internal conflict, where and when the action occurs are essential information if we are to understand conflict and character. In fact, setting working upon character is the essence of conflict in this book.

The writer makes the setting clear in descriptions. Each reader may have a personal catalog of mentally pictured settings—a beach, a farm, or a cabin—but the writer does not depend upon the reader's experience or upon recollection of settings. If the writer wants to make the setting integral to this story, the writer must describe it in concrete details, relying on sensory pictures and vivid comparisons to make the setting so clear that the reader understands how this story is closely related to this particular place.

By contrast, if the unskilled writer insists that setting is significant, and yet creates a setting superficial in concept and shallow in depiction, the reader may then reject all of the story's reality, from character through action and unifying idea. A one-dimensional setting cannot be convincingly integral, and therefore little that happens seems believable.

The title *Willie Goes to the Seashore* suggests that the setting is an integral part of the action; the seashore must be so interesting that Willie will have an exciting time. The actual case is quite different. The little cottage and the sandy beach are the setting. Willie, moving in quick succession from one to another of the activities one expects at the shore, seems to move *over* the setting rather than *in* it, finding neither conflict nor involvement in any of the activities the setting suggests. Setting does not come alive to involve character in plot. So what is exciting about a seashore? Why would Willie want to live there all the time? The setting has failed as an integral part of the story, since it does not influence character, conflict, or idea.

Integral Setting

We say a story has an **integral setting** when action, character, or theme are influenced by the time and place, since, as Eudora Welty says, setting has "the most delicate control over character . . . by confining character, it defines it."[1] These characters, given these circumstances, in this time and place, behave in this way.

> Setting, by confining character, defines it. —*Eudora Welty*

When we open to Chapter 1 of Patricia MacLachlan's *Sarah, Plain and Tall,* we are immediately drawn into the integral setting. Caleb sits close to the fire, the dogs "beside him on the warm hearthstones," a pioneer home, apparently. Anna looks out the window to the prairie that reaches out and touches "the places where the sky came down. Though winter was nearly over, there were patches of snow and ice everywhere." A dirt road crawls across the plains, and there are "fields and grass and sky and not much else." The wind seems to blow Papa into the house. When Sarah comes in answer to Papa's ad for a wife, the family is relieved to find that she enjoys farm life, even to climbing up the ladder on "the mound of hay for bedding, nearly half as tall as the barn, covered with canvas to keep the rain from rotting it." Because the issue is whether Sarah, who loves the dunes and sea of Maine, can be happy as a prairie wife and mother, we must see her involved with and enjoying the prairie farm. The setting is integral.

Knowing the nature of the river in which Tony dares Joel to swim is essential to plot and theme in *On My Honor* by Marion Dane Bauer. We read of the red-brown water "slithering" under the bridge. Chemicals and sewage are not visible, but Joel knows they are there. Although the water flows past like "a refreshing massage," he doesn't want to put his face in it; "the river smelled of decaying fish," and divided in a sharp *V* at the boys' waists. We know not only about the pollution but also about the threat of strong current to an inexperienced swimmer like Tony.

Brian, the protagonist in *Hatchet* by Gary Paulsen, is the sole survivor of the crash of a single-engine plane in Alaska; his only survival tool is his hatchet. To believe in his struggle with isolation in the rugged surroundings he must make habitable, we must see the setting clearly. A stone ridge near the lake that the plane has crashed into yields a cavelike shelter:

> At one time in the far past it had been scooped by something, probably a glacier, and this scooping had left a kind of sideways bowl, back in under a ledge. It wasn't very deep, not a cave, but it was smooth and made a perfect roof and he could almost stand in under the ledge. . . . Some of the rock . . . had . . . been pulverized by the glacial action, turned into sand, and now made a small sand beach that went down to the edge of the water in front . . . .

Here, once he can build a fire, Brian finds protection from the black flies and mosquitoes that blanket his body.

Setting is clearly shown in Bruce Brooks's *Everywhere,* the story of a boy who with his black friend Dooley tries "soul switching." The narrator is afraid his grandfather is dying, but Dooley has a secret method of being sure that it doesn't happen. Find an animal that has some resemblance to grandfather and at the moment when it seems the sick man's soul is about to leave his body, substitute that of the animal—in this case a turtle. As he awaits fearfully some indication that his grandfather is dying, the narrator seems to have a heightened awareness of everything around him. His description of each detail is significant, particularly because he regrets never having shown his grandfather this hideaway:

> I followed [Dooley] out the gate and down the alley. It was paved with crushed coke, which crunched beneath our sneakers. When we reached the edge of the field past the old dairy building, I touched him on the elbow and angled off across it. He followed. . . . Pretty soon we came to some persimmon trees, and I cut through them to the path I had made myself over the previous four or five summers, and we wound downward through denser woods that started to thicken with cedars and pines.

Backdrop Setting

The term **backdrop setting** comes, of course, from the theater. For example, some of the action in scenes from Shakespeare or from many musicals takes place on the apron of the stage before a featureless curtain, or before a flat, painted scene of an unidentified street or forest. Soliloquy, dialogue, action, or character confrontation concerns us; where the characters are positioned matters, but less than our seeing and hearing them, and following them in the developing conflict. Yet, while the street or forest is unidentified, it may have importance. It may have some subtle meaning that suggests the forest as a place of physical or spiritual darkness, and the busy street as a reminder of society.

A clear example of a children's story with backdrop setting is *Winnie-the-Pooh*. A. A. Milne's Christopher Robin might live anywhere at all—from England's Land's End to Lancashire, or from America's Bangor to Sacramento. Action occurs on the bank of a stream, or by a big oak tree with a honeybee hive. While time and place are not specific, they may suggest something about the action or characters when Pooh, Eeyore, Rabbit, and his assorted friends-and-relations set off on an "Expotition" to the North Pole. The Forest—with a capital *F*—is of course the proper place for Pooh and Piglet to track the fearful Woozle/Wizzle, but there is minimal description of the beech tree beyond its being in the middle of the Forest. It is the tension among the characters that matters and dominates.

Pippi Longstocking, Astrid Lindgren's heroine, might also live anywhere. Pippi's chaotic home, Villa Villekula, figures minimally in the story action as we admire Pippi's found treasure. Our eyes and ears focus instead on Pippi as she shows her skills as a Thing Finder, plays tag with the policeman, or tops the ladies' gossip with her own nonsensical servant problems. Pippi's house is important to us only because it must be a remarkable place; Pippi does such ridiculous things there.

In both *Winnie* and *Pippi,* setting is generalized and universal; its vividness exists in our minds merely as the place where the interesting action occurs. We do not know, for example, what Rabbit's house looks like; what matters is the memorable view of Pooh's legs serving as towel racks. Although time and place have importance, they do not influence the character and plot in the same ways that an integral setting does.

> Time and place in backdrop setting do not necessarily influence action or character.

Setting in *Charlotte's Web*

Our touchstone, *Charlotte's Web,* is an excellent example of integral setting literally described. This story could have occurred nowhere but on a farm, in fact only on a farm that has the traditional farm animals. This is not a sprawling ranch or a grain-growing industry, because such farms have concerns other than pigs and their barnyard friends. The Arable farm is near a country road, since Fern catches the school bus at her front door. There is a brook for playing in, with wonderfully oozy, sticky mud. This farm has a dump—or how could Templeton find essential words for the web? It has meadows that show seasonal changes, maples that redden with anxiety, and a big pasture that frightens a timid piglet. This farm, with an orchard where apples fall and the gander's family feasts, is no generalized farm; there is no other farm quite like it, where fog and rain, crickets and song sparrow are all parts of the place, the setting. However, most important of all, this farm has a barn that houses a variety of animals—or how could sheep, pigs, and geese become acquainted, advising, consoling, and taunting one another? White shows the Zuckerman barn as soon as Wilbur sees it. The reader, too, knows its smells, its sights, and its warmth:

> The barn was very large. It was very old. It smelled of hay and it smelled of manure. It smelled of the perspiration of tired horses and the wonderful sweet breath of patient cows. It often had a sort of peaceful smell—as though nothing bad could happen ever again in the world. It smelled of grain and of harness dressing and of axle grease and of rubber boots and of new rope. And whenever the cat was given a fish-head to eat, the barn would smell of fish. But mostly it smelled of hay, for there was always hay in the great loft overhead. And there was always hay being pitched down to the cows and the horses and the sheep.

No one could confuse this setting with any generalized backdrop, since each item in the description shows the singularity of this setting, home of Wilbur, Charlotte, and Templeton. We know this place as well as Wilbur does, and because its description is so vivid, we are alerted to its importance in the total story.

To know the exciting Fairgrounds, we must:

> . . . hear music and see the Ferris wheel turning in the sky . . . smell the dust of the race track where the sprinkling car had moistened it . . . smell hamburgers frying and see balloons aloft . . . hear sheep blatting in their pens.

At night the lighted Ferris wheel revolves in the sky, the gambling machines crackle, the merry-go-round makes music, and a voice calls numbers from the beano booth. In the morning we hear sparrows stirring, roosters crowing, cows rattling chains, and cars whispering on the roadway.

The Fair is an essential part of the story, and it is therefore necessary that the reader see, hear, smell, and even touch and taste it. Wilbur's character is fully revealed at the Fair, where, experiencing threatened failure and final success, he remains humble but radiant. Wilbur's conflict, furthermore, cannot be resolved without the Fair. Wilbur must have time to grow, and then must prove himself worthy of being saved; the fall Fair is a traditional proving time for farm animals. Charlotte's efforts to prolong Wilbur's life produce no certainty of success until the Fair—he wins the prize for attracting so many visitors.

White must also show temporal change, since character growth and conflict, as well as several of the story's thematic discoveries, are dependent upon the passing of time. White must make us see the seasons as they exist, merge, and change. As we hear, see, and smell, we are aware of time passing, and of weather and landscape changing.

Spring is the time for pigs to be born; rain drips from the eaves, runs crookedly between the pigweed, and gushes from the rainspouts. Summer is everyone's holiday; lilacs are blooming, bees are dropping in on the apple blossoms, and horses are pulling the noisy mower. Birds sing and nest. However, since summer cannot last forever, the crickets' song prepares us for fall and the important Fair time. Uneasy sheep break out of their pasture, and the gander's family invades the orchard. Although little of the story's action occurs in winter, even winter is not slighted. The pasture is frozen, the cows are standing in the sun beside the straw pile, the sheep are eating snow, and the geese just hanging about. Then, to complete the year's cycle and to prove that Wilbur has survived butchering time and that Charlotte's eggs have hatched, White returns to spring and its strengthening light, new lambs, nine goose eggs, and Charlotte's old web floating away.

The time element is important here. As the year passes, Wilbur matures from panicky child to responsible adult. In the passing of a full year we know that his victory over society is complete. We have had time to see the truth of such themes as the growth of friendship and of maturity, and the inevitability and acceptance of death. The integral setting has helped to make all of these clear.

Functions of Setting

Setting That Clarifies Conflict

As *Charlotte's Web* demonstrates, an integral setting plays an important part in conflict. Time setting for a story can be any time, past, present, or future. A future time may be very threatening. In British writer Robert Swindell's *Brother in the Land,* time is a frightening future just after nuclear war. Danny, one of the few survivors, must bury his mother, see his father killed by marauders who steal his food stores, and watch while his little brother Ben dies of radiation sickness. We see the devastated land, the flattened city, and the individual homes and places of business left without windows, walls, or furnishings. People drink from puddles of Black Rain, scratch for edible roots, and bed down where they find shelter in places that are dank with the odor of decay. Here, understanding setting is essential to understanding character and conflict as well as theme.

Place, too, can be ominous. In H. M. Hoover's *The Lost Star,* setting, although an alien world, is recognizable in many ways. Lian, who has spent much of her life in similar enclosures, finds the inside of the lumpies' quarters comfortable; gravel crunching beneath boots, she has proceeded to the enclosure through a vine-covered opening to a cavelike space, a wall of brilliant green with sunlit leaves, and around a curve, a doorway machine-tooled and circular as though it opened into a monstrous vault. As she knocks on the wall with her knuckles, it rings as though it is not rock but formed metal. These descriptive images and comparisons enable readers to see setting.

Historical fiction has a responsibility to show how environment, too affects action. For example, turn to the austere Puritan New England setting of *The Witch of Blackbird Pond,* into which Kit Tyler is transported from her West Indies birthplace. Author Elizabeth Speare does not rely merely on our history-book knowledge of that time and place when witchcraft was feared; she clarifies setting by her description of the austerity of life among the Puritans: the house with hand-rubbed copper, indicative of hard work; the heavy, fortresslike door; the dim little mirror; and the severe wooden bench. Speare weaves description of the house itself into a description of Kit's tasks in a typical day. Meat must be chopped, vegetables prepared, and the pewter mugs polished with fine sand and reeds. Throughout the day Kit stirs the kettle of boiling soap with a stick, the lye fumes stinging her eyes and the heavy stirring tiring her muscles. Even the easiest task, making corn pudding, keeps her leaning over the smoky fire that burns her watering eyes. Walking through the little town to church with Kit, we see severity in the straight, cold lines of functional buildings with punitive devices. The unpainted Meeting House, the whipping post, the pillory, and the stocks are frightening evidence that Kit is now in a rigid and uncompromising environment, one for which her carefree Barbados upbringing has not prepared her.

Russel of Gary Paulsen's *Dogsong* is in search of his identity. Is he an Eskimo of the old ways? Or a more modern member of the mechanized society that is taking over the Arctic North? His father cannot help him through his restlessness, but suggests he see Oogruk, the oldest Eskimo, a shaman. Coming into the "government box" house, Russel notes the unusual home. "Inside it was almost pitch-dark. The windows were covered with smoke grime, and the room was full of smoke from the lamp on a box in the corner, a seal-oil lamp with a moss wick that threw a tiny yellow glow around the room." As he drives Oogruk's dogs through the storm, "There was a driving sharp snow with the wind. Not heavy snow, but small and mean and it worked with the force of the wind to get inside clothing, in the eyes, even blow up into the nostrils." Tracking a man lost in that storm, Russel finds it worsening by the minute. "The only advantage they had was that the storm was almost straight out of the north. They could fight dead against the wind and that was a bit easier than going side-on where the team would have been blown over."

Paulsen is in top form when he writes of struggles to survive in the wilderness. His stories about Tucket take place in the West, in midcentury. *Tucket's Ride* is the story of Francis and his adopted family as they move West in search of his own family. Captured by Commancheros, outlaws who trade with the Commanche Indians, they ride without stopping to eat or sleep, ruthlessly driving horses and children. Fear that Francis and his family will be sold provides tension enough, but the desolate setting heightens their anxiety.

All day they rode, stopping only once to loosen and retighten cinches, to take a sip of water and a bit of jerky. All day and into the night they kept riding. . . . Finally, out in the flats of the prairie, they came upon a cut, a wide canyon that didn't show until they were almost on top of it.

> The leader led them down a winding trail wide enough for one horse along the canyon wall. Far below Francis could see a group of small shacks in a stand of cottonwoods—little more than brush huts covered with skins—and a winding stream. . . . He could make out a fairly large herd of horses. . . . Some wagons were parked near the shacks. As they dropped down the canyon wall, Francis could hear dogs barking.

Rosemary Sutcliff, writer of historical fiction, takes great care that we see the wilderness of Britain in A.D. 600, the setting for *The Shining Company*. During the hunt for the white hart, we read:

> I was running, running, as it seemed, the heart out of my breast . . . branches snatching at me, roots clawing at my feet, and always ahead of me the music of the hounds. By and by the land began to lift under us, and the trees thinned and fell back, the crowding damp oaks giving place to birch as we drew up towards the open surge of the great hills, and the sky opened to us, turning wide and shining.

We see the slave-master relationship of the times in the exchange between body-servant Conn and Prosper; Conn asks if he might learn from the smithy how to forge weapons, but Prosper explains that once he learned a trade he would become free. Even such details as how the lord Gerontius shaved are helpful in assuring us that we are living vicariously in a time long ago.

> My father was sitting in the high chair with the lion feet, rubbing his chin with a lump of pumice stone. . . . My father still went clean-shaven in the Roman way, with razor and goose grease when need be, with pumice when the traders brought any.

Historical fiction can make the past come alive, make it become reality. One of the shames of twentieth-century American history is the incarceration of Japanese-Americans in camps during World War II—an event in history that, like slavery, most citizens would like to forget. Although Japanese immigrants had lived for many years in the United States, the bombing of Pearl Harbor awakened suspicions about their loyalty. When, in *Journey to Topaz* by Hoshiko Uchida, we read of the educated and assimilated Sukanes, we are shocked to hear how the family of four is divided, forced to live in a horse stall for a time, then shipped off to the Topaz camp in Utah. We understand the parents' sorrow and the children's anger. The camp is "white powdery dust, covering everyone in a smothering blanket . . . flour-dusted cookies that had escaped from a bakery":

> There wasn't a single tree or a blade of grass to break the monotony of the sun-bleached desert. It was like the carcass of a chicken stripped clean of

any meat and left all dry, brittle bone. . . . They sank into [the road] with each step as though they were plowing through a snow bank.

It was bad enough. . . . for the dust just hung in the air, sifting into her eyes and into her nose and mouth with each breath.

The fact that a setting occurs in the historical past does not mean that the setting must be integral. In Lois Lowry's *Autumn Street,* for example, which is set in World War II days, aside from the absence of Elizabeth's father, the time plays little part in the story of the white girl–black boy friendship.

Not true historical fiction, but a semiautobiographical story of rural life in an earlier time and another place, *Homesick: My Own Story* is Jean Fritz's fictionalized memories of her years in China, a country she loved, but loved less than her parents' native United States. The non-Chinese spend each summer away from the cities, either in the mountains or at the ocean—and despite the beauty of the summer setting, with its Rattling Brook and the multitudes of wild flowers—there is no setting like that of rural living near "Washington, PA," where she feels rooted. The grape arbor, the yard pump, the rooster that crows when the family laughs, the wonderful climbing trees, the garden peas waiting to be shelled, the hand-cranked washing machine—all these elements are new and exciting to China-born Jean. The contrast between the two settings accentuates the conflict Jean feels as she yearns for her homeland.

Regional literature, too, must show how time and place affect story. Sometimes we must know a mode of living or of making a living in order to understand the story's conflict. In such a case the setting may be integral. *Where the Lilies Bloom,* for example, shows setting as a power shaping the lives of those who live in the Smokies. The Cleavers create a setting beautiful enough to hold the characters' loyalty, and yet so wild that it offers Mary Call's family little on which to subsist. Weaving descriptions of setting into action, the writers show wildcrafting, a tedious labor (of collecting medicinal plants) with small rewards, native to this particular lush wilderness. Mary Call's struggle to keep her family together is the more convincing because we see the setting with which she struggles.

Time, particularly in fantasy, has a way of lengthening or shortening, depending upon the make-believe world the writer creates. We know how time is relative: when we're entertained, time goes quickly; when we're bored, time drags endlessly. But the writer of fantasy takes other liberties with time, perhaps by making one event, or one life, last through centuries or be over in seconds.

Setting as Antagonist

Sometimes setting itself is the antagonist, as it is in *Julie of the Wolves.* Even fog, one of nature's milder elements, frightens Miyax, who had never given it much thought. As it streams and rolls up the wolf slope, making the

Setting in a historical past is not necessarily integral.

wolves invisible one by one, she remembers that fog imprisons people—in fog they cannot hunt. As noted earlier, the setting for Burnford's *The Incredible Journey* is an essential part of the story, since the Canadian wilderness is not only setting but antagonist. Without clear descriptions of the dense brush, forest land, and wilderness river, such a novel would have no believable conflict to hold the reader. However, on the opening page of the novel, Burnford prepares us for the conflict; the rugged country of northwestern Ontario is introduced on the first line of the first page, and the description continues for a page and a half:

> . . . [A] vast area of deeply wooded wilderness—of endless chains of lonely lakes and rushing rivers. Thousands of miles of country roads, rough timberlanes, overgrown tracks leading to abandoned mines, and unmapped trails snake across its length and breadth. It is a country of far-flung, lonely farms and a few widely scattered small towns and villages, of lonely trappers' shacks and logging camps.

In *The Talking Earth,* nature is the antagonist that Jean George describes effectively, the natural setting she knows so well. Billie Wind fights fire in Lake Okeechobee, where, in the searing heat, she sees snakes and restless alligators zigzagging just below the water's surface.

> [S]he was struck by a blast of hot air, more searing than the one she had felt in the boat. It smelled of burning grass. And then she knew, she knew why the animals ran and why the island seemed to rise.
>
> . . . Now she could see flames through the trees. Running to the shore, she pushed back the limbs and looked out. Orange blazes licked the sky like serpents' tongues. They shot downward and devoured the grass. They spat black smoke as the many-tongued beast came rushing toward Billie Wind.

Were she not so schooled in the survival tactics of her Seminole heritage, Billie Wind would not survive, but even so, the setting seems heavily weighted against her.

Tituba of Salem Village by Ann Petry demonstrates how setting makes clear to us Tituba's position in her new New England home. Sold from Barbados, where life was easy and pleasant, where she could bathe each morning in the ocean, where she might see through the window the bay as an extension of the kitchen, and where breezes but no chill winds blew, Tituba meets nothing but the bitter winter and wind of New England; the bare trees and shrubs that make her fear they are all dead. The contrast of benign nature in the islands and the rigorous and rigidly controlled life as a slave in the austere Reverend Parris's tiny house prepares us for the conflict. The natural way of life in which Tituba had collected healing herbs for her mistress contrasts with the suspicions surrounding healing by a black woman. As a singular woman in Puritan society, she is suspect because of her color, and suspicions increase because of her skills at spinning, weaving, and healing.

Setting That Illuminates Character

In many examples we have been discussing, setting influences character. Notice the effect of isolation and crowding upon the protagonist's fear in that unusual autobiography *Anne Frank: The Diary of a Young Girl.* We must see the stiflingly cramped atmosphere of the Secret Annexe or we cannot experience the yearning for freedom and privacy that Anne expresses during the twenty-five months of the family's hiding from the Nazi soldiers who are rounding up the Jews for imprisonment. We must see Anne's surroundings as we follow her tensions with her parents and fellow prisoners, her awakening sense of self, and her curiosity about growing up. Just two days after the family crowds into the Annexe, Anne writes as though it is an adventure:

> Our little room looked very bare at first with nothing on the walls; but thanks to Daddy who had brought my filmstar collection and picture postcards on beforehand, and with the aid of paste pot and brush, I have transformed the walls into one gigantic picture. This makes it look more cheerful, and, when the Van Daans come, we'll get some wood from the attic, and make a few little cupboards for the walls and other odds and ends to make it look more lively.

But thirteen months later, we have another picture, this time of the efforts necessary when bedtime approaches:

> *Nine o-clock in the evening.* The bustle of going to bed in the "Secret Annexe" begins. . . . Chairs are shoved about, beds are pulled down, blankets unfolded, nothing remains where it is during the day. I sleep on the little divan . . . chairs have to be used to lengthen it. A quilt, sheets, pillows, blankets, are all fetched from Dussel's bed where they remain during the day . . . creaking in the next room: Margot's concertina-bed being pulled out! Again, divan, blankets, and pillows, everything is done to make the wooden slats a bit more comfortable. It sounds like thunder above, but it is only Mrs. Van Daan's bed . . . shifted to the window.

The setting becomes overwhelming in its effect upon every aspect of the characters' lives. Bickering, quarrels, arguments, and rages result from the pressures of close confinement.

Confinement in one room for two years, with extremely rare opportunities to walk outside, surely has impact on a character. That is also the case in Johanna Reiss's *The Upstairs Room,* the autobiographical account of the author's life during the Holocaust. Annie at first does not understand and is resentful about why she cannot go to school, to the shops, or outside to play. As her confinement continues in the home of a Dutch farm family, she grows in understanding, but at the age of 11 is still resentful. She does not realize the life-and-death danger to her host family should she and her sister Sisi be found, nor does she see why 20-year-old Sisi has more privileges than she does. Her resentment and frustration are like those of most children and are therefore believable.

Maia Wojciechowska's prize-winning novel *Shadow of a Bull* depends upon setting to illuminate both character and conflict. Manolo's internal struggle concerns his efforts to withstand community pressure to become a bullfighter like his adored father who is memorialized by the town, and hold to his own wish to become a doctor. Here is what Manolo has grown up with in his Spanish town:

> Everywhere he turned, he found shrines to his father. In people's homes pictures of his father were kept alongside those of the saints. In every cafe there was his father in hundreds of photographs and dozens of posters: fighting the bull, waiting for the bull's charge, standing over the bull he had killed. . . . The town had placed in the main square of Arcangel a great statue of his father and a bull, taller than any building. . . . His father's lean hands held the mulete, the cloth carved in stone seemed to blow in the wind.

Setting and Mood

As several of the preceding examples demonstrate, setting affects mood. Setting is sometimes sentimentalized, as it is in Frances Hodgson Burnett's *The Secret Garden:*

Setting, too, can be sentimentalized.

> On that first morning when the sky was blue again, Mary wakened very early. The sun was pouring in slanting rays through the blinds and there was something so joyous in the sight of it that. . . .
>
> . . . She clasped her hands for pure joy and looked up in the sky, and it was so blue and pink and pearly and white and flooded with springtime light that she felt as if she must flute and sing aloud herself, and knew that thrushes and robins and skylarks could not possibly help it. . . .
>
> . . .
>
> . . . And the secret garden bloomed and bloomed and every morning revealed new miracles. In the robin's nest there were eggs and the robin's mate sat upon them, keeping them warm with her feathery little breast and careful wings.

In the early pages of *Shadow in Hawthorn Bay,* Janet Lunn shows the benign Scottish setting of Mary's childhood: the brilliant sky, a pasture blazing gold, small lakes ringed with new green, cows grazing on the ridges, hills rising and falling, and fields in flower. After her emigration to join her cousin, Mary's habitat changes to the wilds of Canada. "She [heard] the sounds of the woods at night as though she had just wakened from a sleep—wolves howling nearby, owls hooting, frogs croaking, other unfamiliar cries and calls, and all around her rustlings and gruntings in the underbrush." Everything is strange to Mary, the trees, the woodland streams, the land contours, the animals, even the healing plants growing in marshes rather than on the hilly slopes. To Mary their strangeness is ominous, haunting, and until she feels at home in the north woods, she feels like an unsettled stranger.

Epic style is grand style, vivid and resonant; and setting—like character and action—can be pictured in elevated language. In keeping with the heroic subject, the setting of the epic *Gilgamesh* as retold by Bernarda Bryson is described in words of great dignity:

> The world of Gilgamesh was hemmed in by the mighty mountains of Mashu that were the edge between day and night. It was circled by the Bitter River that flowed round and round it unceasingly, and that had no beginning and no end. No one knew what lay beyond the river, since the very touch of its waters was death. . . .
>
> To the west was the void into which the sun set. There opened those rocky caverns through which the sun passed under the earth and back into the Eastern Garden where his home was and whence he arose again in the mornings. So much was known.

The setting of Ian Serraillier's retelling of the epic *Beowulf the Warrior* also has solemn majesty; its description produces a mood of great dignity. Serraillier sketches the setting briefly with phrases that ring with grandeur. Book One begins with a description of the vast and splendid hall Heorot, scene of Grendel's monstrous deeds and of Beowulf's selfless struggle:

> Hrothgar, King of the Danes, glorious in battle
> Built him a huge hall—its gleaming roof
> Towering high to heaven—strong to withstand
> The buffet of war. . . .
> The long hall . . .
> The floor paved with stone, the roof high-raftered.

As Beowulf battles with Grendel in a struggle of awesome violence, this huge hall shudders. The struggle is greater, and therefore the victory is greater, because of the mood created by the splendor of setting.

The big old house on a hill in *The House of Dies Drear,* once a stop on the Underground Railroad, has many tunnels and caves, which Virginia Hamilton describes. The house sits on "an outcropping, much like a ledge." It

> loomed out of the mist and murky sky, not only gray and formless but huge and unnatural. It seemed to crouch on the side of a hill high above

Epic style is grand, vivid and resonant, and setting is pictured in elevated language.

the highway. And it had a dark, isolated look about it that set it at odds with all that was living.

> The face of the ledge was rock, from which gushed mineral springs. . . . Running down the face of the ledge, the springs coated the rock in their path with red and yellow rust . . . .

"It's bleeding," Thomas says softly. A mysterious atmosphere surrounds the house.

In Avi's *Shadrach's Crossing* the author maintains mystery by picturing the island's rugged wildness, its isolation and inaccessibility.

> Lucker's Island . . . was only a mile and a half at its widest. . . . The middle of the island consisted of rolling, sandy dunes, with low, wind-cut scrub pine bushes and patches of coarse grass. Here and there were piles of stones, and at the southern end, stretches of pebbles. But mostly it was sand. . . . During the last hurricane . . . [h]ouses had been blown flat, as though pressed by hands.

The vacant house where Shad meets his friend Davey, a place abandoned the year before, is the most private place for conferring: "Old wallpaper curled from walls. Floorboards had begun to twist and lift. . . . The front room, as if it were the bottom of an hourglass, had started to fill with sand." To find help in catching the smugglers, Shad and his little brother Brian try to cross the marsh to the mainland:

> Very quickly, the water reached over Shad's ankles. The black bottom became so stirred up that when he looked down he couldn't see his toes. Once, twice, he suddenly sank into a hole of black ooze. but for the most part the bottom held firm. . . . The water was almost up to his waist. Underfoot, the bottom was becoming thicker, softer. . . . But there was no other way to go. No matter which way they turned, they sank into soft, sucking mud. . . . The clutching mud made each step an effort. In the time it had taken to cover ten feet before, Shad could only move three.

In some cases, there is minimal text to evoke setting, but the pictures make it clear. *Where the Wild Things Are* and *Peter Rabbit* are notable examples.

Setting as Symbol

Symbols may operate in setting as they may in other elements of literature. A **symbol** is a person, object, situation, or action that operates on two levels of meaning, the literal and the figurative or suggestive. When we first become aware of symbols, we have a tendency to run wild, to read into stories all sorts of fanciful overtones not legitimately supported by the story.

What seems important here is that only fairly obvious symbols will be understood by most children.

The simplest of symbolic settings are those that suggest that the forest is both a literal setting and a symbol for the unknown; the garden is both a literal setting and a symbol of natural but cultivated beauty; sunlight may symbolize goodness, while darkness is evil. In such a way some of the settings in folktales have symbolic meanings. Hansel and Gretel, as well as Snow White, are lost in the fearful and unknown—the forest. The forest is also the domain of ogres and giants, mysteriously frightening creatures. Despite their backdrop qualities, these symbolic settings often set the mood in traditional tales.

Symbols may be combined to create **allegory,** as they are in some stories for children. According to Northrop Frye, allegory translates into images.[2] To be a true symbol, the object must be emphasized or repeated, and supported throughout the entire story; it represents something quite different from its literal meaning. But stories for children operate on a fairly literal level. Ideas of good and evil may be translated into characters, actions, or setting, which then become symbols for ideas.

In this sense the Narnia series by C. S. Lewis is allegory. However, the Narnia books are also highly successful when read on a literal level; the young reader may or may not see the ideas symbolized by characters or setting. A child may read through the series with great excitement, think a bit, then exclaim "He's talking about good and bad!" and then reread them all, this time on an allegorical or symbolic level.

In contrast, the Forest seems a natural place for Pooh and Piglet to hunt a Woozle/Wizzle; to extend the meaning of the Forest to the point of calling it a symbol for evil is pretentious and pointless. Hannah, the supposed Quaker witch in *The Witch of Blackbird Pond,* does not live in the dark forest; a kind and harmless woman, she lives in the benign and sunny meadows. Speare chooses this setting for Hannah's home to assist in creating conflict, but calling the setting symbolic seems heavy-handed.

> A true symbol is emphasized, repeated and supported.
> —*Northrop Frye*

Special Issues of Setting in Children's Literature

Like adults, children will accept as much or as little setting as the story seems to call for. Like adults, too, they expect that when a setting is important to understanding the story, they will be made to see, to hear, perhaps even to smell the setting—to sense the setting in any way relevant to the mood, conflict, and characters in the story. But younger children will be less likely to sit still for long descriptions that take them away from the conflict and characters. For them, and for many adults as well, setting interwoven with action is the most interesting and readable. Once this setting is established, any reader of any age expects the writer to be consistent. At times we all accept settings as escapes. The scene of an exotic ball or lavish banquet in a folktale undoubtedly was a satisfying escape for the poor and oppressed who heard these stories told in the past; today setting in some adventure and science fiction stories also seems to function as escape. But once again, we return to the principle that the essential setting should be integrated with character and conflict, and that it not be a mere digression. Since folk literature and fantasy seem to be more common in literature for children than for adults, their special considerations bear closer examination.

Folktale settings may be a means of escape to an easier life.

Traditional Literature

In most folktales action and theme are the focus of interest and the setting is backdrop. The action is usually brisk and little time is spent describing time and place. The setting is a vague long-ago-and-far-away that avoids pinning down time and place. Such a setting also suggests magically one of the most pleasurable aspects of the folktale: maybe-it-happened-here, maybe-yesterday! Thus such a setting also anticipates the equally pleasurable possibility that perhaps-it-could-happen-again, perhaps here! We have noted in our discussion of character that in a folktale the protagonists are so general and universal that what happens to them might happen to anyone. Similar vagueness in setting reinforces the possibility of adventures for us, the readers.

Folktale settings often follow the "once upon a time" formula. A random sampling of tales from Grimm—the tales best known to a majority of Western readers—reveals the following settings, or lack of them, in their opening lines; little is added within the stories:

Once upon a time there lived an old man and his wife who for a long time . . . .

Once upon a time there was a king who had twelve daughters . . . .

Once upon a time in deep winter, when the snowflakes were falling like feathers . . . .[3]

Occasionally we read a simple variation: "At the edge of a great forest lived a woodcutter and his wife." Folktale settings from other cultures seem to vary little from the patterns of Grimm, with little more specific definition of time and place than the Native American "My grandfather told me . . . ." It is the nature of the folktale—originally told to an audience who might become restless—to plunge into conflict and action. Such generalized settings can demonstrate more clearly a universal theme: The kindness of the daughter is rewarded; she lives happily ever after in the palace of the prince.

Laurence Yep says, in the introduction to *The Rainbow People,* "Trying to understand Chinese-Americans from these tales is like trying to comprehend Mississippian ancestors by reading a collection of Vermont folktales. Some tales come from a common heritage; but others are specific to the region." One thinks of the particular settings of the Captain Stormalong tales of New England, and those of Big John from the mining regions, as well as Pecos Bill from the Southwest. Just as the people enrich our society, all of these stories enrich their readers.

The African tale retold by Gail E. Haley in *A Story, A Story* begins: "Once, Oh small children around my knee. . . ." A Kaffir tale of South Africa, *Mufaro's Beautiful Daughters,* retold and illustrated by John Steptoe, also begins traditionally: "A long time ago, in a certain place in Africa, a small village lay across a river and half a day's journey from. . . ." *The Name of the Tree,* a Bantu tale retold by Celia Barker Lottridge, begins: "Once, long ago, in the land of the short grass, there was a great hunger." Southeastern Alaska is the scene for the *pourquoi* tale *How Raven Brought Light to People:* It begins, "Long ago when the earth was new. . . ."

The Orphan Boy, a Maasi story told by Tololwa M. Mollel, however, plunges into the action: "As he had done every night of his life, the old man gazed deep into the heavens." The resulting story seems less a folk tale and more an original creation of the writer.

Other folk literature seems equally vague about setting. The fable omits setting altogether, going immediately into action and its didactic point:

A certain Wolf, being very hungry, disguised himself in a sheep's skin.

A mischievous Shepherd's Boy used to amuse himself by calling "Wolf! Wolf!"

Many of the fables are only a few sentences long, and, since they exist to point a moral, setting is quite logically unimportant. The lesson is universal, unlimited by time or place. Myths happened "in ancient Greece," or "in the days of the giants," and designation of time and place is barely relevant. What matters is not location of specific action, but pinning down the locale to a cultural world. Here, too, simplicity in setting reinforces the universal qualities of the myths, their comments upon human vanity or greed.

Legends, those unauthenticated stories handed down from tradition and regarded by the public as figuratively possible or even true, are by their definition related to historical events or people. This relationship narrows somewhat their time and place. For example, Robin Hood's adventures occur in Sherwood Forest since, according to history, that is where Robin Hood lived. Often, however, the legends refer to mystical events occurring centuries later than the lifetime of the character, and caused supposedly by the character's onetime presence. The oases of the Egyptian desert, for example, are said by legend to have sprung up wherever the fleeing Joseph, Mary, and infant Jesus stopped to rest.

In fables, setting exists as backdrop for the stated moral.

Fantasy and Science Fiction

Setting in fantasy is a special consideration, since fantasy often begins in a setting of reality and moves to a fantasy realm, then back again. Such a book as *Alice in Wonderland* moves easily from the real to the fantastic by the device of a dream; Dr. Seuss's *And to Think That I Saw It on Mulberry Street* is a fantastic daydream, a parade framed by what the narrator actually saw on the way home from school. Other transitions are more complex. In Susan Cooper's *The Dark Is Rising*, the world that Will enters is filled with the mysterious and the supernatural—integral parts of the setting and essential to the story. The castle where Will meets the Old Ones, who for centuries have been battling evil, is the setting for Will's discovery that by the exercise of his willpower he can actually bring change. Reluctantly, he learns that he must accept his power in order to use it for good:

> [He looked] across the room at the light and shadow dancing side by side across the rich tapestries on the stone walls, and he thought hard, in furious concentration, of the image of the blazing log fire in the huge fireplace behind him. He felt the warmth of it on the back of his neck, and thought of the glowing heart of the big pile of logs and the leaping yellow tongues of flame. *Go out, fire,* he said to it in his mind, feeling suddenly safe and free from the dangers of power, because of course no fire as big as that could possibly go out.

The fire goes out. Next Will sees that each of the many tapestries on the castle walls has its own frightening image, some as terrifying as "the empty-eyed grinning white skull of a horse, with a single stubby broken horn in the bony forehead and red ribbons wreathing the long jaws." Threatened by the rising of evil, the Dark, Will sees clearly his responsibility to use the special power given him.

In the fantasy *Alice's Adventures in Wonderland*, Lewis Carroll sets all logic awry, including the logic of setting. A rabbit hole extends deep into a strange, unbounded world, and time moves in all directions to create a setting essential to our experience of the story. To us as well as to Alice, time and place are illogical and confusing; they influence nonsensical behavior that defies every rule. In defiance of time and the related laws of growth, Alice grows and shrinks; the Mock Turtle's lessons lessen; the tea party murders time by going on forever; the White Rabbit tries fruitlessly to catch up with time. As for place, nothing seems to be where it is expected to be, and nothing can be counted upon to be in the same place at another moment. The great hall with glass table and tiny door vanishes, and Alice finds her way into a tidy little room. Turning her back on the tea party, Alice walks through a door into a tree—only to find herself back in the long hall with the glass table and the tiny door. Finally, cause and effect—which occur in that order and are logically related to time—defy time to appear in nonsensically reversed order: sentence first, verdict later.

Summary

Setting is of two principal types. First, it may be a backdrop for the plot, like the generalized backdrop of a city, street, or forest against which we can see some of the action of a play. In traditional literature, setting is usually backdrop, so generalized that it becomes universal. Or setting may be an integral part of the story, so essential to our understanding of this plot, these characters, and these themes that we must experience it with our senses. Backdrop or integral—the choice is the writer's. The integral setting may not only clarify the conflict, it may also help the reader understand character, may be cast as the antagonist, may influence mood, or may act as symbol. Often the sense of place prepares the reader to accept the story and the writer's personal view of life and its significance.

Whether setting is integral or backdrop does not constitute a judgment about the quality of a piece of writing. What is important, however, is that understanding may develop only when we realize that this particular setting is essential to this story. And, if setting is essential to our understanding, the writer must make the reader see, hear, touch, and perhaps even smell the setting. It is as much the writer's task when writing for children as for adults to evoke setting, described either in paragraphs or in phrases woven into action, by the details of color, sound, figurative comparisons, and other stylistic means.

Notes

1. Eudora Welty, *Place in Fiction* (New York: House of Books, 1957), p. 22.
2. Northrop Frye, "Theory of Symbol," in *Anatomy of Criticism* (Princeton, N.J.: Princeton University Press, 1957), pp. 71–128.
3. Alfred David and Mary Elizabeth Meek, eds., *The Twelve Dancing Princesses* (Bloomington: Indiana University Press), 1974.

Recommended Books Cited in This Chapter

Avi. *Shadrach's Crossing*. New York: Random House, 1983.
Bauer, Marion Dane. *On My Honor*. Boston: Houghton Mifflin, 1986.

BROOKS, BRUCE. *Everywhere*. New York: Harper & Row, 1990.

BURNETT, FRANCES HODGSON. *The Secret Garden*. 1911. Reprint. New York: Viking, 1989.

BURNFORD, SHEILA. *The Incredible Journey*. Boston: Little, Brown, 1961.

CARROLL, LEWIS. *Alice's Adventures in Wonderland*. 1865. Reprint. New York: Macmillan, 1963.

CLEAVER, VERA, AND BILL CLEAVER. *Where the Lilies Bloom*. Philadelphia: Lippincott, 1969.

———. *The Why's and Wherefore's of Littabelle Lee*. New York: Atheneum, 1973.

COOPER, SUSAN. *The Dark Is Rising*. New York: Atheneum, 1973.

FRANK, ANNE. *Anne Frank: The Diary of a Young Girl*. Garden City, N.Y.: Doubleday, 1967.

FRITZ, JEAN. *Homesick: My Own Story*. New York: Putnam, 1982.

GEORGE, JEAN. *Julie of the Wolves*. New York: Viking, 1972.

———. *The Talking Earth*. New York: HarperCollins, 1993.

HALEY, GAIL. *A Story, A Story*. New York: Macmillan, 1970.

HAMILTON, VIRGINIA. *The House of Dies Drear*. New York: Macmillan, 1968.

HOOVER, H. M. *The Lost Star*. New York: Viking, 1979.

LEWIS, C. S. The Chronicles of Narnia. New York: Macmillan, 1951–56.

LINDGREN, ASTRID. *Pippi Longstocking*. New York: Viking, 1950.

LOTTRIDGE, CELIA BARKER. *The Name of the Tree*. New York: Macmillan, 1989.

LOWRY, LOIS. *Autumn Street*. New York: Dell, 1986.

LUNN, JANET LOUISE. *Shadow in Hawthorne Bay*. New York: Scribner's Sons, 1986.

MACLACHLAN, PATRICIA. *Sarah, Plain and Tall*. New York: Harper & Row, 1985.

MILNE, A. A. *Winnie-the-Pooh*. New York: Dutton, 1926.

MOLLEL, TOLOLWA M. *The Orphan Boy*. Boston: Houghton Mifflin, 1991.

PAULSEN, GARY. *Dogsong*. New York: Simon & Schuster, 1985.

———. *Hatchet*. New York: Bradbury, 1987.

———. *Tucket's Ride*. New York: Delacorte, 1997.

PETRY, ANN. *Tituba of Salem Village*. Binghamton, New York: Vail-Ballou, 1964.

POTTER, BEATRIX. *The Tale of Peter Rabbit*. London: Warne, 1902.

REISS, JOHANNA. *The Upstairs Room*. New York: Harper & Row, 1987.

SENDAK, MAURICE. *Where the Wild Things Are*. New York: Harper, 1963.

SERRAILLIER, IAN. *Beowulf the Warrior*. New York: Walck, 1961.

SEUSS, DR. *And to Think That I Saw It on Mulberry Street*. New York: Hale, 1937.

SPEARE, ELIZABETH. *The Witch of Blackbird Pond*. Boston: Houghton Mifflin, 1958.

STEPTOE, JOHN. *Mufaro's Beautiful Daughters*. New York: Lothrop Lee, 1987.

SUTCLIFF, ROSEMARY. *The Shining Company*. New York: Farrar, Straus, & Giroux, 1990.

SWINDELL, ROBERT. *Brother in the Land*. New York: Holiday House, 1984.

UCHIDA, HOSHIKO. *Journey to Topaz*. New York: Scribner's, 1971.

WHITE, E. B. *Charlotte's Web*. New York: Harper, 1952.

WOJCIECHOWSKA, MAIA. *Shadow of a Bull*. New York: Simon and Schuster, 1964.

YEP, LAURENCE. *The Rainbow People*. New York: HarperCollins, 1992.

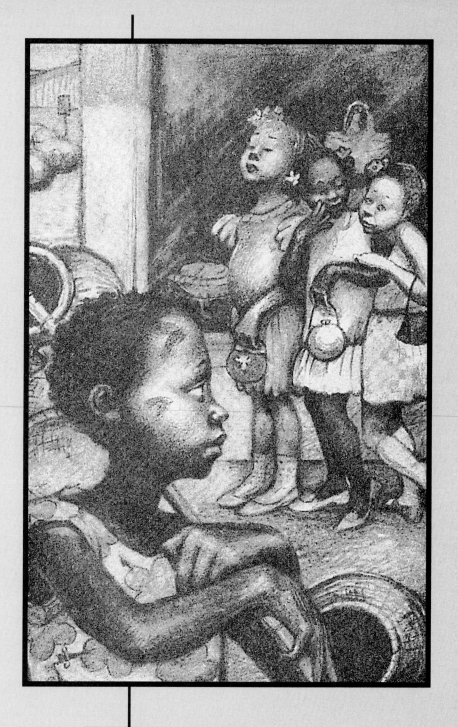

Do You Know Me?
Nancy Farmer (ill. Shelley Jackson)

8

Point of View

Try changing the point of view in a story. What happens?

Whenwehear the term **point of view,** we commonly think of opinion or attitude: "From my point of view, women's rights are . . ." Sometimes we think of a personal angle or perspective: "That may be true for you, but I'm a student, and . . ." But point of view has special meaning for literature. As we read a story, we may be aware that we are seeing the events through the eyes—and mind—of one character. Or we may feel that we are objective observers watching the events unfold before our eyes. The writer wants to tell us this story. Whose view of the story the writer tells determines the point of view. Who sees the events determines how the story will develop.

As we all know, two people to whom the same incident happens simultaneously can have different versions of the event. Each responds out of past experience, or from belief in right and wrong behavior, as well as from the more obvious differences in the physical and emotional effects of the incident. Each version of the facts is a personal truth.

A similar situation exists in literature. As readers we describe point of view depending upon who sees and tells about the action. The same story is a different story, depending upon which side of the story we see. In the case of Louise Fatio's *The Happy Lion,* the story depends upon which side of the cage door the zoo lion is on. The Happy Lion thinks his visitors are pleasant, civil people. They nod, they bow, they greet him, and feed him— when he is inside the cage. But the day the keeper forgets to close the door, the Happy Lion walks out and meets his friends in their territory. One faints, one screams, and another throws a bag of vegetables in his face. Now the Happy Lion's friends have become puzzling strangers. Since the point of view is what we would call limited omniscient, and we know the Happy Lion's innocent thoughts, we are completely sympathetic to his puzzlement. When he calls the people foolish, we agree, since we know this lion is not vicious nor predatory. He's just taking a walk. However, if we didn't know the protagonist's thoughts, we'd be as frightened as the human citizens of the Lion's town. It is all a matter of point of view—whose thoughts we know, whose view of the action we follow.

Types of Point of View

Point of view is determined when the writer chooses who is to be the narrator and decides how much the narrator is to know. The first possibility a writer might consider is the **first-person point of view,** used when a story is told in first-person "I." In such storytelling, the reader lives, acts, feels, and thinks the conflict as the protagonist experiences and tells it, just as Karana does in *Island of the Blue Dolphins.* Occasionally the first-person narrator is not the protagonist, but a minor character who observes the action and tells us what the protagonist is doing.

The second possibility is the **omniscient point of view.** Here the writer, telling the story in third person (he, she, they), is all-knowing or omniscient about any and every detail of action, thought, and feeling—conscious or unconscious—in past, present, or future; if the writer chooses, he or she may recount any and all details. This omniscience is White's choice for *Charlotte's Web.*

A third possibility is the **limited omniscient point of view,** in which the writer, again telling the story in third person, concentrates on the thoughts, feelings, and significant past experience of only the central character or protagonist, as Wilder does in her Little House stories. Occasionally the writer may choose to be omniscient about several—though not all—characters; this choice, too, is sometimes called *limited omniscient.*

The fourth possibility is the **objective (dramatic) point of view,** again using third person, as, for example, in Burnford's *The Incredible Journey.* The meaning of this term seems clear when we refer to the fictional reality of drama or motion picture. A camera seems to record—it cannot comment or interpret. There is no one there to explain to the reader what is going on or what the characters think or feel. The camera selects and we see and draw our own conclusions.

First-Person Point of View

The first-person narrator is limited; like us, he or she cannot tell what another character thinks unless told by that other character. Although the narrator sees the action of another character, the narrator, again like us, can only speculate about what the other is thinking. A hasty tucking in of a shirt or a nervous shaking of the head gives evidence from which the narrator may draw conclusions, just as we draw conclusions. However, unless the second character says aloud what he or she thinks, the first-person narrator, again like us, can only guess.

The first-person narrator who tells the story may be either the protagonist or a minor character observing the action. For example, Karana, the protagonist in *Island of the Blue Dolphins,* is a first-person narrator. At no time does Karana pretend to know what is in the minds of others, not her brother, the hunters, Tutok the Aleut stranger, or the animals. Tutok comes out from the brush quickly; Karana says, "She must have been waiting nearby." That possibility is all that Karana can know about Tutok's motives. Tutok hugs Karana when she receives the shell necklace. Karana says, "She was so pleased that I forgot how sore my fingers were." From a hug—action from another character—Karana concludes that Tutok is pleased. Although Karana knows her dog Rontu very well, she describes only his actions, never his thoughts, concluding that the dying Rontu wishes to bark only because he always had:

> [Rontu] raised his ears at the sound, and I put him down, thinking that he wished to bark at [the gulls] as he always did. He raised his head and followed them with his eyes, but did not make a sound.

Had O'Dell violated the first-person point of view by telling us Rontu's feelings, we might have turned our concentration from Karana, and the story would have been less real.

As we can see clearly from this passage, one of the strongest assets of first-person narration is its great potential for pulling the reader into what appears to be autobiographical truth. Because Karana's thoughts are interesting to us, we sympathize with her. Because she is believably limited in what she can admit to knowing, she is consistently credible. Because solitary Karana—like solitary Robinson Crusoe—tells her own realistic story, the vicarious experience of survival is a powerful reality, convincingly immediate to the reader. If the story had been filtered through an omniscient writer, the immediacy of the experience would be less intense. The intervention of someone who wasn't there but who still knows and can tell it all would create an intervening omniscience between the solitary protagonist and the reader. The story would then be more remote, less immediate, and less intensely real.

First-person point of view creates a sense of autobiographical truth.

Clearly the danger in first-person narration lies in the possibility of "I" ignoring his or her limitations, reporting thoughts of others, and predicting when such prediction would not naturally fall within "I's" ability to predict. Credibility is then lost.

The lives of the Blackfeet Indians of Canada in the 1800s were filled with the struggle to survive as well as great harmony with the cycles of growth and natural change. In her first-person novel *Sweetgrass,* Jan Hudson graphically shows both the struggle and the harmony. Although at the age of 15 she is the oldest unmarried woman in her tribe, Sweetgrass cannot convince her father she is mature enough to be first-wife-who-sits for Eagle Sun. She must continually prove herself. In consistent first-person narration, we see Sweetgrass's struggles with her anger at her father, with her wish to be with Eagle Sun, with her envy of her betrothed or married younger cousins, and finally with her desperate battle against smallpox and starvation. There seems no better way to understand the customs and mores of the Blackfeet culture and its role demands than seeing into the protagonist's mind as she wrestles with what she would like to do and what she as a dutiful daughter and tribe member must do.

Matters of vocabulary and word usage are restrictions, as the person telling the story is limited to diction compatible with age and personality. Vicky Austin's view of events in Madeleine L'Engle's *A Ring of Endless Light* is shaped by her 16-year-old experiences. The story opens at the funeral of Leo's father, where Vicky comments: "I looked at Leo and his face was all splotchy as though he had cried and cried, but he hadn't cried, and he needed to." Later that day, she comments:

> I held Leo and he held me and we rocked back and forth on the old elm trunk, weeping. . . . And I discovered that there is something almost more intimate about crying that way with someone than there is about kissing, and I knew I'd never again be able to think of Leo as nothing but a slob.

And of Adam she says, "He wasn't particularly gorgeous . . . but he had a kind of light within that drew me to him like a moth to a candle." This is the diction of a 16-year-old speaking her feelings and thoughts, and not presuming to know what she cannot know: "I don't think Adam realized how nervous I was."

Cynthia Rylant uses first-person point of view in her novel *A Fine White Dust,* showing Pete's thoughts and feelings as he is caught up in The Man's preaching. Realizing, therefore, the impact of The Man's persuasiveness on Pete's dedication to a new role, we are prepared for his disenchantment with The Man, who has betrayed Pete's trust.

First-person point of view is effective in *Coast to Coast.* By following Birch's thinking, Betsy Byars shows the close relationship of 13-year-old Birch to her grandfather. While helping to get his house ready for a yard sale prior to his move to California, she finds a box of her grandmother's poems, a treasure that makes her want even more to be close to her grandfather. She persuades him to do what he has long dreamed of doing: take his Piper Cub across country to California. While on the flight, Birch wants to speak of what is on her mind; she has just found evidence she may have had a twin sister. But Pop is uncommunicative and preoccupied with the flight. As we follow Birch's thinking, she conveniently speaks it all aloud to the dog Ace:

Diction is compatible with age and personality of the narrator.

It was about a baby that died, Ace, on my birthday. And all of a sudden I knew that poem meant one of two things. Either my mom's natural baby died, or lived just a little while. . . . And so maybe . . . someone else in the hospital had had a baby and was going to put her up for adoption, and that was me.

In their travels across the states, Birch and her grandfather become closer.

Occasionally a writer experiments successfully with different points of view, as do Paul Zindel in *Pigman* and Alice Childress in *A Hero Ain't Nothin' but a Sandwich*. Using first-person point of view, each of Childress's characters tells the story from her or his own perspective of events and relationships. From the total of their stories, we see events, characters, plot, and theme, as well as setting. The story, set in the inner city, concerns Benjie's experience with drugs, and to be convincing, each of the speakers must reveal self through distinctively personal diction:

[*Benjie:*] My block ain't no place to be a chile in peace. Somebody gonna cop your money and might knock you down cause you walking with short bread and didn't even make it worth their while to stop and frisk you over.

[*Grandmother:*] This house is my jail, only I pay rent. I'm afrald to go out in the street alone, day or night. Bad boys will beat [us] and take away our little money.

[*Nigeria Greene, teacher:*] Bernard Cohen is not to be believed. His whole mission in teaching is to convince Black kids that most whites are great except for a "few" rotten apples in every barrel. It burns me.

[*Benjie's mother:*] I try to keep the neighbors out of my business because every friend has a friend, and if I can't keep a secret, how can I ask them not to tell what I told?

Avi's use of first person narrator in *Nothing but the Truth* presents an interesting situation, that of the unreliable narrator. Although the jacket blurb suggests that the issue confronted is the importance of communication, another more important idea is that false communication can wreak havoc. Bent upon squeezing from his teacher an unearned grade so that he can run track, Phillip is totally rebellious. He blames his poor grades not on neglected homework but on a popular teacher; to goad her, and to annoy her in class, he hums the national anthem under his breath, and when she reprimands him, Phillip claims patriotic motives. Phillip's parents believe him, his story is publicized, his teacher humiliated, and his classmates angry. No one hears "nothing but the truth," and only Phillip himself knows what he has done.

Written in the "I" form of letter narration, *Letters from Rifka* by Karen Hesse is set in 1919, when Jewish Rifka is detained on Ellis Island. Writing imaginary letters to her Russian friend on the margins of a volume of Pushkin's poems, Rifka records her impressions of the States, and of the immigration process; again the first-person point of view creates a convincingly personal account.

At one time small children found stories written in first person difficult to follow, but in recent years many books written in a childhood vernacular make the voice of a young narrator far easier to recognize. For example, a first-person story is easy for younger readers to follow in the letter-and-diary format Beverly Cleary uses in *Dear Mr. Henshaw*. She moves from letters to letters-in-a-journal, and in salutations from "Dear Mr. Henshaw" to "Dear Mr. Pretend Henshaw," then to straight journal entries.

So successful in maintaining point of view is Joan Blos in *A Gathering of Days: A New England Girl's Journal* that we search for a footnote.[1] We wonder where Blos discovered this journal, for it seems too real to be a work of fiction.

Omniscient Point of View

A distinct change from the limitations of the first-person point of view occurs when the writer chooses the freedom of the omniscient point of view. The writer in this case may recount relevant information about any and every character—their thoughts, ideas, and feelings about themselves as well as others. The writer may flash back into past experiences, feelings, and thoughts; or forward into what will happen in the future. The omniscient writer may relate anything he or she believes is relevant to the story, moving around, in, and through the characters, knowing everything, explaining motives, and giving the reader helpful information. We see in William Armstrong's *Sounder,* for example, how the boy feels when his father has been taken to jail. "The loneliness that was always in the cabin . . . was heavier than ever now. It made the boy's tongue heavy. It pressed against his eyes, and they burned. It rolled against his ears. His head seemed to be squeezed inward, and it hurt." In adult fiction, details may be more subtly and less obviously related to the conflict and characters, but in children's stories, the writer concentrates on what is essential to the reader's understanding.

White finds the omniscient point of view best for *Charlotte's Web*. The objective, third-person statement that Fern wore a very pretty dress to the Fair has little significance until the young reader has the omniscient writer's interpretation: because she thought she'd see boys. When Wilbur learns of Charlotte's bloodthirsty appetite, he thinks that although Charlotte is pretty and clever, she is everything he doesn't like—scheming and fierce. The reader is as uncertain as Wilbur until White adds that fears and doubts go with new friendships. We know why Templeton finds the dirty junkyard his favorite spot; he thinks it's a good place to hide. If we had merely heard speeches and seen actions, we might have interpreted the details quite dif-

Adult fiction may have details subtly related to character and action.

ferently. White knows and tells what is in the minds of all his characters: Fern thinks the world is blissful; Lurvy feels weak at the sight of the dew-covered words in the miraculous web; Wilbur can't bear loneliness; Templeton is miserable when his rotten egg breaks. And when Wilbur tries to spin a web, Charlotte watches him delightedly, pleased that he is no quitter. White is truly the omniscient narrator. The reader knows everything because of the point of view.

Limited Omniscient Point of View

Often a story is told from a limited omniscient point of view. Here the writer chooses to see action through the eyes of one character—occasionally several characters—and to report that character's thoughts. In children's literature, this character is usually the protagonist. The writer shows not only what the character sees and hears, but also what the character feels and believes. The writer is inside as well as alongside the character.

When Dicey of *Dicey's Song* by Cynthia Voigt is asked in her classroom if her portrait-essay of a person she knows is really her relative, Dicey stands accused of showing fiction as fact, and even of plagiarism. She lifts her chin, and deliberately concentrates on something else—the sailboat Gram has let her refinish:

> She didn't answer. There was no way anybody could make her answer. In her mind, she made a picture: the little boat, she'd have painted it white by then, or maybe yellow—it was out on the Bay beyond Gram's dock and the wind pulled at the sails. Dicey could feel the smooth tiller under her hand; she could feel the way the wooden hull flowed through the water.

This is Dicey's story, her mind and feelings.

In Wilder's *Little House in the Big Woods,* we know from limited omniscient narration what pioneer life was like to a child. First, however, Wilder shows us the universal child Laura. Laura had never had more fun than when she fell from a stump into the soft snow and made pictures shaped like herself. Like everything else in the Wilder series, the understanding of Santa Claus and the giving of Christmas gifts are suited to the child's view of reality. "Santa Claus did not give grown people presents, but that was not because they had not been good. . . . It was because they were grown up, and grown people must give each other presents." Through Laura's innocent point of view we get the literal interpretation of a Bible story. As Adam names the animals, Laura envies him his clothing:

> Adam sat on a rock, and all the animals and birds, big and little, were gathered around him anxiously waiting to be told what kind of animals they

were. Adam looked so comfortable. He did not have to be careful to be keep his clothes clean, because he . . . wore only a skin around his middle.

Because through limited omniscience we see Laura's simplicity and innocence, we accept her account of pioneer life. In detailed description Laura tells us what butchering an animal was like to the frontier child. As one detail follows another, from playing with the pig's bladder to roasting the pig's tail, the modern city child who knows only that meat comes from the supermarket is prepared to believe the truth of butchering on the frontier. By recognizing the feelings of childhood, the reader accepts the particular and specific routines and actions of Laura's life—different though they are from the reader's own. Wilder is successful in large part because she chooses Laura's point of view.

Yolanda of *Yolanda's Genius* by Carol Fenner is smart, tough, and a new arrival in Grand River; she defends and cares for her little brother Andrew, and finally persuades the great BeeBee King of Andrew's musical genius. Yolanda, whose thoughts are always on one of two things—Andrew or food—arranges for Andrew to fake being lost at Chicago's big blues concert weekend, and, when "found," to be seen on the stage with celebrities. There Andrew plays his harmonica and his pipe, imitating all the sounds of the city from the wind off Lake Michigan and the shushing or roaring of the crowd to the strength and queenliness of oversize Yolanda. Andrew's musical genius is recognized. Because the point of view is limited omniscient, we know the thoughts and feelings of both Andrew and Yolanda. Six-year-old Andrew closes his eyes through it all and finally decides to learn to read—so he can read music. For Yolanda, being both smart and independent are good, but having a new best friend to share things with is wonderful.

To cite another example, when Van, the boyfriend of Jamie's mother in Carolyn Conan's *What Jamie Saw,* tries to throw baby Nin against the wall, Jamie catches her, and the three of them escape to live in friend Earl's tiny trailer in the woods. Jamie's "nosey" teacher finds help for the three cold, hungry people, and slowly they begin their painful efforts for a normal life. The story is told in limited omniscient point of view: Jamie worries about Nin's safety, and while the baby sleeps in a drawer, he wonders if she'd fit if he pushed the drawer in when he was in a hurry. Perhaps he could punch holes in the drawer, as he had when he kept bugs in a jar. When Van shows up, Jamie lifts infant Nin from the drawer, then hides under the bed, crawling in first, then pulling her in after him. Characters are few in this short novel, but its effectiveness is largely due to knowing Jamie's mind as we live within his body.

Gary Paulsen, telling a story quite different from his usual action/suspense novels, writes *Sisters/Hermanas* about two girls, both 14 years old, seeking their own ways to similar goals. Rosa from Mexico sells herself on the streets to send money home to her mother, meanwhile dreaming of wealth as a beautiful model. Traci sells her individuality to fulfill her and her mother's dream of financial success, bought by beauty and superficiality. The two girls' paths nearly cross when Traci, shopping for the perfect outfit, finds Rosa hiding from immigration officials. Traci looks into the eyes of the young streetwalker, and sees herself. In alternating chapters, the similarity of the two girls' motives is revealed. The novel is very short, bound as two related stories told in limited omniscient point of view, one in English and the other in Spanish.

Objective (Dramatic) Point of View

In the objective or dramatic point of view, the writer does not enter the minds of any of the characters. The action speaks for itself as it unfolds and the reader hears speeches and sees action. The term *dramatic,* of course, comes from *drama,* where characters reveal themselves by what they say, what they do, and what others say about them. Drama permits the audience to see and hear, but to draw inferences only from what it sees and hears. Inner thoughts or feelings must be revealed by visible action. In most plays there is no interpreter standing at stage left to tell the audience what thoughts run through the speakers' minds. The audience must sometimes figure out for itself the meaning of the actions and speeches, deciding from a character's voice inflections or actions what—beneath or in spite of the words—may lie in that character's mind.

The objective or nearly objective point of view in some stories makes heavier demands on the imagination and understanding of the reader. Adults guess that when a character looks at the floor, scuffs the dust with a toe, or twists a lock of hair, that person is shy or embarrassed, but the ability to interpret body language is a skill few children have. It is the writer's responsibility when using the objective or dramatic point of view to describe and report action that, since it is without interpretation, must be within the child's understanding.

The objective point of view demands that the reader use imagination and understanding.

The Incredible Journey is an example of the use of omniscience for the minor human characters and of relative objectivity for the major animal characters. Realistically, we can never know what, if anything, is in the minds of the three animals:

> The old dog walked gingerly into the shallow water, shivering . . . turning his head away. Once more the Labrador swam the river, climbed out . . . shook himself, and barked. There was no mistaking the command. The old dog took another reluctant step forward, whining piteously, his expressive tail tucked under. . . . Again the Labrador swam across . . . .

Because we see the reluctant step of the old terrier, hear the piteous whine, and note the tucked-under tail, we draw conclusions about how the dog feels. Burnford does better than most writers of animal stories, but even she uses animal/human comparisons, calling the terrier a white cavalier; he is like a "shipwrecked mariner after six weeks at sea on a raft."

Allan W. Eckert, in his portrayal of the badger in *Incident at Hawk's Hill,* is perhaps more successful; his objectivity falters less frequently. Eckert mentions instinct and experience as aids to the badger as she digs a tunnel five feet into the earth to a point she chooses for a nesting chamber. He describes the digging, the earth moving and scattering, and the choosing of a spot fifty feet away to start a longer escape tunnel connecting with the chamber. An incredible engineering feat now accomplished with unerring skill, she wheezes with fatigue. We observe actions, but we do not know thoughts.

Special Issues of Point of View in Children's Literature

Why all these words about point of view? Is it that important?

Yes, it is. Credibility of the story often depends upon a successfully maintained point of view. If we didn't know what Wilbur was thinking in *Charlotte's Web,* we'd wonder why he runs madly about once he gains his freedom. Or how in the world a spider and a pig—two creatures most of us would find unappealing—could forge a friendship. And what motivates that rat, anyway? The three pets of *The Incredible Journey,* who wander across the Canadian wilderness, would be characters from fantasy if we knew what they thought. The resulting destruction of realism would mar the story. Speculate as we may about whether our own lost pets would care about returning home, we have here a reassuring confirmation of their reciprocated loyalty—it doesn't happen only in the newspapers. In the Little House series, Wilder's remarkable consistency in using the growing child Laura's view helps us understand the frontier. It is instrumental in making the frontier real to children. "Enough of forest animals, frontier heroes and the legends about them; this is what it was like for a child like me."

The point of view of seventh-grader Anastasia Krupnik in Lois Lowry's books by that name (*Anastasia at This Address,* for example) is successfully maintained. She is interested in boys, and yet realizes that the boys unfortunately aren't ready for romance. As we follow her thinking, we see her fantasies about an older man, an "SWM" whose ad she answers—an action she now has misgivings about. She finds herself in a corner. Lowry keeps the humor coming: she never condescends or laughs *at* Anastasia while she takes the youthful point of view. We find ourselves understanding just how

A story's credibility may depend upon a consistent point of view.

confusing the vocabulary and actions of the adult world are to a 13-year-old. After all, you'd think that having one's earlobes pierced might logically be called a lobotomy.

Maturity of the Reader

It is not possible, nor even relevant, to make authoritative statements about the best or most successful point of view for children's literature We can make a few sensible inferences, however. The first-person point of view may present difficulties for the smallest child. Because the child is just learning his or her own "I" identity, he or she may have trouble identifying with the strange "I" of the story. But new stories in the "real words" of the vernacular are currently easier to understand.

> There is no "best" point of view in a story for children.

The older child, on the other hand, may find first-person stories exciting proof of understanding, and of the capacity to project self into another "I." First-person seems to be an increasingly popular choice of point of view in stories for older children. When Twain wrote *Huckleberry Finn* in first person, he probably had adult readers in mind, but when Robert Louis Stevenson wrote *Kidnapped* and *Treasure Island,* he must have wished to involve young readers in you-are-there adventures. Since that time we have had many more first-person stories for older readers, and currently there is an abundance of them; they seem to have proliferated since Emily Neville's *It's Like This, Cat* (1963). Like David's conflict with his father in the book, conflicts in these stories often explore the growing-up tensions in a child or young adult.

A skillful writer can make variations in point of view easily understood by a reader. *Antar and the Eagles* by William Mayne begins with Antar's point of view, limited omniscience that despite conversation with his family stays only with Antar's thinking. Without permission, Antar has climbed the ladders to the church steeple to his father. "They saw on one side the sea glittering under the sun, and on the other the distant mountains, where snow lay all summer. Below them all the town lay busy not knowing it was being watched." But this is a fantasy. Antar is snatched away by the Great Eagle to live with eagles so that he may complete the mission of retrieving from a distant star the eagle egg that will hatch to become the next Great Eagle. During Antar's stay in the nest with fledglings, he learns the language of eagles, and the point of view now includes what they think and feel as well. "They want" Antar to climb the mountains and are "extremely annoyed" when he slides and tumbles; they "insist" that he continue to climb, "but let him take the zigzag way." After a time, they are talking to Antar, who understands their language: "You must climb higher. . . . You

> A skillful writer may vary the point of view.

will fly from the height and glide down to the Great Eagle's pinnacle. There is no other way for you to get there." The gradual way in which Antar and the eagles come to communicate in eagle language convinces us to suspend our disbelief. Had Antar and the eagles understood one another immediately, credibility would have suffered.

Paul Zindel employs a variation of the first-person point of view in his novel *Pigman*. Using alternate first-person chapters, the two protagonists—one a boy, the other a girl—each give a personal view of the events. In a somewhat similar way, William Mayne in *Drift* tells two versions of the same story. The first 13 chapters are third-person limited omniscient as the white boy Rafe tells what happened when he and the Native American girl Tawena get lost in the storm while idly hunting Bear: the ice of the lake breaks, and they are unable to return to their village; Tawena "disappears," and Rate is led home by two Native American women seeking ransom. Chapter 14 begins "Tawena's Story." Now events are shown through Tawena's mind, and we realize that she had been close behind Rafe during the long trek through forest, under the waterfall and in the wolf pack, helping where possible to remain hidden, and guiding by pretending to be the voice of Bear, messenger of the god Maneto. The two stories, each with its own point of view, completely support and verify each other.

As for the objective point of view, children are inexperienced in drawing conclusions from speeches and from descriptions of actions; they may find the dramatic point of view hard to understand. This necessity for objectivity, therefore, presents a particular kind of challenge to the writer whose audience is the small child. If the story relies, however, on pictures showing the characters' feelings through facial expressions—as they may in picture books—the interpretive words about emotions and thoughts are not so essential.

Inexperienced in drawing conclusions from action, children may find omniscience easiest.

Animal Realism

Animal realism is a popular kind of story for children that presents special problems in point of view. Look back at *Charlotte's Web*, a story in which the characters are animals. White's story is not a realistic story about pigs and spiders and rats that live in barns; we know that. Such a story would have to show characters living and moving like animals, making animal noises. It would have to be told from a point of view that does not imagine or report the thoughts of nonhumans acting human. White had no intention of being realistic; he chose to portray his animals living as animals and yet similar to people. So successful is White that we have a distinct feeling that they *are* people. In fact, since they all think and worry and love and hurt and laugh and needle one another as people do, White's animal story reveals human truths of friendship and continuity, death and maturity. His careful control of what is animal and what is human in each character, never confusing the two, is a source of his success.

The objective or dramatic point of view, however, seems to be the logical choice for a realistic animal story. *Black Beauty* by Anna Sewell presents a distinct contrast. The book may give the impression of being a realistic story because the horses lead "horse lives." *Black Beauty*'s first-person narrator, however, is a horse using human language to tell us his horse emotions and thoughts. Sewell inconsistently mixes and confuses Black Beauty's animal and human natures. The point of view destroys realism. The horse's feelings would be believable—if we assumed that animal feelings are identical to our own. It is, furthermore, inconsistent with realism that we should know the animal's feelings by anything but observation and speculation, although perhaps accompanied by a hearty dose of our sympathy. Black Beauty, speaking in the first-person "I," says, "Day by day, hole by hole, our bearing reins were shortened, and instead of looking forward with pleasure to having my harness put on . . . I began to dread it." Black Beauty decides to do his duty despite his discomfort. But worse things come; the sharp bit cuts his tongue and his jaw, and he froths at the mouth. He feels "a pressure on my windpipe, which often made my breathing very uncomfortable . . . my neck and chest were strained and painful, my mouth and tongue tender, and I felt worn and depressed." While it is perhaps true that the story makes us feel like a horse, as Frances Clarke Sayers says,[2] the reverse is more nearly accurate; this horse feels the way we would feel if we human beings were living in horses' bodies. In a realistic animal story we expect to find at least a relatively objective point of view, whether the story is for child or adult.

Choice of point of view, as we can see, affects the reader's acceptance of a story. Some writers of animal stories manage to avoid the temptation of sentimentality; they seek to convey the reality of animal life by picturing the animals' natural habitat, showing the impact of predators, weather, seasons, and maturity cycles on animal lives. Such a writer is Felix Salten, author of *Bambi*. Sometimes Salten successfully evokes wonder; through the mind of Bambi the deer, the reader watches the approach of winter, feeling the cold rain and hearing the shushing of falling leaves. It pleases Bambi "to see the milk-white veils of mist steam from the meadow in the morning. . . . They vanished so beautifully in the sunshine. The hoar frost . . . with such dazzling whiteness delighted him too." Salten clearly and believably carries the suspense through a winter in which Bambi's first enemy is starvation and his second is Man. However, when Salten depicts as human Bambi's affection for his doe, or his admiration for the wise owl, the other information— the accurate natural history—seems less reliable. Salten begins to falsify when he humanizes even the leaves and is totally omniscient. By assuming

Choice of point of view affects acceptance of a story.

unlimited knowledge, he causes us to question his otherwise accurate portrayal of nature and its forces. Such complete omniscience may be traceable to the translation, but it creates doubts about what is really true.

In Bruce Coville's compilation of horse stories and poems, called *Herds of Thunder, Manes of Gold.* the quality is consistently high, each story maintaining the point of view of the human owner or observer, each one consistently and convincingly accurate. Coville's own retelling of "The Taming of Bucephalus," of how Alexander the Great met the horse that carried him to conquer Europe, is as convincing as any. In "White Horses," Anne Eliot Crompton tells the story from the point of view of a cave girl grown to womanhood, and in Peter Roop's "Prairie Lightning," the Native American grandfather tells his grandson of another horse of great speed. Nathaniel Hawthorne tells of the capture of the winged horse Pegasus by Bellerophon, but as is often the case when Hawthorne writes for children, his coy asides disturb the mood of the otherwise interesting tale. The overall quality of the stories, however, makes the book a pleasure for lovers of horses.

Fantasy

If fantasy is to be successful, we must willingly suspend disbelief. If the story's characters, conflict, and theme seem believable to us, we find it plausible and even natural to know the thoughts and feelings of animal characters or tiny people. In fact, the story may be so good that we wish it *were* true. This persuasion that the writer wishes to bring about—persuasion that "what if" is really "it's true"—is most successful when the writer is consistent about point of view.

Point of view is an essential part of our appreciation of Mary Norton's *The Borrowers.* Norton's central characters are diminutive; we see most of the action through the eyes of young Arrietty. The Clock family is only six inches tall, and everything in the story, from postage stamps to primroses, is seen in relationship to the characters' size. If we are to believe that Arrietty is so tiny, we must enter the dimensions and scale of her world. Pushing through the grass, she is startled by something glittering and discovers, "It was an eye. Or it looked like an eye. Clear and bright like the color of the sky. An eye like her own but enormous." While "human beans" find a walk across the carpet easy, to tiny Arrietty it is like pushing through a dense field of grain. She moves off the rug to the shiny floor beside the wall where she can run; she "loved running. Carpets were heavy-going—thick and clinging, they held you up." Beneath a table is a great expanse of the unknown, dark as a cave, "a great cavern of darkness. . . . Chair legs were

A story may be so good we wish it were true.

everywhere and chair seats obscured her view." The yard and garden are huge; here is Arrietty's glimpse:

> A greenish beetle, shining in the sunlight, came toward her across the stones. She laid her fingers lightly on its shell and it stood still . . . when she moved her hand the beetle went swiftly on. An ant came hurrying in a busy zigzag. She danced in front of it to tease it and put out her foot. . . . Cautiously she moved . . . in amongst the green blades. As she parted them gently with her bare hands, drops of water plopped on her skirt. . . . pulling herself up now and again by rooty stems into this jungle of moss and wood-violet and creeping leaves of clover . . . she sat down suddenly on a gnarled leaf of primrose.

No wonder we suspend disbelief and are convinced the Clock family lives. Not only do we know that safety pins and postage stamps have a way of disappearing, but we see everything from furniture to flowers from the point of view of Arrietty, who lives in our world, though seeing everything from a six-inch height. The scale is relative to a tiny borrower, and point of view is thoroughly consistent.

This same strongly established point of view and its detailed development helps to account for some of the greatest successes in children's fantasy. One thinks of Carroll's *Alice's Adventures in Wonderland* and of the fantasies of Ursula Le Guin and Robin McKinley.

Stories of Various Cultures

Stories of children from other countries are a particular problem for the writer. Early in the twentieth century, a series of books was published about children of other lands—*The Eskimo Twins, The Japanese Twins,* and others—by Lucy Fitch Perkins. These stories stressed what seemed to be peculiarities of life in other countries. We read of flat and unreal children living in exotic and uninhabitable lands. Fascinating as it all was to learn about children eating whale blubber or octopus, or wearing wooden shoes or tatami sandals, the stories now seem condescending. At this point in our discussion of children's literature, however, we recall that once we believe in the reality of character, we believe in the vicarious experience of the character's way of life. How can a story about other countries show how life is lived there without making the country and its people weird and wondrous, strange and unbelievable?

Children, like adults, see first the obvious differences in people: he has black hair and I have blonde; she is tall and I am short. From these outward physical traits, we shift our attention to more subtle differences, like names, houses, pets, and games—differences we all expect and look for. One effective way in which the writer can picture a different country accurately, make the story credible, and at the same time present the truth of human nature is to make careful use of point of view. An objective point of view in a story about life in Morocco, for example, might leave a child puzzled by uninterpreted facts. Some degree of omniscience, however, achieves several results. First of all, since we can know thoughts, the character can more easily be shown to be like us. Then, once we recognize these similarities, we accept the character as believable. From this acceptance of the character we can move on to believe the character's way of life is different but interesting, rather than strange or beneath us—a significant contribution to international understanding.

Varying cultures may be more easily understood through omniscience.

Point of view also reveals other things about people. Through Meindert DeJong's use of limited omniscient point of view in *House of Sixty Fathers*, North American readers not only discover experiences unfamiliar to themselves and to this Chinese child, but also how familiar parts of American experience must look to a child of another land. We, who automatically peel paper from chewing gum and pop it into our mouths to chew continuously and without purpose, find the action nothing unusual, but Tien Pao is mystified. Here he rides for the first time in a jeep, a "small, open carriage": "The man behind the strange wheel did things with his hands and feet. The carriage suddenly roared, shot ahead. It hopped and jumped and bounced in swiftness over the little road. It went still faster." Each aggressive action Tien Pao sees is committed by impersonal war equipment, every kind act by a human being whom Tien Pao comes to know.

An interesting corollary to consider beside *Sixty Fathers* is *Dragonwings,* Laurence Yep's story of a Chinese immigrant boy coming to California, the "Golden Mountain." As he approaches the California coast, he is disappointed; it is only "a brown smudge on the horizon," the wooden houses "like shells of wood which terrible monsters had spun about themselves." As the narrator tries to learn the new language, the "letters keep on rearranging themselves in the most confusing patterns." Because they can use their great powers for good or evil, the Chinese immigrants call the Americans "demons"—demons whose calendars, even, are not properly arranged, not based sensibly on the movements of the moon or on the ten-day week.

Because we are aware of their feelings, we find ourselves breathlessly involved in the Chinese family's lives, and are fearful for their safety. Although their lives are different from our own, they are themselves like us. We see people, countries, cultures, and ways of life—all through the point of view and wide eyes of a child—and are persuaded that a child is a child in any culture.

Summary

Point of view, an integral part of storytelling, determines the view the reader gets of events, character motivation, suspense and climax, and theme. There are four major kinds of point of view: first-person with an "I" narrator, omniscient with an all-knowing writer, limited omniscient with focus on one or a few characters, and objective or dramatic with a report only of what can be seen and heard. Each one, when suited to story and reader, accomplishes a significant task.

Since the limited experience of children makes it hard for them to draw their own inferences from objective description of action and speech, the writer often clarifies the story by use of some degree of omniscience. The pleasure of literature comes from style, character, plot—all of the literary elements. In literature for children, understanding of character and the other elements is aided by a sensitive choice of point of view adapted to subject matter, type of conflict, and expected maturity level of readers.

Notes

1. Joan Blos found that in writing *A Gathering of Days* in journal form, she did not have to invent details of doubtful authenticity, since diaries rarely include as many details as novels. For example, see *The Voice of the Narrator in Children's Literature,* edited by Charlotte F. Otten and Gary D. Schmidt (New York: Greenwood, 1989).

2. Frances Clarke Sayers, "Walt Disney Accused," in *Children and Literature: Views and Reviews,* edited by Virginia Haviland (Glenview, Ill.: Scott, Foresman, 1973).

Recommended Books Cited in This Chapter

ARMSTRONG, WILLIAM. *Sounder.* New York: Harper & Row, 1969.

AVI. *Nothing but the Truth.* New York: Orchard, 1991.

BLOS, JOAN W. *A Gathering of Days: A New England Girl's Journal, 1830–32.* New York: Scribner's, 1979.

BURNFORD, SHEILA. *The Incredible Journey.* Boston: Little, Brown, 1961.

BYARS, BETSY. *Coast to Coast.* New York: Delacorte, 1992.

CHILDRESS, ALICE. *A Hero Ain't Nothin' but a Sandwich.* New York: Coward, 1973.

CLEARY, BEVERLY. *Dear Mr. Henshaw.* New York: Morrow, 1983.

COMAN, CAROLYN. *What Jamie Saw.* Arden, N.C.: Front Street Press, 1995.

COVILLE, BRUCE, ed. *Herds of Thunder, Manes of Gold*. New York: Doubleday, 1989.

DeJONG, MEINDERT. *The House of Sixty Fathers*. New York: Harper, 1956.

ECKERT, ALLAN W. *Incident at Hawk's Hill*. Boston: Little, Brown, 1971.

FATIO, LOUISE. *The Happy Lion*. New York: McGraw, 1954.

FENNER, CAROL. *Yolonda's Genius*. New York: Simon & Schuster, 1995.

HESSE, KAREN. *Letters from Rifka*. New York: Henry Holt, 1992.

HUDSON, JAN. *Sweetgrass*. New York: Putnam, 1989.

L'ENGLE, MADELEINE. *A Ring of Endless Light*. New York: Farrar, Straus & Giroux, 1980.

LOWRY, LOIS. *Anastasia at This Address*. Boston: Houghton Mifflin, 1991.

MAYNE, WILLIAM. *Antar and the Eagles*. New York: Doubleday, 1989.

NORTON, MARY. *The Borrowers*. New York: Harcourt, 1965.

O'DELL, SCOTT. *Island of the Blue Dolphins*. Boston: Houghton Mifflin, 1960.

PAULSEN, GARY. *Sisters/Hermanas*. Translated into Spanish by Gloria de Aragon Andojar. New York: Harcourt, 1993.

RYLANT, CYNTHIA. *A Fine White Dust*. New York: Bradbury, 1986.

SALTEN, FELIX. *Bambi*. New York: Grosset & Dunlap, 1929.

STEVENSON, ROBERT LOUIS. *Kidnapped*. 1886. Reprint. New York: Scribner's, 1913.

———. *Treasure Island*. 1883. Reprint. New York: Scribner's, 1911.

TWAIN, MARK. *Huckleberry Finn*. 1884. Reprint. New York: Dutton, 1955.

VOIGT, CYNTHIA. *Dicey's Song*. New York: Random House, 1982.

WHITE, E. B. *Charlotte's Web*. New York: Harper, 1952.

WILDER, LAURA INGALLS. *Little House in the Big Woods*. 1932. Reprint. New York: Harper, 1953.

YEP, LAURENCE. *Dragonwings*. New York: Harper & Row, 1975.

ZINDEL, PAUL. *Pigman*. New York: Harper & Row, 1968.

Hiawatha
Henry Wadsworth Longfellow (ill. Susan Jeffers)

9

Style

Is it possible to identify the sources of distinctive style?

Let us now consider the literary element that makes language memorable—its style. Frequently someone asks, "But does the writer know what he or she is doing with words?" Yes. The author has added, subtracted, experimented, and substituted, creating the style that best tells his or her story. The skilled writer chooses words that become setting, plot, character, and theme to make a piece of literature.

Style is basically words, *how* an author says something as opposed to *what* he or she says. From infinite numbers of words available, the writer chooses and arranges words to create a particular story, the words and arrangement best for that story. Rufus Moffat, for example, on the first day of school, "felt a slight impulse to run home and play as he used to. Play what? . . . Mud pies? he asked himself sarcastically. Pooh! He was too old for all that business now. He was going to school. Soon he would be going home to lunch." This is Rufus, his own style—that is, author Eleanor Estes's choice of the style suited to situation and character in *The Moffats*.

By contrast, Scott O'Dell's formal and restrained language and simple sentence structure constitute the style suited to the setting, conflict, and character in *Island of the Blue Dolphins*. The protagonist, who lives a life totally dependent upon nature, says in the opening lines: "I remember the day the Aleut ship came to our island. At first it seemed like a small shell afloat on the sea. Then it grew larger and was a gull with folded wings. At last in the rising sun it became what it really was—a red ship with two red sails." O'Dell uses nature comparisons throughout the survival story. Ramo has eyes "half-closed like those of a lizard lying on a rock about to flick out its tongue to catch a fly." An invader's beard is combed until it "shines like a cormorant's wing." Karana says the enemy's mouth is "like the edge of a stone knife." A school of friendly dolphins dives in and out "as if they were weaving a piece of cloth with their broad snouts." The sea elephants have faces "like wet earth that has dried in the sun and cracked." Word pictures and comparisons describe characters, action, and setting, but in a style suited to this story of a protagonist who lives with her antagonist, nature. The styles of *The Moffats* and *Island of the Blue Dolphins* could not be interchanged. In each case the style is right for that particular story.

Similarly, the style of *The Midwife's Apprentice* is suited to the medieval setting. Karen Cushman's sentences are sometimes long and rhythmic, as though the story were being told to attentive listeners. She often lists the tasks of apprentice Alyce, and the ancient healing herbs with their curative powers. She takes and stores "in her brain and her heart what she heard the midwife say and do about babies and birthing and easing pain":

> She discovered that an eggshell full of the juice of leeks and mallows will make a labor quicker, that rubbing the mother's belly with the blood of a crane can make it easier, that birthwort roots and flowers can strengthen contractions in a reluctant mother, and that, if all else fails, the midwife can shout into the birth passage, "Infant, come forward! Christ calls you to the light!"

In fiction, style at its best increases not only our pleasure in words and sounds, but also our belief in the characters' reality. We come to know them through the words they say, through the words that describe how they look and how they act. We are eager to believe in the characters' experiences, following the plot and visualizing the action described in the chosen words. Through words, we see, hear, and even smell the setting while we realize its effect upon characters and conflict. Style is the product of all the choices the writer makes.

These choices are, of course, an entirely personal matter, since style and writer are inextricable. Mark Twain's style is no more Ogden Nash's style than Twain is Nash. One writer deals with the nature of reality or fantasy in one way; another expresses his or her vision in quite another way. A writer does, of course, vary her or his own style. Since one story differs from another, styles will differ as the writer suits style to story. Notice how O'Dell's restrained and dignified style in the opening of *Island* differs from his brisk and active language in the opening of *The King's Fifth*. This is not Karana but a different character:

> It was eight bells of the morning watch, early in the month of June, that we entered the Sea of Cortés. On our port bow was the Island of California. To the east lay the coast of New Spain.
> I sat in my cabin setting down in ink a large island sighted at dawn, which did not show on the master chart. The day was already stifling hot, so I had left the door ajar. Suddenly the door closed . . . .

A writer's style is a personal choice dependent upon setting, plot, and characters.

Style is not something applied to a finished piece of writing; rather, it is the writing, conveying both the idea and the writer's view of the idea. Henry James says that each word and every punctuation mark directly contribute to meaning; the content of a story and how it is told are inseparable.[1] Tone, word choice, grammatical structure, devices of comparison, sound, and rhythm all are style. All of these elements vary with the author's purpose, as the idea, the incidents, and the characters vary. Style gives the whole work its distinction and makes the story memorable.

Originality and style are not the same, but they are related in the sense that a writer is himself or herself an original. Nor should novelty be confused with style, for novelty is sometimes mere gimmickry—as it often is in Paul Zindel's novels, for example—rather than unique and personal expression. If the writer's way of telling the story and its truth is distinctively the writer's own, then that expression has a personal mark, and the style should become the best possible one for a particular work. Reading a work aloud is a pleasurable way to discover style as senses awaken, rhythms appear, and comparisons become vivid.

Devices of Style

The most easily identified element of style is the writer's use of certain specific devices of language. Many of these stylistic devices are listed in dictionaries of literary terms; our chief concern here is with those most often used in children's literature.

Connotation

Connotation is the associative or emotional meaning of a word. Connotative meaning, when added to dictionary meaning, or **denotation,** adds significance and impact to a term. Charlotte, for example, is not as big as a thimble, or as small as a fingernail, or as round as a button—all denotative comparisons which might convey her proper size and shape but which have no emotional impact. Charlotte is, instead, "about the size of a gumdrop." Now there's a reassuring comparison for a bloodthirsty spider. The stomach of gluttonous Templeton is not bulbous, or enlarged, or even like a ball. Instead, "as big around as a jelly jar" expresses comparative size and shape, but adds pleasant connotations. No spider egg sac ever had the appeal of Charlotte's; it is neither orange nor pink, but peach-colored and looks like cotton candy. The images of cotton candy, jelly jar, and gumdrop are all favorites with children; each of these comparisons describes size, color, and shape, but adds pleasant and positive emotional meaning.

Imagery

By far the most frequently used device, and the most essential, is imagery. **Imagery** is the appeal to any of the senses; it helps create setting, establish a mood, or show a character. We use imagery in our everyday conversations to describe sounds, smells, and sights. We say the sky is sapphire blue, the carpet is celery green, a jacket is fire engine red; we describe the nature of a sound as clanging, buzzing, humming, or thundering. We say that tastes are bitter, sweet, or salty, that smells are acrid or musty, and that texture is scaly or slimy.

The writer, too, relies on imagery to give the reader impressions of what the writer wishes to depict. But verisimilitude, or description to duplicate reality, is not the writer's only goal; suggestion and release of the imagination are important. The writer, by the choice of details and of the words used to describe the details, stirs the reader's imagination; the impact may be recognition or delight.

Charlotte's Web demonstrates the use and effectiveness of imagery. In the opening pages of the third chapter, Wilbur has just come to live in the manure pile of the Zuckerman barn, and we explore the building with him. No barn was ever more real, more suggestive of security and activity. The imagery convinces us as we smell the variety of smells, feel the warmth and coolness, and see the clutter of equipment. We may not settle down snugly in the manure pile, but we are as much at home in the barn as Wilbur is.

White describes the silence of the barn, but by sound imagery of a negative kind. The quiet itself is described by White's noting the absence of the customary noises; animals are so quiet that we hear only the weather-vane:

> The sheep lay motionless. Even the goose was quiet. Overhead, on the main floor, nothing stirred: the cows were resting, the horses dozed. Templeton had quit work. . . . The only sound was a slight scraping noise from the rooftop, where the weather-vane swung back and forth.

When Wilbur first arrives at the fairgrounds, that setting is created for the reader by imagery. As White lists the senses one by one, a specific image appeals to each:

> They could hear music and see the Ferris wheel turning in the sky. They could smell the dust of the race track where the sprinkling cart had moistened it; and they could smell hamburgers frying and see balloons aloft. They could hear sheep blatting in their pens. An enormous voice over the loudspeaker . . .

White relies on imagery to make the reader aware not only of setting but also of character and action. When Wilbur gets his buttermilk bath, we see him; he stands with closed eyes, feeling the buttermilk trickling over his sides. When he greedily opens his mouth and tastes the delicious buttermilk, Wilbur's childlike character is revealed. He stands in the pig trough and drools with hunger, while White itemizes the slops, each particle a distinctly visual image with a taste of its own:

> It was a delicious meal—skim milk, wheat middlings, leftover pancakes, half a doughnut, the rind of a summer squash, two pieces of stale toast, a third of a gingersnap, a fish tail, one orange peel . . . the scum off a cup of cocoa, an ancient jelly roll, a strip of paper from the lining of the garbage pail, and a spoonful of raspberry jello.

As we visualize slops, each item has color and shape in our minds. At the same time, White appeals to taste by listing foods a child knows and likes. And finally, the variety has the distinct quality of slops, since it is punctuated by a fish tail and a bit of garbage pail liner. Imagery not only helps create setting, but pictures action and character as well.

Figurative Language

Another device of style is **figurative language.** The writer uses words in a nonliteral way, giving them meaning beyond their usual, everyday definitions and thereby adding an extra dimension to meaning. Personification, simile, and metaphor are the most common kinds of figurative language in stories for children.

Children's stories often make use of **personification,** the giving of human traits to nonhuman beings or inanimate objects. In *Charlotte's Web* a large cast of nonhuman characters is personified, from Wilbur to the maple trees and even crickets:

> The crickets sang in the grasses. They sang the song of summer's ending. . . .
>   The sheep . . . felt so uneasy they broke a hole in the pasture fence. . . .
> The gander discovered the hole and led his family through. . . . A little maple tree . . . heard the cricket song and turned bright red with anxiety.

We hear the crickets singing, rather than chirping. The sheep are "uneasy," the goose "family" eats apples, and nearby the "anxious" maple turns autumn colors. Human qualities are given to everything. Where Salten fails in *Bambi,* White is successful because his personification is fresh and the story is fantasy, not sentimentalized realism.

One of the simplest figurative devices is the **simile,** a stated comparison between unlike things, using *as, like,* or occasionally, *than*. Straw fluttered down "like confetti" at the exciting news from the Fair loudspeaker. When Charlotte is weary, she is swollen and listless and feels "like the end of a long day." These very specific comparisons are easy to see, since they are directly stated. Their combination of imagery and comparison makes them distinctive enough to stir the reader's imagination.

Implied comparisons, such as the sapphire sky and the celery green carpet, examples mentioned earlier, are called **metaphors.** They are sometimes so neatly put, so recognizably clear that we scarcely notice them—like the familiar "beads" of water decorating Charlotte's web. As Charlotte catches and stings her insect fare, she metaphorically "anaesthetizes" them. Templeton hears the Fair is a figurative "paradise," where he'll find a "veritable treasure" of leftovers, enough for "a whole army of rats." Paradise is great happiness, treasure great wealth, and army a vast number; all are metaphors.

Hyperbole

We are so accustomed to exaggeration as humor that we scarcely recognize it as a figure of speech; we often stretch a comparison to create **hyperbole.** When, for example, Mrs. Zuckerman is scared to death, or Wilbur threatens to die of a broken heart, the author uses hyperbole that has become part of our daily conversation. But when Templeton, grousing that he did not come to the Fair to be a newsboy, refuses to "spend all my time chasing down to the dump after advertising material. . . . Next thing you'll want . . . is a dictionary," his grumbling and sarcasm are hyperbole. Wilbur uses self-pitying hyperbole when he says, "I'm less than two months old and I'm tired of living." But we may laugh at the words of the sheep whose hyperbole is sheer imaginative extremism. He speaks to Templeton: "If Wilbur is killed and his trough stands empty day after day, you'll grow so thin we can look right through your stomach and see objects on the other side."

Much of Robert Newton Peck's *Soup's Hoop* is sheer nonsense hyperbole. Rob and Soup's new friend Piffle Shootsensinker, a seven-foot native of Pretzelstein, is unable to play basketball without the music of his native spitzentootle. So that Piffle can help Learning School win the basketball game, the two boys create a spitzentootle from this and that. Throughout the story, Rob speaks in hyperbole. Janice is the school scourge who, when she knocks out a fellow student's tooth, would take it home, "stuff it full of sugar, and watch it ache." When she lassos the boys, she finds a bug "not quite the size of a Shetland pony," and thinks it might fancy "a nasal excursion." The cereal the boys eat is called Soppies, because when touched by milk it is fit "only to be eaten by . . . starving maggots." In the earth-floored cellar, the boys see a rat, big "as a golden retriever. A kid could have throwed a saddle on that rat and rode it to school." In each case, the image such exaggeration creates in our minds is visually vivid.

Understatement

The reverse of exaggeration is **understatement,** or playing down. Like hyperbole, it may be used for comic effect. When Fern bites into a raspberry with a concealed "bad-tasting bug" and gets "discouraged," discouragement seems minimal. When Avery removes from his pocket the frog that has traveled back and forth on the barn swing all morning, scrunched and dried in a tight pants pocket, we read that the frog seems tired from a morning of swinging. Merely tired?

Like Karana in *Island of the Blue Dolphins,* Jan Hudson's *Sweetgrass* does not mention her sorrow but, and with restraint, describes factually the tragedy of the death of the protagonist's baby sister:

> Her tiny tummy was swollen already, puffed out like that of a corpse of many days. . . . Soon her shape would not be human at all.
>
> I knew what had come amongst us, then. Only one sickness killed so fast and turned its victims to foul black dung. Smallpox. The white man's smallpox had stolen into our camp and was now bent . . . over our little baby.
>
> I stumbled out and vomited into the snow.

We watch as Sweetgrass searches for a blanket to wrap around the decaying corpse, as she considers ways in which to satisfy burial customs and yet make it possible for her to stay and nurse Almost-Mother and her two brothers, and finally, knowing she cannot properly satisfy custom, makes her compromises. Restraint marks the descriptions, restraint that avoids sentimentality and yet convinces us that Sweetgrass grieves for her baby sister while she struggles.

Allusion

One figure of speech, **allusion,** probably has meaning only to the mature reader, since it relies on recognition of a reference to something in our common understanding, our past, or our literature. No adult will miss an allusion—for example, to a disastrous experience, an exam perhaps, when it is called "my Waterloo." White adds an opportunity for pleasure for the adult reader when he alludes to the call of the white-throated sparrow that must have come all the way from Boston, "Oh, Peabody, Peabody, Peabody!" Some adults may recognize reference to the Peabody sisters of Salem, but if not, no meaning is lost; it remains a New Englander's description of the bird song, as well as a standard description of the birdcall. One of the delights of *Alice in Wonderland* for Victorian readers was the wealth of allusions they could recognize, although contemporary readers, young and old, may miss them. Allusion is difficult for children to catch, since it relies on a background they lack.

Symbol

A **symbol** is a person, object, situation, or action that operates on two levels of meaning, the literal and the figurative or suggestive. Certain symbols are universal: the dove is the symbol for peace, a flag symbolizes a certain country. Other symbols are particular to a story. Clearly, the necklace of shells Karana gives to Tutok in *Island of the Blue Dolphins* is a symbol of friendship. Less obvious is the Borrowers' emerald watch among all the unneeded and unmissed items borrowed from Aunt Sophie's household. We might call it a symbol for the latent materialism in Pod, and particularly in Homily.

In a picture book, too, symbol can help us understand a thematic point. *Fly Away Home* by Eve Bunting tells of a homeless father and his small son who live at the airport, moving constantly so as not to call attention to themselves. When a bird flies in, the boy watches it dash itself repeatedly against windows, trying to be free. Wounded, then rested, it finally manages to "fly away home," just as the boy hopes he and his father will be able to fly away to a home.

Book titles can also be symbolic. *Shadow of a Bull* represents the shadow of Manolo's father's fame hovering over him as he struggles to decide how to spend his life—as a bullfighter or as a doctor to bullfighters.

A symbol, then, has significance beyond its literal self. At times we may think that a repeated sight or object is a symbol, but because the writer does not connect it with an idea, a mood, or some other meaning, it fails as a symbol. Clay in Paula Fox's *Monkey Island* uses a red crayon to add his own graffiti to others on the walls of the elevator of the welfare hotel. Seeing a tiny "Stop" crayoned here and there, its red color standing out from the other scrawls, we think it is a symbol for something. Vaguely, it connects with the problems in Clay's life as a homeless and abandoned child, but unfortunately its significance is never made clear, and we can merely guess.

> To be a symbol, a term needs meaning beyond its literal meaning.

Puns and Wordplay

An imaginative writer who enjoys the pleasure of words is tempted to echo words of other literary works. When White says that Templeton has no "milk of rodent kindness," we may recognize an echo from *Macbeth*. Wilbur is lured back to his pen by the promise of slops and the goose warns, "It's the old pail trick, Wilbur. Don't fall for it!" We hear echoes of "the old shell game." A sly grammatical error slides in, one that parents frequently correct in their children: "He also has a smudge on one side where he lays in the manure." And instead of correcting the grammar—*lies* for *lays*—Zuckerman corrects the facts: "He lays in clean straw." Then White adds a bad **pun** using another word: "untenantable" is implied.

> "If that ancient egg ever breaks, this barn will be untenable."
> "What's that mean?" asked Wilbur.
> "It means nobody will be able to live here on account of the smell."

Finally, White plays with words in still other ways. Naive Wilbur uses faultless logic when he argues with the lamb that he is not less than nothing: "I don't think there is any such thing as less than nothing. Nothing is absolutely the limit of nothingness. It's the lowest you can go. . . . If there were something that was less than nothing, then nothing would not be nothing . . . ."

Onomatopoeia

One sound device called **onomatopoeia,** or words that sound like their meanings, dominates an occasional paragraph of *Charlotte's Web.* For example, as White describes Wilbur eating his slops, he uses the onomatopoeic words "swishing and swooshing," which suggest Wilbur's happy gluttony. While these slushy sounds suggest one kind of eating, the explosive sounds of "gulping and sucking" describe another.

Alliteration

Another easily recognized sound device is **alliteration,** repetition of initial consonants: "They *s*ang the *s*ong of *s*ummer's ending." The effect of the sentence is musical, but its movement is slow and the music sad and final. By contrast, the Zuckerman dump becomes exciting as visual imagery rhythmically piles up in interesting debris, layer upon layer. Alliteration then adds to the pleasure of the passage: "*b*roken *b*ottles . . . *d*iscarded *d*ishmops . . . last *m*onth's *m*agazines."

Assonance

A device that enhances meaning by the repetition of similar vowel sounds within a phrase is called **assonance.** When we hear the crickets' song, "*a* sad, m*o*n*oto*n*o*us s*o*ng, the neutral *a* and the similarly sounded *o*'s suggest the feeling of sorrow and sameness. Reading the passage aloud shows how sadness and monotony are here extended by assonance.

Consonance

The close repetition of consonant sounds is called **consonance.** In the phrase "emp*t*y *t*in cans and dir*t*y rags and bi*t*s of me*t*al and broken bo*t*tles," repetition of the abrupt *t*'s in varying positions in the words emphasizes the idea of ragged remains of unrelated items—junk. Again, reading the sentence aloud is the best test for sound devices, since sound rather than spelling shows how meaning is affected.

Rhythm

So closely is **rhythm**—from the Greek word meaning flow—associated with poetry and verse that we often forget that it is also part of prose. Stories that are read aloud to children can make particularly effective use of rhythm, which in prose is sometimes called **cadence.** White uses the word *and* to create rhythm as he shows the Zuckerman dump, an accumulation of one item after another, each joined to the others by *and*. Reading aloud is the test for rhythm as it is for other sound devices. Here is . . .

> . . . an astonishing pile of old bottles and empty tin cans and dirty rags and bits of metal and broken bottles and broken hinges and broken springs and dead batteries and last month's magazines and old discarded dishmops and tattered overalls . . . and useless junk of all kinds, including a wrong-size crank for a broken ice-cream freezer.

The rhythmic list slows to a halt with the last comma, followed by the final, jerking phrase filled with abrupt and explosive consonants: "a *wr*ong si*z*e cran*k* for a *br*o*k*en ice-cream *fr*eezer." The changed rhythm brings the astonishing pile to an end.

An unusually effective example of cadence occurs in White's description of the rope swing as it flies back and forth. The first phrases of the passage anticipate "and jumped," and then the swinging begins. Again, by reading aloud, we hear each of the phrases shorten as the arc of the swing shortens. Abruptly the words bring the swing to a halt, and the swinger jumps to the ground:

> Then you got up all your nerve, took a deep breath, and jumped. . . . The rope would twist and you would twist and turn with the rope. Then you would drop down, down, down out of the sky and come sailing back into the barn almost into the hayloft, then sail out again (not quite so far this time), then in again (not quite so high), then out again, then in again, then out, then in; and then you'd jump off and fall down and let somebody else try it.

Rhythm ceases completely with the series of short, explosive words and phrases at the end of the paragraph. As the successive phrases shorten, we find pleasure in the description of action as well as in the understanding of the experience. Rhythm is the key.

Special Issues of Style in Children's Literature
Trite Versus Fresh Style

A story written in clichés is dull, just as a person who thinks in clichés is dull. Some of the drabbest stories for children are often those that tie into children's television shows, like *The Muppets* or *Sesame Street*. Other popular fiction for children may rely on its subject matter, exclusively focused on early adolescence. Many of Judy Blume's books are written in trite language. Here there are no surprises. For lack of figurative or connotative language or appeals to the senses through imagery, nothing is vivid. In *Then Again, Maybe I Won't*, the first-person narrator has just found that his friend is shoplifting:

> The salesman told me the mitt I liked was $37.50. I thought that was a lot of money. . . . I'd have to think about it. . . . I walked back to the cash register where Joel was waiting. I wanted to know if he thought $37.50 was too much for a mitt. But I never asked him because he was smiling his crooked smile and humming some tune.
>
> I thought, oh no! Please, Joel. I don't want to be sick again. I don't want to go back to the hospital. I know what you've done. I can tell by just looking at you. What'd you take this time, Joel?

We've heard this before. Or even worse—we feel we must have, even if we know we haven't. There are no surprises. Nothing is distinctive here. The first-person narrator gives us no sense of the personality of the speaker because the words spoken in vernacular lack individuality and freshness. Similarly, the style of Peter and Connie Roop's writing in *Keep the Lights Burning, Abbie* is monotonous, although the subject—Abbie Burgess, the girl who, left alone in 1856, kept Maine lighthouse lamps burning—is potentially interesting. Simple sentences repeat words and information unnecessarily, and the reader grows impatient waiting to get on with the action.

Story and style work together for a coherent whole, but occasionally we encounter a combination that seems an uncomfortable mix. Such is the case with Walter Wangerin, Jr.'s *Elizabeth and the Water-Troll*. The story begins with a long and rhythmic line that promises a folktale, but in folktales we know who is good and who is not. Here we are confused by the ugly Troll who lives in the Well of Despair and whose picture resembles that of a conventionally drawn devil who "grins" and "creeps"; his teeth "flash," as he "speaks through his fangs," and his "claws [come] toward her face" as he "snarls." This Troll, we are to believe, loves Elizabeth, and yet the terms describing him describe a fearful monster, terms quite unlike those describing Beauty's sad and lonely but kind and thoughtful Beast in that folktale. Held to his breast, Elizabeth "feels his hurt as though it were her own," "a suffering," "a pain" we know nothing of, unrevealed to us now or later; he is "an injured creature whom she loves." Is his ugliness or his loneliness the source of his sadness? What causes her to love him? Further stylistic dissonance occurs in such double-negative phrases as "No, I won't trust nobody, nobody, since everybody lies." "He is frowning on account of a difficult thought." Her father rushes "out of doors. 'Happy day! I know where Elizabeth's at!'" Abrupt shifts in what at times is folktale style, then ungrammatical colloquialism, prevent our feeling compassion for the Water-Troll or believing in Elizabeth's love for him.

In contrast, vernacular language may be clear and descriptive, like that of a young person like Jerome Foxworthy in Bruce Brooks's *The Moves Make the Man*. Jerome, a basketball player, strings his words together without breaks or pause; we feel and hear and see the shot, a pleasure in many sensory ways:

> . . . [C]radling the ball and at the last minute pulling my left hand away like Oscar Robertson and snapping that lubricated right wrist and knowing, feeling it right straight through from the tips of the fingers that had let fly the ball and touched it all the way to the last, straight down the front edge of my toes just before they hit the ground again, that the shot was true, feeling the swish and tickle of the net cords rushing quick down my nerves, and landing square and jaunty in time to watch, along with everybody else, as the ball popped through the net without a single bit of deceit, so clean it kicked the bottom of the cords back up and looped them over the rim, which is called a bottoms up and means you shot perfect and some people even count them three points in street games.

Although Jerome does not lapse into the vernacular, he manages to sound like a credible boy.

Using rap in the title *The Mouse Rap* by Walter Dean Myers makes style immediately significant. Each chapter begins with a piece of rap like, for example, the lines that open Chapter 2:

> *Phoomp! Phoomp! . . . Phoomp! Phoomp!*
> *Phoomp Phoomp Phoomp! Phoomp! Phoomp! Phoomp!*
> High waters run fast, still waters run deep
> 'Cause a man look old don't mean he asleep
> Those old-time dudes were big and bold
> And I'm glad I heard their stories told
> They were sometimes right, and sometimes wrong
> Their days were short but their stash was long
> A million bucks will blow your mind
> But your hand can't spend what your eyes can't find
> *Phoomp! Phoomp! . . .*

Rap style (in a book!) may convince some older readers that there might be something in this book. Mouse, the first-person narrator, continues in the rhythm of African-American idioms, and a reader follows the suspenseful story to find the money hidden by a gang years ago.

The style of Gary Paulsen's *The Winter Room* is perfectly suited to the storytelling skills of Eldon, an 11-year-old living on a farm in northern Minnesota. Many of his questions gain from his father and Uncle David only puzzling answers, "with words around the edges." "And sometimes Uncle David is never wrong so that might be the way of it." Time to thrash is Father's favorite time "if there's been good rain and the oats and wheat are good, and his sad time if it's been dry and the oats and wheat didn't make right." Fall is the time when "all the grain is up and the barn is full of hay and the fields are tucked in with haystacks waiting to be used and everything is done." Eldon describes arguing with his brother:

> Wayne says there aren't any divisions in things. We had a big fight one time over whether or not there was a place between days when it wasn't the day before and it wasn't tomorrow yet. I said there were places, divisions in things so you could tell one from the next but he said no there wasn't and we set to it. By the time we were done I had a bloody nose . . . .

In Paulsen's survival story *Hatchet,* Brian finds seventeen leathery turtle eggs and knows that to survive he must eat them raw. He sharpens a stick to poke a hole in the shell, widens it with a finger and looks inside to see a yolk of dark yellow. We watch him as he brings the egg to his lips, closes his eyes, squeezes the flexible shell, and swallows as fast as possible. Despite its oily taste, it was an egg. "His throat tried to throw it back up, his whole body seemed to convulse with it, but his stomach took it, held it, and demanded more." The vivid sensory images show Brian's struggle to do what he must to survive.

Retellings and Translations

When a story is no longer protected by copyright laws, publishers may ask different writers to retell the story in "simple" language. *Peter Rabbit,* for example, has been retold countless times, sometimes with didactic messages for children or with new and trite illustrations. Hans Christian Andersen's "The Ugly Duckling" is another such example. For instance, a major children's author, a Newbery Award winner, retells the classic Andersen story in such choppy sentences and drab phrases that it loses all its artistry; sensory appeals vanish with the vanished setting, and characters change to become dull and uninteresting. It is then a plot summary, not the story:

> Once upon a time there was a proud Mama Duck. She was sitting on four eggs, waiting for them to hatch.
>
> . . .
>
> Every day she said, "Quack! Quack! Just wait till my babies come out of their shells. I always have such beautiful ducklings!" . . .
> "Quack! Quack!" the Mama Duck said. "Look at them! How beautiful!"
> "Peep! Peep!" the baby ducks said. "Look at us!"
> Then the Mama Duck looked at the last egg. "Quack! Quack! What's the matter with you? Why don't you hatch?" . . .
> Finally the last shell went *Crack.*

. . . "Quack!" she said. "Oh, no! Something's wrong!" For the last baby duck was not beautiful. He was big and ugly. "Oh, no! How could I hatch an Ugly Duckling?"

Now look at what Andersen actually wrote, as translated by R. P. Keigwin.[2]

Summertime! How lovely it was out in the country, with the wheat standing yellow, the oats green, and the hay all stacked down in the grassy meadows! And there went the stork on his long red legs, chattering away in Egyptian, for he had learnt that language from his mother. The fields and meadows had large woods all around, and in the middle of the woods there were deep lakes.

Yes, it certainly was lovely out in the country. Bathed in sunshine stood an old manor house with a deep moat round it, and growing out of the wall down by the water were huge dock-leaves; the highest of them were so tall that little children could stand upright underneath. The place was as tangled and twisty as the densest forest, and here it was that a duck was sitting on her nest. It was time for her to hatch out her little ducklings, but it was such a long job that she was beginning to lose patience. She hardly ever had a visitor; the other ducks thought more of swimming about in the moat than of coming and sitting under a dock-leaf for the sake of a quack with her.

At last the eggs cracked open one after the other—"peep! peep!"— and all the yolks had come to life and were sticking out their heads.

"Quack, quack!" said the mother duck, and then the little ones scuttled out as quickly as they could, prying all round under the green leaves; and she let them do this as much as they liked, because green is so good for the eyes.

"O, how big the world is!" said the ducklings. And they certainly had much more room now than when they were lying in the egg.

"Do you suppose this is the whole world?" said their mother. "Why, it goes a long way past the other side of the garden, right into the parson's field; but I've never been as far as that. Well, you're all out now, I hope"—and she got up from her nest—"no, not all; the largest egg is still here. How ever long will it be? I can't bother about it much more." And she went on sitting again.

Here are a manor house, a deep moat, enormous dock-leaves so huge children can stand beneath them, a dense, figurative forest all tangled and twisted, an onomatopoeic "scuttling," the nonsensical granting of permission to the ducklings to look all around because green is so good for the eyes, the understatement about the size of the world—right into the parson's fields. The stork speaks Egyptian, and a patient mother continues her lonely vigil waiting for her last egg to hatch.

Our memories of *Tom Sawyer* include adventures and characters as we recall Tom's runaway trip to the pirate island, his surreptitious night visit to Aunt Polly, and Tom, Huck, and Joe as they attend their own funeral. We remember hunting treasure by moonlight and getting lost in the cave, but we may not be aware that these memories are so vivid because of Twain's style; his use of the right word in the right place.

Twain meticulously describes Tom's and Becky's wandering farther and farther away from the cave mouth, intrigued by the possibility of exciting discovery. Notice the imagery and the figurative devices in Twain's description:

> Presently they came to a place where a little stream of water, trickling over a ledge and carrying a limestone sediment with it, had, in the slow-dragging ages, formed a lace and ruffled Niagara in gleaming and imperishable stone. Tom squeezed his small body behind it in order to illuminate it for Becky's gratification.

A reteller of *Tom Sawyer* matter-of-factly substitutes monosyllables and clichés and eliminates the allusion to Niagara Falls.[3] While Twain's Tom *squeezes* behind the ruffled Niagara, the reteller's Tom *steps* behind the falls:

> Soon they came to a place where a little stream, carrying limestone matter with it, had formed a falls of beautiful stone. Since Tom was small, he stepped behind the falls with his candle so that Becky might see the lacy stone lighted in all its glory.

Twain's description is filled with imagery; he uses details to describe the cave:

> In one place they found a spacious cavern from whose ceiling depended a multitude of shining stalactites of the length and circumference of a man's leg. They . . . presently left it by one of the numerous passages.

The reteller eliminates the long words; he substitutes for stalactites a trite comparison to ice that fails to create a picture, and he turns the children's awed exploration into a pleasant walk through a hallway:

> In one place they found a cave from whose top hung something that looked like ice. Parts of this were nearly the size of a man's leg, and when Tom held his candle up toward them, they shown in the light. The children walked all about this cave, wondering and admiring, and finally left by one of the halls.

Twain shows the children wondering, admiring, marveling, and being bewitched by turns. He creates mounting suspense, his imagery showing the enormous, endless caverns and corridors of the cave. His verbs change from those of appreciative awe to verbs of vigorous action that show Tom's fear and arouse fear in the reader: seizing, hurrying, darting, striking, chasing, plunging. However, when the reteller substitutes more ordinary

Retelling does not always improve a story, but may instead make the story drab.

verbs—saw, flew, put out, hurried—the action loses its suspense. As for the cave, Twain's is a labyrinth of endless passageways and a limitless lake; we fear that Tom and Becky will never find their way out. In the reteller's version of the story, two children merely come to a small hall.

We might point out many more contrasts in the two versions of *Tom Sawyer,* each one showing how the loss of freshness in style results in the loss of suspense in the action, depth in the characterization, and vividness in the setting. The two stories are vastly different, even though the same events are carefully reported in the retelling. The reason for the difference is not what happens, but how the writer selects and uses words to show what happens. This is style.

Translations may present other problems. In an otherwise beautifully translated story, *The Island on Bird Street* by Israeli author Uri Orlev, translator Hillel Halkin occasionally lapses from informal language into American slang. Polish Alex, the first-person narrator who is hiding in the ruins of the Warsaw ghetto of Holocaust days, is "bushed" (exhausted); feels "like a dope"; and is told to "shut up." Although these lapses seem trivial, in an otherwise seamless narrative that is totally convincing—rooted as it clearly is in the reality of Orlev's experience—they call attention to the story as a translation from another language in a way that *Island of the Blue Dolphins* does not. Lest these brief comments detract too much from an excellent and engrossing narrative, notice the convincing language describing Alex's scavenging efforts.

> A word or phrase of slang may be so out of place that it disrupts credibility.

> I decided to make just one bundle of clothes. Into it went a few things that fit me, the suits for father, the coat, and some towels and sheets. I found a beat-up Polish army hat, the kind tough Polish kids like to wear, and stuck it happily on my head. Then I filled a second blanket with books and dragged the two bundles to the entrance to the cellar, where I took them apart and carried in a few things at a time. Before it got dark I went back again and took a mattress. I picked a nice soft one. And then I made one last trip for a folding chair that I managed to fit through the opening too.

Stories of Other Periods and Places

Word choice, or **diction,** should give the reader the flavor of the time, the place, and the events; this the writer does by use of language that seems native to the period and locality of the story.

Fantasy is maintained in *The Moorchild* by Eloise McGraw not only by using folktale elements like the changeling traded for a human being, but also by the rich cadences and unusual figurative language. Eavesdropping on the activities of the "Folk," "they boasted of their pranks around the cookfires; one had stripped a farmer's honeycombs, another emptied a fisherman's basket as fast as he filled it. . . . [Life] as it was meant to be . . . went on, seamlessly, until she and the other younglings had finished their nighttime learning and began to go abroad by day—to find out about dogs and iron and crosses, and humans who were not safely asleep but awake and wary." Here fantasy creates another world or society that uses its own vocabulary. An argument becomes an argle-bargle, a trundle bed a truckle bed, a fool a lackbrain, disciplinary detention a tether, and to hurry is to skimble-skamble. When the moorchild is angry, she "vents her baffled spleen," and when meaning is clear, it is "clear as a shout." Flavor and color are appropriate in *The Moorchild;* they apply to time, place, characters, and genre.

The same statement can be made of Ozark diction in *Where the Lilies Bloom.* As she works her way wildcrafting through dense weeds high as her head, Mary Call is "alone on this blasted mountain working myself to a frazzle." She thinks she must "have moss growing inside [her] head where [her] brains should be." "Nobody but a poor dement" would take on "three snot-nosed kids to raise." "If I had the sense of a rabbit or even half that much, I'd just take off across that bald over there and go down the other side of it . . . and never look back." Although the times and places of their lives are different from our own, the styles of these two novels give us universal characters in whose experiences we believe.

Another example, *Anpao: An American Indian Odyssey* by Native American author Jamake Highwater, is written in the style and form of the oral tale. The holy man Wasicong tells the story of Anpao's lengthy and dangerous quest, a task set for him by the beautiful Ko-ko-mik-e-is, whom he wants to marry. With his contrary twin Oapna, he must travel to the Sun and get his permission for the marriage. As we follow Anpao, the storyteller maintains a serious, mystical tone achieved by the evocation of the natural world, the formality of the language, and the long cadences of oral telling:

> Once again the sacred pipe was lighted and, under the new stars and among all the people of the land, it was passed around the great circle where the twins sat with the old swan-woman. The campfire rose into delicately twisting flames and the drums sang. . . .
>
> Oapna had fallen asleep while the old woman told her story, and he lay wrapped in a blanket of swan feathers. But even in his sleep he seemed to ebb and drift in the new light of the Sun.

Laurence Yep's novel *The Star Fisher* tells of a 15-year-old Chinese-American girl who has moved from the big city of Toledo to a small town in West Virginia, there to face the bigotry of an insular society that has never met anyone of Chinese heritage. Yep's story chronicles a variety of

Style is also compatible with setting.

discriminatory experiences met by the children in school and in the town, a situation comparable to that in the old Chinese tale for which the book is named. It tells of star fisher birds, mystical creatures or changelings who are not at home on earth as people but nevertheless must stay. The necessity for each of us to understand groups in a multicultural society is well served by the realistic story. It is, however, interesting to note the difference in style between the narrator Joan's language as she tells the Chinese folktale to her little sister and her speaking style for the rest of the story:

> "[The three women] were dressed in silken gowns—though the farmer could not decide what color they were because they seemed to change every moment. Around the women's shoulders were cloaks of golden feathers that rippled with a soft light of their own like the sunlight on the surface of a pond."

The melodious language of the folktale evokes images of beauty through such terms as "silken gowns," "cloaks of golden feathers," "rippled," "sunlight on the surface"; the remaining narrative is the crisper speech of a schoolgirl:

> I snatched up Bobby's [lunch bag] just before the wind sent it swirling away. And as I sat folding up old paper bags, I could hear the laughter and happy shouts all around me; and I felt as I were trapped inside some glass cage—cut off from the laughter and happy voices that surrounded me.

Grab Hands and Run by Frances Temple is the story of escape to the North made by fugitive slaves. Not only is it a pleasure to be caught up in the excitement of a successful escape, but the account is made stylistically interesting by its vivid imagery and figurative language. Fear grips the small family, "making a hole in my brain," thinks Felipe. "Mama is like a balloon about to burst, a volcano ready to explode." A voice "comes from the shadow of a boathouse at the end of the dock. A man steps out suddenly, silently. He has on a leather hat and a gray serape. He smells of fish and sour tequila, and his eyes in the lantern light are red and vivid. . . . The man's voice comes out in short growls." Style increases suspense as the reader wonders if the newcomer is friend or foe.

Stories of other cultures and times make special demands upon the writer. Before we can accept them as believable, we must first believe that the characters are human beings like ourselves. To understand the new culture, we must see the particular differences between our own lives and those of other people. Style makes the difference.

High Fantasy

Since the most significant struggle in all human experience is that between the forces of good and evil, it seems appropriate that the language of high fantasy should have dignity. Spicing her serious tone and elevated diction with occasional humor—in descriptions of her pets, the foltstza and the yerig, for example—Robin McKinley uses long, complex sentences and slow cadences in *The Hero and the Crown*. Here elevated language appears in the final lines of the novel as we read of the years following Aerin's defeat of the dragon Mauer and the ascent of Tor and Aerin to the throne:

> Perhaps the memory of the reek of Mauer's despair made her a little forgetful too, for she began to think of the wide silver lake as a place she had visited only in dreams; for the not quite mortal part of her did sleep, that she might love her country and her husband.

Summary

Few of us are content with plot summary as a substitute for the story itself. What happened to the ugly duckling or to Mary Call was not merely plot, since action alone does not make absorbing hours of reading. Helpful as Charles and Mary Lamb are in *Tales from Shakespeare,* the book is no substitute for Shakespeare, and a quick look at a book of plot summaries reminds us that *Tom Sawyer* and *Little Women* were never like this. Any good story is words, many words, selected and arranged in a manner that best creates character, draws setting, recounts conflict, builds suspense to a climax, and ties it all together with some significance.

Style involves the use of comparisons or figurative language appropriate to the story; imagery that describes for the senses what is happening or how things look; exaggeration or understatement to entertain or to heighten feelings; allusions to people or events already known; wordplay with puns or echoes; and sound devices to give pleasure and to heighten meaning. Appropriateness and freshness—the sense that these words are the best possible words for this particular story—are not only the style of the story; they *are* the story.

Notes

1. Henry James, *The Art of Fiction and Other Essays* (New York: Oxford University Press, 1948).
2. Hans Christian Andersen, *The Ugly Duckling,* translated by R. P. Keigwin, illustrated by Adrienne Adams (New York: Scribner's, 1965).
3. *Tom Sawyer,* adapted by Albert O. Berglund (Glenview, Ill.: Scott, Foresman, 1949).

Recommended Books Cited in This Chapter

ANDERSEN, HANS CHRISTIAN. *The Ugly Duckling*. Translated by R. P. Keigwin. New York: Scribner's, 1965.

BROOKS, BRUCE. *The Moves Make the Man*. New York: Harper & Row, 1984.

CARROLL, LEWIS. *Alice's Adventures in Wonderland*. 1865. Reprint. New York: Macmillan, 1963.

CLEAVER, VERA, AND BILL CLEAVER. *Where the Lilies Bloom*. Philadelphia: Lippincott, 1969.

CUSHMAN, KAREN. *The Midwife's Apprentice*. New York: Houghton Mifflin, 1995.

ESTES, ELEANOR. *The Moffats*. New York: Harcourt, 1941.

FOX, PAULA. *Monkey Island*. New York: Orchard, 1991.

HIGHWATER, JAMAKE. *Anpao: An American Indian Odyssey*. Philadelphia: Lippincott, 1977.

HUDSON, JAN. *Sweetgrass*. New York: Philomel, 1989.

McGRAW, ELOISE. *The Moorchild*. New York: Simon & Schuster, 1996.

McKINLEY, ROBIN. *The Hero and the Crown*. New York: Greenwillow, 1985.

MYERS, WALTER DEAN. *The Mouse Rap*. New York: Harper & Row, 1990.

O'DELL, SCOTT. *Island of the Blue Dolphins*. Boston: Houghton Mifflin, 1960.

———. *The King's Fifth*. Boston: Houghton Mifflin, 1966.

ORLEV, URI. *The Island on Bird Street*. Translated by Hillel Halkin. Boston: Houghton Mifflin, 1984.

PAULSEN, GARY. *Hatchet*. New York: Bradbury, 1987.

———. *The Winter Room*. New York: Orchard Press, 1989.

PECK, ROBERT NEWTON. *Soup's Hoop*. New York: Dell, 1992.

STEMPLE, FRANCES. *Grab Hands and Run*. New York: Orchard Press, 1993.

TWAIN, MARK. *The Adventures of Tom Sawyer*. 1876. Reprint. New York: Macmillan, 1966.

WANGERIN, WALTER. *Elizabeth and the Water-Troll*. New York: HarperCollins, 1991.

WHITE, E. B. *Charlotte's Web*. New York: Harper & Row, 1952.

WOJCIECHOWSKA, MAIA. *Shadow of a Bull*. New York: Simon & Schuster, 1964.

YEP, LAURENCE. *The Star Fisher*. New York: Morrow, 1991.

Alice's Adventures in Wonderland
Lewis Carroll (ill. John Tenniel)

10

Tone

Can you identify tone in a children's novel? Why does it matter?

We hear the command from old cowboy movies—"Smile when you say that!" and we know what the speaker means: "If you call me your friend, a smile will say you mean it, a frown will mean the opposite." Although identical words are used, friend or enemy can change meaning by adding a smile. The same words spoken by a teacher to a child acquire a different tone for different situations by the change in voice inflection. Pulling a rebellious child into the classroom, a teacher says, "Come on!" Encouraging a child to try the new word puzzle, the teacher says, "Come on!" Rejecting a long-winded excuse from the child who must clear the work table, the teacher says, "Come on!" Each time the words have different meanings because inflection, or vocal tone, changes meaning.

Just as tone of voice reveals how a speaker feels about his or her subject, **tone** in literature tells us how the author feels about his or her subject. In literature, however, we cannot rely upon inflection in a writer's voice. We rely entirely upon words. Words express the writer's attitude toward his or her work, subject, and readers. Without vocal inflection to help convey tone, the writer must choose words with great care.

The author's **style** conveys the tone in literature. Sentence structure, word choice, patterns, arrangements—all influence style. Figures of speech are chosen for their sounds, as well as for their meaning. All these choices create the style and determine the tone of the writing, revealing the attitude of the writer toward both the subject and the reader.

You may feel that tone is too subtle a literary element to be found in children's literature. But this is not so. For example, most readers would agree that Kipling's tone in *Just So Stories* is humorous. Kipling's way of saying "This is the way it all happened—just so" is his own unique combination of matter-of-fact and humor:

> So the Elephant's Child went home across Africa frisking and whisking his trunk. . . . When he wanted grass he plucked grass up from the ground, instead of going on his knees as he used to do. When the flies bit him he broke off the branch of a tree and used it as a fly-whisk: and he made himself a new, cool, slushy-squshy mud-cap whenever the sun was hot.

We suspend our disbelief and say wouldn't-it-be-fun-if, toying with the idea that it might really have happened this way. Because we like the pompous Bi-Coloured-Python-Rock-Snake, and the Crocodile with his "musky tusky mouth" who stretches the "mere smear nose" into a handy trunk, we play along with Kipling's "facts" about how the elephant got his trunk. The tone here is the feeling resulting from all the elements working together—the mock-serious situation Kipling is reporting, the tongue-in-cheek characterization, the playful language, the deliberately overplayed, pretentious style. The humorous tone results from all of these.[1]

Tone cannot be isolated from word in the story.

Tone in the *Just So Stories,* like tone in any writing, cannot be isolated from the words of the story. More specifically, words of all kinds, as well as the sounds of these words, show tone, and tone influences meaning. "Frisking," "whisking," and "plucking" are playful and lighthearted kinds of action expressed in short vowels and quick consonants. Their kinds of action are quite different from the action suggested by, for example, "slamming, banging, and breaking." If the light, rapid sounds of "fly whisk" became "flyswatter," tone would become more serious; if the Elephant Child's "schloopy-sloshy mud-cap all trickly behind the ears" became instead an objectively described "cold, messy, runny mudpie dripping behind the ears," the harsher consonants and the longer vowels would influence and change the tone. Kipling's choice of playful words and quickly moving cadences makes his pretense of factual reporting into humorous spoof.

We have noted the literary meaning of point of view as the mind or minds through which we see the story—the voice telling the story, whether a character or an omniscient author. Tone is different. It is the author's attitude toward story and readers. By the writer's choice of materials, the writer almost inevitably reveals something about his or her own personality. If the author were telling the story orally, voice tone would reveal attitude and self; since the author is telling the story in print, the choices of words must be the means of showing attitude.

Tone in *Charlotte's Web*

How do we discover tone? We can often describe a writer's tone but are not aware of how we discovered it. Tone seems to creep into our consciousness without our being aware of it. But tone, like the showing of action, depiction of character, and description of setting, is created by the writer's choice of words. If we look carefully at a few passages from *Charlotte's Web*, we may see how White's tone is revealed.

The first pages of the book are filled with kindness and affection: Mr. Arable looks at Fern "with love," and speaks to her "gently." Fern kisses her father and mother, pleased that the runt pig is safe. White describes the setting and the characters in the same kinds of affectionate terms. The action—Wilbur spinning a web, for example, or fainting at his honors—is humorous and yet affectionate.

The chapter "Summer Days" begins with a description of setting:

> The early summer days on a farm are the happiest and fairest days of the year. Lilacs bloom and make the air sweet, and then fade. Apple blossoms come with the lilacs, and the bees visit around among the apple trees. The days grow warm and soft. School ends, and children have time to play and to fish for trouts in the brook.
>
> . . . All morning you could hear the rattle of the machine as it went round and round, while the tall grass fell down behind the cutter bar in long green swathes. Next day . . . the hay would be hauled to the barn in the high hay wagon, with Fern and Avery riding at the top of the load. Then the hay would be hoisted, sweet and warm, into the big loft, until the whole barn seemed like a wonderful bed of timothy and clover. It was fine to jump in, and perfect to hide in.

In this selection, there are nothing but pleasant sensory images—fragrant lilacs, apple blossoms visited by friendly bees, children fishing for trout. Summer work goes on, but the sights and sounds are pleasant; work is another kind of sensory pleasure—rhythmic "round and round," colorful "long green swathes," sweet-smelling clover, a soft timothy bed for playing in. The abstract terms "happiest," "fairest," "warm," and "soft" describe the days, while "wonderful," "fine," and "perfect" describe the fun the days bring. Both the abstract words and the vivid appeals to our five senses have pleasant connotations. Summertime is not marred by a single unpleasant image or connotation. Summer fun is also humorous; Avery carries in his pocket a stiff, warm trout to be fried for dinner, or finds a slender grass snake and pockets it. Like the rest of the story, this chapter is filled with descriptions of a serene and pleasant world. White loves the summertime, the farm, the children, and the animals. Although White later builds suspense to a strong climax, his affectionate descriptions of all that summer brings have assured us that he will not permit disaster to come. While his emphasis upon the cycle of seasons prepares us for change, he never suggests in his choice of words that the change will bring tragedy or despair. Summing up White's attitude toward his story, we can best characterize it as humorous affection. As White goes on to compare a gray spider to a gumdrop, the contours of a gluttonous rat to a jelly jar, and to describe a pig as ter-rific, radiant, and humble, we see affection and humor in all that happens in the story. White's word choices—style—have determined tone.

Humor

Humor is an important tone in children's literature. Much of the humor comes from situation, that is, incongruous happenings that make children laugh. The cow jumping over the moon, the barber shaving a pig—these situations are funny to a small child. Situation or action is also the source of humor in Astrid Lindgren's *Pippi Longstocking* and Robert McCloskey's *Homer Price*. But these stories are more than pie-throwing cartoons; they have invention and absurdity expressed in straightforward language.

Other stories depend for their humor upon style or unexpected phras-ing as well as upon situation. Ludwig Bemelmans's *Madeline,* for example, in which the diction is precise and brief, not only shows a humorous situa-tion, but also describes the situation in fresh and unexpected wording, rhythm, and rhyme. The crack upon the ceiling whose habit it is to look like a rabbit is situation nonsense; it is also humorous absurdity because of the unexpected internal rhyme and the personification that accompanies cracks having habits. The source of humor in *Winnie-the-Pooh* does not lie in the situation alone—sailing off on an overturned umbrella or disguising oneself as a black cloud. The humor rises as much from the quiet, almost solemn wording of conversations and descriptions surrounding the absurdities.

Few writers use humor as skillfully and pervasively as does Betsy Byars. Open any of her stories to any page, and you are likely to find reason for chuckling. In *The Burning Questions of Bingo Brown,* for example, the class bully moves into the house next door to Bingo, a bully so objectionable that he insults everyone.

> Mamie Lou's insult was, "Mamie Lou, you are a perfect 10. Your face is a two, your body is a two, your legs are a two . . . ."
> Tom Knott's was, "Tom, your nose is so big it has its own zip code."
> Melissa's was, "Melissa, you have the face of a saint—a Saint Bernard."
> "Harriet, you may not have invented ugliness, but you sure are the local distributor."

In *Bingo Brown, Gypsy Lover,* Bingo pedals to the post office to mail his Christmas gift earrings to Melissa.

> Bingo stepped up and took the post office pen. He had always wanted a reason to use this pen.

On the inside of the card he wrote, "Well, here they are, Melissa. I hope you like them. I wish I could see your ears with them in them."

He regretted that "them in them." It wasn't topnotch writing. But the post office pen didn't erase.

He added:

Merry Christmas forever.

Open another of Byars's books, *The Blossoms and the Green Phantom*, and again find not only the humor of language but the humor of situation. Pap, hearing a puppy whine from the dumpster, climbs up to rescue it, and because of his weak knees, falls into the dumpster. From there he scares a woman depositing her trash, falls asleep exhausted from trying to get out, and then is grateful to the police for rescuing him. "It would be a terrible, terrible thing for a man to die in a dumpster."

Meanwhile, the Green Phantom, Junior's space ship made of helium-filled garbage bags and an air mattress, gets caught on Mr. Benson's chicken house roof; when Junior climbs up to reach it, he gets stuck. "[M]aybe I should just do the sensible thing and stay up here for the rest of my life." To Junior, the Green Phantom is the most beautiful thing in the world, and now it is going around the world. Considering their adventures, it is true, as Junior says, that "we Blossoms have never been just anybody."

A humorous tone carries Phyllis Shalant's *Beware of Kissing Lizard Lips* as each of the agonies of early adolescence comes along, from "muscles like pimples" to first boy-girl parties and unexpected hormone rages. Zach spends every spare minute trying to grow in both height and strength, and will try anything. After he connects with Nikki who can teach him tae kwon do, he joins her at the ice rink despite his wobbly ankles.

> Zach took a deep breath and pushed off with his right leg. But the ground refused to stay still. He brought his left foot down too quickly, snagging the ice so that he almost tripped. To catch himself, he threw his body backward, except then his right skate began sliding out from under him. To regain his balance, he waved his arms.
>
> "Quack! Quack!" someone called.

The humor of Paula Danziger in *Everyone Else's Parents Said Yes* whips along with jokes and cracks and insults and put-downs. Writing this time about a boy protagonist, Matthew Martin, Danziger's major focus is the tormenting of brothers and sisters and of 11-year-old classmates, boys against girls against boys. Its humor relies to some extent upon "gross" behavior, typical of children at this age.

For younger readers, Ellen Conford's Jenny Archer books are also humorous. In *What's Cooking, Jenny Archer?* for example, Jenny decides to be a creative cook and is commissioned to make school lunches for five of her friends. Her profits are quickly eaten up at the grocery store, and when her clam dip mixtures and her peanut butter with pineapple and cucumber sandwiches aren't acceptable to her customers, they all want their money back, and Jenny decides to write a cookbook instead. In *A Job for Jenny Archer,* Jenny has only 27 cents to buy her mother a fur coat for her birthday. To earn money, she tries dog training and baby sitting, but each ends in disaster. Her venture into real estate sales consists of showing people through her own house—to her parents' dismay.

The consistently humorous tone of Paula Danziger's *Earth to Matthew* is once again a clever and accurate rendition of sixth-grade dialogue. Focusing on the put-downs of boys to girls and girls to boys. she uses vivid and specific language to keep laughter in the air. When Mrs. Stanton, a wonderfully creative and lighthearted teacher, asks for an example of the ecological chain, "how one thing environmentally affects something else," Matthew's response is directed at his nemesis, Vanessa:

> "Like if someone, who will remain nameless, was outside one day and a giant vulture swooped down, captured her, took her back to its nest, and the baby vultures ate her. Then the barfing baby birds fell out of the nest into the water and died, polluting the water with the disgustingness of the nameless person. Then the fish who got sick from the pollution got scooped up into a net and sold to the company that sells stuff to the school cafeteria. Then we all got sick from the polluted fish cakes. That's how it works, right?"

A few paragraphs later, hungry Tyler, who dreads polluted fish cakes for lunch, is disgusted by the class discussion of the ecological impact of disposable diapers; further humorous dialogue of a slightly scatological nature follows—another kind of childhood humor.

In writing *Ali Baba Bernstein,* Johanna Hurwitz shows clearly how well she knows eight-year-olds. Each chapter begins with a different, exact recitation of David's age: eight years, four months, and sixteen days. Tired of being one of many Davids, he has changed his name to Ali Baba, another gambit common to eight- and nine-year-olds. Ali Baba, who fancies himself a detective, follows every false clue to its humorous conclusion. Finally, he invites all of the David Bernsteins in the phone book to his birthday party. The tone is sustained throughout, and there is laughter on every page.

Strong rivalry carries the plot of *Supermouse* by British writer Jean Ure, but humor, in both text and Ellen Eagle's illustrations, is its delight. Long, skinny, smart Nicola is never appreciated, while every little simpering thing her sister Rose does is praised and touted. Because the point of view is Nicola's, we know her resentment and her ways of getting back at Rose. Assigned to walk Ben the dog, Nicola chooses the forbidden building site where she can be alone on the mud mound to act out her fury at Rose:

Nicola, long-leggity in black wool tights and a red plaid skirt that didn't reach her knees, did a little twirl, tiptoe in the mud.

"Such a *dear* little girl—such a *sweet* little girl—"

Primp, preen, simper, simper.

"Just *see* how she can point her toe! See her curtsy—see her pirouette—"

Nicola pirouetted vigorously on the top of her mud bank.

"See her fall flat on ber silly fat face—"

BANG.

Slap, thud, into the mud.

"Nicola *burt* me, Nicola's been *mean* to me . . . boo hoo! Now I'm all *dirty*—"

Absorbed in being Rose, Nicola covered her face and roared, dramatically.

"Yes, and serve you jolly well *right!*"

With a demonic yell, she sprang off the mound. . . . "Silly, simpering, self-righteous *cow!*"

Whooping and hallooing, she danced around the mound.

Nicola's long legs are compared to those of a bird; she looks like a heron, her mother says. Her skin is sallow; she has no waist, though Nicola knows "it was there, in the middle of her body, the same as everyone else's."

Many stories would not be called humorous in tone, and yet they have moments of humor. In Katherine Paterson's *Jacob Have I Loved,* for example, the Captain takes a swing at the tomcat and yells, "Damn it to hell!" Call is shocked, saying that is against the commandments, but the Captain replies, "Call, I know those blasted commandments as well as you do, and there is not one word in them about how to speak to tomcats." Gleefully, Wheeze screeches through her laughter, "I bet there's not one word in the whole blasted Bible on how to speak to cats."

Stories for very young readers need not be written in drab prose, but may be as lively and entertaining as those for older readers. Patricia Reilly Giff, who writes for children in the early elementary grades, successfully holds our attention with humor and real understanding of the concerns of that age group. In *Matthew Jackson Meets the Wall,* for instance, the worries about moving to a new town, a new home, a new school, and new friends are central. Matthew has much to hide: his poor reading and spelling skills, the new house that looks haunted, his cat Barney's disappearance, and the Wall, the boy next door who, he's been told, is fierce. In vivid prose we read how Matthew practices karate stance and shadowboxes to prove to himself that he's tough, but then finds there is nothing to worry about.

We expect children to laugh at situation humor, since it is easy to see. But we underestimate children when we assume that is all that they can find humorous. We limit children's discovery when we limit their exposure to the simplest and most obvious. A double row of beds and a double file of children is the situation humor of *Madeline.* However, "lived twelve little girls in two straight lines" is the sophisticated humor of style. Children deserve this source of humor, too.

Small children can appreciate verbal as well as situation humor.

Parody

Parody is usually a device for older readers, since it relies on the reader's memory of a known piece of writing or of a way of talking. It retains the form of the original but changes the words and the tone for humorous effect. "An hour of freedom is worth a barrel of slops" is a simple parody of an old saying—an ounce of prevention is worth a pound of cure. A parody reminds us of something known, then gives fresh pleasure by duplicating form that contrasts to new and humorous meaning. A clear parody for children is the bedtime story that Charlotte tells Wilbur. It has the traditional beginning, as well as the fluid phrasing, of folk or fairy tale. Within the folktale parody is a description of the struggling fish trapped in the spider web. Read the paragraph aloud and notice its similarity to a prizefight account:

> "There was my cousin, slipping in, dodging out. . . . dancing in, dancing out, throwing her threads and fighting hard. First she threw a left around the tail. The fish lashed back. Then a left to the tail and a right to . . . ."

And again, try square dancing while Charlotte spins her web:

> "Now for the R! Up we go! Attach! Descend! Pay out line! . . . Whoa, girl! Steady now! . . . Now right and down and swing that loop and around and around! O.K.! Easy, keep those lines together! . . ."

The child catches some of the pleasures of White's parody and wordplay, but the adult catches many more; the result is pleasure for everyone. Carroll's literary parodies are extremely witty—Robert Southey's "The Old Man's Comforts" becomes "You Are Old, Father William," for example. But with the exception perhaps of "Twinkle, twinkle, little bat," they are unrecognized by the child—or by most of today's adults, for that matter. White, however, parodies word patterns from three familiar situations—folktale, prizefight, and square dance. Wit explained loses its wittiness, and these need no explanations.

A rare triumph in parody for small children occurs in *Santa Cows,* a picture book by Cooper Edens illustrated by Daniel Lane; success results from children's familiarity with "The Night Before Christmas." Using the exact rhythms and general outline of the original, the story tells of cows floating down through the chimney, singing carols with the family, giving game-play gifts, and stopping to play baseball in the snow of Christmas Eve.

Differing Tastes in Tone

We all bring to a story our own backgrounds and experiences, and the story has a personal meaning for us because we respond out of our own emotional history and present feelings. Readers, however, can only take from a story something already put into the story by the writer; tone is the effect of the writer's words. If two readers describe tone differently, it is often the result of personal definitions of their descriptive terms, or the result of differing personal taste and experience.

Response to literature is a transaction between reader and writer.

Frances Hodgson Burnett's *The Secret Garden* is a story about an unloved little girl sent to live with a grieving uncle, who pays little or no attention to her. Mary's loneliness sends her out into the unkempt but once luxurious garden, where she finds a secret door to a secret garden that she tends lovingly. Finding in the huge mansion an equally isolated and unloved boy named Colin, she joins him, and together they restore the garden and themselves to health. To some readers Burnett's tone may seem cute, coy, or sentimental as her use of the omniscient point of view takes us into the minds of birds and flowers:

> The bulbs in the secret garden must have been much astonished. Such nice clear spaces were made round them that they had all the breathing space they wanted, and . . . they began to cheer up under the dark earth and work tremendously. The sun could get at them and warm them, and when the rain came down it could reach them at once, so they began to feel very much alive . . . .

> The first moment [the robin] set his dew-bright black eye on Dickon he was not a stranger, but a sort of robin without beak or feathers. He could speak robin (which is quite a distinct language not to be mistaken for any other). To speak robin to a robin is like speaking French to a Frenchman. . . . The robin thought he spoke this gibberish to them because they were not intelligent enough to understand feathered speech.

In recent years *The Secret Garden*[2] has once again become loved by many children. The many beautiful colored and black-and-white illustrations by Shirley Hughes placed throughout the story in a recent edition no doubt play a part, as does a reawakened interest in fantasy, to say nothing of the successful musical of recent years. But perhaps after a lengthy run of severely despairing books, violent films, and news stories about the horrors of reality, *The Secret Garden* returns readers to a peaceful and hopeful world where children enjoy innocent play and awaken love in an idealized world.

The tone of *Winnie-the-Pooh* may seem to some readers whimsically affectionate. Pooh and Piglet do not converse in fragments the way we do, but in long, complex sentences filled with "that" clauses. And all the time, what they discuss so gravely is near nonsense:

> "I think that I have just remembered something. I have just remembered something that I forgot to do yesterday and shan't be able to do tomorrow. So I suppose I really ought to go back and do it now."
>
> "It isn't the sort of thing you can do in the afternoon," said Piglet quickly. "It's a very particular morning thing, that has to be done in the morning, and, if possible, between the hours of—What would you say the time was?"

One reader calls the tone whimsical and playful. Another reader, thinking the playfulness and sentiment excessive, reads Christopher Robin's words, "Oh, Bear . . . how I do love you!" and says this is not a lightly affectionate tone, but sentimentality—an adult talking the way children never talk. The same words are used by the writer; two different readers receive them. The differing opinions might be called a matter of taste. Children, like adults, have their personal preferences. They may not define their reactions in terms of tone, but they may think the Pooh stories are "funny," or "silly," or "boring." On questioning them, we may find that these children are responding to what they see as Milne's attitude toward his material and his readers—in other words, tone.

Tone Related to the Author's Choice of Materials

Any kind of tone can be found in any kind of genre of children's literature. A fantasy, for example, may be serious in tone to fit its serious themes, as Robin McKinley demonstrates in *The Blue Sword*. Or the tone may be lighthearted, as it is in *The Wind in the Willows,* which—with its little universe of peace, its pictures of natural beauty, and its variety of friendly and harmless animal characters in a quiet country setting—shows in its tone Grahame's attitude toward his characters and his story. In gentle and kindly acceptance, Grahame not only observes but enjoys the differences among the characters, their styles of living, their preferences, and their habits. Bountiful leisure, filled with lunches, snacks, picnics, and breakfast extending into lunchtime, and all surrounded by profound good will, occupies a benevolent world.

First, notice how the setting reflects Grahame's tone. Rat loves his river. When the brown flood water "all drops away and shows patches of mud that smells like plum-cake, and the rushes and weeds clog the channels," Rat "can potter about dry-shod over most of the bed of it and find fresh food to eat." That is when Rat loves his river best. "Plum-cake" and "potter about" are connotative of comfort and happiness. The river is Rat's world and its banks are covered with his friends. Mole learns to love it, too, to enter "into the joy of running water."

Badger is the perfect host in his house "behind comfortable-looking doors," a cozy home with "wide hearth," chairs grouped "sociably," "spotless plates" winking from the shelves, and rafters hung with stored harvest: "The ruddy brick floor smiled up at the smoky ceiling; the oaken settles, shiny with long wear, exchanged cheerful glances with each other; plates on the dresser grinned at pots on the shelf, and the merry firelight flickered and played over everything without distinction." Everything in Badger's house is friendly; each item is personified and made to smile, to glance cheerfully, to grin, to play and be merry.

Mole's home, too, although it is also underground, has a welcoming front yard that shows love of home and a hospitable welcome: "A garden-seat stood on one side of the door. . . . On the walls hung wire baskets with ferns in them . . . a skittle-alley, with benches along it and little wooden tables marked with rings that hinted at beer-mugs." Here, also, the setting shows tone: the pleasant game court, lined with spectator benches and tables, shows a generous host who serves his friends refreshments in leisurely comfort.

This same kindness and acceptance appear in the characters' attitudes toward one another. Impetuous braggart Toad is "the best of animals. . . . So simple, so good-natured, and so affectionate. Perhaps he's not very clever—we can't all be geniuses; and it may be that he is both boastful and conceited. But he has got some great qualities, has Toady." Such terms as "accepting," "kindly," "friendly," or "genial" might describe tone, but all spring from the close relationship between the idyllic country setting and the gentle, accepting characters.

In her several books about Lynn, Mouse, and Mrs. Toggle the witch, Phyllis Naylor tells a spooky story, successfully awakening the reader's fear. As we note their behavior in a totally realistic story of the two girls in school, at home, on their bikes, in the cemetery where they talk staring up at the clouds, we are convinced by her matter-of-fact tone that these are normal girls and everyday occurrences and behaviors. But in *The Witch's Eye,* whenever the glass eye—all that remained when Mrs. Toggle was killed in her burning house—is present, the tone becomes mysterious. The eye causes Lynn and her little brother, Stevie, to be drawn to the river, to behave cruelly to family and friends, to sing the frightening song that croons, "Hear the shadows whisper back." They even seem to age and become the evil Mrs. Toggle. The eye winks, it sings a spooky song, and seems to bring a flock of crows that circle Lynn's house. Naylor successfully balances the realistic and the fantastic by adhering to suitable tone in each instance.

A humorous tone dominates the first part of *The Watsons Go to Birmingham* by Christopher Paul Curtis. Ten-year-old Kenny is taunted by his teasing older brother, King Cool Byron, who continually works at being a bad boy. When Kenny and his sister Joetta complain about wearing piles of warm clothes that their Southern mother insists upon lest they "freeze solid," By claims it's true. Furthermore, they mustn't ever look inside the garbage trucks with the huge mouths because early each morning the workers pick up all the bodies so frozen they "won't bend in the middle" and disposes of them. The tone becomes serious, however, once the family reaches Birmingham, where the Watsons experience racism. Now By is strong and tender, comforting the panicked family when the Sunday School where Joetta is thought to be is bombed. Tone changes as the situation changes.

Tone is hopeful in Lois Lowry's *The Giver*. A new society is examined, and its shortcomings suggest its end. In the impersonal society, people are in artificially constructed groups of spouses and "newchildren" known by their functions assigned by the governing council. As the Receiver of history and memories, Jonas the narrator receives all past memories from the elderly Giver. As he learns bit by bit about something called "family"—that something called "love" connected people with one another, that old people were not "released" but kept in the family as beloved grandparents—Jonas becomes uneasy. When he learns that being "released to Elsewhere" is really being killed, he can no longer stay in his honored role as Receiver, but with baby Gabriel, whose development is ominously slow, he takes off on his bicycle for an old-fashioned community. Optimism wins as he sees one ahead.

Literature for children should and usually does touch on the particular concerns of children in today's world; one of these is the single parent. Ivy Ruckman in *Who Invited the Undertaker?* focuses on Dale's worry about the depression of his mother, Cathy, following her husband's death, and about the family's financial struggle. As children often do, Dale seeks a partner for his mother. Although his letter to the personal ads describing her interests draws women callers because he alludes to her only as "C," Dale does manage to set up a meeting with John that seems promising. The title of the story relates to the young undertaker-in-training who is at-

Tone need not remain the same; as a story's tension rises, tone may change.

tracted to his mother and may be fun, but is also struggling financially. John has the advantage. Cathy becomes a fighter for all single parents when she insists that father-son and mother-daughter programs are discriminatory. Although these are serious issues, Ruckman maintains a humorous tone in dialogue and in sustaining Dale's point of view.

Such a mixture is also apparent in Phyllis Naylor's *Reluctantly Alice,* a story filled with Alice's concern for her father's happiness, but also with humor and the usual traumas of a seventh-grade girl who wants everyone to like her. Elizabeth and Pamela talk about seeing boys naked. They have made a pact to tell each other everything, even embarrassing things, and not to laugh:

> "Well . . ." Elizabeth raised her shoulders and took a deep breath, then stared down at her feet. "I'm twelve years old, I'm in junior high, but I've—I've never seen a boy naked."
>
> I was waiting for her to get to the point, then realized that *was* the point.
>
> "So?" I said. "Elizabeth, you can still graduate."

Science fiction and high fantasy need carefully controlled tone to persuade us to suspend disbelief willingly, as does H. M. Hoover in *The Lost Star.* The protagonist Lian seems at home in the environment of Balthor, where her aircar has crashed; familiar with many of the space sights, sounds, and inventions, Lian accepts them. Carried by the sense that Lian is comfortable here, and yet that Lian like us wishes her parents were not too busy to rescue her, the reader goes along with each of Lian's discoveries.

Throughout the high fantasy *A Wizard of Earthsea* by Ursula Le Guin, the elevated language, often with long and sonorous line, emphasizes the seriousness of the struggle between good and evil in the soul of Ged. Le Guin preserves such departure from ordinary language when she describes the otak, a small animal Ged carries with him on his travels. By using inverted word order, she sets the otak apart from earthly animals. "They are small and sleek, with . . . fur dark brown or brindle. . . . Their teeth are cruel and their temper fierce, so they are not made pets of. They have no call or cry or any voice." Although not all high fantasy is written in so formal a tone, such word choice seems highly appropriate.

Ian Serraillier in his retelling *Beowulf the Warrior* uses the language of today and yet retains the tone and qualities of the folk epic as it was first recorded a thousand years ago. The intent of the folk epic is serious, since the long narrative centers on a national hero and makes clear the values of a people. Serraillier has respected this intent by maintaining a consistently dignified tone. He keeps the elevated language, the compound synonyms or kennings, the imagery, the alliteration, and the extended metaphors. In the passage below, Beowulf and his band set sail:

> They ran up the white sail. And the wind caught her,
> The biting wind whipped her over the waves.
> Like a strong bird the swan-boat winged her way
> Over the grey Baltic, the wintry whale-road.

The voyage across the sea is no happy, lighthearted sail across the bay; Beowulf and his valiant warriors face a sea worthy of their courage.

Hand-to-hand combat with a monster has a dignity heightened by long, rhythmic lines, richly connotative terms, and alliterative descriptions with long vowels and hard consonants:

> Spilling the benches,
> They tugged and heaved, from wall to wall they hurtled.
> And the roof rang to their shouting, the huge hall
> Rocked, the strong foundations groaned and trembled.

The long sounds (extended *a*'s and *oo* sounds, slowly moving consonants— *l*'s, *g*'s, and *r*'s, for example) make the poetic lines move slowly to create a sense of dignity that accompanies the awesome struggle. After Beowulf defeats Grendel, Hrothgar praises Beowulf, and thereby shows his own generous and humble nature. But here shorter vowel and consonant sounds quicken the pace and so lighten the tone:

> . . . the grateful King,
> All glooming gone, his countenance clear and cloudless
> As the sky in open radiance of the climbing sun,
> Gave thanks to God for deliverance. "Beowulf," he said,
> "Bravest of men, I shall love you now as my son.
> All I have is yours for the asking."

The epic hero of *Gilgamesh* is a king "who fears nothing," is "lofty and unconquerable." His friend Enkidu is equally strong. Together they have even greater strength, and so mighty a love of each other that together they can conquer the monster Humbaba, the scourge of Gilgamesh's people. In hand-to-hand combat, the two defeat the monster:

> Humbaba grasped the horns of Enkidu and began to flail his body against a tree. . . . Gilgamesh roused himself. . . . The earth reverberated with the sound, and distant mountains shook. . . .
>
> Gilgamesh felt pity in his heart. He withdrew his sword and put down his axe, while the monster Humbaba crept toward him, groveling and wailing for help.

The qualities of loyalty as well as moral and physical strength in Gilgamesh combine with his love of action and adventure, and his determination to free his people from the scourge of Humbaba. In her retelling, Bernarda Bryson has retained the lofty tone of awe at great moral strength and awakens admiration for a hero as great as Beowulf.

Rosemary Sutcliff has retold the hero tales of Anglo-Saxon Beowulf and of Finn MacCool and Cuchulain of Ireland, Wales, and Scotland. Sutcliff too retains the elevated style of the epic, even while she describes characters that to us seem horribly bloodthirsty. These were days of fierce combat and intense loyalty to king and country; the story is filled with such wars. Notice the style of Cuchulain's story *The Hound of Ulster:*

> For a long time after the fight at the ford and the death of Ferdia, for a long while after the wounds of his body were healed, it was as though Cuchulain were wounded in his mind; he had no joy left to him even in hunting, no joy in harp song, nor in the touch of [his wife] Emer's hands. But little by little, as the months passed into years, that wound also healed, though maybe the scar of it never ceased its aching. . . . The fire of life burned high in him again, and he answered as of old to the call of any adventure that came his way.

In the retelling of the epic about Finn MacCool, the supernatural element common to the epic often intervenes, particularly as related to war. Here is a gentler passage about Finn's marriage to Saba, one of the Fairy Kind, but the language is nonetheless serious and dignified rather than sentimental.

> So she became Finn's wife, and their happiness was like the happiness of the immortals in the Land of Youth where spring never turns to winter, and magic birds sing always in the branches of the white apple trees whose blossom never falls, even when the apples sweeten and turn gold.

Special Issues of Tone in Children's Literature
Condescension

When someone looks down upon us, treating us as though we are unintelligent or immature, we call this attitude condescension. In the original writings of the Greeks, Homer, Hesiod, and Pindar, the myths conveyed religious truth; they expressed the depth and seriousness of ancient faith. As Edith Hamilton says, we know Greek mythology best through the Greek writers who believed in what they wrote. One of Hamilton's examples is the story of Perseus and the Gorgon's head, a story that moves us, its brief descriptive phrases giving horror and urgency to the tale:

> And they are three, the Gorgons, each with wings
> And snaky hair, most horrible to mortals.
> Whom no man shall behold and draw again
> The breath of life.

By contrast, in Nathaniel Hawthorne's retelling in *A Wonder Book,* the Gorgons become snake-fairy-butterfly concoctions:

> Why, instead of locks of hair, if you can believe me, they had each of them a hundred enormous snakes growing on their heads, alive, twisting, wriggling, curling, and thrusting out their venomous tongues, with forked strings at the end!. . . . and they looked very dazzling, no doubt, flying about in the sunshine.

By making the Gorgons into cartoonlike characters, Hawthorne has turned the tone of the story almost into ridicule; in descriptions of the hero himself—Perseus who slew the Gorgon Medusa—there is none of the expected dignity. Instead, in casual, quick-paced language, Hawthorne describes Perseus as pathetically vulnerable. His turning to stone would be a "very sad thing to befall a young man." Perseus' motives seem selfish and glory-seeking, as he "wanted to perform a great many brave deeds, and to enjoy a great deal of happiness in this bright and beautiful world." Perseus could hardly keep from crying. He felt "greatly ashamed . . . like a timid little schoolboy." "What would my dear mother do, if her beloved son were turned into stone?" "Dear me . . . I shall be afraid to say a syllable." All grandeur is lost in this version.

The tone in Hawthorne's retelling of the myth is not respectful but condescending. He seems to be saying to the reader, "Now, children, isn't this a silly little story about foolish people?" There is no awe at the size of Perseus' task, no admiration for the courageous and liberating act. The myths of ancient people, myths that have come to us from those who believed in them, were filled with reverence and mystery, since by myth human beings were attempting to explain the wonders of human beings and of nature. Hawthorne, although he may have followed the traditional details, has changed the myth completely by his condescending tone.

A modern example of condescension is Walt Disney's *Wonderful World of Knowledge,* Volume 10, which does include the traditional details of the myths. Although the diction is condescending, it is not as offensive as the illustrations: Pluto is Icarus and King Arthur; Mickey Mouse is Jason, Roland, Sigurd, and Galahad; Tinker Bell is one of the ondines, or water sprites, from the Norse Eddas. Despite color reproductions of classical artworks showing myths, the total effect is destroyed by the cartooned heroes.

Does this condescending tone matter? When a retelling so completely violates the original tone or the spirit in which it was told, the story is changed beyond recognition; a child meeting such condescension may be turned off by tone that talks down, and he or she may never be encouraged or interested enough to find a better version of the myth. In original fiction, too, literature that talks to children as "dear little readers" demeans them; they may even be insulted. No one likes condescension, and the child who meets it may reject the pleasures and discoveries of literature.

Talking down to children may discourage them from reading.

Sentimentality

Sentimentality, or the overuse of sentiment, is a kind of condescension. Thornton W. Burgess, still in print and on the library shelves after many years, in telling his story *Mother West Wind's Animal Friends* is not only trite in language but also sentimental in tone. Burgess creates talking animals that have few traits to convince us either of their likeness to people or of their animal natures—except that those with wings fly, and those without, walk. Open a Burgess story and find this:

> Then old Mr. Toad picked up his cane and started down the Crooked Little Path to the Green Meadows. There he found the Merry Little Breezes stealing kisses from the bashful little wind flowers. Old Mr. Toad puffed out his throat and pretended that he disapproved, disapproved very much indeed, but at the same time he rolled one eye up at jolly, round, red Mr. Sun and winked.
>
> "Haven't you anything better to do than make bashful little flowers hang their heads?" asked old Mr. Toad gruffly.

The many capitalized nouns and adjectives, the personification of breezes, flowers, and sun, the repetition of words and phrases ("disapproved, disapproved very much indeed") and the clichés ("anything better to do") do little to convey conflict or to make the story move. Peter Rabbit (a nod to Beatrix Potter) and the "little meadow people and forest folk" are organizing an Easter Egg Rolling for everyone in the Green Meadows, the Purple Hills, and the Green Forest. The long-winded combination of sentimentality and the omniscient point of view create a coy tone and fail to reveal character or to describe actions. Burgess lacks respect for his readers and his characters; his condescension makes a shallow story.

By contrast, Scott O'Dell in *Island of the Blue Dolphins* never condescends, never demeans Karana's life by sentimentality. Her people have always lived on the windswept island, dependent upon themselves and their own capacities to use what is provided by nature and to avoid death at nature's impersonal hands. A product of this culture, living close to the elements, Karana quietly accepts what faces her. Life is sometimes cruel; humans survive by self-control. Ramo's being killed by wild dogs does not make Karana wild in her grief; we sense instead her feeling of inevitability and of necessity for restraint:

> All night I sat there with the body of my brother and did not sleep. I vowed that someday I would go back and kill the wild dogs in the cave. I would kill all of them. I thought of how I would do it, but mostly I thought of Ramo, my brother.

Even the death of a loved one can be described without sentimentality.

O'Dell's restraint makes us feel sympathy for and understanding of Karana in her isolation and loneliness; there is no sentimentality here.

Nor is there sentimentality in Katherine Paterson's portrayal of Jess's grief at the death of his friend in the flood waters. In *Bridge to Terabithia* we read that Jess's stomach "felt so odd." And yet, the morning after the news, pancakes doused in syrup taste "marvelous." Jess's sister accuses him of not caring, and he is puzzled: "The coldness curled up inside of him and flopped over." As Jess's mother and sister talk, he "could hear them talking and they were farther away than the memory of a dream." He cannot leave the table, but he doesn't know what to do. Then, his mind a blank, he mumbles, "What little girl?" Paterson's depiction is not sentimental, filled with sighs and tears and sobs; we nonetheless see that Jess is shocked and grief-stricken.

The Winter Room is dedicated to the author's father. Gary Paulsen might easily have let his story of boyhood in northern Minnesota fall into the trap of sentimentality, but he doesn't. In the second chapter, "Spring," he describes his family, including his parents, his brother Wayne, and his elderly Uncle David. Spring on a northern farm, the rooms and furnishings in the house, the farm buildings, the weaning of the calves, playing cowboys with his brother, and Wayne's jump from the hay mow to the old horse's back are the matters of the chapter. In later ones, the first-person narrator tells the stories Uncle David told in the Winter Room (the parlor used only in winter), and concludes with a moving tale about a "strong young man" who could split a log from the ends by swinging two axes, one axe in each hand to meet perfectly in the center. To the narrator's horror, Wayne calls Uncle David a liar, and then, hiding in the loft, the boys see old Uncle David enter the barn and quietly, with great strain, manage the old trick. The story's poignancy comes from Paulsen's underplaying the incident while we see how the old man yearns for his youth and strength—and tries one more time to prove his strength to himself.

Missing May by Cynthia Rylant is a tale of love. Summer misses May, the most loving human being anyone can imagine; in the little trailer, May was the source of all good for her husband Ob as well. Since May's death, life is empty. Ob is about to give in to grief, but Summer tries to keep him involved, to find new purpose for his life. A new focus for Ob is Cletus, an odd but beloved boy. It seems that love does not die but can keep adding new love objects. Without sentimentality, tone here supports theme.

Janet Taylor Lisle also avoids sentimentality in *Afternoon of the Elves,* the story of friendship between healthy Hillary and Sara-Kate, her impoverished neighbor. Sara-Kate's village of tiny elf houses made from twigs is the focus for their play—empty houses and invisible elves. Little by little, Hillary recognizes them to be the empty houses Sara-Kate lives in with her sick mother—unfurnished, cold, and without electricity or telephone. Sara-Kate must resort to theft and hiding so that she and her mother can eat and survive. We suspect some of these conditions, but follow Hillary's gradual discoveries as, with her, we appreciate Sara-Kate's pride and her insistence upon privacy.

The dedication in Bruce Brooks's *Everywhere* reads, "For my dad, and his," another dedication that might easily make a story lapse into sentimentality. In this case, the slim book tells of the 10-year-old narrator's experience of his grandfather's heart attack, and the remarkable "soul switch" his African-American friend Dooley manages with the help of a box turtle, some nail polish, and a frozen chicken neck. Dooley, nephew of Lucy the nurse, knows some Native American lore that will get the soul of the turtle to switch with that of the dying man, so that the boy's grandfather will not die. The boy remembers making things with his grandfather, regrets that he has never shown him his secret place by the stream, fears as he climbs to the bedroom window and sees the old man's body jerking in what may be death throes. Then he calms as he makes eye contact with the old man. The story is filled with the love of boy and grandfather, but despite the brush with death never becomes maudlin or tearful.

Sensationalism

Sensationalism, which we have noted in our discussion of plot, is another kind of tone. Paula Fox's *The Slave Dancer* and the Colliers' *My Brother Sam Is Dead,* for example, might have been sensational in many places. The writers, however, have carefully chosen words that convey meaning and control tone but avoid sensationalism.

A sensational tone occurs in many books published for children. Pop stars are often accused of sensationalism in their concert appearances and song lyrics, resorting to highly flamboyant behavior to pull in the crowds. In fiction, sensationalism often appears as the gratuitous and unwarranted inclusion of violence, or perhaps explicit sexuality, for the sake of selling

Sensationalism is common in "escape" fiction.

books. Writers and publishers are not above such unnecessary and excessive sensationalism, and at times this tone takes over. Like overused sentimentality, sensationalism may dull the reader's reaction to emotional pain or physical discomfort in real life.

When Robert Cormier's *The Chocolate War* was first published in 1974, some criticism was leveled at what at first glance seemed sensational violence in the final boxing match that punished Jerry Renault for his refusal to join in the Vigils' behavior. That section of the novel, however, is an integral part of the whole and not added for sensational reasons; we know that unfortunately such behavior is not uncommon among the young. Cormier, who wrote *The Chocolate War* for his adult audience, was persuaded to make some changes for a younger audience. He remains a fine writer whose work continues to reflect the concerns and lives of young adults, while offering well-developed characters and strong themes.

Other stories with sensational segments are out there now. When first published, Judy Blume's *Forever* was much castigated for what by today's standards seems tame sexual allusion. A quick glance at books for young adults shows that Blume's book has been overtaken by those that include everything from four-letter words to a 16-year-old as mistress to a man of forty, a book in which the writing is not sensational, although some may consider the topic so.[3]

One kind of tone misunderstood by those who castigate folktales or nursery rhymes for their violence is **distanced tone.** One critic defines distance as the "degree of dispassionateness with which reader or audience can view the people, places, and events in a literary work.[4] *Aesthetic distance* is defined as the "effect produced when an emotion or experience . . . is so objectifed by the proper use of form that [it is] independent of immediate personal experience."[5] It depends upon the reader's ability to recognize the separateness of art and reality. Form, as we have noted earlier, is strong in folktales, in their plotting as well as their characters, and because they are unlike anything known to them, readers do not identify with the characters or situation.

Didacticism

Didacticism, or preaching, is expected of sermons that point to moral lessons, and teaching from textbooks that spread before us the truths of concept or fact.[6] In folk literature, the fable exists only to make visible or tangible a moral lesson. In fact, that may be one of the pleasures of the fable: Once we hear it, we enjoy saying, "I know what that story means." Fable form requires didacticism, but in other imaginative literature it is a negative quality. Perhaps one reader sees an obvious theme that appears didactic, while another reader will not find the story to be teaching or preaching, but merely to be developing a second theme. In the same way, a biblical parable may evoke two similar responses.

By giving the protagonist a few personal traits and setting him or her into a narrative, the writer may seem to have created a story. (Remember our earlier discussion of *Willie Goes to the Seashore*.) Since pleasure comes from a good story told well and understanding grows from a discovery about human nature, this kind of story often fails as literature.

Look, for example, at the picture book *I Want to Be a Homemaker*. Jane's mother gives her advice about her doll children. She says that they need good food—milk, eggs, vegetables, meat, and so forth—so they will grow. As Jane pours tea into her doll teacups, her mother adds that some foods will build bones and others muscles. Others give "pep" for running, jumping, and playing. "You see, Jane, we need many kinds of food." Moments later Jane tells a visitor about her doll children, who sometimes won't behave, won't brush their teeth, often get their feet wet, and even run into the street. Mother replies that a good homemaker is a teacher all day long.

Such a story seems to have been conceived only in order to teach. Characters are undeveloped, conflict is nonexistent, and style is dull. All that survives is a didactic message: homemakers—i.e., women—must know about child care. While *Homemaker* is an extreme and unfortunate example of sexist stereotyping, many "stories" seem to have as their purpose the underlining of a moral or the teaching of a lesson. Pleasure and understanding are lost.

> "I'll teach the readers a lesson" seems to be some writers' motive.

Didacticism we will always have with us. The degree of acceptance varies with the reader, but the pleasure is diminished for many when the moral seems more important than the characters and their significant experiences.

Changing Values

Styles in writing change—for children as they do for adults. Sometimes it is tone that forces the retirement of a onetime classic. Such, it seems, may be the case in E. Nesbit's *Five Children and It,* a book that continues to appear on lists of classics but is no longer read by many children. While an occasional child today may still respond to the playful fantasy of *Five Children,* it is perhaps the sentimental and condescending tone that has retired it from the active shelf. Lamb, who is too old to be called a baby today, kisses the gypsy woman, "a very nice kiss, as all his kisses are, and not a wet one like some babies give." Robert asks Lamb to "come and have a yidey on Yobby's back." Sentimental and stereotyped characterization combines with condescension toward gypsies, "Eyetalians," and "Red Indians."

> Tone in a classic of the past may retire it from today's list.

Condescension and whimsy also contrast artificially the views of children and adults on what is real and true:

> . . . Grown-up people find it very difficult to believe really wonderful things, unless they have . . . proof. But children will believe almost anything, and grown-ups know this . . . they tell you that the earth is round like an orange, when you can see perfectly well that it is flat and lumpy; and why they say that the earth goes round the sun, when you can see for yourself any day that the sun gets up in the morning and goes to bed at night like a good sun as it is, and the earth knows its place, and lies as still as a mouse.

By contrast, look at Eleanor Estes's *The Moffats,* or Beverly Cleary's *Ramona and Her Father,* two other family stories. We might call the tone of such stories "wonder"—a kind of wonder that says "Aren't everyday, ordinary things remarkable?" Ramona, who has made herself a crown of burs and now must have her hair cut off in order to remove them, begs Daddy not to cut any more than he has to. "Does it look awful?" she asks. And her father replies with humor, "It will never be noticed from a trotting horse." Ramona lets out a "long, shuddery sigh, the closest thing to crying without really crying." When Ramona, whose father has lost his job, wishes she might earn a million dollars like the boy on the hamburger commercials, her father replies:

> "I'll bet that boy's father wishes he had a little girl who fingerpainted and wiped her hands on the cat when she was little and who once cut her own hair so she would be bald like her uncle and who then grew up to be seven years old and crowned herself with burs. Not every father is lucky enough to have a daughter like that."

Although the events of *Five Children* are fantastic and those of *Ramona* are humorously everyday, *Ramona* is far more successful in its creation of a sense of surprise. True, the children of *Five Children* live in an era more remote and foreign, but time distance is not the issue, since to a child time is not measured by decade. Possibly, what makes one story old-fashioned and relegates it to book lists and what keeps the other alive and read may be to a great extent tone, or how the authors feel about their subjects and readers. Our tastes in tone change. Baby-talk was more acceptable in Victorian fiction than it is today.

Variety of Tone

Some writers vary tone as the situation in the story changes; they use various tones to comment on people as individuals and as social groups. While such a story can often be read as a fast-paced, character-conflict-theme story, the perceptive reader who catches the shifts and shading of tone may find added pleasure in the story. As the readers recognize human manners and behavior, they also discover the author's attitude, and a whole new level of pleasure can be uncovered.

We can note the various tone shifts in Andersen's "The Ugly Duckling." Andersen is sometimes humorous, sometimes tender, often critical, and even, sometimes, almost cynical. The child may read "The Ugly Duckling" often during the early years; because of the range of tone, at each reading the child discovers a new tone and added meaning.

Alice Childress, as she changes point of view with each chapter in *A Hero Ain't Nothin' but a Sandwich,* shows each of the speakers with a different tone. The principal's tone is resigned: "No matter what I do or don't do there are drug addicts." Benjie is naive when he says of his addiction, "I kicked once and I can kick any time I wanta." Walter the pusher, angry and protesting that anyone who sells anything is a pusher, says he is "pushin' for cops, when you get right down to it. You heard me! When I pay off, what the hell you think I'm payin' with? . . . I gotta hustle ten bags before I can pay the fuzz five singles, dig?"

Jean Fritz, too, varies tone. In the foreword to *Homesick: My Own Story,* she calls the book "my story, told as truly as I can tell it."[7] In an accepting and reminiscent tone touched with occasional gentle humor, Fritz observes people and events through the eyes of a child. When Jean's mother takes over her education, she insists upon arithmetic, figuring how long a train takes between Hankow and Peking at x miles an hour, stopping y times on the way. Jean, who hates arithmetic, protests the unnecessary study: "I knew that grown-ups never figured out such problems; they just looked at timetables." When Jean meets American girls and is asked to speak some Chinese, she obliges with Chinese insults, then refuses to translate: They are "worthless daughters of baboons," with big turtles for mothers. But Fritz is often serious. When her nurse Lin Nai-Nai returns from her home in beseiged Wuchan, Jean finds her swaying in her chair, trouser legs rolled, foot bindings gone, "her stumps of feet, hard little hooves with toes bent under," painful from running "like a stumbling duck."

And one further example. Accustomed as we might be to the idea of an omnipotent God speaking in stentorian tones to warn of the flood, it comes as a surprise when Rosemary Harris in *The Moon in the Cloud* describes the voice of God very differently. Speaking conversationally, a still small voice says that "the people are grown exceedingly wild. They worship idols, they take too many wives in marriage and discard those that displease them. They care for nothing and nobody—and they're violent." Noah hears a gentle sighing voice as God describes the coming flood. "A clean sweep . . . I had in mind. Everything mean and small and violent done for."

Tone may vary within the story itself.

The quiet tone of voice that accompanies God's appearance as rings of brilliant color makes God a benevolent but disappointed creator who wants not to punish but to erase the mistakes of human behavior.

Few stories have greater variety and complexity in tone than *Tom Sawyer,* a story that offers great excitement on the level of character and plot alone. Mark Twain ranges over human attitudes from tenderness to sarcasm, from delight to cynicism. In his depiction of boyhood and adolescence, Twain admits that life is varied and contradictory; he uses tone to show its complexity and perversity. In reading the following passages from the novel, notice Twain's distance from, and yet smiling acceptance of, the self-deception and self-absorption of the young:

> [*On crushes:*] He had been months winning [Amy]; she had confessed hardly a week ago; he had been the happiest and the proudest boy in the world only seven short days, and here in one instant of time she had gone out of his heart like a casual stranger whose visit is done.

> [*On ceremony:*] The oath was complete. They buried the shingle close to the wall with some dismal ceremonies and incantations, and the fetters that bound their tongues were considered to be locked and the key thrown away.

Twain, in commenting on human behavior, is sly and faintly satirical:

> [*On theft:*] There was no getting around the stubborn fact that taking sweetmeats was only "hooking," while taking bacon and hams and such valuables was plain simple stealing—

> [*On the forbidden:*] Huckleberry was cordially hated and dreaded by all the mothers of the town, because he was idle and lawless and vulgar and bad—and because all their children admired him so, and delighted in his forbidden society, and wished they dared to be like him.

Although we remember *Tom Sawyer* as a happy book, Twain is ironic, sarcastic, even cynical at times:

> [*On showing off:*] [The Sunday school superintendent] by bustlings and activities. [The librarian] by making a deal of the splutter and fuss that insect authority delights in. [The teachers] by bending sweetly over pupils that were lately being boxed.

> [*On accusation:*] The public are not slow in the matter of sifting evidence and arriving at a verdict.

And finally, on public sentimentality he becomes almost sardonic:

> This funeral stopped the further growth of one thing—the petition to the governor for Injun Joe's pardon . . . a committee of sappy women . . . in

deep mourning . . . wail around the governor, and implore him to be a merciful ass and trample his duty underfoot . . . scribble their names to a pardon petition, and drip a tear on it from their permanently impaired and leaky waterworks.

By giving his novel a great variety of tones, Twain has increased the scope and significance of his story. He has shown what pleasure can come from observing all of life and from taking a stand on any and every aspect of it. By varying tone yet maintaining an overall attitude of humor and enjoyment of each experience, he has not only managed to create a novel of suspense and excitement, but also one that continues to amaze and delight, no matter what the age of the reader or the number of rereadings.

There are kinds of tone that seem unsuited to children's stories. Satire with its intent to reform is often too intellectual an exercise. It demands breadth of experience and ability to see and interpret exaggeration and understatement. Some stories are so strong that they carry the child's interest and the satire may be missed completely without loss to the reader—the *Alice* books, for example. As overall tone, sarcasm with its intent to wound is also too complex and thus questionable for children. To children, all experience is a subject for wonder. Condemnation, as well as fear and pessimism, seem to have little place in their literature; without experience to place these negative tones in perspective, they may be overwhelmed and moved to despair.

For a time, children's literature took increasingly honest looks at all areas of life, adding suffering, pain, and futility to stories for young readers. As long as these negative attitudes are not unrelieved, they have their place. However, children are less able than adults to defend themselves against despair, and so find the pessimistic messages more meaningful if they are presented within a story in which the tone is basically hopeful.

In addition to our opportunity to live with Laura her frontier life, the tone of Laura Ingalls Wilder's Little House books may be a significant reason for their popularity. In each of the nine successive volumes, Laura is older and the reader follows with interest as she grows and matures, but an additional appeal is the consistent tone of quiet security. Indians, wild animals, hard work and deprivation, many moves and new houses, long and bitter winters, the long wait for Pa's return, and Mary's blindness surely hold us, but despite these and other inevitable uncertainties, they are never sensationalized. In fact, some might say the stories are sentimental because hardships are minimized—or even forgotten—when we once again glimpse the firelit room, and hear Pa's fiddle and the click of Ma's knitting needles. Laura's contentment with her life holds us as it concludes each volume.

What matters is that tone for children's literature be, if not optimistic, at least positive, or perhaps objective. For children, all the world is opening

Stories of other times and places let the reader enjoy experiences vicariously. Factual tone helps.

up; there is much to be appreciated and marveled at—and improved upon. If limiting tone to optimism and affirmation narrows it too much, we may consider only condescension and unrelieved sensationalism or despair as unsuitable. But if we defend these kinds of tone, we must remind ourselves of the functions of literature. Futility and despair do not give pleasure or necessarily increase understanding; there are dozens of other possible attitudes that may do this for young readers.

Summary

Tone, the author's attitude toward subject and readers, is an integral part of story, since it is created by the writer's choice of words. It is not created by any single, obvious decision of the author; instead it is the result of all the choices made in telling the story. Tone can make the same story—one of heroes and valiant deeds, for example—either a series of trivial anecdotes or a monument to human valor. Tone can fill us with affection and acceptance, or rouse us to examine and to laugh at ourselves.

Notes

1. For further discussion of style and its relationship to humor in Kipling's *Just So Stories,* see Lukens, "Kipling's Humor in All Its Promiscuous Parts" in *Studies in American Humor,* Winter, 1986–87, pp. 255–266.

2. See To the Instructor for comments about changes made in onetime classics (including *The Secret Garden*), changes necessary to appeal to today's children. Peter Hunt in *Children's Literature Quarterly* for Winter, 1996–97.

3. Today's crop of novels for young adults, some fine and some disappointing, underlines the injustice of the continuous ban on that insightful novel *The Catcher in the Rye,* the story of Holden Caulfield's yearning for an ideal world.

4. C. Hugh Holman, *A Handbook of Literature,* 3rd ed. (Indianapolis: Odyssey Press, 1972) p. 164.

5. Ibid., p. 8.

6. Joanna Gillespie, in her article, "Schooling through Fiction" (*Children's Literature,* New Haven: Yale University Press, 1986), quotes from early literature for children, part of the Sunday School movement: "It has been my design . . . to direct the minds of children to subjects of higher importance than those which generally occupy the pages of books put into their hands. . . . The silly stories which their fathers read in their childhood will soon be, perhaps in a double sense, 'tales of other times!'" (quote from writer William M'Gavin, 1849).

7. Jean Fritz has reconstructed her China childhood with true incidents but feels that the possibility of inaccuracy in chronology necessitates calling *Homesick: My Own Story* fiction.

Recommended Books Cited in This Chapter

BEMELMANS, LUDWIG. *Madeline*. New York: Viking, 1939.

BROOKS, BRUCE. *Everywhere*. New York: Harper & Row, 1990.

BRYSON, BERNARDA. *Gilgamesh: Man's First Story*. New York: Holt, Rinehart & Winston, 1967.

BURNETT, FRANCES HODGSON. *The Secret Garden*. 1911. Reprint. New York: Viking, 1988.

BYARS, BETSY. *Bingo Brown, Gypsy Lover*. New York: Viking, 1990.

———. *The Blossoms and the Green Phantom*. New York: Delacorte, 1987.

———. *The Burning Questions of Bingo Brown*. New York: Viking, 1988.

CHILDRESS, ALICE. *A Hero Ain't Nothing but a Sandwich*. New York: Coward McCann, 1973.

CLEARY, BEVERLY. *Ramona and Her Father*. New York: Morrow, 1977.

COLLIER, JAMES LINCOLN, AND CHRISTOPHER COLLIER. *My Brother Sam Is Dead*. New York: Four Winds, 1974.

CONFORD, ELLEN. *A Job for Jenny Archer*. Boston: Little, Brown, 1988.

———. *What's Cooking, Jenny Archer?* Boston: Little, Brown, 1989.

CORMIER, ROBERT. *The Chocolate War*. New York: Pantheon, 1974.

CURTIS, CHRISTOPHER. *The Watsons Go to Birmingham*. New York: Delacorte, 1995.

DANZIGER, PAULA. *Earth to Matthew*. New York: Delacorte, 1991.

EDENS, COOPER. *Santa Cows*. Illustrated by Daniel Lane. New York: Greenwillow, 1991.

ESTES, ELEANOR. *The Moffats*. New York: Harcourt, 1941.

FOX, PAULA. *The Slave Dancer*. Scarsdale, NY: Bradbury, 1973.

FRITZ, JEAN. *Homesick: My Own Story*. New York: Putnam, 1982.

GIFF, PATRICIA REILLY. *Matthew Jackson Meets the Wall*. New York: Doubleday, 1990.

GRAHAME, KENNETH. *The Wind in the Willows*. 1908. Reprint. New York: Scribners, 1953.

HARRIS, ROSEMARY. *The Moon in the Cloud*. New York: Macmillan, 1982.

HOOVER, H. M. *The Lost Star*. New York: Viking, 1979.

HURWITZ, JOHANNA. *Ali Baba Bernstein*. New York: Morrow, 1985.

KIPLING, RUDYARD. *Just So Stories*. 1902. Reprint. New York: Doubleday, 1946.

LE GUIN, URSULA K. *A Wizard of Earthsea*. Berkeley: Parnassus, 1968.

LINDGREN, ASTRID. *Pippi Longstocking*. New York: Viking, 1950.

LISLE, JANET TAYLOR. *Afternoon of the Elves*. New York: Orchard, 1989.

LOWRY, LOIS. *The Giver*. New York: Doubleday, 1993.

MCCLOSKEY, ROBERT. *Homer Price*. New York: Viking, 1943.

MCKINLEY, ROBIN. *The Blue Sword*. New York: Greenwillow, 1982.

MILNE, A. A. *Winnie-the-Pooh*. New York: Dutton, 1926.

NAYLOR, PHYLLIS. *Reluctantly Alice*. New York: Atheneum, 1991.

———. *The Witch's Eye*. New York: Delacorte, 1990.

O'DELL, SCOTT. *Island of the Blue Dolphins*. Boston: Houghton Mifflin, 1960.

PATERSON, KATHERINE. *Bridge to Terrabithia*. New York: Crowell, 1978.

PAULSEN, GARY. *The Winter Room*. New York: Orchard, 1989.

RUCKMAN, IVY. *Who Invited the Undertaker?* New York: Harper, 1991.

RYLANT, CYNTHIA. *Missing May*. New York: Orchard, 1992.

SERRAILLIER, IAN. *Beowulf the Warrior*. New York: Walck, 1961.

SHALANT, PHYLLIS. *Beware of Kissing Lizard Lips*. New York: Dutton, 1995.

SUTCLIFF, ROSEMARY. *The Hound of Ulster*. New York: Dutton, 1963.

TWAIN, MARK. *The Adventures of Tom Sawyer*. 1876. Reprint. New York: Macmillan, 1966.

URE, JEAN. *Supermouse*. New York: Morrow, 1984.

WHITE, E. B. *Charlotte's Web*. New York: Harper, 1952.

WILDER, LAURA INGALLS. The Little House books. 1932–43. Reprint. New York: Harper, 1953.

Madeline's Rescue
Ludwig Bemelmans

11

From Rhyme to Poetry

Children naturally respond to the rhythms and rhymes of verse, but some never move on to poetry. Are these children missing anything you can describe?

When do children first meet literature? If they are lucky, they meet it in infancy, as early as the time they are making valiant efforts to "pat-a-cake, pat-a-cake, baker's man." Because nursery or Mother Goose rhymes use the elements of literature and the devices of style, and because the rhymes are sources of pleasure and understanding, we can legitimately call them the earliest literature for the youngest child. These **rhymes** are brief stories which have been passed orally from generation to generation, and are the beginning of poetry for children.

Nursery Rhymes

Few narratives in literature for child or adult are told with the joyful economy of the nursery rhyme. Many of them, like "Pussy cat, pussy cat, where have you been?" are the most tightly constructed stories. "Sing a song of sixpence, a pocketful of rye" tells a complete tale in three short verses. "Three wise men of Gotham" could hardly be more condensed:

> Three wise men of Gotham
> Went to sea in a bowl.
> If the bowl had been stronger,
> My story had been longer.

Small children—whose attention spans are limited—are introduced to brief fictional tales in rollicking rhythms and rhyming forms. While the rhymes are not poetry, they are the most natural introduction to poetry.

Literary Elements

Many of the Mother Goose or nursery rhymes are the simplest and briefest of stories. The **characters** are the Queen of Hearts who made some tarts, the old woman tossed up in a basket, and Old Mother Hubbard whose cupboard is bare. **Setting,** too, is quickly sketched in some rhymes. Amazingly, the Old Woman lives in a shoe, and Peter Pumpkin Eater's wife lives in a pumpkin shell. The brief narratives have simple **plots.** The crooked man uses his crooked sixpence to buy a crooked cat which "caught a crooked mouse/And they all lived together in a little crooked house" for a happy closed ending. Action in these stories varies from the simplest of tumbles taken by Humpty Dumpty to the more complex involvements of "The House That Jack Built" and "Who Killed Cock Robin?"

Ideas also occur in Mother Goose rhymes, ideas a small child can grasp. Some of the simple rhymes are surprisingly clear in their insights, and oftentimes the short verse-stories have slight **themes.** "Life is a fleeting thing," we discover from "Solomon Grundy":

Solomon Grundy
Born on Monday,
Christened on Tuesday,
Married on Wednesday,
Took ill on Thursday,
Worse on Friday,
Died on Saturday,
Buried on Sunday,
That's the end
Of Solomon Grundy.

Because of Dapple Gray, we know that "a pet is worth more than money":

I had a little pony; his name was Dapple Gray.
I lent him to a lady to ride a mile away.
She whipped him, she slashed him,
She rode him through the mire—
I would not lend my pony now
For all that lady's hire.

A child's understanding is increased in other ways.[1] Curiosity about the environment is roused when the commonplace is made exciting. The trip to the grocery store is no longer ordinary: "To market, to market, to buy a fat pig"; and a walk beside the flower beds is time for "Mistress Mary's garden" with "silver bells and cockle shells and pretty maids all in a row."

Style

In a pleasant, regular beat of rhymes there is **rhythm** that may correspond to breathing and the heartbeat within us; rhythm is a way into poetry:

> Hickory, dickory, dock.
> The mouse ran up the clock.
> The clock struck one,
> And down he run,
> Hickory, dickory, dock.

The quick rhythmic movement makes a child jump to a beat:

> Jack be nimble, Jack be quick.
> Jack jump over the candlestick!

Children clap hands to "The Farmer in the Dell," and swing their arms to "London Bridge." Rhythm, which is determined by patterns of accented and unaccented syllables and by long or short vowels, moves the lines quickly and happily.

The variety of **sound effects** in nursery rhymes, although simple, acquaints children with poetic devices and gives pleasure. "A tisket, a tasket," "Hey, diddle, diddle," "Hickety, pickety," or "Rub-a-dub-dub" use **internal rhymes, assonance,** and **consonance. Alliteration** occurs in "Daffy-down-dilly," or "Peter Piper picked a peck of pickled peppers"; consonant and vowel repetitions exist in "Tommy Snooks and Bessie Brooks went walking out one morning." There is **onomatopoeia** in "Hark, hark, the dogs do bark!" and "Bow-wow-wow, whose dog art thou?" The enjoyable sounds of tongue-twisters are endless challenges. And of course the usual **end rhyme** is pleasing:

> Little Boy Blue, come blow your horn!
> The sheep's in the meadow, the cow's in the corn.
> Where's the boy who looks after the sheep?
> Under the haystack fast asleep!

Figurative language is another stylistic trait of Mother Goose rhymes. Dishes and spoons, ravens and daffodils, cats and mice and ladybugs are excitingly **personified.** "Frogs and snails and puppy dogs' tails" contrast to "sugar and spice and everything nice," **metaphors** for "bad" and "good" qualities in the little boys and girls. Jack Sprat and his wife figuratively—or literally if we prefer—"lick the platter clean"; in **simile** form, a snail is "like a little Kyloe cow."

As for **tone,** humor with delight is more prevalent than any other. There is laughter in

> Barber, barber, shave a pig.
> How many hairs will make a wig?
> Four and twenty, that's enough.
> Give the barber a pinch of snuff.

And there is seriousness in

> Ding Dong Dell, Pussy's in the well!
> Who put her in? Little Johnny Green.
> Who pulled her out? Little Johnny Stout.
> What a naughty boy was that
> To try to drown poor pussy cat
> Who never did him any harm
> But killed the mice in his father's barn.

Verbal **irony** is found in

> A diller, a dollar,
> A ten o'clock scholar,
> What makes you come so soon?
> You used to come at ten o'clock,
> And now you come at noon.

Wonder at romance and possible adventure are awakened in the melodious "Bobby Shafto's gone to sea," or in "I saw a ship a-sailing."

Emotional intensity may be more commonly thought of as a quality of fine lyric poetry, but there is also intensity in children's play and the rhymes that accompany this play. Children chant a teasing rhyme, "Tattle-tale, tattle-tale, hanging on a dog's tail!" Carried along by rhythms and sounds, children sing out variations on names:

> Sally-bum-balley, tee-alley-go-falley,
> Tee-legged, tie-legged, toe-legged Sally.

Or in the universal taunts of childhood, children adapt verses to their playmates' names:

> Janie's mad and I'm glad,
> And I know how to please her.
> A bottle of wine to make her shine,
> A bottle of ink to make her stink,
> And all the boys to tease her.

Caught up in what Robert Frost calls the catchiness of rhythm and rhyme, children recite and improvise.

In the nursery or folk rhymes, children also find the intrigue of riddles. They ask each other rhythmic or rhyming questions:

What can go up the chimney down,
But can't go down the chimney up?

They are surprised that "umbrella" is the answer. And children don't forget this involved question:

As I was going to St. Ives,
I met a man with seven wives.
Each wife had seven sacks;
In each sack were seven cats;
Each cat had seven kits.
Kits, cats, sacks, wives,
How many were going to St. Ives?

In addition to the rhymes we commonly call Mother Goose, children are made ready for poetry by many other folk rhymes that may have general similarities and local geographical variations. Children from many parts of the country know the ball-bouncing rhyme "When Buster Brown was one/He learned to suck his thumb." Some children, perhaps from a particular section of a particular state, seem to share common variations of similar rhymes, like the jump-rope verses with the refrain

Here comes the doctor,
   Here comes the nurse,
Here comes the lady
   With the alligator purse.

Other rhymes seem to appear by some magic, known at first only to an inside group on a particular playground. If the rhymes are catchy enough, they are soon carried across the country by a child who moves away, or by a visitor who returns to a hometown. It seems unlikely that those who have jumped rope to this rhyme will forget it:

Fudge, fudge,
Call the judge.
Mama's got a baby.
Ain't no girl,
Ain't no boy,
Just a plain old baby.
Wrap it up in tissue paper.
Put it on the elevator.
First floor, miss!
Second floor, miss!

Third floor, miss!
Fourth floor—
Kick it out the door.[2]

Nonsense

Nursery rhymes and sidewalk jingles merge with nonsense; there is no line of demarcation. While each is joyful in itself, both prepare the child for poetry. When the cow jumps over the moon, that's nonsense. Of all the animals that Adam named, the least likely moon-jumper is the stodgy cow. Nonsense plays upon our delight in the illogical and the incongruous, upon our pleasure in words cleverly used or misused, upon some secret yearning to see the immutable laws overturned. The best nonsense can do all of these things. Edward Strachey wrote in 1894 in his introduction to Edward Lear's *Nonsense Omnibus* that nonsense is not "a mere putting forward of incongruities and absurdities, but the bringing out of a new and deeper harmony of life in and through its contradictions." Strachey called nonsense the "true work of the imagination, a child of genius, and its writing one of the Fine Arts."

Children thrive on nonsense. They make up and invert words or make illogical comparisons; one child tells another "It's cold as a bumblebee out!" and both children roll on the floor in glee. They repeat nonsense words in series, just for the pleasure of tasting and hearing their sounds: "Eenie-beenie-pepsi-deenie"; "Hogan-Bogan-Mogan was her name." Nonsense relies upon rhythm, sound patterns, figurativeness, compactness, and emotional intensity—the intensity of laughter that may be repeated, stored in the memory, then shared again and again.

Rhythm and Sound

The **limerick** form, first popularized by Edward Lear in the nineteenth century, is the most traditionally structured nonsense verse. It clearly shows how important to nonsense are rhythm and sound:

> There was an Old Person of Ewell,
> Who chiefly subsisted on gruel;
>   But to make it more nice,
>   He inserted some mice,
> Which refreshed that Old Person of Ewell.

Suitable to the tone—lighthearted laughter—the rhythm is quick, with the syllables more frequently unaccented than accented. The sounds are short, with happy rather than serious overtones.

Compactness and Surprise

Much of the humor in nonsense verse comes from the surprise of names, events, or words. Look, for example, at Harry Behn's "Circles," which surprises us by the consistency of its plural word endings, all distorted to rhyme with "compasses."

> The things to draw with compasses
> Are suns and moons and circleses
> And rows of humptydumpasses
> Or anything in circuses
> Like hippopotamusseses
> And hoops and camels' humpasses
> And wheels on clownses busseses
> And fat old elephumpasses.

Laura E. Richards, who had a gift for nonsense, confuses an unlikely pair, elephants and telephones, in her verse "Eletelephony." "The Owl and the Eel and the Warming Pan" is made up of perfectly assorted incongruities, since more unlikely characters and events would be hard to assemble:

> The owl and the eel and the warming-pan,
> They went to call on the soap-fat man.
> The soap-fat man he was not within;
> He'd gone for a ride on his rolling-pin.
> So they all came back by the way of the town
> And turned the meeting-house upside down.

The lighthearted treatment of disaster or the slightly macabre are often subjects for nonsense; nonsense verses often comment on current fads as well, as does X. J. Kennedy in "A Choosy Wolf":

> "Why don't you eat me, wolf?" I asked.
>
> "It wouldn't be much fun to.
> Besides, I'm into natural foods
> That nothing has been done to."

In the rhythm and rhyme of nonsense, ordinary creatures become extraordinary, as this anonymous verse notes:

> What a wonderful bird the frog are—
> When he stand he sit almost;
> When he hop, he fly almost.
> He ain't got no sense hardly;
> He ain't got no tail hardly either.
> When he sit, he sit on what he ain't got almost.

Perhaps Lewis Carroll wrote the most compact and intense nonsense, so witty that not a word is wasted, not a sound is out of place. "The White Rabbit's Verses" from *Alice in Wonderland,* for example, uses over forty pronouns, and yet has only five nouns to which the multitude of pronouns might refer. The 24 lines are written in such logical word order—subject, verb, complement—that they thoroughly convince us of their truth. And yet, when we finish the six verses, we have no idea what we are now convinced of.

Carroll's most admired nonsense is "Jabberwocky," a mystifying tale of valor:

"Twas brillig, and the slithy toves
    Did gyre and gimble in the wabe;
All mimsy were the borogoves,
    And the mome raths outgrabe.

"Beware the Jabberwock, my son!
    The jaws that bite, the claws that catch!
Beware the Jubjub bird, and shun
    The frumious Bandersnatch!"

He took his vorpal sword in hand:
    Long time the manxome foe he sought—
So rested he by the Tumtum tree,
    And stood awhile in thought.

And as in uffish thought he stood,
    The Jabberwock, with eyes of flame,
Came whiffling through the tulgey wood;
    And burbled as it came!

One, two! One, two! And through and through
    The vorpal blade went snicker-snack!
He left it dead, and with its head
    He went galumphing back.

"And hast thou slain the Jabberwock?
    Come to my arms, my beamish boy!
O frabjous day! Callooh! Callay!"
    He chortled in his joy.

'Twas brillig, and the slithy toves
    Did gyre and gimble in the wabe;
All mimsy were the borogoves,
    And the mome raths outgrabe.

Perhaps the best-known popularizer of nonsense verse in the past decades has been Ogden Nash, many of whose verses are known by adult and child alike. Nash's nonsense employs rhythm and made-up words. For compactness, one could not improve on

Dentists' anterooms
Give me tanterooms.

Poetry

We move from nursery rhymes and nonsense to poetry with a feeling, perhaps, that now the discussion will become somber and difficult to follow. Not so. Something about the idea of getting meaning beyond amusement from brief groups of words in short lines, each line or phrase usually beginning at the left margin, seems to frighten many readers. Strange to say, we can read along easily in paragraphed pages, but if the same words are placed in stanza form, the meaning seems less quickly apparent, and we are lost.

Prose and Poetry

The difference between poetry and prose is not as great as it may seem. Much of what we encounter in poetry we have already met in rhymes or in prose. Flow or cadence in prose may become more regular in poetry and be called rhythm, or meter. Sound patterns in prose, like alliteration and onomatopoeia, exist in poetry to even greater degree. Connotative meaning in prose acquires heightened significance in poetry. Figurative language that compares unlike things exists in prose, but occurs more frequently in poetry. What seems to take us by surprise and to make us feel that the two forms are totally different lies elsewhere.

The principal difference between prose and poetry is *compactness*. A single word in poetry says far more than a single word in prose; the connotations and images hint at, imply, and suggest other meanings. In a sense, the poet distills meaning in brief and vivid phrases. Economy and suggestion evoke our response.

Compactness can be a challenge rather than a mystery.

The characteristics of poetry that set it apart from prose are essentially *rhythm, sound patterns, figurativeness, compactness,* and *emotional intensity*. The last two qualities are to a large extent the results of effective use of rhythm, sound patterns, and figurative language to produce compressed expression in words. This compactness in turn results in emotional intensity, a particular quality of poetry.

Analysis of rhythm in such metrical patterns as anapestic or iambic, or of such line patterns as dimeter or tetrameter, seems irrelevant to our discussion of rhythm in poetry for children. We focus here not on naming the forms of meter, but on the *use* of rhythm.

One question seems in order. What is the difference between poetry for adults and poetry for children? Once again, we say that the difference is not in kind, but in degree. We may arbitrarily divide poetry for adults by theme and subject—love or nature lyrics, death or war lyrics, for example. Adults are also concerned about the passage of time, the inevitability of death, and the changing of relationships. Just as the interests of adults are the subjects of their poetry, the concerns of childhood are the subjects of children's poetry. Since much of childhood is spent in play, or in wonder at what is common and yet not commonplace, what surrounds children in their constantly unfolding world are the subjects of children's poetry.

Some poetry appeals to both children and adults, and it seems impossible and unnecessary to designate it as poetry for either group. However, in discussing rhyme and poetry for children, we *can* be somewhat more concise, although no less arbitrary. Nursery or Mother Goose rhymes are the happy rhythmic verses of early childhood; they can also be said to include riddles, chants, and tongue twisters. As the inventive rhymes focus more on the incongruous and the surprising or unexpected, they become more nonsensical, and we tend to call them nonsense rather than nursery rhymes. Where the division comes, anyone or no one can say. When nonsense seems masterfully created, we may find ourselves calling it poetry, and yet where poetry and nonsense begin and end—again, anyone and no one can say. What does seem important is that we appreciate the particular qualities of language form that are distinctively poetic. In our discussion of the arbitrary categories—nursery rhymes, nonsense, and poetry—we are focusing in varying degrees upon these qualities. The essential point remains that poetry is poetry, and that poetry for children differs from poetry for adults in degree, but not in kind. Subject matter may differ, but our standards remain the same.

Many have tried to define poetry, and most have found such definitions difficult. A. E. Housman sardonically calls poetry a secretion, "whether a natural secretion, like turpentine in the fir, or a morbid secretion like the pearl in the oyster." Robert Frost calls it simply "a performance of words." Most definitions of poetry, however, return to at least one central idea derived from the Greek origin of the word. A poet is a *maker,* and poetry is *made;* every word counts.

"Being inspired" sounds passive. "Making" a poem takes energy and effort.

Unlike the word "created," which implies inspiration and mystery, the term "made" suggests materials and effort. If poetry is made, it does not emerge perfect from the writer's pen. Like anything that is made, poetry follows a pattern of development: conception, effort, technical discipline, and refining and polishing before the maker is pleased with the thing made. Most likely the poem is written and rewritten; words are crossed out; substituted for, perhaps replaced with, earlier words; rewritten, crossed out, substituted for again—until the maker-poet feels the poem is finally right. Of course, effort alone does not make a poem, any more than it makes good fiction. Skill, patience, and the critical judgment of the disciplined mind are a more likely combination.

Verse and Poetry

First, let us say that **verse** differs from poetry. What matters is not that we distinguish between them, congratulating the poet for poetry and denigrating the versifier for verse. That is not the issue. Once again, we are aware of a continuum; at one end is trite doggerel and at the other the finest of lyrics. Such distinction may suggest that verse is of a lower order than poetry, which is, by one definition, the most imaginative and intense perceptions human beings can express concerning themselves, others, and their relationships to the world outside themselves. Another definition—noble emotions, noble thoughts, expressed by noble minds—seems a forbidding description. Far more inviting is Shelley's statement. "Poetry is the record of the best and happiest moments of the best and happiest minds." Such a definition includes an extensive part of the continuum.

The content of poetry is emotion; its contribution to human beings is significance. Perhaps one person will insist that beauty—and beauty is a matter of preference—must illuminate a familiar object with newness and sensitivity; as Coleridge says, poetry's immediate object "is the communication of pleasure," again an end achieved through a wide spectrum of sources. Or, as Wordsworth says, it is "the spontaneous overflow of powerful feelings recollected in tranquility." Note that these statements suggest both joyful intensity and serene happiness, but not all poetry is tranquil or serene. Some is somber, even upsetting. Such feelings may come to us from what one critic might call verse and another poetry, but the possibility of such emotions arising from the experience of doggerel seems highly unlikely. Emily Dickinson had criteria for poetry that few poets can achieve; her statement surely sets poetry apart. "If I read a book and it makes my whole body so cold no fire can ever warm me, I know that it is poetry. If I feel physically as if the top of my head were taken off, I know that it is poetry."

Given the inevitability of difference of opinion, and perhaps even the irrelevance of making a distinction, it might still be worthwhile to look at how some critics have defined verse. They maintain that while poetry is an end in itself, verse has a specific purpose. Poet-critic T. S. Eliot, for example, who seems almost to dismiss verse as "a superior amusement," describes poetry by contrasting it to verse. He says that while feeling and imaginative power are found in real poetry, verse is merely a matter of structure, formal metrical order, and rhyme pattern. Its structure, furthermore, may seem more important than its meaning. Proverbial wisdom occurs in verses as simple as "A stitch in time/Saves nine." The purpose of

According to T. S. Eliot, the structure of verse often seems more important than its meaning.

other verses is to sell diet drinks and chewing gum; still others convey traditional sentiments. We know what greeting card verse is, and, perhaps without knowing why, have a feeling that it is not poetry. Some of such verse is humorous, some sentimental, and some so incongruous that it may provoke a condescending smile: "To love a father is no fad/When he's a father like my dad."

Verses can be pleasant and entertaining; they can remind us of sentiments and ideas with which we agree, but often their expression is trite and awkward, with rigid metrical structure, ordinary images, obvious rhymes, or phrases twisted to produce rhyme. They are not poetry as T. S. Eliot has described it—the distilled and imaginative expression of feeling. Notice, for example, the pointlessness of Annette Wynne's "I Keep Three Wishes Ready," a verse with an incongruous, marching rhythm that takes over the meaning. Here the speaker expects to meet a fairy and has three wishes ready. But fairies float, they flit, they drift—never march. Prose would say more clearly and with greater brevity the idea expressed in 16 lines filled with empty, throwaway words.

We have a tendency to see the name of a poet, like Robert Frost or John Ciardi, and assume that everything that person writes is fine poetry. That is not the case. Both Frost and Ciardi, as well as many, many other poets, have written verse—some clever and some pedestrian. We assume, too, that Robert Louis Stevenson's *A Child's Garden of Verses* has been around so long, it is all poetry. Or that A. A. Milne, who delights us with his Winnie-the-Pooh tales, is writing poetry in *When We Were Very Young*. The division may sometimes be difficult to distinguish, but the difference between verse and poetry lies in intensification of feeling and in distillation of language, not in regular end rhymes and predictable figures of speech.

Large quantities of both verse and poetry are available to children. With exposure, children grow in awareness of the pleasure that artful poetry can bring. Greater experience with imaginative poetry can lead children to an awareness and appreciation of Walter de la Mare's "rarest of the best." But children enjoy verse as well; each has its place.

Kinds of Poetry

We sometimes simplify the classification of poetry and say there are two kinds of poems: **narrative,** situational or story poetry; and **lyric** or song poetry. Two familiar examples of narrative poems are Alfred Noyes's "The Highwayman" and Robert Browning's "The Pied Piper of Hamelin," found in many anthologies.

Poems may use a narrative form as well as convey emotion. Kaye Starbird often mingles slight narrative with personal poetry rich in imagery and
figurative language, as in "That Morning in June":

That morning in June when I wakened
   at sunrise
And walked alone,
I followed a path through the country,
   half-hidden
And overgrown,
Where everything, everywhere glittered
   and sparkled.
Everything shone.

Along with the shimmering grass near
   the dewy
Path that I took,
The tipped-over bowl of the sky had
   a gleaming
And polished look,
And so did the glimmering fishes
   that circled
The see-through brook.

It seemed as if Someone important
   had ordered
The world to shine.
And suddenly everything listened
   and glistened,
Each leaf, each vine
And even the numberless needles
   on every
Steeple-topped pine.

In case (when I'm older) I find I'm forgetful
Of things I've known.
I hope I'll remember forever that morning
I walked alone,
That morning when everything,
   everywhere sparkled.
Everything shone.

One type of narrative, the **ballad,** comes to us from traditional or
folk literature. Other ballads are of known authorship; both may show

supernatural intervention, themes of physical courage and love, and incidents common to ordinary people. Developing the story through dialogue and using little characterization or description, ballads traditionally have abrupt transitions, are frequently incremental in structure, and rely upon refrains. "John Henry," like other folk ballads originally sung, flows with songlike cadence, and exemplifies many ballad qualities.

Other poems are **lyrics,** or songlike poems that use sounds, rhythms, and figurative devices to express emotional response to some brief moment of experience, as does Carl Sandburg's familiar "Fog," or the less familiar "Forms of Praise" by Lillian Morrison.

> Basketball players
> already tall
> rise on springs
> aspiring for the ball,
> leap for the rebound
> arms on high
> in a dance
> of hallelujahs.

Some adult poems are a pleasure to both children and adults, and most children's poems can be enjoyed by adults. The intense experience of lyric poetry, however, is often given to children in some kind of situation or story form.

Rhythm

Look now at the characteristics of poetry, several of which are known to children through rhymes and nonsense. The recurrence of stress is called **rhythm.** In our discussion of rhythm in prose, we mention cadence or flow, but when rhythm is set into a more regular pattern as it often is in verse or poetry, we speak of **meter.** The poet uses rhythm to enhance the feeling that the poet's words express. In choosing the rhythm for a poem, whether it be unvarying metrical form or more freely flowing lines, the poet makes several commonsense choices. When we are happy, we speak quickly; when we are sad, or serious, or matter-of-fact, our words come more slowly. In the same way, the poet uses a quickly moving line with many unaccented syllables and short vowels to express lightheartedness in lines that may move as quickly as those of the limerick. When the poet is expressing serious thoughts, the rhythm moves more slowly, with longer vowels and a higher proportion of accented syllables. Within the line, rhythm may also vary as the poet wishes to stress an idea or a single word. And within the poem, the rhythm slows or quickens to vary the mood or shift the tone.

The best poetry uses rhythm to add meaning to words, as does Robert Francis's "The Base Stealer." The sense of the baseball player poised on base, almost on, back again, teasing with sideways shuffles and teetering motions, is clearly shown by the irregular rhythm and the increasingly quick vowels.

Poised between going on and back, pulled
Both ways taut like a tightrope-walker,
Fingertips pointing the opposites,
Now bouncing tiptoe like a dropped ball
Or a kid skipping rope, come on, come on,
Running a scattering of steps sidewise,
How he teeters, skitters, tingles, teases,
Taunts them, hovers like an ecstatic bird,
He's only flirting, crowd him, crowd him,
Delicate, delicate, delicate, delicate—now!

As we note the variation in phrase length, the surprise of the longer phrasing of "come on, come on," then the short vowels, the plosive *t*'s and *c*'s, the sibilant *s*'s, we recognize how the quickening rhythm leads up to an admonitory "Delicate, delicate, delicate, delicate," and the final emphatic "now!" sending him off to steal the base.

In a few tight lines, Arnold Adoff uses rhythm in "Let the Biter Beware" to produce sharp images of what dangers lie ahead for the candy-lover. Irregular beats and line length reproduce the jerky chewing, as caramel and nuts lurk, ready to glue or shock:

In the center of each

                        pale
                        milk
c h o c o l a t e lump
there is a hard nut
waiting to bump your
front tooth into the
d e n t i s t ' s c h a i r

In the center of each
                        dark
                        deep
c h o c o l a t e h u n k
there is a car a mel
chunk just waiting to
                        glue
your teeth to geth er
                  for ev er.

T a k e
c a r e .

Abrupt and halting rhythm and frequent accented syllables in Myra Cohn Livingston's "74th Street" create the sense of a beginner on roller skates, struggling to get and maintain balance, then to take another jerky stroke.

Hey, this little kid gets roller skates.
She puts them on.
She stands up and almost
flops over backwards.
She sticks out a foot like
she's going somewhere and
falls down and
smacks her hand. She
grabs hold of a step to get up and
sticks out the other foot and
slides about six inches and
falls and
skins her knee.

    And then, you know what?

She brushes off the dirt and the
blood and puts some
spit on it and then
sticks out the other foot

    again.

The astonishing news that a single stroke, shown almost entirely in words of one syllable that create a jerky rhythm, has resulted from all this activity is the delight of the poem.

One caution: When we read prose, we pause at punctuation marks, but the poet also starts and stops lines in units of meaning; this requires that at the end of the line we must also make a stop, minute though it may be. Here ending lines with conjunction or adverb, like "and" and "almost" forces the rhythm into even more abrupt pauses, just like the jerkiness of the skater's strenuous efforts and continuous failures.[3]

Robert Louis Stevenson creates the movement of the swing arc by his use of regular and lilting rhythm in "The Swing":

How do you like to go up in the swing,
    Up in the air so blue.
Oh, I do think it the pleasantest thing
    Ever a child can do!

Up in the air and over the wall,
    Till I can see so wide,
Rivers and trees and cattle and all
    Over the countryside—

Till I look down on the garden green,
  Down on the roof so brown—
Up in the air I go flying again,
  Up in the air and down!

But notice, by contrast, the rhythm of "Falling Snow." The words fall into a regular, thumping pattern of beats, a strong accent on every second syllable and a far cry from the gentle and noiseless falling of actual drifting flakes that accumulate so slowly. The hard, rhythmic beat denies the meaning rather than enhances it:

See the pretty snowflakes	/˘/˘/˘
Falling from the sky;	/˘/˘/
On the walk and housetop	/˘/˘/˘
Soft and thick they lie.	/˘/˘/

Here regular meter seems more important to the writer than the experience of snow; rhythm in this verse exists for itself, because a marching rhythm cannot describe falling snow.

As Eve Merriam says about "Inside a Poem," rhythm is important:

It doesn't always have to rhyme,	˘/˘/˘/˘/
but there's the repeat of a beat, somewhere	˘/˘˘/˘˘/˘/
an inner chime that makes you want to	˘/˘/˘/˘/˘
tap your feet or swerve in a curve;	/˘/˘/˘˘/
a lilt, a leap, a lightning split:—	˘/˘/˘/˘/

The quick, changeable beat contributes to meaning, saying that poetry is joyful discovery of meaning, assisted by rhythm. Here the first line is a serious statement about rhyme, and Merriam's rhythm enforces the factual meaning of the line by regularity and uniformity. The first line has four accented syllables, as do all the others. The second line has the same number of accented syllables, but the line's rhythm picks up speed with the use of two additional unaccented syllables, a ratio of six light to four heavier syllables. The more unaccented syllables, the more quickly the line runs, and the more lightness the meaning acquires. Line 3 also has four accented syllables, but it includes five unaccented ones; in line 4 the final anapestic foot ˘˘/ also adds to the lightness and the unexpected quality of the rhythm. Again in line 5, there are four accented syllables, but this time the internal punctuation interrupts the rhythm. The scansion looks the same as that of the first line. ˘/˘/˘/˘/, but the commas cause us to stop and start, stop and start. The surprise we feel as we pause for the two final *t*'s of "lilt" and "split" and the final *p* of "leap," when added to the short vowels and the plosive consonants, is all part of what Merriam is saying about rhythm: rhythm need not be absolutely regular, but it should suit meaning. The idea of "Inside a Poem"—while a poem need not rhyme, its rhythm exists to clarify meaning—is clear. Note too that while Merriam says a poem need not rhyme, she uses rhyme, but in unexpected places. The sound of "rhyme" reappears in "chime" a bit later; "repeat of a beat" and "swerve in a curve" are not the regular and predictable rhymes occurring in end positions, but rhymes nonetheless. Merriam uses rhyme as she uses rhythm—not as an end in itself as the versifier does, but as a means to enforce meaning.

Sound Patterns

In "Lost," Carl Sandburg uses musical devices and sound patterns that are exceptionally helpful as they add to meaning. The poet personifies the fogbound boat as a lost child, and the harbor as a mother:

> Desolate and lone
> All night on the lake
> Where fog trails and mist creeps,
> The whistle of a boat
> Calls and cries unendingly,
> Like some lost child
> In tears and trouble
> Hunting the harbor's breast
> And the harbor's eyes.

The long sounds of the words "calls and cries" are not the only lonely ones, since every line echoes the feeling of desolation. The long vowels in "lone," "all," "long," "fog," "trails," and "creeps" give added duration to the words. Sandburg calls the vessel a "boat," its long *o* adding to the loneliness far more than would the word "ship" with its short *i* sound. Consonants are largely liquid *l*'s and *r*'s or nasal *m*'s, *n*'s, and *ng*'s held together with sibilant *s*'s. The long vowel duration and the consonants that further pull and stretch the words, called **phonetic intensives,** create the slow groping of the fogbound ship. The sounds of the two lines dealing with the "mother," the protective harbor, are quite different. Because vowels are short and decisive, and the words are spoken more swiftly, the effect of the lines is reassuring.

As for rhythm, stressed syllables in "Lost" are far more frequent than unstressed syllables, and the effect is a slowly moving poem—movement like a fogbound boat. Sound devices combined with imagery and figurativeness have created a visible and audible scene. The short poem has given us a fresh picture, and its sound has strengthened both the meaning and the impact.

Figurativeness

As we noted in our discussion of style, figurative language is a means by which a writer says one thing in terms of another, and by which the writer makes comparisons. It is this quality of which Christopher Fry speaks when he says that poetry "has the virtue of being able to say twice as much as prose in half the time, and the drawback, if you do not . . . give it your full attention, of seeming to say half as much in twice the time."

When a poem makes either implied or explicit comparisons, the images called up may acquire connotative meaning, or may be seen in a fresh way. For example, Dorothy Aldis in "On a Snowy Day" describes a fence post topped by the little white cylinder of snow; the personified posts wear metaphorical marshmallow hats. The shapes are aptly compared and the metaphor and image are not only vivid, but also connotatively pleasant.

In "Mama Is a Sunrise," Evelyn Tooley Hunt uses figurative language effectively, comparing Mama by implication to the quiet warmth and light of sunrise:

When she comes slip-footing through the door,
   she kindles us
   like lump coal lighted,
   and we wake up glowing.
She puts a spark even in Papa's eyes
and turns out all our darkness.

When she comes sweet-talking in the room,
   she warms us
   like grits and gravy,
   and we rise up shining.
Even at night-time Mama is a sunrise
that promises tomorrow and tomorrow.

"Slip-footing" is Mama's quiet step as she sets her children glowing, kindling them just as she kindles the spark in Papa's eyes. We say that we "turn on the light," but the poet says Mama "turns out the darkness." Her sweet talk warms the family to make them rise shining. Using tactile and taste imagery, the simile of warming "like grits and gravy" provides pleasant connotations. The final lines state clearly that at night, too, Mama is just as reassuring that all will be well "tomorrow and tomorrow," when another pleasant sunrise is in store. This is not a mother who flips the windowshade to a loud snap and cries out "Rise and shine!" These children are eased serenely into day.

The moon is a favorite object for poets' contemplation; its changes are mysterious to us all, and particularly to the child. Emily Dickinson's poem noting the moon's changes begins with a figurative picture of the crescent moon:

The moon was but a chin of gold
   A night or two ago—
And now she turns her perfect face
   Upon the world below—

> Her forehead is of amplest blond;
>   Her cheeks like beryl hewn—
> Her eye unto the summer dew
>   The likest I have known.

If the crescent moon is "but a chin of gold," then the full moon must be a "perfect face," with forehead, cheeks, and eyes. The metaphor is perfectly suited to the changing shape of the moon.

Vachel Lindsay in his figurative description of the phases of the moon begins with the full moon:

> The Moon's the North Wind's cooky.
> He bites it day by day,
> Until there's but a rim of scraps
> That crumble all away.

A cookie, rich in connotative meaning particularly for children, begins as whole and round, and ends in crumbs.

Like the jigsaw puzzle already put together, the poem with obvious figurative comparisons—the moon is a golden ball—denies the reader the excitement of a personal search and discovery. When the figurative comparisons are ineptly chosen, they confuse meaning rather than reveal it.

Because of figurative language, Nikki Giovanni's brief poem "the drum" can say a great deal in just five lines. The impenetrable drum, sealed and resonant, is impossible to invade, says daddy. But the speaker doesn't care. This child will make his own life as he pleases, pounding, sounding and succeeding.

> daddy says the world is
> a drum tight and hard
> and i told him
> i'm gonna beat
> out my own rhythm

The poet's use of metaphors may delay our discovery of meaning. However, at the same time, these comparisons make the puzzle more intriguing and the discovery more exciting. Look, for example, at the completely compatible figurative devices that John Updike uses in his poem "October," each one a reference either to autumn weather or to Halloween:

> The month is amber,
>   Gold, and brown.
> Blue ghosts of smoke
>   Float through the town.
>
> Great V's of geese
>   Honk overhead,
> And maples turn
>   A fiery red.

Frost bites the lawn.
  The stars are slits
In a black cat's eye
  Before she spits.

At last, small witches,
  Goblins, hags,
And pirates armed
  With paper bags,

Their costumes hinged
  On safety pins,
Go haunt a night
  Of pumpkin grins.

Sometimes we may be puzzled by the figurative language in a poem; the more complex the poem, the more subtle the metaphors may be. The simplest way to check the meaning and suitability of comparisons is by means of simple "this = that" equations. The similes and metaphors in Lilian Moore's "Bike Ride" form a series of figurative comparisons:

Look at us!

We ride a road the sun has paved with shadows.	sun = paving machines shadows = pavement
We glide on leaf lace across tree spires over shadow ropes of droopy wires.	leaf lace = shadow pattern spires = steeplelike shadows of tree tops ropes = telephone wire shadows
We roll through a shade tunnel into light.	tunnel = overhanging branches
Look! Our bikes spin black-and-white shadow pinwheels.	pinwheels = shadows of whirling bicycle wheels

"We ride through the shadows on the road" is a summary statement of the lines, but surely the experience of these words is not the same as the poem.

The rightness of Moore's figurative comparisons has made a fresh experience from what might have been an ordinary one.

As the reader pictures the tiny but fierce-looking iguana, then, little by little, the dragon, Alice Shertle's subtle figurative comparison in "Iguana" becomes clear and reasonable, fantastic but plausible. Why not guard emerald and ruby treasures, invincible?

> O, for the breath of flame
> once more!
> For wings that climbed
> the spires of the skies
> when heroes came
> against me for the prize
> and I was in my prime.
> The world was different
> once upon a time.
>
> Once more to hold
> within my smoldering coils
> the gleaming gold,
> my hoard
> a dragon's spoils . . .
> The ring that glittered
> colder than a star,
> the sheen of armor
> that the hero wore,
> the clinking coins,
> the green and crimson stones
> that winked at me
> among the heroes' bones . . .
>
> It was a different world, before.
> O, for the breath of flame
> once more!

Imagery, the appeal to our senses, makes additionally vivid the figurative comparisons, as we clearly see in Dorothy Aldis's "Fourth of July Night":

> Pinwheels whirling round
> Spit sparks upon the ground,
> And rockets shoot up high
> And blossom in the sky—
> Blue and yellow, green and red
> Flowers falling on my head . . . .

Blossoming flowers and pinwheels spitting sparks make the bright display a picture in our minds. In *Hailstones and Halibut Bones,* Mary O'Neill uses another figurative device called, **synesthesia,** in which stimulation of one sense (colors, sight) results in our seeing concrete images of smells and sounds as well.

Imagery further stretches our perceptions to see details and figurative comparisons otherwise only vaguely noted. Cats are sleek and fat, plump and thin, make unpleasant screeching noises as well as pleasant humming ones. Rosalie Moore tells us these facts in her poem "Catalog"; she compares their graceful jumping to skin slipping from a grape, and their refusal to move from a sleep spot to immovable City Hall. Aileen Fisher also personifies the cat, giving a clear visual metaphor in her poem "At Night":

> When night is dark
> my cat is wise
> to light the lanterns
> in his eyes.

The value of such images is clear when we contrast these poems to verse that minimizes sensory appeal. As Herbert Read says, "Poetry is not made up of words like pride and pity, or love and beauty. . . . The poet distrusts such words and always tries to use words that have a suggestion of outline and shape, and represent things seen as clear and precise as crystal."[4] For example, although Stevenson, in his poem "The Swing," successfully duplicates the rhythm of the swing, his terms are not sensory. "Rivers," "trees," "cattle," "countryside," and "pleasantest thing" make little appeal to our senses. Although the roof is brown, we do not see truly vivid sights. We do not smell, hear, taste, or touch them, and both reader and poem are the poorer for lack of sensory appeal.

Whispers, on the other hand, are a very common part of life, and might be vaguely described. But whispers are titillating, bringing secrets for cherishing, then for sharing, and perhaps for embellishing. Once whispers were merely audible, but never again, because "Whispers" by Myra Cohn Livingston captures other sensory qualities. Notice, too, the pleasant connotations of the many sensory appeals:

> Whispers
>   tickle through your ear
>   telling things you like to hear.
>
> Whispers
>   are as soft as skin
>   letting little words curl in.
>
> Whispers
>   come so they can blow
>   secrets others never know.

Whispers will never be the same, because not only do we hear them, but we feel whispers when they "tickle," "blow," and are "soft as skin"; we see them as the "words curl in." Because of the connotative meanings of the words, we delight in whispers, feeling their tender softness and seeing their spiral curl headed for listening ears.

The best chosen words for a poem add by **connotations** new dimensions of meaning to words we have always known. However, sometimes the connotations of words are distracting rather than helpful in uncovering the meaning of the poem. This is the case in "Feeding the Fairies," where fairies are compared to hens and roosters:

> Fairies, fairies, come and be fed,
> > Come and be fed like hens and cocks;
> Hither and thither with delicate tread,
> > Flutter around me in fairy flocks.

First, the title deceives us. Instead of finding ourselves in a quiet grove or a magic circle where we might hope and expect to find fairies, we are taken to the barnyard where clucking, pecking chickens live their unmagical lives. Next the chickens' "flutter" and "delicate tread" (an incongruous phrase because *delicate* connotes the opposite of *tread*) have connotations incompatible with the fragile appearance and delicate movement of fairies. The connotations are wrong for this comparison.

Compactness

Poetry exists as an end in itself. It has no mission or message beyond discovery, beyond the emotion and thought of the reader as he or she explores the lines. A poem is best said in few and artfully chosen words; it follows that if we change a word, we change the poem. Nothing can be altered in Langston Hughes's simple yet eloquent lament for a lost friend:

> I loved my friend.
> He went away from me.
> There's nothing more to say.
> The poem ends,
> Soft as it began—
> I loved my friend.

Hughes's purpose is not to instruct or to inform us, but through his words to make us experience profound loss. Change a single word and we change the experience. "I miss my friend" is no substitute for these six lines; the poem says far more than that. Even the repeated last line does not repeat the first idea, but adds to it. So compact is the poem that it can bear no paraphrase; it says twice as much in half the time.

Poems are brief and condensed. The poet must make the best possible use of each word, often choosing one term to convey many meanings, or relying on connotation to extend our awareness of the experience.

Emily Dickinson compresses the experience of reading a book into a poem of eight lines. To make her poem compact she relies upon three figurative comparisons, each one expanded in meaning by its richness in connotations:

> There is no frigate like a book
>   To take us lands away,
> Nor any courser like a page
>   Of prancing poetry—
> This traverse may the poorest take
>   Without oppress of toll—
> How frugal is the chariot
>   That bears the human soul!

Dickinson does not say that a book is like a mere boat, or even a sailboat; she calls up romance by using the term "frigate." Frigates are sailing vessels used by explorers seeking new lands, by pirates pursuing treasure and adventure, by merchants carrying silks and spices from the Orient to far-flung shores. A book is like a "courser," not a mere horse. "Courser" connotes knights charging off on missions fraught with danger and the promise of rescue. No car or wagon could have the mystery of a "chariot," a fragile royal cart flying along behind the hoofs of a thoroughbred. Other words as well, like "prancing," "frugal," and "toll," are rich in connotative meaning. Specific terms with rich meanings expand the ideas in the compact comparisons. By means of these connotations, the total experience of a book becomes adventure, wealth, discovery, suspense, intrigue, danger, romance, and a multitude of other possibilities. This poem, like the one Eve Merriam describes in "How to Eat a Poem," has nothing unnecessary, nothing to throw away—not a seed or a pit, a stem or a core or a rind.

Intensity often derives from compactness, and brevity exists in Jim Hall's "White Trash," a title with double ironic meaning. The many images and figurative comparisons are accurate, more effective in poetry than prose:

> Now it's Styrofoam pellets
> that blow across the yard.
> They settle in the new grass
> like the eggs of Japanese toys.
> It's a kind of modern snowing.
>
> The boy next door opened a box,
> and took out the precious present
> and shook these white spun plastic
> droplets into the wind.
> It's how his family thinks.

Hundreds of them. Shaped like
unlucky fetuses or the brains
of TV stars.

Now they burrow in the lawn,
defy the rake, wriggle like the toes
of the shallow buried.

They'll be there when we're gone.
Bright tumors, rooted in the dark.
Crowding the dirt. Nothing makes them
grow. But nothing kills them either.

Emotional Intensity

Like fiction at its best, poetry at its best lets us enjoy an old experience with new insight or understand one that we have never met. However, unlike the writer of fiction, the poet condenses the experience. Poetry attempts to capture the reader where he or she is, and to involve the reader briefly but intensely.

The successful poem is an intense emotional experience. "There Is No Frigate" is an experience of a book. It is not a description of a book, or of the feelings a child might have while reading a book. By its richly connotative words and its varied sensory images, the poem becomes an intense emotional experience. The same can be said of McCord's "Pickety Fence"; the poem is not a prosy description of a fence or the sounds a child might hear when drawing a stick along a picket fence. Because of its sounds and rhythms, the poem is an emotional experience of a picket fence. The poem has used the devices of poetry—rhythm, sound, compactness—to give us insight into the experience.

We have noted how rhythm, sound, and figurative language contribute to compactness, and compactness to emotional intensity. Langston Hughes writes out of the black experience but gives nonetheless a universal reaction to waiting for a dream to come true. "Dream Deferred" has emotional intensity, intensity created particularly by his skillful use of unusual figurative comparisons and sensory appeals:

What happens to a dream deferred?

Does it dry up
like a raisin in the sun?
Or fester like a sore—
And then run?
Does it stink like rotten meat?
Or crust and sugar over—
like a syrupy sweet?

Maybe it just sags
like a heavy load.

Or does it explode?

From the poem we have an intense emotional experience of frustration. A festering sore, stinking meat—these are ugly images causing us to experience the emotions that accompany frustration. The images connote neglect, usefulness turned to decay. What was a simple sore is now painfully infected; what was edible meat is now stinking uselessness.

Countee Cullen's speaker in "Incident" evokes both our sympathy for the black child and shame about the white racist, all in a few brief lines of the following poem:

> Once riding in old Baltimore,
>   Heart-filled, head-filled with glee,
> I saw a Baltimorean
>   Keep looking straight at me.
>
> Now I was eight and very small,
>   And he was no whit bigger,
> And so I smiled, and he poked out
>   His tongue, and called me, "Nigger."
>
> I saw the whole of Baltimore
>   From May until December;
> Of all the things that happened there
>   That's all that I remember.

Poetry can point out stereotypes as well. In four short lines, Janet Wong reminds readers of their prejudices:

> "Asians are supposed to be good at math."
> Mr. Chao can't figure me out.
> "Asians are quiet. Asians like numbers."
> Me, I like to shout.

Negative Qualities in Poetry

The negatives of literature—**didacticism, sentimentality,** and **condescension**—make their appearances in poetry, too, but only in poor poetry. These qualities are often expressed in words with distracting connotations, in trite comparisons, commonplace imagery, repetitious and unvaried beat, or in sound unsuited to meaning and tone. Kipling's didactic verse "If" is representative of the preaching verse adults often hear in the so-called inspirational speech. But children are even more often subjected to verses with preaching purpose, and Abbie Farwell Brown's "A Music Box" is one. The first stanza sets up a metaphor; the two that follow preach a sermon:

> I am a little Music Box
>   Wound up and made to go,
> And play my little living-tune
>   The best way that I know.
>
> If I am naughty, cross, or rude
>   The music will go wrong,
> My little works be tangled up,
>   And spoil the pretty song.
>
> I must be very sweet and good
>   And happy all the day,
> And then the little Music Box
>   In tune will always play.

Intrigued with the metaphor, we are fooled into thinking that "A Music Box" will be a pleasurable experience; then we learn that our sins spoil the song. By the final stanza—"I must be very sweet and good"—we are thoroughly disenchanted, disappointed that what began by intriguing us ends by instructing us to be happy models of perfection.

As for sentimentality and condescension, a poem that speaks to a worm about pain, assuming its pain to be comparable to the pain a person might feel if jumped on by a giant—that poem surely condescends to readers as it tries to rouse our emotions beyond justification:

> No, little worm, you need not slip
> Into your hole, with such a skip;
> Drawing the gravel as you glide
> On to your smooth and slimy side.
>
> For my part, I could never bear
> Your tender flesh to hack and tear,
> Forgetting that poor worms endure
> As much as I should, to be sure,
> If any giant would come and jump
> On to my back, and kill me plump,
> Or run my heart through with a scythe,
> And think it fun to see me writhe![5]

It is not the subject of the poem that is inappropriate for poetry; it is the sentimental tone. Notice, by contrast, the quality of wonder in Elizabeth Madox Roberts's poem "The Worm," in which the poet duplicates a childhood experience, relying almost exclusively upon imagery to draw us into experiencing the children's intent wonder. As the children dig with broken shell, tin, and spade, they find a small clod with a worm inside:

> We watched him pucker up himself
> And stretch himself to walk away.
> He tried to go inside the dirt,
> But Dickie made him wait and stay.

The children marvel at the sheen of the soft, wet skin, and they forget to dig their wells. Like children everywhere, they wonder if the worm knows it is a worm:

> And while we tried to find it out,
> He puckered in a little wad,
> And then he stretched himself again
> And went back home inside the clod.

Digging up a worm and looking at it intently can be an experience of poetry, an experience so compact that even adults become children once again during their involvement in 24 lines. In Roberts's poem there is neither sentimentality nor condescension.

The best poetry is made with care and artistry. Sometimes, in fact, poetry is found in paragraph form; the writer has chosen each word for its imagery and connotative power, asking of the reader concentration and imagination to discover meaning. On the other hand, prose and prosaic writing is sometimes put into the form usually reserved for poetry—irregular lines and stanza arrangement. But by failing to use words rich in connotative meaning, by failing to make figurative comparisons or to use rhythm to enhance meaning, the writer has written prose. Line or stanza arrangement has not made poetry out of prose.

The best prose and the best poetry are both written with care and skill. The difference lies primarily in the compactness and the intensity of the expression. Figurative devices, rhythmic flow, and sound patterns occur in prose. There is then no line to be drawn between prose and poetry; the difference is simply in degree. As rhythm becomes more regular, imagery more vivid, and statements more compact, emotions become more intense. The reader feels the increased intensity and becomes aware of the expression as poetry.

Summary

Rhymes and sidewalk jingles are many children's first experience with literature, and surely their first introduction to verse and poetry. The rhymes may not only provide an easy and loving bridge between the parents' childhoods and the new generation, but their simple stylistic devices of rhythm, sound, and comparison, their colorful characters involved in elementary tensions, and their occasional themes about the lives of human beings are sufficient reasons for including them as literature for the youngest child. They may or may not influence children's understanding, but the joy they give is undeniable.

The nursery and nonsense rhymes of childhood contain on different levels many of the elements of literature—of poetry and its style. Rhymes give pleasure through story and sounds. Nonsense delights us by its inventiveness, its unexpected turns and surprises. With its rapid rhythms and unexpected rhymes, and its topsy-turvy, no-sense way of looking at the logic of life, nonsense provides children with a great deal of pleasure—whether the joy is awakened by a patterned limerick, a gem of concentrated wit, or by children's own creations. Nonsense, too, is a way into poetry.

Poetry stands as an aesthetic experience in itself. Rhythm, sound, and connotation expand meaning; imagery heightens our sensory awareness; and apt figurative comparisons tempt our imaginations. A distilled representation of an experience, poetry at its best permits the reader to participate, but without the burden of didacticism or sentimentality.

Since the whole range from rhyme to nonsense to imaginative poetry is available to children, it seems only fair to introduce them to it all. Led easily from simple rhymes and nonsense to poetry, children, as Herbert Read says, deserve to be enticed and invited, wheedled and persuaded by poetic art. The experience of the best efforts of skillful poets is enlarging; it gives pleasure and promotes understanding. To keep that pleasure forever, children should be allowed to memorize what *they* choose—because we are all different.

Notes

1. Myra Cohn Livingston, in "Don't Cook Mother Goose," *New York Times Book Review,* July 26, 1988, calls attention to occasional new versions of Mother Goose that refuse "to free fancy," but interpolate "didacticism, moralism, and parochialism"; "they destroy the charm to tongue and ear and blind the child's inner eye."

2. Francelia Butler, in her study of jump-rope rhymes around the world, seems

to have discovered more brutality and violence in rhymes from America than in those from other countries. See "Over the Garden Wall/1 Let the Baby Fall: The Poetry of Rope-Skipping." *Children's Literature,* Vol. 3 (Storrs, Conn.: *Journal of the Modern Language Association and the Children's Literature Association,* 1974). Violence, however, is not peculiar to children's rhymes. Consider the recent controversy about song lyrics for young adults.

3. Listen to a recording of a poet reading his or her own poetry. Line breaks are recognized by the poet.

4. Herbert Read, "What Is Poetry? An Afterthought," in *This Way, Delight* (New York: Pantheon, 1956), p. 140.

5. Ann Taylor (1782–1866) published verses during a period when instruction was the only excuse for poetry to be published for children. *Original Poems for Infant Minds,* written by Ann, Jane, and their brother Isaac, was published in 1804.

Books Containing Poems Cited in This Chapter*

ADOFF, ARNOLD, ED. *Chocolate Dreams.* New York: William Morrow, 1989.

ALDIS, DOROTHY. *Hop, Skip and Jump.* New York: Putnam, 1934.

BEHN, HARRY. *The Little Hill.* New York: Harcourt Brace, 1949.

BROWN, ABBIE FARWELL. *Pinafore Palace.* ed. Kate Douglas Wiggin and Nora Archibald Smith. New York: Doubleday, 1907.

CARROLL, LEWIS. *Alice's Adventures in Wonderland.* 1865. Reprint. New York: Macmillan, 1963.

CULLEN, COUNTEE. *On These I Stand.* New York: Harper & Row, 1927.

DICKINSON, EMILY. *The Complete Poems of Emily Dickinson.* Boston: Little, Brown, 1960.

FISHER, AILEEN. *Out in the Dark and Daylight.* New York: Harper & Row, 1980.

FRANCIS, ROBERT. *The Orb Weaver.* Middletown, Conn.: Wesleyan University Press, 1948.

GIOVANNI, NIKKI. *Spin a Soft Black Song.* Toronto: Collins Publishers, 1985.

HUGHES, LANGSTON. *Selected Poems of Langston Hughes.* New York: Knopf, 1926.

JANECZKO, PAUL, ed. *Looking for Your Name.* New York: Orchard Books, 1993.

KENNEDY, CHARLES W., ed. *Anthology of Old English Poetry.* London: Oxford University Press, 1960.

KENNEDY, X. J. *The Phantom Ice Cream Man: More Nonsense Verse.* New York: Atheneum, 1979.

LEAR, EDWARD. *Nonsense Omnibus.* New York: Frederick Warne, 1943.

*Because of their very nature, anthologies and collections of poetry are not always consistent in their quality. Therefore, the list here is a list only of books containing poems cited in the chapter.

LINDSAY, VACHEL. *The Congo and Other Poems*. New York: Macmillan, 1914.

LIVINGSTON, MYRA COHN, ed. *What a Wonderful Bird the Frog Are*. New York: Harcourt Brace Jovanovich, 1973.

———. *Whispers and Other Poems*. New York: Harcourt Brace Jovanovich, 1958.

MERRIAM, EVE. *Inside a Poem*. New York: Atheneum, 1962.

MOORE, LILIAN. *Think of Shadows*. New York: Atheneum, 1980.

MORRISON, LILIAN. *The Sidewalk Racer*. New York: Lothrop, Lee & Shepard, 1968.

NASH, OGDEN. *The Face Is Familiar*. Garden City, N.Y.: Garden City Publishers, 1941.

O'NEILL, MARY. *Hailstones and Halibut Bones*. New York: Doubleday, 1989.

RICHARDS, LAURA E. *Tirra Lirra: Rhymes Old and New*. Boston: Little, Brown, 1955.

ROBERTS, ELIZABETH MADOX. *Under the Tree*. New York: Viking, 1930.

SANDBURG, CARL. *Chicago Poems*. New York: Harcourt Brace Jovanovich, 1944.

SCHERTLE, ALICE. *Advice for a Frog*. New York: Lothrop, Lee & Shepard, 1995.

STARBIRD, KAYE. *The Covered Bridge House*. New York: Four Winds, 1979.

STEVENSON, ROBERT LOUIS. *A Child's Garden of Verses*. New York: Watts, 1966 (first published, 1885).

UPDIKE, JOHN. *A Child's Calendar*. New York: Knopf, 1965.

WONG, JANET S. *Good Luck Gold and Other Poems*. New York: Macmillan, 1994.

WYNNE, ANNETTE. *More Silver Pennies*. New York: Macmillan, 1938.

My Dream of Martin Luther King
Faith Ringgold

12

Biography

Some children get "hooked" on biography, and others may never discover it. What reasons for leading children to biography can you identify?

Sometimes curiosity leads children to wonder about people. How did this writer start writing? Who proved the world is round? Who wondered about the stars? Who led millions of people to understand racism? What made women become nurses?

Biography Defined

Biography is the history of the life of an individual. It includes three essentials: facts, a concept that the facts relate to, and an attitude toward the subject and the reader. First of all, the facts are expected to be accurate, up-to-date, and authentic as they depict the subject and the period in which the subject lived. The objective biographer must include or omit events and details as they suit the interests and age level of the readers for whom the biography is intended. As for concept, we assume that the subject of the biography is worth reading about, just as it is worth the writer's time in research and writing. A subject for biography has done something or been something, discovered or demonstrated something that makes her or his life significant—more significant, say, than your life or your sister's or brother's. As for attitude, the attitude of the writer reflects interest and enthusiasm. If the writer finds the subject worth writing about, she or he finds the subject worth writing about with the skill we call style. The skillful biographer uses words imaginatively, even in the simplest biographies for younger readers. Autobiography, written by the subject, cannot be totally objective because the narrated events are filtered through the writer's consciousness. A particularly moving series of personal accounts can be found in Julius Lester's collected slave narratives, *To Be a Slave.*

Biography often gives a picture quite different from traditional stereotypes. The cruel emperor and successful conquerer of Chingis Khan might seem a strange figure for a biography for the picture-book crowd, but writer-illustrator Demi seems to have been tempted by the story's colorful and unusual opportunities for illustration. Each page of the brief text is accompanied by an elaborately detailed picture of the action. The account does not glorify cruelty, but instead rewards loyalty and military skill.

We often turn to the lives of significant people because we wish to discover more about what it was like to be alive and aware in a period of history we have just discovered. Or we may become curious about the "what if" of being a frontier hero—"What if I had been one?" Or a winning athlete, or a worker in the slums. We may be wondering how people become writers or architects. Or we may have discovered that once people didn't know about bacteria, and we wish to know about that discovery and its relationship to disease. Curiosity, wonder, the possibility of discovery—a number of related motives may lead us to read about the lives of individuals.

Curiosity leads the reader into a subject and on beyond it.

The Writer's Obligations

Within the definition of biography—biography is the history of the life of an individual—are two terms, *history* and *individual,* and each presents a separate obligation for the writer. The first term, *history,* implies facts, and biography, like all nonfiction, should be factually accurate. Information about the life of the subject comes from such sources as letters, journals, diaries, court records, newspaper accounts, recorded conversations, and interviews, wherever feasible. Although not all biographies for children include a bibliography, it is a useful addition. A quick glance at the foreword or acknowledgments may also tell something about the writer's research, and perhaps suggest other readings to the curious child. A closer look at the text itself will reveal dates, quotations, places, and names as they fit into the narrative. But again, the numbers of such details depend upon the age of the intended readers. Such data make the book seem factually authentic, and other information can be taken on faith.

The term *history* implies another obligation on the part of the writer: History when properly written is reported objectively. The respected historian neither shows personal bias nor assumes omniscience about thoughts and feelings of historical figures. The conscientious biographer, despite interest in the subject, is bound by similar limitations; he or she does not get into the mind of the subject, but limits the information to verifiable matters and to emotions, fantasies, or thoughts the subject has spoken of or recorded. For example, in *The Double Life of Pocahontas,* Jean Fritz is faithful in her documentation; notes and bibliography are complete enough for the child reader. As extensive as her research seems to have been, Fritz could not know what Pocahontas thought as she was being "civilized" by the British at Rock Hall. "Perhaps she thought [she would] become one of them. . . . In her long skirts she may already have felt less like an Indian." John Rolfe and Pocahontas "probably first met at church. . . . Perhaps he was falling in love." Partiality yields to fact and objectivity.

By definition, a biography is about an *individual,* and here lies a second responsibility. Children who become interested in the lives of presidents, for example, often have difficulty sorting out the life of one president from the life of another, because aside from living in different historical periods, presidents in children's biographies may become stereotypes of all that is good. Their differences are slight: Washington is honest, Lincoln compassionate, Wilson scholarly, Theodore Roosevelt nonconforming but commanding. Servants to society like Jane Addams, Clara Barton, or Florence Nightingale are unselfishly devoted to helping others; freed slaves like Amos Fortune may be cardboard figures of self-denial. The process of writing biography, like that of writing informational books, is a process of constant decision-making: what to select and what to omit. The biographer wishes to show the individual as a believable human being, complete with such flaws as occasional self-interest, irritability, or faulty judgment. Although there is a trend toward showing the less admirable traits in the character of the subject, writers usually ignore socially disapproved behavior. Poor biographies, however, often ignore completely any negative qualities and present only the good. The result is sometimes a book colored by an approving tone that may be disproportionate to the subject's achievements or character, and in any case is unrealistic.

In *Christopher Columbus,* Susan Heimann gives her subject credit for his achievements; nonetheless, she does show him as a believable human being. Columbus, in writing about the Native Americans in the newly discovered land, says of them: "They ought to be good servants and of good skill . . . they would easily be made Christians, because it seems that they belonged to no religion." Heimann goes on to say that Columbus has revealed in these words that while the one public motive for the voyage—bringing religion to the natives—is still important, it now seems to come second to "using" these people as skillful servants. Since children often read biography because of curiosity about a hero to emulate, it seems important that the subject of the biography not be so unreal, or so saintly, that the reader feels emulation is impossible. When honestly described, the subject is real enough to encourage the reader to similar efforts and achievements.

Facts and objectivity are essential.

Biography and Fiction

We see the terms *biographical fiction* and *fictional biography* and wonder what they mean. Both admit that the writer has dramatized or invented parts that perhaps cannot be verified, or that the writer wishes to make facts into a story to show how the subject *might* have behaved, given his or her character. The problem for the writer of biography for children lies to a great extent in the answers to two basic questions: How much fact shall I include? How much narrative may I invent?

F. N. Monjo, for example, used some of the facts of Lincoln's life along with a fictional storytelling device: Lincoln's son Tad is the first-person narrator of *Me and Willie and Pa*. Tad tells, among other things, of crawling into Pa's bed when he was lonely after Tad's brother Willie's death. The book uses historical facts, but the child's interest is held by the imagined narrative. A biography as brief as a picture book can also be effective nonfiction, telling only the most significant events. *The Glorious Flight* by Alice and Martin Provensen tells of Louis Blériot, his five children, and the family's fascination with the clacking flying machine overhead. Blériot's keen interest turns to obsession, and he builds one machine after another, until in 1909 Blériot XI flies the twenty miles across the English Channel. The text does not try to describe differences in the eleven models, but the book pictures them one by one.

For younger children, some invented narrative seems acceptable.

Biography for the older child might fall closer to the factual end of the spectrum; the older child can absorb more facts and may require less story. Too much factual detail, however, makes the page dense with the capital letters of places, people, and events, and the appearance is that of an encyclopedia. The response to such a biography may be, "This is more than I really want to know." And yet, too much dramatization or inclusion of probable dialogue prompts the response, "What can I really believe?" Carl Sandburg, in writing about his biography of Lincoln, stated that he did not invent dialogue or incident to prove a point; he adhered to fact. And yet Sandburg's work, from which *Abe Lincoln Grows Up* is drawn, is unsurpassed as a definitive biography of young Lincoln, both for accuracy and interest. It is possible to stick to the facts and to write an interesting book. But if the writer does dramatize, these inventions should be historically true to the times and not merely possible, but probable. Such dramatization often occurs when the subject of the biography is long dead and has left few written records.

The carefully researched *Lincoln: A Photobiography* by Russell Freedman is very convincing, largely because Freedman quotes from Lincoln's handwritten notes and occasional journals. He catches the tone of Lincoln's writing, interpreting what happens in light of the insights gained from personal glimpses. Lincoln's last day, for example, rings true to what we know of his compassion. After lunch he "revoked the death sentence of a Confederate spy." And he pardoned a deserter, signing his name with the comment, "Well, I think this boy can do us more good above ground than under ground!" Members at the last cabinet meeting heard his wish that no retaliatory "bloody work" be done, adding that blood enough had been lost.[1]

People who live active lives are naturally and easily made interesting for children; when adventure is part of the subject's life, the narrative pulls the reader along. However, biographies of philosophers, poets, or musicians who lived quietly with little drama or action in their lives are more difficult to make interesting, especially for younger readers. The obligation remains, however, for the biographer to focus upon the nature of the person as well as upon the exciting events of his or her life. Where the subject's achievement is less filled with action or adventure, the writer faces the necessity of holding interest in the subject and yet keeping invented action to a minimum. This dual responsibility is not easy to fulfill, particularly when the subject has left few recorded statements. Invention is sometimes the biographer's compromise.

Tone and Style

The reader of biography ought to expect suitable tone and appropriate style. In five different accounts of Columbus's landing in what he thought to be the Indies, the biographers refer to the "Indians" and explorers in different ways. One account seems to call undue attention to the Indians' nakedness, and by using quiet verbs and exotic descriptions creates a romantic, fairytale tone. Notice the effect of "scarlet" instead of red, for example:

> Columbus and his men saw a new beautiful world.
> Here were brown men with no clothes at all. Their bodies were painted red and other bright colors. . . . They were pleased to take gifts of bells and beads and scarlet caps. They were a gentle and friendly people.

A second biographer seems to condescend because he places quotation marks around "talk" and "told," as he describes in minimal terms the sign language used by both the Indians and the explorers:

> Columbus finally managed to "talk" to the Indians by making signs with his hands. The Indians made signs too. They "told" Columbus he was welcome.

A third account by its tone of wonder makes the Indians seem like children and the explorers seem, even to the reader, to be like gods.

> [All Columbus saw] were naked, red-skinned savages. They threw themselves to the ground and worshiped Columbus and his bearded men. . . .

> They thought that gods had descended from the heavens on white-winged birds. They led the white gods to their homes.

And a fourth writer, Susan Heimann, wins our belief by narrating facts in a convincingly objective tone:

> Curiosity quickly overcame fear on the part of the people of the island, and soon they came out to meet these strange men from another world. These "very handsome people" were Tainos. . . . Columbus called them Indians. He described them as gentle and helpful in every way. They wore no clothes, and many of the men painted their bodies.

Jean Fritz, in *Where Do You Think You're Going, Christopher Columbus?* seems to be showing Columbus as a very ordinary man who has miscalculated the distance to the Indies as well as what the "Indians" would look like, his impressions gained from the inaccurate hearsay descriptions of Marco Polo and Sir John Mandeville.

> . . . The only sign of gold was the gold rings that the natives wore in their noses. Indeed, that was all they wore. The people were as naked, Columbus said, "as their mothers bore them," which of course, was pretty naked. Otherwise, they were normal looking. They didn't have umbrella feet or eyes on their shoulders.

Fritz's description of the Indians retains the light, humorous tone of the whole book, and therefore it does not condescend to the Indians any more than to anyone else. The biography seems essentially accurate, and a thoroughly enjoyable "story" complete with endnotes.

The number and variety of books about Columbus recently published for the quincentennial or five-hundredth anniversary of the "discovery" of America seems infinite. A brief look at several merely suggests the variety of publications in which the occasion has been commemorated. Look first of all at one of the most controversial, *Encounter,* Jane Yolen's imaginative and sympathetic picture book narrated in first person by a Native American boy who distrusted the explorers from the start and whose distrust proved to be merited when he was taken captive. The worst elements of the explorers' behavior seem very real when we see their effect on a young boy. Another, *A Picture Book of Christopher Columbus,* pictures an oddly static assortment of events in the explorer's life, including his marriage and a plea to King John II of Portugal, who seems to be pictured as a woman. *Meet Christopher Columbus* says in halting and hesitant style that Columbus was advised to tell Queen Isabella of Spain about his plan. "He wrote to her. She was very interested. She asked Columbus to come and tell her more about it. If she liked it, she would give him the ships herself. If she did not like it, she would not let him go at all."

The oversized history book by Richard Humble called *The Voyages of Christopher Columbus,* in the Exploration Through the Ages series, is beautifully illustrated with pictures of Indians, small maps, large action pictures aboard sailing ships, and glimpses of the explorers' clothing and of Columbus on his death bed. Dates make the account authoritative, and rarely noted facts are interesting additions. For example, it was later Spanish arrivals who made slaves of the Native Americans. In comparison to other accounts, the tone of this book seems to cover up the explorer's character flaws.

In *Christopher Columbus,* part of the Junior World Biographies, Norman L. Macht begins his Columbus story with the influential effect of the writings of Marco Polo as he described the exotic wealth of the Grand Khan of China. In the sixteenth century, people feared that at the equator the sea was boiling hot, ships would burn up, and monsters would eat the sailing crews. They also feared that if the earth was truly round it would be impossible to turn around and sail upward toward home. The text, using a more critical tone, reveals Columbus's weakness as governor of Hispaniola, his harsh treatment of rebels, and his irritability as he saw others who had sailed with him going out now to achieve a new glory while he stayed behind in Spain to plead endlessly with the monarchs for new ships and sailors.

The same individual may be quite different in different biographies.

An interesting variation is *The Log of Christopher Columbus* by Christopher Columbus, selections by Steve Lowe. Here are Columbus's own words, telling how he kept two records of progress, one that he believed to be truthful and the other that assured the crew they were not far from home. He knows that mutiny threatens his life, that his sightings of floating weeds and tiny shore birds are keeping hope alive. The linoleum-cut illustrations are highly effective. A very personalized account is found in *Christopher Columbus: From Vision to Voyage* by Joan Anderson, whose use of an omniscient point of view and sympathetic tone lets us know what Columbus thinks:

> Christopher, having secretly planned to make a dramatic gesture, pulled
> an egg from his pocket and placed it on a table. "Your Majesty," he said,
> "I implore you to make this egg stand on its end. . . . You see," he said,
> "you can do anything you want if you know how."

The elegant photographs by George Ancona show well-researched period costume, and the effect is a good story, the product of an imaginative writer.

Many other Columbus books are longer and more detailed. Nancy Smiler Levinson, in her author's note to *Christopher Columbus: Voyager to the Unknown,* has the objectivity of the historian as she tells of the difficulties of researching events five hundred years old, the early translations that seem to contradict one another, and the controversy regarding which island was Columbus's first landfall. *Christopher Columbus: The Great Adventure and How We Know About It* by Delno C. and Jean M. West includes artifacts, the legend of an unknown pilot, navigational instruments, a variety of ancient maps, cargo carried to Spain, Viking predecessors, and local foods as well as accepted historical truth.

Discovering Christopher Columbus: How History Is Invented by Kathy Pelta does what the title suggests: matter-of-factly tells how research is done. A myriad of information is recounted, beginning with the difficulties of tracing the explorer's history because the few written accounts (many in Latin) differ widely: his name is different in Italy, Portugal, and Spain, and his signature and the burial place of his bones are even in question. At one time regarded as superhuman, he was considered a genuine hero; later discoveries show him also to have been tyrannical and hypocritical. Note is made of Alice Gould, credited with research that clarified the crew's wages, duties, and origins; her work has been called by historian Samuel Eliot Morison "the most valuable piece of Columbian research in the present century." This book concludes with notes about many sources of information and suggests that children may wish to pursue them further. All in all, not only is the book interesting, but its tone makes it seem highly authentic.

All these books are merely a few of those about Columbus available to children.

Look next at a group of biographies of Martin Luther King. The first, *Martin Luther King, Jr.: A Man Who Changed Things,* is part of a series called "Rookie Biography." The book bores the reader immediately by its simple sentences in repetitive form:

> Next Martin studied in Boston.
>> There he met a girl.
>> Her name was Coretta Scott.
>> She was pretty and smart.
>> On their first date, Martin
>> asked her to marry him.

Happy Birthday, Martin Luther King is a bare-bones account of his life. Racist society is briefly described in a few sentences about drinking fountains, restaurants, and segregated schools, while King's philosophy of nonviolent protest is oversimplified into "Love one another in peace."

Martin Luther King, Jr, and the March Toward Freedom, however, plunges immediately into showing reasons for readers to know about King. "Movements are born when many people share a belief that things must change. But every great movement needs a leader. Often it takes a single person to shape a clear vision of how the world can be." Unfortunately, not all of Rita Hakim's writing is interesting; she, too, falls at times into simple, repetitive sentences. In chapters with titles like "The Minister and the Boycott," "The Movement," and "The March on Washington," the narrative follows the principal events in King's life. His "I Have a Dream" speech is partly quoted, and Mahatma Gandhi's method of nonviolent protest explained. The book ends with a useful list of suggestions for books, movies, and places to look for further information.

As one of the series called "World Leaders: Past and Present," Nancy Shukur's *Martin Luther King* begins with the significant March on Washington. In preparation for his speech, King has spent the entire night wondering if the crowds would be significant and if his words would be heard beyond the Mall. By the time 250,000 people, most of them black, have gathered, the narrative has reached a suspenseful point. Shukur's style is clear and forceful, and the newspaper clippings and photographs effective in following King's short life. Beginning with the second chapter, the book tells of King's schooling, his doubts about the church's leadership in civil rights, his time in jail, and the impact of Gandhi's teachings on his thinking. Attractively formatted, the book is effective.

A number of picture books also tell King's story. Faith Ringgold's *My Dream of Martin Luther King* is unlike others. In the narrator's dream, great crowds of people of all creeds and colors are gathered, each with a bag containing ignorance, fear, and hatred. The essential facts of King's life and times—his family, the country's racism, nonviolent protest, Rosa Parks—all are there in the narrator's illustrated dream, but the crack of an assassin's gun ends King's life. When the dream crowd gathers to mourn his death, they empty their bags of hatred and racism, which go up in a burst of flame as, "emblazoned across the sky," words are seen by the crowd: "Every good thing starts with a dream." The biography is effective, a personal reaction to King's life and work.

Martin Luther King by Rosemary L. Bray, paintings by Malcah Zeldis, is an unusual mix of lengthy text on a full 10-x-12 inch page across from a full-size illustration. It tells of the bus strike initiated by Rosa Parks, encouraged by the NAACP, and organized by King. Apparently the book is for a picture-book audience, but it deserves a more appropriate format. The text is not oversimplified, but well written and surprisingly complete, showing King as what he was: a martyr to civil rights.

Writers of biography may use all of the devices of style. In *Stonewall*, stylist Jean Fritz describes Stonewall Jackson as experiencing painfully hard years between the deaths of his father and his mother. She calls this time a figurative "hard knot at the very root of his character." Using imagery and onomatopoeic language, she tells us that he lived with his mother's relatives for a time, where the "rumble of wagon wheels, the slip-slopping of water, the buzzing of machinery formed a background music for all the farmwork." Life on his uncle's farm was rough; men "from all over the country came and . . . bet and drank and smoked and swore and spit and carried on." Using five sentences of repeated subject-verb order, Fritz's style, because here it contrasts with her usual sentence variety, emphasizes Jackson's determination: "He decided . . . he had to find rules for his life and then follow them strictly. He wasn't going to let life just happen to him. He wasn't going to be like his father and slip carelessly into errors and from errors to ruin. He was going to be in charge."

The biographer, facing the need to arouse and hold the reader's interest, may be tempted to create sympathy for the subject and to make a tear-jerker out of early trials. One biographer of the composer Beethoven as a young man has made from very brief factual information a sentimental story of Beethoven's being victimized by a tyrannical teacher. He says, "Poor Ludwig!" and describes his day as long, hard, and wearying. Ludwig stumbles off to bed, but is shaken awake in the middle of the night and called a lazy rascal. Then he is made to stay awake and write music. His unreasonable teacher stands over him, thunders at his drowsiness, forces the exhausted boy back to work, then goes to bed leaving the weary boy struggling with fatigue as he finishes the writing. Here again, it is not the facts we question so much as the tone.

Paderewski the pianist might have been treated with equal sentimentality as he goes off to the Warsaw Conservatory. However, in *Paderewski*, Charlotte Kellogg is unsentimental: "More than discouraging was his first experience in a piano class. 'Not hands for playing,' the teacher declared. 'That thumb, that third finger, too short.' He gave Ignace a trial, then told him to leave, to take up some other instrument."

Concepts and Didacticism

Concept is needed in biography as it is in other literature; our preoccupation with fact must not blind us to idea.

Buddhism is one of the world's major religions, and Susan Roth in *Buddha* introduces her subject by recounting Buddha's mother's dream of his princeliness before his birth. Buddha's childhood in a totally protected environment, where he was pampered in every conceivable way, left him ignorant of aging, pain, illness, and poverty, but following his marriage he moved outside the palace and saw the real world. He then devoted himself to simplicity and prayer for the unfortunate. Buddhists are increasing in numbers in North America, and Roth's lyrical text and vivid collages introduce Buddha to small children.

The title *Invincible Louisa* suggests a concept behind the biography; the same can be said for *Carry On, Mr. Bowditch,* or *Up From Slavery.* Other biographies, while they may not indicate the unifying idea in their titles, do have a concept that is implicit within them, perhaps the reasons for the writer's having chosen these people as subjects. This leader unified his or her country; this scientist persisted until research bore fruit; this athlete overcame difficulties; this composer was an innovator. Any of these reasons for writing the biography can unify the account to make it a coherent whole.

Biographies need facts, but also idea—a reason for the choice of subject.

Concept unifies Fritz's biography *Stonewall*, a nickname that characterized Jackson's determination in everything, from his health to his battle plans. "I'm going to make a man of myself if I live. What I will do, I can do." Self-control that dictated posture, prayers, and health maintenance picture Stonewall as standing erect to keep his alimentary canal straight:

> [He put] himself on a diet of stale unbuttered bread and lean meat. No tea, coffee, or stimulants of any kind. And he exercised. Fast walks accompanied by leaps and arm-whirlings. . . . One arm, he decided, was heavier than the other so he developed the habit of thrusting the heavy one up in the air at regular intervals. This way the blood would run back into the body . . . and lighten the arm.

However, having a reason to choose a subject for biography does not give the writer license to preach. Intent upon making a point about the worthiness of the subject, the writer may lapse into didacticism. Writing of Louisa May Alcott's early life, Cornelia Meigs insists that we recognize the idealism behind her father Bronson Alcott's efforts to form the perfect social community. Such insistence intervenes between the readers and Louisa, the real subject; it shakes a finger at the readers to make them accept Meigs's views. In *Invincible Louisa*, she writes:

> We must remember, however, that Bronson and his friends, wise in some ways, mistaken in others, had the courage to find out, by the only possible means, where they were right and where they were wrong. There is only one method of testing a system of living; that is by living it.

Louisa saw Concord soldiers march away to the Civil War, and such a picture is relevant to the biography. But here, too, Meigs intervenes:

> There is no experience in the world that can ever match that of seeing soldiers go away, of seeing the gaiety and the excitement and of knowing the black and hopeless tragedy which is behind it all. There is little that is so terrible as seeing strong, wholesome young men, every one of them beautiful in the flush of their high patriotism, as watching them go and knowing that they are surely to die.

Some biographies have strong themes, as does *Be the Best You Can Be* by Kirby Pucket with Greg Brown. Because the book is autobiographical and is for the picture-book set, the theme as expressed in the title seems didactic. There is further didacticism on the last page, under the heading "Kirby's Extra Innings," where quotations from athlete Kirby tell children to "Say Nope to Dope," "Get an Education," and "Treat People Right." In a sense, it is healthy for young readers to discover that some athletes strive for more than merely the high salary and have some principled views on life. Pardoning the didacticism is left to the reader.

There is information coupled with vitality in *Carry On, Mr. Bowditch*. Jean Lee Latham tells of Nathaniel Bowditch's discovery of a new and simpler way to make lunar calculations at sea. Without preaching, she simultaneously explains the process, records the action, and reproduces the excitement of discovery:

> Tonight ought to be a good one for a lunar. The moon was due to pass over a star that was bright enough to see in spite of its nearness to the moon. . . . Just when the moon neared the bright star, a cloud got in the way. Nat shrugged and sighed. There ought to be a better way to work a lunar! He studied the glittering heavens. Was there another star bright enough tonight—that the moon would pass over? Of course not. He knew that. That one . . . the moon would pass below it . . . that one . . . the moon would pass above it . . . that one . . .
>
> The idea hit Nat so suddenly that he gasped. He raced below and for the second time that night crashed into Prince's cabin without knocking.

The straightforward, factual tone of Russell Freedman's *The Wright Brothers* carries conviction. Letters add personal touches of feeling, both optimism and disappointment, and photographs illustrate the efforts of the bachelor brothers as they confront flight problems of lift, propulsion, and control. Bishop Wright's two sons Orville and Wilbur worked to improve machines by Lilienthal, Langley, and Chanute. Their favorite niece wrote of the two brothers' early helicopter, made of cork and cloth, harbinger of their intense interest in flight, as particularly fascinating. Newspaper accounts tell of the curious crowds that gathered at Kitty Hawk as they tried one variation after another in search of perfect solutions. The brothers first camped on the Outer Banks of North Carolina, played their harmonica and mandolin—and thought. They thought alike, rising each morning filled with enthusiasm and new ideas to try out. The effect of the biography is that these were real men with enormous curiosity and imagination, who without years of schooling were persistent in their project, loving it not for imagined financial rewards but for the joy of invention.

Many of the facts in *Eleanor Roosevelt: A Life of Discovery,* also by Freedman, are taken from Eleanor Roosevelt's own writings—her letters, newspaper columns, and autobiography—along with transcriptions of interviews and conversations with those she knew, as well as from a variety of other carefully researched sources. The unifying concept comes from one of her own statements, used as an epigraph: "You gain strength, courage and confidence by every experience in which you really stop to look fear in the face. . . . You must do the thing you think you cannot do." Roosevelt's early years and the first years of her marriage to Franklin were filled with experiences for which she looked fear in the face, doing what she felt she could not do—but did. In 1946, the plain and awkward child once demeaned by her beautiful mother was a grown woman given a standing ovation in the United Nations. Freedman's biography concludes with a return to the concept expressed in the words of the epigraph: "And having learned to stare down fear, I long ago reached the point where there is no living person whom I fear, and few challenges I am not willing to face."

The man who in 1853 opened Japan to world trade was Commodore Perry, and in the opening paragraphs of *Commodore Perry in the Land of the Shogun* by Rhonda Blumberg, we read of the people's panic at the arrival of the mysterious ship filled with "aliens," monsters the Japanese fear, arriving with the threat of horrors: "Great giants puffing smoke." "Alien ships of fire" might invade to kill, kidnap, or destroy all of Japan, Land of the Rising Sun. Over a period of weeks spent in the harbor, the curious Americans come to respect the courteous and inquisitive Japanese, and an amicable diplomatic relationship develops. This well-researched book, whose footnotes defend its accuracy, is illustrated with numerous drawings and a few black-and-white photos.

An illustrated collection of brief biographies of six Native American chiefs, Freedman's *Indian Chiefs* describes the life histories of men who were chiefs because they were advocates of either peace or war. Within tribes there were often leaders who advocated compromising with the white traders and settlers, and others who wished to drive them all back to the territories where, in their treaties, they had promised to stay. Hence, there were chiefs of war and chiefs of peace. Freedman discusses Red Cloud of the Oglala Sioux, Santana, of the Kiowa, Quanah Parker of the Comanche, Washake of the Shoshone, Joseph of the Nez Percé, and Sitting Bull of the Hunkpapa Sioux.

Summary

Biography is the history of the life of an individual. The word *history* implies fact, and the term *individual* requires that the portrayal avoid stereotyping and show the subject as unique. Readers choose biography out of curiosity about a person, curiosity aroused perhaps by having read a reference to that person, or by a reference to a discovery or a period in time. A well-written biography helps the reader toward knowledge—knowledge as contrasted to mere information or fact. Naturally, techniques are therefore subordinated to this end. Within each biography, the reader seeks facts, concepts, and the writer's attitude toward subject. Curiosity or wonder, the motivation for children, is stimulated by the quality of what they read, tempting them to discover more about people and their relationships to far-off times, scientific concepts, or ways of solving society's problems.

Since the order in which facts and concepts are presented influences how well readers understand, a chronological narrative is usually best for younger children. Tone influences biography, just as it does imaginative literature. Condescension looks down upon the subject, sentimentality distorts it, and propaganda invalidates it. Style, although it must be clear and factual, need not be banal or trite; imagery, figurative language, and varied sentence structure stimulate a reader's response: I want to know more.

Notes

1. See "Abe, Honestly and Otherwise," by Henry Mayer, *New York Times Book Review*, February 12, 1989, p. 24, for a comparison of Lincoln biographies for children.

Recommended Books Cited in This Chapter

ANDERSON, JOAN. *Christopher Columbus: From Vision to Voyage*. Photographs by George Ancona. New York: Dial, 1991.

BLUMBERG, RHODA. *Commodore Perry in the Land of the Shogun*. New York: Morrow, 1985.

BRAY, ROSEMARY L. *Martin Luther King*. Illustrated by Malcah Zeldis. New York: Greenwillow, 1995.

COLUMBUS, CHRISTOPHER. (Steve Lowe, ed.) *The Log of Christopher Columbus*. Illustrated by Robert Sabuda. Blue Ridge, Pa.: Philomel, 1992.

DEMI. *Chingis Khan*. New York: Henry Holt, 1991.

FREEDMAN, RUSSELL. *Eleanor Roosevelt: A Life of Discovery*. Boston: Houghton Mifflin, 1993.

———. *Indian Chiefs*. New York: Holiday House, 1987.

———. *Lincoln: A Photobiography*. New York: Tichnor & Fields, 1987

———. *The Wright Brothers*. New York: Holiday House, 1991.

FRITZ, JEAN. *The Double Life of Pocahontas*. New York: Putnam, 1983.

———. *Stonewall*. New York: Putnam, 1979.

———. *Where Do You Think You're Going, Mr. Columbus?* New York: Putnam, 1980.

HAKIM, RITA. *Martin Luther King, Jr. and the March Toward Freedom*. Brookfield, Conn.: Millbrook Press, 1991.

HEIMANN, SUSAN. *Christopher Columbus*. New York: Watts, 1973.

HUMBLE, RICHARD. *The Voyages of Christopher Columbus*. Illustrated by Richard Hooks. New York: Watts, 1991.

KELLOG, CHARLOTTE. *Paderewski*. New York: Viking, 1956.

LATHAM, JEAN LEE. *Carry On, Mr. Bowditch*. Boston: Houghton Mifflin, 1955.

LEVINSON, NANCY SMILER. *Christopher Columbus: Voyager to the Unknown*. New York: Lodestar, 1990.

MACHT, NORMAN L. *Christopher Columbus*. New York: Chelsea House, 1992.

MONJO, F. N. *Me and Willie and Pa*. New York: Simon & Schuster, 1973.

PELTA, KATHY. *Discovering Christopher Columbus: How History Is Invented*. Minneapolis: Lerner, 1991.

PROVENSEN, ALICE AND MARTIN PROVENSEN. *The Glorious Flight*. New York: Viking, 1983.

RINGGOLD, FAITH. *My Dream of Martin Luther King*. New York: Crown, 1991.

ROTH, SUSAN. *Buddha*. New York: Doubleday, 1994.

SANDBURG, CARL. *Abe Lincoln Grows Up*. New York: Harcourt Brace, 1931.

SHUKUR, NANCY. *Martin Luther King: World Leaders Past and Present*. New York: Chelsea House, 1985.

WEST, DELNO C., AND JEAN M. WEST. *Christopher Columbus: The Great Adventure and How We Know About It*. New York: Atheneum, 1991.

YOLEN, JANE. *Encounter*. New York: Harcourt Brace, 1992.

HANDLE

CUTTING WHEEL

HANDLE

SPUR GEARS

A can opener has a sharp-edged cutting blade or wheel that slices into the lid. A toothed wheel fits beneath the lip of the can, and rotates the can so that the cutting wheel is forced into the lid. Two further toothed wheels — one above the other — form a pair of spur gears (see p.41) to transmit the turning force from the handle.

The Way Things Work
David Macaulay

13

Nonfiction

How does nonfiction become propaganda?

Adults range widely in their reading interests, from the financial page of the daily newspaper to a favorite comic strip, and on to particular curiosities, whether they be genealogy or strip-mining. In between, they experience floods of enthusiasm for "everything *that* writer ever wrote" to "everything I see about the Internet." And yet we are continually surprised at the diversity in children's taste or at their sudden enthusiasms for horses or baseball players. People are alike, and often we find that the interesting adult with a multitude of curiosities is the grown child whose reading may have begun with an omnivorous—and simultaneous—devouring of animal fantasy and atomic fission.

What does interest a child in nonfiction? Of course, older children may go in search of information, but small children frequently find fiction and nonfiction shelved in the same section of their libraries. In search of another good book "like the one last week about the ducklings in the park," they encounter another good book—but this time it is about the color wheel and how one color merges with another to form tones and shades and tints and other colors. Both books may be equally fascinating. At other times, children who have moved away from the picture book section may happen upon a shelf where there are cataloging numbers on the spines of the books, instead of just the initial *E* or *J*. And there, wonder of wonders, are all kinds of books about how animals really live, and eat, and raise their babies, and fight to survive. From this discovery, children may take off on a nonfiction binge. In all of this meandering there seems to be a thread that holds one book or group of books to another—curiosity.

The line between fiction and nonfiction is a fine one in books for children. In a great many storybooks, there is much information about the world, animals, people, history, nature. After all, we learn about spinnerets and the parts of the spider's legs in *Charlotte's Web*. But when we discuss nonfiction, we are really less interested in how suspense is built and more interested in how facts are presented; less interested in character and more in discovery of the relationship and application of concepts to society or the natural world. Sometimes the writer uses a chronological arrangement of some kind, a narrative, that makes the nonfiction resemble fiction. Sometimes the writer speaks of "you" and "we" to make the explanation personal or like a story. However, the fact remains that the functions of fiction and poetry are pleasure and understanding, while the purpose of nonfiction is the discovery of factual or conceptual information. Although we look at the two somewhat differently, pleasure derives from both.

In the pages that follow we shall notice that the nonfiction writer is concerned with *facts* first of all. But in addition to facts, the writer tries to show the reader that these facts add up to or lead into a *concept,* just as the facts about chemical composition inside the egg lead us to the concept of how it becomes an embryo and then a chick. Affecting our acceptance of fact and concept is *tone,* the writer's attitude toward the subject and the readers. We shall be concerned with all three.

Nonfiction Defined

Anyone who has spent time with a child knows that children have enormous curiosity and delight in satisfying that curiosity. They are filled with questions that lead to more questions, which, when answered, lead to still other questions. Many of these questions can be answered by the right nonfiction book, whether it is a book about a single topic like trees, an explanation of a concept like energy, or a book that awakens awareness to an issue like overpopulation. As Margery Fisher says in *Matters of Fact,*[1] an information book evokes many responses:

> A child uses information books to assemble what he knows, what he feels, what he sees, as well as to collect new facts. His reaction to something as ordinary as a loaf [of bread] may be, at one time or another, one of wonder, excitement, interest, aesthetic pleasure, physical satisfaction, curiosity.

When adults seek answers, they may turn to encyclopedias; a solid page of factual information does not frighten or confuse them. Their experience helps them sift out the specific items they need from the mass of information; they can extract the essential from the nonessential, the clear from the too complex. The child, to whom the world is new and perhaps confusing, may also, with the help of a book, recognize order in what he or she already sees or knows. This recognition of order and this assembling and sorting help to organize and stabilize the multitude of surrounding facts. The curious child moves from order to comparison, and on to new understanding of concept. To satisfy such needs, the child must have books that combine individuality with clarity in a combination of words that give significance to the subject and make it clear.

Wonder as Motivation

The limited experience of the child poses specific problems for the nonfiction writer. First the writer must satisfy curiosity without squelching a sense of wonder; yet the writer must avoid suggesting miracles. "Wonder" connotes curiosity and interest, while "miracle" connotes mystery and the unknowable. The successful writer of nonfiction opens a door to discovery but does not suggest that the facts are miraculous or beyond ultimate comprehension. There are facts as yet unknown and principles as yet undiscovered, it is true, but if the child is to be led to discovery, the child must feel that the search will be rewarding and will not merely dead-end at unknowable mystery.

Adults usually choose their nonfiction for utilitarian purposes; they need to know. However, to a child, for whom everything in the world is astonishing, wonder is more often the motivation. Curiosity is the force that leads to discovery of all kinds. It led, for example, to the discovery of electricity; the unexplained needed explanation.

In *How Did We Find Out About Electricity?* Isaac Asimov begins his explanation with a narrative situation very similar to the reader's search for answers. Something piques a boy's curiosity, as it does the reader's. Asimov takes us back 2,500 years, to the village of Magnesia on the coast of Turkey, where a shepherd boy uses an iron-tipped stick to help him climb. As the iron sticks to a stone, the boy is mystified, but he can find nothing sticky on either surface. The odd rock comes to the attention of a wise man named Thales, who was a person we would call a scientist; Thales experiments with the stone and discovers that it attracts only iron. Asimov's account follows a pattern very similar to that which our curiosity follows as it is provoked by the unusual; we notice, we experiment, we seek to discover what we can, and when we need help we go to authority.

While Asimov stimulates wonder in one way, Jean George in her Thirteen Moons series relies on facts both truthful and surprising. Simple, clear language that yet avoids ordinary terms sets the stage for *The Moon of the Salamanders:* "In the third moon of the year the first thaw came. Warm winds blew for days and nights. Lakes of ice turned to water. The snow slipped away. The frost let go of the soil." Notice how ice "turns to water" rather than melts; snow does slip away because the change in form seems almost invisible, and the hard grip of frost does "let go." George is not timid about mature language, but tells of "ephemeral ponds," that are "sequestered" among trees; words that follow make meaning clear. Cold ponds, flat areas we do not think of as having defined edges, are "filled to their brims," and a "dark stage" is set for the "ancient ritual" of the sala-manders. The language, as quiet as the woods itself, evokes wonder, as the salamanders "act out a strange and ancient drama just as they did 330 million years ago." Other fascinations may lie ahead in *The Moon of the Salamanders.*

In the opening paragraphs of *The Sea Around Us,* Rachel Carson, writing for more mature readers, rouses wonder by means of surprise. First Carson reminds us that we cannot really know how the oceans were formed, since there were no people there to see and to report:

> Beginnings are apt to be shadowy, and so it is with the beginnings of that great mother of life, the sea. Many people have debated how and when the earth got its ocean, and it is not surprising that their explanations do not always agree. For the plain and inescapable truth is that . . . in the absence of eyewitness accounts, there is bound to be a certain disagreement.

Carson goes on to suggest the range of estimated age for rocks found on the earth—2.3 billion to 2.5 billion years, an astonishing figure for us who find a month or a year a long time. As we follow Carson's speculations about the earth changing from a ball of whirling gases to a molten mass, and then to patterns of layered materials, our wonder is aroused, and we are led into Carson's hypothesis about the origins of the oceans.

The function of the nonfiction book for children, as for adults, is to give this desired information. If the book is to stimulate the child to reach for more, it must be written with strict attention, not only to factual accuracy, but also to tone and style that attract and lead to discovery.[2] The successful nonfiction book manages to supply information and yet make the reader sense that discovery is open-ended. There is more to be known, and finding out is exciting. Because the attitude of wonder is stimulated, we assimilate the facts and come to understand a concept.

Informational Books

Organization and Scope

Common sense tells us that facts cannot be dumped upon a reader all at one time; in that situation we would have to make order out of masses of information, a task for an authority, not for an inquirer. The writer of non-fiction must select the key ideas, put them in simple forms, relate them to facts already known or to concepts already understood, and from this point begin to clarify. Breaking down the ideas into component parts that can be easily understood, the writer arranges them in coherent sequence from *sim-*

Coherent sequence for information is essential.

plest to *most complex,* from *familiar* to *unfamiliar,* or from *early develop-ment* to *later development,* as Peter Spier does in *Tin Lizzie,* for example.

Since this task is not as easy as it sounds not all writers are successful in finding the natural order. Some writers—like some teachers we may know—have a difficult time communicating concepts to those without backgrounds comparable to their own. These writers may have the under-standing, but they lack the capacity to recall what it was like when they were uninformed and needed elementary and orderly explanations.

An Indian Winter is skillfully written by Russell Freedman. The his-torical facts of Prince Maximilian's trip up the Missouri River to learn about the Mandan Indians of North Dakota are set out in a carefully re-searched book. Verifying his story are the journals of Maximilian and the many paintings of his companion, the artist Karl Bodmer. During a severe winter, Bodmer illustrates family and tribal customs as well as painting por-traits and landscapes. Authenticity in the narrative account is further strengthened by Bodmer's illustrations, painted at the time of the difficult trip, creating a convincing picture of the Mandans and their neighbors the Hidatsas.

By contrast, as occasionally happens in picture books, pictures some-times seem to have been conceived before text; that is the case in *The Stream,* a book that was probably intended to show how water gets to a stream. It begins with clouds, moves to underground water, then to snow melting into a stream. Next come waterfalls, rivers, lakes, reservoirs for cities; then to the ocean and back to the dry mountains where heavy rainfall evaporates into the clouds. Although at first glance the circle seems com-plete because it begins and ends with clouds, the movement itself is not co-herent. Another book, *Follow the Water from Brook to Ocean,* begins with the sound of rainfall and water dripping from eaves into gutters, then moves to the brook beside the house, to a stream, a big river, and then to puddles. Rain and snow go through the ground to a brook where algae, frogs, salamanders, and trout live; no acknowledgment is made that algae live in stagnant water and trout in quickly moving streams. Next we move from brook and stream to underground rock and a spring, and on to how moving water carves the land and otters live there. The Grand Canyon ex-emplifies water carving rock, but we move immediately to the flatlands and a meandering stream, to dams, electricity, garbage, and on to the mouth of a river, where the word "delta" goes unexplained. Too much is covered; the process backtracks, and all is disjointed.

The writer of *Rivers and Lakes* does not know how much to focus on or where to quit, and also has problems of logical order. The table of con-tents begins with looking at rivers and lakes, showing how rivers begin in runoff from the mountains, meander through slightly sloping lands in the middle, and at the end move through flatlands to the ocean, order that surely seems logical. Then the text moves to how water shapes the land, shapes civilization, forms lakes, then is controlled; how water is used at work and at play, how people live beside rivers and lakes; and concludes with the "The Story of Rivers and Lakes," a return to the earlier order once anticipated. All this is followed by facts and figures. The reader follows the water's movement to the ocean, then must return to the river banks to see its effects. A more logical order would show the shaping of land, civilization and lakes *as* the water moves.

True, water is a complex topic, its uses many, its forms varied, but by limiting the text to a clear explanation of a simpler issue in *The River,* David Bellamy is successful. The text begins with clear water, goes on to how clean water becomes polluted and then restored so that pike, gulls and frogs can live in and beside it once again. Wendell Tanghorn in *Glacier* uses a logical order and sticks to his more limited subject of how glaciers are formed and how they melt and move from between ten feet to a few inches in long or brief time periods, showing how ice cracks off and moves, taking with it huge boulders and dropping them off along the way. An excellent and beautifully illustrated book, *Oceans* by Seymour Simon, begins with the startling news that 70 percent of the earth's surface is water, then writes of ocean depths and water quantities, how water moves up and down on the surface and below it. It then explains horizontal movement like currents, tides, tidal waves, crests and troughs, storm-driven waves, and surf and its effect on flat beaches. Simon concludes with how people use the ocean as a wastebasket and points out that there are limits to such use if we want oceans to be able to renew themselves. The organization is logical and easy to follow.

Organizing text from early to later developments is clearly shown in David Macaulay's *Cathedral.* Beginning with the gratitude of some thirteenth-century French villagers for peace, health, and plenty, we learn how a medieval architect is hired to design a cathedral to the glory of God. We read of the designing of the cathedral, the hiring of master craftsmen who own shops staffed with apprentices learning trades, and the addition of laborers, many just returning from the Crusades. Cutting the timber, quarrying the stone, clearing the site, building workshops and forges, digging the foundation proceeds to walls, piers, buttresses, temporary wooden frames, and then arches, and up, up to beams, vaulted ceilings, and towers, and finally to sculpture placed in niches. Process, from beginning to end, is a logical plan for organization.

David Macaulay has written and illustrated another remarkable book called *The Way Things Work.* In large, clear drawings with a limited color palette, he shows how everything works, from nail clippers to nuclear power plants, from axles to holograms. The book defies description. Macaulay's illustrations and his text—somewhat reminiscent of *Gulliver's Travels*—are amazingly clear. Lest we feel overloaded with information, a

Organizing may proceed from early development.

fanciful text about the wooly mammoth provides a thread of regular humorous breaks to show how difficult a process is without the simple and ever more complex machines of human invention.

Although in *The Wright Brothers: How They Invented the Airplane* Russell Freedman is telling the history of the airplane, he leaps ahead in Chapter 1 with an account of the first dramatic flight, lasting one minute and thirty-six seconds. Then he returns to the chronology of experimentation that led to that exciting minute. Notice the opening sentences in the first five chapters, each one an attention-grabber:

> No one had ever seen what Amos Root saw on that September afternoon in 1904.

> "From time to time we were [like] little children," Wilbur Wright once said, "my brother Orville and myself lived together, played together, and, in fact, thought together."

> While the Wright brothers were building bicycles in Dayton, an engineer named Otto Lilienthal was conducting gliding experiments from the top of a small hill in Germany.

> Otto Lilienthal's gliding experiments in Germany, and his dramatic death in 1896, had aroused the Wright brothers' curiosity.

> The experiments that Wilbur and Orville had carried out with their latest glider in 1901 were far from encouraging.

With a very different subject, the history and culture of a society, *People of the Breaking Day* uses chronology to describe the family relationships and responsibilities, lifestyles, trading, and sports of the Wampanoags, who lived in southeastern Massachusetts. The final and fitting topic that Marcia Sewell treats is burial customs and procedures.

Narrative Form

In nonfiction for the younger child, the writer may weave information into a narrative. Robert McCloskey in his picture book *Time of Wonder* demonstrates that a slight unifying narrative can convey information about the New England shore. The island has a very old rock at the point, a rock that was hot as fire when it was new to a new world, and as cold as ice when the weight of the glacier ground into it. The seal sniffs, while the fishhawks and eider ducks listen and watch. The colors of the fern change from green to yellow and brown. The robins have flown, and the swallows have left their boathouse nest, but their places are taken by birds that rest in migration as they fly south. Gulls and crows fuss and feud, and hummingbirds find the late petunias. Trees that have fallen during the storm leave jagged holes where their roots have been, and we understand the wind's power. A snow-white heap of shells left long ago by the Indians crumbles at a touch, and

Narrative may provide sequence in books for small children.

we realize that once the Indians lived where we are standing, before the white man came. We have moved down the beach, discovered a bit about geology, seen the effect of the storm on the trees, and then sensed the aging agelessness of the Maine seacoast. These facts have been tied together by the slight narrative.

To cite another example from picture books, *Sugaring Time* by Kathryn Lasky takes us chronologically from trail-breaking through the snow to the sugar maples, cutting runner marks on the trail, tapping trees with drill and bit, then collecting into a gathering tank the maple sap that runs like a river, and finally boiling the sap, with the accompanying tasks of skimming, temperature testing, and fire stoking.

Although Jeanne Bendick does not use a continuous narrative to hold together her book *Why Can't I?* she does use the device of children wondering about the things they see. From a series of comparisons, we discover why we can't breathe under water like a fish or walk on the ceiling like a fly. On the bottom of each of the fly's six feet is a pad of stiff and sticky hairs. As the fly walks on a smooth surface, these pads flatten and make the fly stick. Able to hold more than just the fly's weight, they keep him on the ceiling. "The bottoms of *your* feet are smooth and slippery," she points out. "You can make them a *little* sticky by wearing sneakers. But you're still too heavy to walk up a wall or across the ceiling." The relating of the facts to the reader, the "I" of the title and the "you" of the text, makes these facts personal, interesting, and remarkable. Comparisons make the facts understandable, and each comparison has some narrative quality. The young reader is involved in this explanatory situation by the simplest of narrative elements.

A remarkably able effort to show the devastation of the Great Fire of Chicago in 1871 is found in *The Great Fire* by Jim Murphy. The many illustrations and news stories taken from periodicals of the day, the quoted personal recollections of fire survivors, the carefully researched facts about a Chicago made almost entirely of wood before and after the fire—all add up to a disaster of highly personal proportions. *The Great Fire* owes much of its success to Murphy's use of concrete and specific language to make the fire credible. The awesome destruction of four square miles of the booming wooden city becomes real as we read newspaper accounts and survivor narratives. Careful research details the effect of sweeping winds of tempest strength, alight with coals and embers that land on rooftops, church steeples, and protective blankets, then cross the river to ignite another area. Human errors in judgment are often caused by spreading panic, and sobbing parents fruitlessly seek their children, many of them among the dead. Over 100,000 are left homeless. Updrafts catch strange items like a burning shirt and send them aloft among the flying embers. A leather cap misshapen from the heat, a burst fire hose, a dribble of water from another, a dead fire engine awakened by a hammer tap, and an undertaker's coffins being held upright out of the fire by young boys, as well as 50,000 tents pitched by General Sheridan's troops, detail the devastation.

What history portrays as a city's disaster becomes a disaster for individuals who lose lives, homes, livestock, and businesses. For example, the first call of "Fire!" is made by Daniel "Peg Leg" Sullivan, whose wooden leg gets caught in the uneven floor of the O'Leary barn; hopping on his other leg, he is hit by a calf racing for the door, hangs on to it, and is saved. This fire as personal disaster becomes more and more clear. Account after account of efforts to save the sick or infirm, the animals, homes, and businesses, is interesting in itself; the wealth of individual stories means far more than numbers of victims. For example, William Lee, checking on his 17-month-old child, who was crying, looks out the window and sees the sky lit by flames that generated flying embers:

> Lee hesitated a moment, shouting to his wife to take care of the baby and rushed out of the house. He ran the three blocks to Bruno Goll's drugstore, determined to do what no one else in the neighborhood had thought about doing: turn in a fire alarm. At this point, the fire was barely fifteen minutes old. What followed was a series of fatal errors that set the fire free and doomed the city to a fiery death.

Occasionally, however, because the writer is intent upon narrative suspense, he or she may not make the facts clear. In *How People Live in the Big City,* for example, we wander through the city learning that some people live in very tall buildings with walls of glass. We read that such buildings sometimes are called glass houses, but we do not discover that they are far more often called apartment houses until the term is used later. We learn that riding on the stairs that move is like "floating up, up, up," but not that these stairs are called an "escalator." Some writers seem to fear that words of more than two syllables will not be understood by children, but children's vocabularies are filled with big words: after all, *hamburger* has three syllables, and *refrigerator* five.

Sometimes, for the sake of the narrative, information is completely lost or so distorted that it is untrue. *When the Root Children Wake Up,* for example, is a misleading fairy tale explaining the coming of spring:

> Wide awake at last, in their root house, the root children work busily on their new Spring dresses. Each chooses the color she loves best—violet, yellow, blue, white, orange, or red—and with needle, thread and thimble, sews happily till her work is done.
>
> The root boys . . . wake up the sleeping insects—the beetles, grasshoppers, lady-bugs. . . . They sponge them and brush them and paint their shells with bright Spring colors . . . .

Personification is not the only cause for distortion here; the writer in her eagerness to interest the reader in an account of the changes brought by spring has replaced facts with additional fantasy.

An account need not be personal to be interesting.

In writing of the pecking order among hyenas, Alice L. Hopf in *Hyena* is accurate without personifying animals. "Hyenas have order and rank in their packs. Because females are larger than males, they stand at the top. Or two females are the leaders in each pack, with others ranged below. . . . [T]he female . . . leads the pack on the hunt . . . decides where and when to go. She takes her packmates on a boundary-marking expedition or rushes ahead into battle with the neighboring packs of hyenas." Citing the work of several naturalists, Hopf describes the ways of animals that seem a hybrid of dogs and cats. She adds that Sir Walter Raleigh did not believe Noah would have saved hyenas in the Ark because he would not have saved hybrids.

Robert McClung is highly successful at weaving facts of nature into narrative form. In a factually accurate narrative called *Possum,* McClung faces the reality of the possum's life. We follow a family of nine babies and discover that they are easy prey; one is caught by a fox, another by a great horned owl, a third by a rattlesnake, another by a giant snapping turtle, and a fifth is run over as it crosses the road. These are the facts of life in the possums' world: nine babies, four survivors. Within the narrative form, *Possum* remains factually accurate. A more ambitious purpose unifies McClung's *Samson, Last of the California Grizzlies.* In this vivid narrative, Samson, to satisfy the frontiersmen's craving for excitement, is pitted against Diablo the bull:

> The crowd roared as the two great beasts tangled again. Samson crouched low, trying to seize the bull's head in his huge paws, while Diablo thrust his horns downward in a deadly twisting sweep. As Samson rolled sideways to parry the blow, the tip of one of the bull's horns caught in a link of the chain that held the bear. There was a sudden loud snap as the chain broke, and Samson rolled free.

Here is a verifiable narrative of action on the frontier; there is sympathy for the two struggling animals forced to fight till death, but there is no sentimental distortion.

Style

Style cannot be separated from meaning.

How the writer uses language is style. In nonfiction, as in fiction or poetry, style is an integral part of meaning, and not merely decoration or embellishment added to explanations and descriptions. Style is part of all written matter. Some writers of nonfiction neglect artistry in language as a means of making their subjects interesting, while others are keenly aware of their responsibility to use language effectively.

As we note in the work of Jean George, simplicity need not be either trite or banal. Comparisons are one means of making concepts clear to the reader, and some writers use comparisons simply and effectively. Irving Adler in *The Story of Light* uses a reference to the familiar Aladdin story. Aladdin rubbed a lamp to summon the Jinni. We flick a switch to summon light. Adler goes on to remind us of how difficult it is to get rid of light; it streams in through windows and drapes, or through keyholes. Light cannot be held by force; although we try to grab it, it slides through our fingers. But if we learn about its tricks, we can put the energy of light to work. Referring next to the common experience of bumping into things in the dark, Adler then compares light to a messenger that guides people around obstacles.

In *Volcano: The Eruption and Healing of Mount St. Helens,* Patricia Lauber is also successful in her use of comparisons. Explaining how a blast of steam tore the mountain open, she says that the water was heated by the magma rising inside. Then, by means of a comparison, she goes on to tell how this could happen:

> Normally water cannot be heated beyond its boiling point, which is 212 degrees Fahrenheit at sea level. At boiling point, water turns to gas, which we call steam. But if water is kept under pressure, it can be heated far beyond its boiling point and still stay liquid. . . . If the pressure is removed, this superheated water suddenly turns, or flashes, to steam. As steam it takes up much more room—it expands. The sudden change to steam can cause an explosion.

Frequent comparisons are particularly helpful in the explanations of complex ideas or startling facts. In one picture book, for example, we read the factual statement that the temperature on the sun's surface is close to 10,000 degrees Fahrenheit, and that the temperatures at the sun's center may be close to 32,000 degrees. But we have no frame of reference for these facts. Referring to familiar temperatures like our body heat of around 98 degrees, or water that boils and steam that scalds at 212 degrees would make such high temperatures with so many zeroes even more startling and somewhat more comprehensible.

Some writers simplify their texts by relying upon the simplest sentence structure—subject, verb, complement. Such writers risk losing the interest of children who may weary of the monotonous rhythm created by repeating word patterns. In *What's Hatching Out of That Egg?* Patricia Lauber, in describing the many animals that hatch from eggs, is factually accurate, and the picture-book format is inviting. The style, however, is jerky and halting. Describing the hatching of a monarch butterfly, she uses short simple sentences: "The young animal will spend its days flying about and feeding. But it will no longer eat leaves." Children, after all, do talk in compound and complex sentences; they are more able to read complex sentence forms than some writers assume. *The First Book of New Zealand* is filled with generalizations that suggest that all New Zealanders are alike—an unjust and

Repetitious sentence structure may put the reader to sleep.

inaccurate statement. The style of the book is often monotonous and repetitious as well. We are lulled into boredom and disbelief by its declarative sentences, the drumbeat of omniscient authority:

> The New Zealanders of today are law-abiding, practical, and conscientious people. They dislike extremes of any kind. They usually own their own homes. The houses are surrounded by flower gardens, for New Zealanders like to plant and grow things. . . .
>
> Maori women practice as doctors and dental assistants; they teach school where both the Maoris and *pakehas* are students. They also work as news commentators on the radio. Maori girls are extremely clever.

Take a Trip to Argentina is filled with informative detail, but its brief sentences make it read haltingly. Its failure to relate or compare details about Argentina to what readers know about the United States diminishes the impact of the information. We find ourselves asking questions:

> The picture shows Cordoba, Argentina's second largest city. It was founded in 1573. [When was Boston founded?] . . . Argentina declared itself independent on July 9, 1816. [How many years after the United States declared its independence?] . . . It consists of a 254-member House of Deputies [like our House of Representatives?] and a 46-member Senate [like ours?]. Argentina is a republic and an elected President is Head of State. [Are we a Republic? We elect our President.]

Under the illusion that they are making their meaning more accessible, other writers simplify their language by breaking up compound sentences into halting and choppy fragments:

> How did the glacier do it?
>
> A glacier works just like a plow. But instead of one blade, it has a thousand. For every rock frozen into its bottom acts like a plowshare.

By contrast, notice the clear and vivid description in *Gorilla Gorilla*. In this book we have facts, but they are given to us in sentences of varying length, with words and phrases in varying orders:

> The hoots grew louder and faster, faster and faster still. Suddenly the huge leader thrust himself to his short legs. He tore up great clumps of bush and vine, tossed them with a furious heave high into the air, and began to thump his massive chest like a frenzied drummer. The drumming boomed and leapt into the leafy jungle, across the high meadows and jutting cliffs of the rain forest—an increasing chorus of beats. The hoots melted into a blurred growl.

Variety in sentence length and construction gives interest to this passage. Further interest in what Carol Fenner wants us to know about gorillas is created by the use of imagery. We hear the drumming and thumping of the huge gorilla, and we see his actions. As the leader is compared in a simile to a "frenzied drummer," the drumming booms and leaps. We see the "leafy jungle" and the "jutting cliffs," and we hear the "blurred growl," words chosen to convey precise meaning by creating sight and sound images. The result of Fenner's style is that we learn the facts of the gorilla's hooting, and of his feats of strength. But by seeing and hearing him in his natural habitat, we also discover something about the concept explored in the book: Captivity influences gorilla behavior.

Any impression that all dress in early America was extremely simple, sensible, and drab is contradicted in *Colonial Living* by Edwin Tunis's word pictures of Dutch apparel. Relying upon imagery for clarity, Tunis vividly describes the New Netherlanders' dress:

> In an age of ballooning britches, a Dutchman's outswelled all others. His hat was a big plumed hat, not too well suited to his stocky build. Shoe buckles seem to have been popular. . . . The prosperous among the Dutch clung to the starched ruff. . . .
>
> Ruffs were a great nuisance and a great expense. They had to be laundered by experts. . . . The starched flutes . . . were arranged on "setting sticks" and fixed into shape with hot metal "poking sticks." Even then it was necessary to wear a wire "under-propper" to hold a ruff up.

Detailed imagery may also serve to make action clear. In vigorous language, Robert Leckie shows and explains the process of loading the Revolutionary War guns in *The World Turned Upside Down*. Notice Leckie's use of action verbs in differing forms:

> [The British soldier] bit the cartridge open . . . [and] sprinkled a little powder on the pan of his piece. Then, placing the musket butt-downward, he poured the rest of the powder down the barrel. Next, he pushed in the ball. Crumpling the paper into a wad, he crammed that in afterward. Finally, seizing his rifle rod, he rammed all—powder, ball, and paper—down tight inside the barrel.
>
> To fire the musket, he placed the butt against his shoulder and pulled the trigger. This released a cock which struck its flint against a piece of steel to send a shower of sparks into the pan. When the powder here ignited, it flashed through a touch-hole into the bottom of the barrel and exploded the charge, which propelled the bullet down the barrel.

A child reading such a description sees that readying the Brown Bess for action was a slow and complicated process, and may understand that wars of bombers and fighters pilots differ from the battles of the American Revolution.

Images and figurative comparisons not only contribute to an interesting style, but they are also the means by which the writer clarifies meaning. To create visual pictures filled with comparisons, Jean George uses color imagery and figurative language. In *The Moon of the Monarch Butterfly,* she expresses wonder at the beauty of the monarch by comparing its wings to stained-glass windows and its antennae to knotted wands:

> Before sundown she came to rest on a wisteria vine that entwined the porch of a small white house in the country. Clinging to a purple flower, she closed her wings above her back, as butterflies do. Her wing tops were burnt orange, their undersides yellow. Black veins spread through them like lead in a stained-glass window and their edges seemed as if the night and day had been knitted together into sparkles of white and black. Her antennas were like wands, slender, with knots on the ends for sensing the flowers, the winds, and other monarch butterflies.

Scientific details and various kinds of eating equipment are made surprisingly clear and easy to understand when Millicent Selsam makes vivid figurative comparisons. In *How the Animals Eat,* the chapter on dinner in the water has several subheadings and captions, each an image suggesting a comparison. Sea Soup, or plankton, is a mixture of tiny animals that drift together with tiny plants. In some animals, Sea Strainers, or gill rakers, work as built-in strainers holding the Sea Soup back for the fish to swallow as water passes out through mouth and gills. A Sea Sword is the upper jaw of the fish grown out into a bony, sharp point; it stabs a hole in a big fish and kills it. A Flexible Snout is a trunklike tube that can poke around among the stones in the mud on the bottom of the sea, picking up little sea animals the same way the hose of a vacuum cleaner sucks up dirt. Each of the metaphors compares in words the unfamiliar manner of eating to something already known to the child. Each verbal comparison becomes vivid and clear. Style, in such cases, can serve as the agent for stimulating wonder and for starting the child's exploration of a subject.

Illustration

The writer of nonfiction relies upon illustration somewhat differently from the writer of fiction. There is no need for characterization, for example, and only occasionally does text evoke mood. In nonfiction, illustration helps to clarify. Sometimes a nonfiction book makes use of photographs, but often photographs can be less valuable than drawings or diagrams, since photos sometimes seem to oversimplify, catching only the external appearances of objects and concepts. Although illustrations are necessary to nonfiction, the writer who cannot achieve corresponding effects of clarity with the use of words is depriving the child of a discovery that words can explain just as pictures can.[3]

A highly useful graphic device is a cross-section or three-dimensional section shown in a line drawing, a representation far more difficult to make clear in a photograph. Growth and change in a bud or flower, for example,

Illustrations should clarify text.

are clearer in a drawing, where the changes and stages can be shown by captions designating time lapse. Views of the object are visible from all angles and positions. In Patricia Lauber's *Volcano,* which is filled with beautiful full-color photographs, the artist uses five colored drawings as verification of text: an air view of the area around Mount St. Helens, affected in differing ways by the eruption; the globe as viewed from Antartica, showing the Ring of Fire of active volcanos surrounding the Pacific; two cross-sections showing the Earth's plates and what happens when they move; and how a small plate colliding with the larger one built the Cascade mountain range. The illustrative combination is most effective.

Special Issues in Nonfiction for Children

Tone

Tone is an important part of nonfiction, just as it is of fiction. Many children involve themselves more easily in a nonfiction account if they feel that a real person is conveying the facts to them. Writers may become persons in their own accounts by using the pronouns "we" and "you." To satisfy further this need for person in the communication, the writer also adopts a particular attitude toward the facts and the readers.

Sometimes the writer of books about nature, science, processes, or other facts names the book *The Wonderful World of*—and we are startled to discover that our city sewer system is wonderful. Although the word *wonder* is overworked, there are a great many subjects about which it is perfectly reasonable to wonder. But when the writer uses the title *The Mystery of Chlorophyll,* he or she adopts a tone of surprise and intrigue. Science and the natural world are not miraculous, because as we discover more about them, their opening mysteries continue to provoke wonder—but become less mysterious. If books of fact are to stimulate the minds of children to further exploration, the writer's tone or attitude might better say, "Remarkable as all this is, we can know it. If we investigate it, we are amazed and enlightened."

Writers of nonfiction, like those of fiction, sometimes fall into a tone of condescension, oversimplifying, thinking of the readers as dear little things, or guarding their ears from the whole truth. In one book about elephants, for example, we are mystified when we read that usually peaceful males, who do not charge unless threatened, get angry and excitable once a year for a few weeks or months. This is a period known as *musth;* apparently we are being protected from awareness of the mating season. Although this condescension may occur in a purely factual account, it seems to appear more frequently in facts tied together with a slight narrative.

History, and particularly remote history, is sometimes narrated in a pattern of condescension. In *The Land and People of Iceland,* Erick Berry

"Mystery" connotes the unknowable.

describes the Vikings, using the accounts in the Sagas, recorded about A.D. 1000. Berry makes these warriors' lives ridiculous: in violent and purposeless battle, they cut off each other's heads. "[At nightfall their heads] were miraculously restored, so that they might all sit down together and feast and drink all night. To resume fighting again next morning. Presumably their morning-after headaches also disappeared by magic." Berry, however, does go on to explain the Vikings early governmental bodies, whose purpose was to settle disputes; "man-made words sought to wipe man-made violence from the land." The clumsy effort at humor seems out of place in a chapter that seriously traces Icelandic history from piracy to democracy.

A capable reader curious about the World War II years would find *I Am an American: A True Story of Japanese Internment* by historian Jerry Stanley a very personal account of the effect of U.S. policy after Pearl Harbor, when anyone of Japanese descent was placed in a camp. Such policy was based upon assumptions, and little evidence that Americans with Japanese ancestry would side with the enemy rather than with their homeland. The book, relying upon the experiences of specific internees, is very readable, a needed look at the other side of that assumption. Generously, the final page quotes Shi Nomura, who says that "one of the greatest things about America is that it admits its mistakes. . . . It's easy to think that this is just a part of Japanese history. But it's really part of American history because this is what America is all about: tolerating different cultures, accepting people who look different."

When Edwin Tunis writes of Native Americans in *Indians*, he manages to treat objectively a subject that is often the victim of intellectual snobbery—superstition. Because of the matter-of-fact tone of the account, we accept the Indians' fears:

> There was no Indian who was even reasonably free from superstition: it covered everything in the world. When every animal and every tree, and every stream and every natural phenomenon was possessed of a spirit, probably malevolent, it took a lot of finger-crossing and wood-knocking to ward off evil. The Indian was afraid of everything . . . of killing snakes and wolves . . . of witchcraft and of the owls he associated with it . . . superstition . . . pervaded all Indian living.

Tone also helps us to believe surprising statements. For example, we may be a bit unsettled to learn on the first page of Milton Meltzer's *All Times, All Peoples: A World History of Slavery* that "white, black, brown, yellow, red—no matter what [your] color, it's likely that someone in [your] family way back, was once a slave." We go on to understand why this might be true; his factual tone convinces us: "It was hard for [the earliest peoples] to feed themselves. . . . That is why, when they raided other people, they killed them instead of taking them prisoner. If the winners had spared the lives of the losers, they would have been unable to feed them." But as farming and food production grew and it was possible for conquerors to feed prisoners, they kept them as slaves. The book's powerful illustrations in black and white further reinforce the credibility of Meltzer's factual tone.

In books about animals, condescension often takes the form of **anthropomorphism,** an attitude that suggests a lack of interesting qualities in the animals themselves and a need to jazz up their lives by making them more nearly human. When pets are given human qualities, we are not surprised, but it seems unacceptable and highly unscientific to attribute human qualities to prehistoric beasts. In one book about dinosaurs, a brontosaurus is called "terribly dumb"; the tylosaurus, described as clever, fierce, and cruel, seems vicious rather than, more accurately, carnivorous. In *Here Come the Wild Dogs,* about the life of a fox family, the father fox thinks to himself:

> What a fine morning for racing with the dogs!
> Excitement!
> Adventure!
> And yes, even danger!

As we follow the race, in which the fox outwits the dogs, we hear the victorious fox say, "What fun!" While these may be reasonable emotions for people, the child reading that the fox has such thoughts and feelings is misled about reality, even led to believe that foxes relish the danger and adventure of being hunted. Animal stories are great favorites with children; it is important that when the child expects a factual report, a factual report is given. Any narrative should be kept within the realm of real possibility. Wild animals' lives are filled with serious battles with hunters, blizzards, mountain lions, wolves, and starvation; books should show far more convincingly than the fox book how an animal responds physically to its natural enemies.

The writer of *Ookie, the Walrus Who Liked People* goes a step further than the writer of the fox book; he regards the walrus as almost totally human.[4] She wasn't much interested in the penguin pool; she didn't think they'd be the sort of creatures that would be fun to play with. The seals, however, were the playmates she liked when she was lonely. The huge yet sleekly graceful walrus becomes cute and coy, like the cartoon characters of animation. Wonder and curiosity do not urge us to discover more about walruses; the account stops discovery short by making the walrus neither human nor animal.

While accounts of the animal world are particularly subject to the condescension of anthropomorphism, some writers, Jean George for one, show great respect for their animal subjects. The reader, while absorbing

Anthropomorphism may be condescension.

detailed information about the gray wolves, acquires at the same time an admiration for their grace and intelligence. In *The Moon of the Gray Wolves,* we watch the wolf as he watches the caribou herd and looks for prey:

> The black wolf waited until the main herd passed around the bend of the Toklat. Then, studying the forest and tundra for laggers, he tightened his muscles and sprang into a trot. His narrowly spaced wolf-shoulders gave him the stride of a horse rather than that of a dog, and in the manner of all wolves he glided along the ridge like a thoroughbred. Stiff, long guard-hairs grew beyond his fuzzy underfur and fended off ice and snow . . . .

We further discover that the wolf is an essential predator, since by "harvesting" the weak and the old, the wolf keeps the caribou herd healthy, and their numbers balanced with the available food supply. Here George's tone is objective and respectful, suitable for her description.

Phyllis and Raimondo Borea are even more factual in tone in their account of *Seymour, a Gibbon*. In order to make the descriptions clear, the Boreas often compare the monkeys' actions to those of people, but they carefully avoid lapsing into personification:

> Gibbons . . . live in family groups—father, mother, one or two youngsters, and sometimes a very old gibbon, perhaps a grandfather or mother . . . only gibbons enjoy this close way of living rather like our own. The family wakes at dawn after a night together in their sleeping tree, because, also like us, the higher primates sleep at night and are up and about during the day.

Although the Boreas compare gibbon families to human families, the two are said to be "perhaps" similar, but never the same. And since the authors cannot know the reasons for the gibbons' morning cries, they only speculate:

> For an hour or more after waking, they greet the dawn and their neighbors with cries that have been called songs and set down on paper like music. . . . Their morning songs may be a way of letting other gibbon families know these particular trees are lived in. The songs may also be just for the fun of it.

Herbert S. Zim is another writer intent upon giving the reader the facts and the facts alone. He makes few human comparisons, and he gives only verifiable information. In *Monkeys,* Zim uses a completely objective and matter-of-fact tone:

Records kept at zoos show that monkeys have a fairly long life span compared to other mammals. A mandrill has been known to live 27 years, a macaque up to 29, and a baboon to 45. But these may be special cases, and wild monkeys, on an average, may not live much over 10 or 12 years.

Didacticism and Propaganda

When a writer chooses a controversial topic such as drugs as a subject for a children's book, he or she is probably impelled by a desire to persuade the readers, or to influence their thinking, about the dangers of narcotics or of smoking. As a result, writers may have a difficult time separating their facts from their propaganda. The writer, however, has as a first obligation the presentation of generalizations supported by factual information. Experiments, statistics, descriptions of studies, and references to authorities should be the meat of the book. If the facts are carefully arranged, the evidence gathers and builds to prove the point. Preachment is unnecessary.

If, on the other hand, the book lacks sufficient evidence and relies upon generalizations that the writer knows to be true but has not bothered to support with evidence for the reader's examination, the book then raises questions that have not been answered. How do we know? Who says so? When did that happen? If these questions are left unanswered by the data, the reader says "That's just opinion; it's never proved." The effect on the reader's mind is a quick write-off: "Propaganda. Pure propaganda." Doubt and distrust result.

Proof needs facts, not generalizations.

Some concepts have been well researched and a variety of experiments has led to the same conclusions—smoking endangers the health of smokers and nonsmokers. Scientists conduct experiments, note results, and draw hypotheses; they then test these hypotheses in an effort to reach a conclusion. But many of these series of experiments are still in hypothetical stages, insufficiently proved. It is most often these hypotheses that turn into propaganda for unproved theories.

The writer of nonfiction has a responsibility to use and to foster the scientific attitude. It is the writer's obligation when dealing with theory not fully proven to make us aware that there are theories and countertheories on the subject. Perhaps—if society is lucky—the child-readers will be so intrigued by the puzzlement of scientists that they themselves will wish to find the solution some day.

Adults often seek nonfiction books because they wish to know a particular expert's opinion or attitude toward a subject. The child, however, not knowing that the facts surrounding a social problem can be interpreted through the individual perspectives of various kinds of experts, approaches a book expecting to find facts and objectivity. The child will then be less likely to detect bias. It seems reasonable to say that children's books that inform should not be propaganda. Freedom to draw our own conclusions from the facts is a precious right. If a writer has a bias, we should expect it to be stated openly at some point.

Unlike adults, children may not detect bias.

The confusing of theory with truth concerns the scientist with integrity. In *The Seeds of Tomorrow,* Ben Bova cites the published projections of eminent scientists from the Massachusetts Institute of Technology regarding the disastrous effects of overpopulation. Listing the kinds of information fed to the computer, he mentions pollution, farm production, famished continents, infant mortality and increased longevity, and depletion of natural resources, then contrasts them with expected birth rates. Science and technology, while they have produced many of these "problems," are essential parts of a better future; "they offer a chance to avert the total world collapse that awaits us." Describing the evolution of *Homo sapiens,* he credits the curiosity of humankind with solving problem after immediate problem, and points to the use of "second generation technology [that] would feed, cure, and protect us without long-term damage to the environment." He makes no effort to preach family planning, but presents the problem in its complexity.

In *Hunger on Planet Earth,* another writer, Jules Archer, focuses primarily on overpopulation as the source of hunger. Noting that wars are often started over too-many-people-too-little-space, he says that wealthy nations have done little to help because food aid only results in higher birth rates. Using a particularly vivid illustration, he says that "each time your heart beats, three more new hearts start to beat elsewhere on earth and three more mouths must be fed," then cites the hard-nosed views of some scientists: "If people breed like rabbits they must be allowed to die like rabbits." Next, the moral argument is cited, followed by mention of countless efforts to solve overpopulation problems at world conferences, acknowledging at the same time the varied objections to family planning. Titles of his final chapters indicate Archer's emphasis on population control: "New Ideas for Feeding Planet Earth" addresses food production, pest control, plant genetics, irrigation, energy innovation, altered diets, sea harvesting, and a variety of other issues. "Controlling World Population." however, is the topic of one whole chapter. Clearly he sees it as paramount.

Look next at three books that mention endangered species with varying kinds of emphasis. The Wildlife Youth Service produces a series of slender books called Animals in Danger, opening each volume with a serious appeal using white letters on a black page to state that animals must stay in their natural environments; people have made life difficult for animals, and we can and must "do something about it." The Asia volume describes snow leopards, tigers, giant pandas, and the Arabian oryx, telling about habitat, history, predation, and efforts to save the species. Its tone is deliberately didactic.

The second, *And Then There Was One* by Margery Facklam, devotes a chapter to each of several ways in which animals become extinct, some of them natural and others the intervention of people. Hunting is not the only cause of extinction; people have found other ways to cause it. Beginning with the Galápagos tortoise, Facklam describes the discovery of the undisturbed tortoises by pirates and sailors in search of food on long voyages. By stacking them up in the ship's hold, sailors enjoyed meat for weeks, eating one 400-pound tortoise after another. Meanwhile, settlers arrived on islands and with them came domestic animals who eat tortoise eggs and young. Another chapter relates to the constant changes in land and climate that necessitate animal adaptation. Animals that adapt survive; others do not. Changes in land conformation made migration possible for dinosaurs: as they moved they may have encountered bacteria or new predators. True, hunters have destroyed whole species, like the passenger pigeon and the mammoth, but people also insist upon manipulating natural populations. Immigrants sometimes missed familiar animals or birds and imported them, only to find they became pests. They then imported other species to control new populations. For example, rats deserting ships became a nuisance in Jamaica, yet the imported mongoose did not control them but ate other species instead. And finally, human intervention like the disaster of the Exxon Valdez oil spill resulted in "no place to live" for some species. The final chapter summarizes the "good news" of human efforts to counteract extinction, including education, zoo breeding and repopulation, animal refuges, and protective laws, but admits that some degree of extinction is inevitable because we cannot change the ways nature makes land and climate changes. The point of view is objective, the examples extensive, and the effect is not didactic but informative.

A book can inform without preaching.

The third, much longer book has a different focus but concludes with a point about species conservation. *Keepers and Creatures at the National Zoo* by Peggy Thomson describes diverse species and their dedicated keepers, each with knowledge and skills suited to that particular species. Keepers describe their work, their training or care techniques, and the varied personalities within the group; their enthusiasm for their work is easily apparent. Thomson, however, maintains objectivity and does not enter the minds of the animal subjects. The keeper of the sea lions says that without the excitement and challenge of natural life, the animals may languish in boredom; her treatment tries to keep that excitement and challenge alive. Asked if the hippos like him, the keeper responds thoughtfully that they are indifferent and would miss not him but the food he brings. The keeper of the gorillas says that nothing is constant and everything is endlessly perplexing; his tossing a bouquet of sunflowers to Sylvia seems to keep her happy. Once our interest in a large variety of species is thoroughly aroused, the final chapter is devoted to zoo changes in animal habitats and to humane treatment: Animals are not purchased from hunters, captured and shipped to zoos, but are now traded by specialists who are breeding species carefully, which after careful retraining are set free in the wild to prevent their extinction.

Summary

Nonfiction informs by attention to facts, capitalizing on children's wonder at all the information available, at all the topics out there. When nonfiction is most effective, it suggests a wealth of information, stimulating in the young reader a wish to know more. Without the natural organization of fiction, informational books may need another kind of planning: Major methods include moving from the simplest to most complex, from familiar to unfamiliar, or from early to later development. Style, which cannot be separated from meaning, is as important to nonfiction as it is to fiction. As the writer avoids repetitious sentence structures, variety results. Illustration of the text may in some cases be central, and text merely clarification of what the reader sees. Or, depending upon the level of intended audience, text may be illustrated by an occasional graphic. A tone of didacticism or preachiness, of "Now you know it all!" is less effective than one more objective, but in either case, without supporting evidence the writer may be writing propaganda.

Notes

1. I am grateful to Margery Fisher for many of my ideas throughout this chapter. Her book *Matters of Fact* (Brockhampton, 1973) is an excellent discussion of what should be expected of nonfiction books for children.

2. Fisher contrasts two terms: A starter makes the child "want to pursue it further. A stopper can be quickly skimmed and will be as quickly forgotten because it gives the deadly impression of being self-contained and yet incomplete" (p. 23).

3. Discovery through words gives the child an opportunity for greater growth. Continual reliance upon illustration for clarity does not expose children to new words or develop in them the habit of using words to express themselves.

4. William Bridges's book is classified as nonfiction.

Recommended Books Cited in This Chapter

ADLER, IRVING. *The Story of Light.* Irvington-on-Hudson, N.Y.: Harvey House, 1971.

ARCHER, JULES. *Hunger on Planet Earth.* New York: Crowell, 1977.

ASIMOV, ISAAC. *How Did We Find Out About Electricity?* New York: Walker, 1973.

BELLAMY, DAVID. *The River.* New York: Potter, 1988.

BENDICK, JEANNE. *Why Can't I?* New York: McGraw-Hill, 1969.

BOREA, PHYLLIS, AND RAIMONDO BOREA. *Seymour, a Gibbon.* New York: Atheneum, 1973.

BOVA, BEN. *The Seeds of Tomorrow.* New York: David McKay, 1977.

CARSON, RACHEL. *The Sea Around Us.* New York: Oxford University Press, 1961.

FACKLAM, MARGERY. *And Then There Was One.* Illustrated by Pamela Johnson. Boston: Little, Brown, 1990.

FENNER, CAROL. *Gorilla Gorilla.* New York: Random House, 1973.

FREEDMAN, RUSSELL. *An Indian Winter.* With illustrations by Karl Bodmer. New York: Holiday House, 1992.

GEORGE, JEAN. *The Moon of the Gray Wolves.* New York: Crowell, 1969.

———. *The Moon of the Monarch Butterfly.* New York: Crowell, 1968.

———. *The Moon of the Salamanders.* New York: HarperCollins, 1992.

HOPF, ALICE L. *Hyena.* New York: Dodd Mead, 1983.

LASKY, KATHRYN. *Sugaring Time.* New York: Macmillan, 1983.

LAUBER, PATRICIA. *Volcano: The Eruption and Healing of Mount St. Helens.* New York: Bradbury, 1986.

LECKIE, ROBERT. *The World Turned Upside Down.* New York: Putnam, 1973.

MACAULAY, DAVID. *Cathedral.* Boston: Houghton Mifflin, 1973.

———. *The Way Things Work.* Boston: Houghton Mifflin, 1988.

MCCLOSKEY, ROBERT. *Time of Wonder.* New York: Viking, 1957.

MCCLUNG, ROBERT. *Samson, Last of the California Grizzlies.* New York: Morrow, 1973.

MELTZER, MILTON. *All Times, All People: A World History of Slavery.* New York: Harper & Row, 1980.

MURPHY, JIM. *The Great Fire.* New York: Scholastic, 1995.

SELSAM, MILLICENT. *How the Animals Eat.* Eau Claire, Wis.: E. N. Hale, n.d.

SEWELL, MARCIA. *People of the Breaking Day.* New York: Macmillan, 1990.

SIMON, SEYMOUR. *Oceans.* New York: Morrow, 1990.

TANGHORN, WENDELL. *Glacier.* Illustrated by Marc Simont. New York: Crowell: 1988.

THOMSON, PEGGY. *Keepers and Creatures at the National Zoo.* New York: Crowell, 1988.

TUNIS, EDWIN. *Colonial Living.* New York: World, 1957.

———. *Indians.* New York: World, 1959.

WORLD WILDLIFE YOUTH SERVICE. Animals in Danger series. Windermere, Fla.: Rourke Corp., n.d.

ZIM, HERBERT S. *Monkeys.* New York: Morrow, 1955.

Children's Book Awards

Children's book awards are listed on the Internet. See the Children's Literature Web Guide, Internet Resources Related to Books for Children and Young Adults (Children's Literature Awards page, copyright © 1997 David K. Brown.). Listed below in alphabetical order is a representative group.

Australian Children's Books of the Year Awards

Australia gives an award for Older Readers (1946) Younger Readers (1982), Picture Books (1956), and Information Books (1993). Listed here are the winners for all categories.

1946   *Karrawingi, the Emu* by Leslie Rees, Sands

1948   *Shackleton's Argonauts* by Frank Hurley, Angus & Robertson

1949   *Whalers of the Midnight Sun* by Alan Villiers, Angus & Robertson

1951   *Verity of Sydney Town* by Ruth Williams, Angus & Robertson

1952   *The Australia Book* by Eve Pownall, Sands

1953   *Aircraft of Today and Tomorrow* by J. H. and W. D. Martin, Angus & Robertson

         Good Luck to the Rider by Joan Phipson, Angus & Robertson

1954   *Australian Legendary Tales* by K. L. Parker, Angus & Robertson

1955   *The First Walkabout* by H. A. Lindsay and N. B. Tindale, Kestrel

1956   *The Crooked Snake* by Patricia Wrightson, Angus & Robertson; Picture Book: *Wish and the Magic Nut* by Sheila Hawkins, text by Peggy Barnard

1957   *The Boomerang Book of Legendary Tales* by Enid Moodie-Heddle, Kestrel

1958   *Tiger in the Bush* by Nan Chauncy, Oxford; Picture Book: *Pickaninny Walkabout* by Axel Poignant

1959   *Devil's Hill* by Nan Chauncy, Oxford
        Sea Menace by John Gunn, Constable
1960   *All the Proud Tribesmen* by Kylie Tennant, Macmillan
1961   *Tangara* by Nan Chauncy, Oxford
1962   *The Racketty Street Gang* by H. L. Evers, Hodder & Stoughton
        Rafferty Rides a Winner by Joan Woodbery, Parrish
1963   *The Family Conspiracy* by Joan Phipson, Angus & Robertson
1964   *The Green Laurel* by Eleanor Spence, Oxford
1965   *Pastures of the Blue Crane* by Hesba F. Brinsmead, Oxford; Picture Book:
        Hugo's Zoo by Elisabeth MacIntyre
1966   *Ash Road* by Ivan Southall, Angus & Robertson
1967   *The Min Min* by Mavis Thorpe Clark, Landsdowne
1968   *To the Wild Sky* by Ivan Southall, Angus & Robertson
1969   *When Jays Fly to Barbmo* by Margaret Balderson, Oxford; Picture Book;
        Sly Old Wardrobe by Ted Greenwood, text by Ivan Southall
1970   *Uhu* by Annette Macarther-Onslow, Ure Smith
1971   *Bread and Honey* by Ivan Southall, Angus & Robertson; Picture Book:
        Waltzing Matilda, illustrated by Desmond Digby, text by A. B. Paterson
1972   *Longtime Passing* by Hesba F. Brinsmead, Angus & Robertson
1973   *Family at the Lookout* by Noreen Shelly, Oxford
1974   *The Nargun and the Stars* by Patricia Wrightson, Hutchinson; Picture
        Book: *The Bunyip of Berkeley's Creek,* text by Jenny Wagner
1975   Picture Book: *The Man from Iron Bark,* illustrated by Quentin Hole, text
        by A. B. Paterson
1976   *Fly West* by Ivan Southall, Angus & Robertson; Picture Book: *The
        Rainbow Serpent* by Dick Roughsey
1977   *The October Child* by Eleanor Spence, Oxford
1978   *The Ice Is Coming* by Patricia Wrightson, Hutchinson; Picture Book: *John
        Brown, Rose and the Midnight Cat,* illustrated by Ron Brooks, text by
        Jenny Wagner
1979   *The Plum-Rain Scroll* by Ruth Manley, Hodder & Stoughton; Picture
        Book: *The Quinkins* illustrated by Percy Trezie and Dick Roughsie
1980   *Displaced Person* by Lee Harding, Hyland House; Picture Book: *One
        Dragon's Dream* by Peter Pavey
1981   *Playing Beatie Bow* by Ruth Park, Nelson
1982   *The Valley Between* by Colin Thiele, Rigby; *Rummage* by Christobel
        Mattingley, Picture Book: *Sunshine,* illustrated by Jan Ormerud
1983   *Thing* by Robin Klein; *Master of the Grove* by Victor Kelleher, Penguin;
        Picture Book: *Who Sank the Boat?* illustrated by Pamela Allen
1984   *A Little Fear* by Patricia Wrightson, Hutchinson; *Bernice Knows Best* by
        Max Dann; Picture Book: *Bertie and the Bear* by Pamela Allen
1985   *The True Story of Lilli Stubeck* by James Aldridge, Hyland House;
        Something Special by Emily Rodda
1986   *The Green Wind* by Thurley Fowler, Rigby; *Arkwright* by Mary Steele;
        Picture Book: *Felix and Alexander,* illustrated by Terry Denton
1987   *All We Know* by Simon French, Angus & Robertson; *Pigs Might Fly* by
        Emily Rodda, illustrated by Noela Young, Angus & Robertson; Picture

Book: *Kojuro and the Bears,* illustrated by Junko Morimoto, adapted by Helen Smith

1988   *So Much to Tell You* by John Marsden, Walter McVitty; *My Place* by Nadia Wheatley; Picture Book: *Crusher Is Coming* by Bob Graham, Lothian

1989   *Best-Kept Secret* by Emily Rodda, Angus & Robertson: *Beyond the Labyrinth* by Gillian Rubinstein, Hayland House; Picture Book: *Drac and the Gremlin,* illustrated by Jane Tanner, text by Allan Baillie, Viking Kestrel

1990   *Come Back to Show You I Could Fly* by Robin Klein, Viking Kestrel; *Pigs and Honey* by Jeanne Baker, illustrated by Jeanne Adams, Omnibus Books; Picture Book: *The Very Best of Friends,* illustrated by Julie Vivas, text by Margaret Wild

1991   *Finders Keepers* by Emily Rodda; *Strange Objects* by Gary Crew; Picture Book: *Greetings from Sandy Beach,* illustrated by Bob Graham

1992   *The House Guest* by Eleanor Nilsson, Viking; *Magnificent Nose and Other Marvels* by Anna Fienberg, illustrated by Kim Gamble, Allen & Unwin; Picture Book: *Window* by Jeannie Baker, Julia MacRae Books.

1993   *Looking for Alibrandi* by Melina Marchetta; *The Bamboo Flute* by Gary Fisher; Picture Book: *Rose Meets Mr. Wintergarden* by Bob Graham

1994   *The Gathering* by Isobelle Carmody; *Angel's Gate* by Gary Crew; *Rowan of Ring* by Emily Rodda; Picture Book: *First Light* by Gary Crew

1995   *Foxspell* by Gillian Rubenstein; *Ark in the Park* by Wendy Orr; Picture Book: *The Watertower,* illustrated by Steven Woolman, text by Gary Crew

1996   *Pagan's Vows* by Catherine Jinks; *Swashbuckler* by James Maloney; Picture Book: *The Hunt* by Norelle Oliver

1997   *A Bridge to Wiseman's Cove,* by James Maloney; Honor Books: *Peeling the Onion* by Wendy Orr; for Older Readers: *Johnny Hart's Heroes* by David Metzenthen

Boston Globe–Horn Book Awards

These awards have been given annually in the fall ever since 1967 by the *Boston Globe* and *The Horn Book Magazine.* Through 1975, two awards were given—one for outstanding text and the other for outstanding illustration. In 1976 the award categories were changed to (and currently are) Outstanding Fiction or Poetry, Outstanding Nonfiction, and Outstanding Illustration. Books published in the United States but written by non-Americans are also eligible.

1967   Text: *The Little Fishes* by Erik Christian Haugaard, Houghton Mifflin
         Illustration: *London Bridge Is Falling Down* by Peter Spier, Doubleday

1968   Text: *The Spring Rider* by John Lawson, Crowell
         Illustration: *Tikki Tikki Tembo* by Arlene Mosel, illustrated by Blair Lent, Holt

1969   Text: *A Wizard of Earthsea* by Ursula K. Le Guin, Houghton Mifflin
         Illustration: *The Adventures of Paddy Pork* by John S. Goodall, Harcourt

1970   Text: *The Intruder* by John Rowe Townsend, Lippincott
        Illustration: *Hi, Cat!* by Ezra Jack Keats, Macmillan
1971   Text: *A Room Made of Windows* by Eleanor Cameron, Atlantic–Little,
        Brown
        Illustration: *If I Built a Village* by Kazue Mizumura, Crowell
1972   Text: *Tristan and Iseult* by Rosemary Sutcliff, Dutton
        Illustration: *Mr. Gumpy's Outing* by John Burningham, Holt
1973   Text: *The Dark Is Rising* by Susan Cooper, McElderry/Atheneum
        Illustration: *King Stork* by Trina Schart Hyman, Little, Brown
1974   Text: *M. C. Higgins, The Great* by Virginia Hamilton, Macmillan
        Illustration: *Jambo Means Hello* by Muriel Feelings, illustrated by Tom
        Feelings, Dial
1975   Text: *Transport 7-41-R* by T. Degens, Viking
        Illustration: *Anno's Alphabet* by Mitsumasa Anno, Crowell
1976   Fiction: *Unleaving* by Jill Paton Walsh, Farrar, Straus & Groux
        Nonfiction: *Voyaging to Cathay: Americans in the China Trade* by Alfred
        Tamarin and Shirley Glubok, Viking
        Illustration: *Thirteen* by Remy Charlip and Jerry Joyner, Parents
1977   Fiction: *Child of the Owl* by Laurence Yep, Harper & Row
        Nonfiction: *Chance Luck and Destiny* by Peter Dickinson, Atlantic–Little,
        Brown
        Illustration: *Ganfa' Grig Had a Pig and Other Rhymes* by Wallace Tripp,
        Little, Brown
1978   Fiction: *The Westing Game* by Ellen Raskin, Dutton
        Nonfiction: *Mischling, Second Degree: My Childhood in Nazi Germany* by
        Ilse Koehn, Greenwillow
        Illustration: *Anno's Journey* by Mitsumasa Anno, Philomel
1979   Fiction: *Humbug Mountain* by Sid Fleischman, Atlantic–Little, Brown
        Nonfiction: *The Road from Home: The Story of an Armenian Girl* by
        David Kherdian, Greenwillow
        Illustration: *The Snowman* by Raymond Briggs, Random House
1980   Fiction: *Conrad's War* by Andrew Davies, Crown
        Nonfiction: *Building: The Fight Against Gravity* by Mario Salvadori,
        McElderry/Atheneum
        Illustration: *The Garden of Abdul Gasazi* by Chris Van Allsburg,
        Houghton Mifflin
1981   Fiction: *The Leaving* by Lynn Hall, Scribner's
        Nonfiction: *The Weaver's Gift* by Kathryn Lasky, Warne
        Illustration: *Outside Over There* by Maurice Sendak, Harper & Row
1982   Fiction: *Playing Beatie Bow* by Ruth Park, Atheneum
        Nonfiction: *Upon the Head of the Goat: A Childhood in Hungary,
        1939–1944* by Aranka Siegal, Farrar, Straus & Giroux
        Illustration: *A Visit to William Blake's Inn: Poems for Innocent and
        Experienced Travelers* by Nancy Willard, illustrated by Alice and Martin
        Provensen, Harcourt
1983   Fiction: *Sweet Whispers, Brother Rush* by Virginia Hamilton, Philomel
        Nonfiction: *Behind Barbed Wire: The Imprisonment of Japanese Americans
        During World War II* by Daniel S. Davis, Dutton

Illustration: *A Chair for My Mother* by Vera B. Williams, Greenwillow

1984 Fiction: *A Little Fear* by Patricia Wrightson, McElderry/Atheneum
Nonfiction: *The Double Life of Pocahontas* by Jean Fritz, Putnam
Illustration: *Jonah and the Great Fish,* retold and illustrated by Warwick Hutton, McElderry/Atheneum

1985 Fiction: *The Moves Make the Man* by Bruce Brooks, Harper & Row
Nonfiction: *Commodore Perry in the Land of the Shogun* by Rhoda Blumberg, Lothrop
Illustration: *Mama Don't Allow* by Thatcher Hurd, Harper & Row

1986 Fiction: *In Summer Light* by Zibby Oneal, Viking Kestrel
Illustration: *The Paper Crane* by Molly Bang, Greenwillow
Nonfiction: *Auks, Rocks and the Odd Dinosaur* by Peggy Thomson, Crowell

1987 Fiction: *Rabble Starkey* by Lois Lowru, Houghton Mifflin
Illustration: *Mufaro's Beautiful Daughters* by John Steptoe, Lothrop
Nonfiction: *Pilgrims of Plimouth* by Marcia Sewall, Atheneum

1988 Fiction: *The Friendship* by Mildred Taylor, Dial
Illustration: *The Boy of the Three-Year Nap* by Diane Snyder, Houghton Mifflin
Nonfiction: *Anthony Burns: The Defeat and Triumph of a Fugitive Slave* by Virginia Hamilton, Knopf

1989 Fiction: *Village by the Sea* by Paula Fox, Orchard Books
Illustration: *Shy Charles* by Rosemary Wells, illustrated by Rosemary Wells, Dial
Nonfiction: *The Way Things Work* by David Macaulay, illustrated by David Macaulay, Houghton Mifflin

1990 Fiction: *Maniac Magee* by Jerry Spinelli, Little, Brown
Illustration: *Lon Po Po: A Red Riding Hood Story from China* by Ed Young, Philomel
Nonfiction: *Great Little Madison* by Jean Fritz, Putnam

1991 Fiction: *True Confessions of Charlotte Doyle* by Avi, illustrated by Ruth E. Murray, Orchard
Illustration: *Tale of the Mandarin Ducks* by Katherine Paterson, illustrated by Leo Dillon and Diane Dillon, Lodestar
Nonfiction: *Appalachia: The Voices of Sleeping Birds* by Cynthia Rylant, illustrated by Barry Moser, Harcourt

1992 Fiction/Poetry: *Missing May* by Cynthia Rylant, Orchard
Illustration: *Seven Blind Mice* by Ed Young, illustrated by Ed Young, Philomel

1993 Fiction: *Ajeemah and His Son* by James Barry, Harper
Honor Book: *The Giver* by Lois Lowry, Houghton
Nonfiction: *Sojourner Truth: Ain't I a Woman?* by Patricia C. and Frederick McKissack, Scholastic
Nonfiction Honor Book: *Lives of the Musicians: Good Times, Bad Times (And What the Neighbors Thought)* by Kathleen Krull, illustrated by Kathryn Hewitt
Picture Book: *The Fortune Tellers,* by Lloyd Alexander, illustrated by Trina Schart Hyman, Dutton

Picture Honor Books: *Raven: A Trickster Tale from the Pacific Northwest,* illustrated by Gerald McDermott, Harcourt; *Komodo!* by Peter Sis, Greenwillow

1994   Fiction: *Scooter* by Vera B. Williams, Greenwillow

Fiction Honor Books: *Flour Babies* by Anne Fine, Little, Brown; *Western Wind* by Paula Fox, Orchard

Nonfiction: *Eleanor Roosevelt: A Life of Discovery* by Russell Freedman, Clarion

Nonfiction Honor Books: *Unconditional Surrender: U. S. Grant and the Civil War,* by Robert Sabuda, McElderry

Picture Book: *Grandfather's Journey* by Allen Say, Houghton Mifflin

Picture Book Honor Books: *Owen* by Kevin Henkes, Greenwillow; *A Small Tall Tale from the Far Far North* by Peter Sis, Knopf

1995   Fiction: *Some of the Kinder Planets* by Tim Wynne-Jones, Kroupe/Orchard

Fiction Honor Books: *Jericho* by Janet Hickman, Greenwillow; *Earthshine* by Theresa Nelson, Jackson/Orchard

Nonfiction: *Abigail Adams: Witness to a Revolution* by Natalie S. Bober, Atheneum

Nonfiction Honor Books: *It's Perfectly Normal: A Book About Changing Bodies, Growing Up, Sex, and Sexual Health* by Robie H. Harris, illustrated by Michael Emberley, Candlewick; *The Great Fire* by Jim Murphy, Scholastic

Picture Book: *John Henry,* retold by Julius Lester, illustrated by Jerry Pinkney, Dial

Picture Book Honor Book: *Swamp Angel* by Anne Isaacs, illustrated by Paul O. Zelinsky

1996   Fiction: *Poppy* by Avi, Jackson/Orchard

Fiction Honor Books: *The Moorchild* by Eloise McGraw, McElderry; *Belle Prater's Boy* by Ruth White, Farrar, Straus & Giroux

Nonfiction: *Orphan Train Rider: One Boy's True Story* by Andrea Warren, Houghton Mifflin

Nonfiction Honor Books: *The Boy Who Lived with the Bears: And Other Iroquois Stories* by Josephy Bruchac, illustrated by Murv Jacob, HarperCollins.

Picture Book: *In the Rain with Baby Duck* by Amy Hest, illustrated by Jill Barton, Candlewick

Picture Book Honor Books: *Fanny's Dream* by Caralyn Buehner, illustrated by Mark Buehner, Dial; *Home Lovely* by Lynn Rae Perkins, Greenwillow

1997   Fiction and Poetry Honor Books: *Lily's Crossing* by Patricia Reilly Giff, Delacorte; *Harlem* by Walter Dean Myers, illustrated by Christopher Myers, Scholastic

Nonfiction: *Lou Gehrig: The Luckiest Man* by David A. Adler, illustrated by Terry Widener, Harcourt; *Leonardo da Vinci* written and illustrated by Diane Stanley, Morrow

Picture Book: *The Adventures of Sparrowboy* written and illustrated by Brian Pinkney, Simon & Schuster

Picture Book Honor Books: *Home on the Bayou: A Cowboy's Story* by G. Brian Karas, Simon & Schuster; *Potato: A Tale from the Great Depression* by Kate Lied, illustrated by Lisa Campbell Ernst, National Geographic Society Fiction and Poetry: *The Friends* by Kazumi Yomoto. New York: Farrar, Strauss & Giroux

The National Book Award for Young People's Literature

This award, formerly a National Book Award/American Book Award from 1969 to 1983, was added to the National Book Awards in 1996. Presented each year, the Young People's category recognizes outstanding contributions to literature for children and young adults in various genres by writers in the United States.

1996   *Parrot in the Oven: Mi Vida* by Victor Martinez. New York: HarperCollins Publishers/Joanna Colter Books, 1996.
1997   *Dancing on the Edge* by Han Nolan. New York: Harcourt Brace Jovanovich.

The Caldecott Medal

Since 1938, the Association of Library Service to Children of the American Library Association has annually awarded the Caldecott Medal to the illustrator of the most distinguished picture book published in the United States in the preceding year. The recipient must be a citizen or resident of the United States. The medal is named in tribute to the well-loved English illustrator Randolph Caldecott (1846–1886).

1938   *Animals of the Bible* by Helen Dean Fish, illustrated by Dorothy P. Lathrop, Lippincott
        Honor Books: *Seven Simeons,* written and illustrated by Boris Artzybasheff, Viking; *Four and Twenty Blackbirds* by Helen Dean Fish, illustrated by Robert Lawson, Stokes
1939   *Mei Li,* written and illustrated by Thomas Handforth, Doubleday
        Honor Books: *The Forest Pool,* written and illustrated by Laura Adams Armer, Longmans; *Wee Gillis* by Munro Leaf, illustrated by Robert Lawson, Viking; *Snow White and the Seven Dwarfs,* written and illustrated by Wanda Gág, Coward; *Barkis,* written and illustrated by Clare Newberry, Harper, *Andy and the Lion,* written and illustrated by James Daugherty, Viking
1940   *Abraham Lincoln,* written and illustrated by Ingri and Edgar Parin d'Aulaire, Doubleday
        Honor Books: *Cock-A-Doodle Doo . . . ,* written and illustrated by Berta and Elmer Hader, Macmillan; *Madeline,* written and illustrated by Ludwig Bemelmans, Viking; *The Ageless Story,* illustrated by Lauen Ford, Dodd
1941   *They Were Strong and Good,* written and illustrated by Robert Lawson, Viking

Honor Book: *April's Kittens,* written and illustrated by Clare Newberry, Harper

1942   *Make Way for Ducklings,* written and illustrated by Robert McCloskey, Viking

Honor Books: *An American ABC,* written and illustrated by Maud and Miska Petersham, Macmillan: *In My Mother's House* by Ann Nolan Clark, illustrated by Velino Herrera. Viking; *Paddle-to-the-Sea,* written and illustrated by Holling C. Holling, Houghton; *Nothing at All,* written and illustrated by Wanda Gág, Coward

1943   *The Little House,* written and illustrated by Virginia Lee Burton, Houghton

Honor Books: *Dash and Dort,* written and illustrated by Mary and Conrad Buff, Viking; *Marshmallow,* written and illustrated by Clare Newberry, Harper

1944   *Many Moons* by James Thurber, illustrated by Louis Slobodkin, Harcourt

Honor Books; *Small Rain: Verses from the Bible,* selected by Jessie Orton Jones, illustrated by Elizabeth Orton Jones, Viking; *Pierre Pigeon* by Lee Kingman, illustrated by Arnold E. Bare, Houghton; *The Mighty Hunter,* written and illustrated by Berta and Elmer Hader, Macmillan; *A Child's Good Night Book* by Margaret Wise Brown, illustrated by Jean Charlot, W. R. Scott; *Good Luck Horse* by Chih-Yi Chan, illustrated by Plao Chan, Whittlesey

1945   *Prayer for a Child* by Rachel Field, illustrated by Elizabeth Orton Jones, Macmillan

Honor Books: *Mother Goose,* illustrated by Tasha Tudor, Walck; *In the Forest,* written and illustrated by Marie Hall Ets, Viking; *Yonie Wonder-nose,* written and illustrated by Marguerite de Angeli, Doubleday; *The Christmas Anna Angel* by Ruth Sawyer, illustrated by Kate Seredy, Viking

1946   *The Rooster Crows* ... (traditional Mother Goose) illustrated by Maud and Miska Petersham, Macmillan

Honor Books: *Little Lost Lamb* by Golden MacDonald, illustrated by Leonard Weisgard, Doubleday; *Sing Mother Goose* by Opal Wheeler, illustrated by Marjorie Torrey, Dutton; *My Mother Is the Most Beautiful Woman in the World* by Becky Reyher, illustrated by Ruth Gannett, Lothrop; *You Can Write Chinese,* written and illustrated by Kurt Wiese, Viking

1947   *The Little Island* by Golden MacDonald, illustrated by Leonard Weisgard, Doubleday

Honor Books: *Rain Drop Splash* by Alvin Tresselt, illustrated by Leonard Weisgard, Lothrop; *Boats on the River* by Marjorie Flack, illustrated by Jay Hyde Barnum, Viking; *Timothy Turtle* by Al Graham, illustrated by Tony Palazzo, Viking; *Pedro, the Angel of Olvera Street,* written and illustrated by Leo Politi, Scribner's; *Sing in Praise: A Collection of the Best Loved Hymns* by Opal Wheeler, illustrated by Marjorie Torrey, Dutton

1948   *White Snow, Bright Snow* by Alvin Tresselt, illustrated by Roger Duvoisin, Lothrop

Honor Books: *Stone Soup,* written and illustrated by Marcia Brown, Scribner's; *McElligot's Pool,* written and illustrated by Dr. Seuss, Random;

Bambino the Clown, written and illustrated by George Schreiber, Viking; *Roger and the Fox* by Lavinia Davis, illustrated by Hildegard Woodward, Doubleday; *Song of Robin Hood,* edited by Anne Malcolmson, illustrated by Virginia Lee Burton, Houghton

1949 *The Big Snow,* written and illustrated by Berta and Elmer Hader, Macmillan
Honor Books: *Blueberries for Sal,* written and illustrated by Robert McCloskey, Viking; *All Around the Town* by Phyllis McGinley, illustrated by Helen Stone, Lippincott; *Juanita,* written and illustrated by Leo Politi, Scribner's; *Fish in the Air,* written and illustrated by Kurt Wiese, Viking

1950 *Song of the Swallows,* written and illustrated by Leo Politi, Scribner's
Honor Books: *America's Ethan Allen* by Stewart Holbrook, illustrated by Lynd Ward, Houghton; *The Wild Birthday Cake* by Lavinia Davis, illustrated by Hildgard Woodward, Doubleday; *The Happy Day* by Ruth Krauss, illustrated by Marc Simont, Harper; *Bartholomew and the Oobleck,* written and illustrated by Dr. Seuss, Random; *Henry Fisherman,* written and illustrated by Marcia Brown, Scribner's

1951 *The Egg Tree,* written and illustrated by Katherine Milhous, Scribner's
Honor Books: *Dick Whittington and His Cat,* written and illustrated by Marcia Brown, Scribner's; *The Two Reds* by Will, illustrated by Nicolas, Harcourt; *If I Ran the Zoo,* written and illustrated by Dr. Seuss, Random; *The Most Wonderful Doll in the World* by Phyllis McGinley, illustrated by Helen Stone, Lippincott; *T-Bone, the Baby Sitter,* written and illustrated by Clare Newberry, Harper

1952 *Finders Keepers* by Will, illustrated by Nicolas, Harcourt
Honor Books: *Mr. T. W. Anthony Woo,* written and illustrated by Marie Hall Ets, Viking; *Skipper John's Cook,* written and illustrated by Marcia Brown, Scribner's; *All Falling Down* by Gene Zion, illustrated by Margaret Bloy Graham, Harper; *Bear Party,* written and illustrated by Willian Pène du Bois, Viking; *Feather Mountain,* written and illustrated by Elizabeth Olds, Houghton

1953 *The Biggest Bear,* written and illustrated by Lynd Ward, Houghton
Honor Books: *Puss in Boots* by Charles Perrault, illustrated and translated by Marcia Brown, Scribner's; *One Morning in Maine,* written and illustrated by Robert McCloskey, Viking; *Ape in a Cape,* written and illustrated by Fritz Eichenberg, Harcourt; *The Storm Book* by Charlotte Zolotow, illustrated by Margaret Bloy Graham, Harper, *Five Little Monkeys,* written and illustrated by Juliet Kepes, Houghton

1954 *Madeline's Rescue,* written and illustrated by Ludwig Bemelmans, Viking
Honor Books: *Journey Cake, Ho!* by Ruth Sawyer, illustrated by Robert McCloskey, Viking; *When Will the World Be Mine?* by Miriam Schlein, illustrated by Jean Charlot, W. R. Scott; *The Steadfast Tin Soldier* by Hans Christian Andersen, illustrated by Marcia Brown, Scribner's; *A Very Special House* by Ruth Krauss, illustrated by Maurice Sendak, Harper; *Green Eyes,* written and illustrated by A. Birnbaum, Capitol

1955 *Cinderella, or the Little Glass Slipper* by Charles Perrault, translated and illustrated by Marcia Brown, Scribner's
Honor Books: *Book of Nursery and Mother Goose Rhymes,* illustrated by Marguerite de Angeli, Doubleday; *Wheel on the Chimney* by Margaret

Wise Brown, illustrated by Tibor Gergely, Lippincott; *The Thanksgiving Story* by Alice Dalgliesh, illustrated by Helen Sewell, Scribner's

1956   *Frog Went A-Courtin'*, edited by John Langstaff, illustrated by Feodor Rojankovsky, Harcourt
Honor Books: *Play with Me,* written and illustrated by Marie Hall Ets, Viking; *Crow Boy,* written and illustrated by Taro Yashima, Viking

1957   *A Tree Is Nice* by Janice May Udry, illustrated by Marc Simont, Harper
Honor Books: *Mr. Penny's Race Horse,* written and illustrated by Marie Hall Ets, Viking; *1 Is One,* written and illustrated by Tasha Tudor, Walck; *Anatole* by Eve Titus, illustrated by Paul Galdone, McGraw; *Gillespie and the Guards* by Benjamin Elkin, illustrated by James Daugherty, Viking; *Lion,* written and illustrated by William Pène du Bois, Viking

1958   *Time of Wonder,* written and illustrated by Robert McCloskey, Viking
Honor Books: *Fly High, Fly Low,* written and illustrated by Don Freeman, Viking; *Anatole and the Cat* by Eve Titus, illustrated by Paul Galdone, McGraw

1959   *Chanticleer and the Fox,* adapted from Chaucer and illustrated by Barbara Cooney, Crowell
Honor Books: *The House That Jack Built,* written and illustrated by Antonio Frasceni, Harcourt; *What Do You Say, Dear?* by Sesyle Joslin, illustrated by Maurice Sendak, W. R. Scott; *Umbrella,* written and illustrated by Taro Yashima, Viking

1960   *Nine Days to Christmas* by Marie Hall Ets and Aurora Labastida, illustrated by Marie Hall Ets, Viking
Honor Books: *Houses from the Sea* by Alice E. Goudey, illustrated by Adrienne Adams, Scribner's; *The Moon Jumpers* by Janice May Udry, illustrated by Maurice Sendak, Harper

1961   *Baboushka and the Three Kings* by Ruth Robbins, illustrated by Nicolas Sidjakov, Parnassus
Honor Book: *Inch by Inch,* written and illustrated by Leo Lionni, Obolensky

1962   *Once a Mouse . . . ,* written and illustrated by Marcia Brown, Scribner's
Honor Books: *The Fox Went Out on a Chilly Night,* written and illustrated by Peter Spier, Doubleday; *Little Bear's Visit* by Else Holmelund Minarik, illustrated by Maurice Sendak, Harper; *The Day We Saw the Sun Come Up* by Alice E. Goudey, illustrated by Adrienne Adams, Scribner's

1963   *The Snowy Day,* written and illustrated by Ezra Jack Keats, Viking
Honor Books: *The Sun Is a Golden Earring* by Natalie M. Belting, illustrated by Bernarda Bryson, Holt; *Mr. Rabbit and the Lovely Present* by Charlotte Zolotow, illustrated by Maurice Sendak, Harper

1964   *Where the Wild Things Are,* written and illustrated by Maurice Sendak, Harper
Honor Books: *Swimmy,* written and illustrated by Leo Lionni, Pantheon; *All in the Morning Early* by Sorche Nic Leodhas, illustrated by Evaline Ness, Holt; *Mother Goose and Nursery Rhymes,* illustrated by Philip Reed, Atheneum

1965   *May I Bring a Friend?* by Beatrice Schenk de Regniers, illustrated by Beni Montresor, Atheneum

Honor Books: *Rain Makes Applesauce* by Julian Scheer, illustrated by Marvin Bileck, Holiday; *The Wave* by Margaret Hodges, illustrated by Blair Lent, Houghton; *A Pocketful of Cricket* by Rebecca Caudill, illustrated by Evaline Ness, Holt

1966   *Always Room for One More* by Sorche Nic Leodhas, illustrated by Nonny Hogrogian, Holt
Honor Books: *Hide and Seek Fog* by Alvin Tresselt, illustrated by Roger Duvoisin, Lothrop; *Just Me*, written and illustrated by Marie Hall Ets, Viking; *Tom Tit Tot*, written and illustrated by Evaline Ness, Scribner's

1967   *Sam, Bangs and Moonshine*, written and illustrated by Evaline Ness, Holt
Honor Books: *One Wide River to Cross* by Barbara Emberley, illustrated by Ed Emberley, Prentice

1968   *Drummer Hoff* by Barbara Emberley, illustrated by Ed Emberley, Prentice
Honor Books: *Frederick*, written and illustrated by Leo Lionni, Pantheon; *Seashore Story*, written and illustrated by Taro Yashima, Viking; *The Emperor and the Kite* by Jane Yolen, illustrated by Ed Young, World

1969   *The Fool of the World and the Flying Ship* by Arthur Ransome, illustrated by Uri Shulevitz, Farrar
Honor Book: *Why the Sun and the Moon Live in the Sky* by Elphinstone Dayrell, illustrated by Blair Lent, Houghton

1970   *Sylvester and the Magic Pebble*, written and illustrated by William Steig, Windmill
Honor Books: *Goggles!* written and illustrated by Ezra Jack Keats, Macmillan; *Alexander and the Wind-Up Mouse*, written and illustrated by Leo Lionni, Pantheon; *Pop Corn and Ma Goodness*, by Edna Mitchell Preston, illustrated by Robert Andrew Parker, Viking; *Thy Friend, Obadiah*, written and illustrated by Brinton Turkle, Viking; *The Judge* by Harve Zemach, illustrated by Margot Zemach, Farrar

1971   *A Story, A Story*, written and illustrated by Gail E. Haley, Atheneum
Honor Books: *The Angry Moon* by William Sleator, illustrated by Blair Lent, Atlantic/Little; *Frog and Toad Are Friends*, written and illustrated by Arnold Lobel, Harper; *In the Night Kitchen*, written and illustrated by Maurice Sendak, Harper

1972   *One Fine Day*, written and illustrated by Nonny Hogrogian, Macmillan
Honor Books: *If All the Seas Were One Sea*, written and illustrated by Janina Domanska, Macmillan; *Moja Means One: Swahili Counting Book* by Muriel Feelings, illustrated by Tom Feelings, Dial; *Hildilid's Night* by Cheli Duran Ryan, illustrated by Arnold Lobel, Macmillan

1973   *The Funny Little Woman*, retold by Arlene Mosel, illustrated by Blair Lent, Dutton
Honor Books: *Anansi the Spider*, adapted and illustrated by Gerald McDermott, Holt; *Hosie's Alphabet* by Hosea, Tobias, and Lisa Baskin, illustrated by Leonard Baskin, Viking; *Snow-White and the Seven Dwarfs*, translated by Randall Jarrell, illustrated by Nancy Ekholm Burkert, Farrar; *When Clay Sings* by Byrd Baylor, illustrated by Tom Bahti, Soribner's

1974   *Duffy and the Devil* by Harve Zemach, illustrated by Margot Zemach, Farrar

Honor Books: *Three Jovial Huntsmen,* written and illustrated by Susan Jeffers, Bradbury; *Cathedral: The Story of Its Construction,* written and illustrated by David Macaulay, Houghton

1975   *Arrow to the Sun,* adapted and illustrated by Gerald McDermott, Viking
Honor Book: *Jambo Means Hello* by Muriel Feelings, illustrated by Tom Feelings, Dial

1976   *Why Mosquitoes Buzz in People's Ears,* retold by Verna Aardema, illustrated by Leo Dillon and Diane Dillon, Dial
Honor Books: *The Desert Is Theirs* by Byrd Baylor, illustrated by Peter Parnall, Scribner's; *Strega Nona,* retold and illustrated by Tomie dePaola, Prentice

1977   *Ashanti to Zulu: African Traditions* by Margaret Musgrove, illustrated by Leo Dillon and Diane Dillon, Dial
Honor Books: *The Amazing Bone,* written and illustrated by William Steig, Farrar; *The Contest,* retold and illustrated by Nonny Hogrogian, Greenwillow; *Fish for Supper,* written and illustrated by M. B. Goffstein, Dial; *The Golem,* written and illustrated by Beverly Brodsky McDermott, Lippincott; *Hawk, I'm Your Brother* by Byrd Baylor, illustrated by Peter Parnall, Scribner's

1978   *Noah's Ark,* illustrated by Peter Spier, Doubleday
Honor Books: *Castle,* written and illustrated by David Macaulay, Houghton; *It Could Always Be Worse,* retold and illustrated by Margot Zemach, Farrar

1979   *The Girl Who Loved Wild Horses,* written and illustrated by Paul Goble, Bradbury
Honor Books: *Freight Train,* written and illustrated by Donald Crews, Greenwillow; *The Way to Start a Day* by Byrd Baylor, illustrated by Peter Parnall, Scribner's

1980   *Ox-Cart Man* by Donald Hall, illustrated by Barbara Cooney, Viking
Honor Books: *Ben's Trumpet,* written and illustrated by Rachel Isadora, Greenwillow; *The Garden of Abdul Gasazi,* written and illustrated by Chris Van Allsburg, Houghton

1981   *Fables,* written and illustrated by Arnold Lobel, Harper
Honor Books: *The Grey Lady and the Strawberry Snatcher,* illustrated by Molly Bang, Four Winds; *Truck,* illustrated by Donald Crews, Greenwillow; *Mice Twice,* written and illustrated by Joseph Low, Atheneum; *The Bremen-Town Musicians,* illustrated by Ilse Plume, Doubleday

1982   *Jumanji,* written and illustrated by Chris Van Allsburg, Houghton
Honor Books: *Where the Buffaloes Begin* by Olaf Baker, illustrated by Stephen Gammell, Warne; *On Market Street* by Arnold Lobel, illustrated by Anita Lobel, Greenwillow; *Outside Over There,* written and illustrated by Maurice Sendak, Harper; *A Visit to William Blake's Inn,* by Nancy Willard, illustrated by Alice and Martin Provensen, Harcourt

1983   *Shadow* by Blaise Cendrars, translated and illustrated by Marcia Brown. Scribner's
Honor Books: *When I Was Young in the Mountains* by Cynthia Rylant, illustrated by Diane Goode, Dutton; *A Chair for My Mother,* written and illustrated by Vera B. Williams, Greenwillow

1984   *The Glorious Flight: Across the Channel with Louis Blériot* written and illustrated by Alice Provensen and Martin Provensen, Viking
Honor Books: *Ten, Nine, Eight* by Molly Bang, Greenwillow; *Little Red Riding Hood,* retold and illustrated by Trina Schart Hyman, Holiday House

1985   *St. George and the Dragon,* retold by Margaret Hodges, illustrated by Trina Schart Hyman, Little, Brown
Honor Books: *Hansel and Gretel,* retold by Rika Lesser, illustrated by Paul O. Zelinsky, Dodd; *Have You Seen My Duckling?* by Nancy Tafuri, Greenwillow; *The Story of Jumping Mouse* by John Steptoe, Lothrop

1986   *The Polar Express,* written and illustrated by Chris Van Allsburg, Houghton Mifflin
Honor Books: *The Relatives Came* by Cynthia Rylant, illustrated by Stephen Gammell, Bradbury; *King Bidgood's in the Bathtub* by Audrey Wood, illustrated by Don Wood, Harcourt

1987   *Hey, Al!* by Arthur Yorinks, illustrated by Richard Egielski, Farrar
Honor Books: *The Village of Round and Square Houses,* written and illustrated by Ann Grifalconi, Little, Brown; *Alphabetics,* written and illustrated by Suse MacDonald, Bradbury; *Rumpelstiltskin,* retold and illustrated by Paul O. Zelinsky, Dutton

1988   *Owl Moon* by Jane Yolen, illustrated by John Schoenherr, Philomel
Honor Book: *Mufaro's Beautiful Daughters,* written and illustrated by John Steptoe, Lothrop

1989   *Song and Dance Man* by Karen Ackerman, illustrated by Stephen Gammell, Knopf
Honor Books: *Free Fall,* written and illustrated by David Wiesner, Lothrop; *Goldilocks and the Three Bears,* retold and illustrated by James Marshall, Dial; *Mirandy and Brother Wind* by Patricia McKissack, illustrated by Jerry Pinkney, Knopf; *The Boy of the Three-Year Nap* by Diane Snyder, illustrated by Allen Say, Houghton

1990   *Lom Po Po: A Red Riding-Hood Story,* translated and illustrated by Ed Young, Philomel
Honor Books: *Bill Peet: An Autobiography* by Bill Peet; *Color Zoo* by Lois Ehlert; *Talking Eggs: A Folktale from the American South,* illustrated by Jerry Pinkney, text by Robert D. San Souci; *Hershel and the Hanukkah Goblins,* illustrated by Trina Schart Hyman, text by Eric Kimmel

1991   *Black and White* by David Macaulay, Houghton
Honor Books: *Puss in Boots,* illustrated by Fred Marcellino, text by Charles Perrault, translated by Malcolm Arthur; *"More More More" Said the Baby: Three Love Stories* by Vera B. Williams

1992   *Tuesday,* written and illustrated by David Wiesner, Clarion
Honor Book: *Tar Beach* by Faith Ringgold

1993   *Mirette on the High Wire,* written and illustrated by Emily Arnold McCully, Putnam
Honor Books: *The Stinky Cheese Man and Other Fairly Stupid Tales,* illustrated by Lane Smith, text by Jon Scieszka; *Seven Blind Mice* by Ed Young; *Working Cotton,* illustrated by Carol Byard, text by Shirley Anne Williams

1994   *Grandfather's Journey* by Allen Say
        Honor Books: *Peppe the Lamplighter,* illustrated by Ted Lewin, text by
        Elisa Bartone; *In the Small Small Pond* by Denise Fleming; *Raven: A
        Trickster Tale from the Pacific Northwest* by Gerald McDermott; *Yo! Yes?*
        by Chris Raschka; *Owen,* by Kevin Henkes
1995   *Smoky Night,* illustrated by David Diaz, text by Eve Bunting
        Honor Books: *John Henry,* illustrated by Jerry Pinkney, text by Julius
        Lester; *Swamp Angel,* illustrated by Paul Zelinsky, text by Anne Isaacs;
        Time Flies by Eric Rohmann
1996   *Officer Buckle and Gloria* by Peggy Rathman
        Honor Books: *Alphabet City* by Stephen T. Johnson; *The Faithful Friend,*
        illustrated by Brian Pinkney, text by Robert D. San Souci; *Tops and
        Bottoms* by Janet Stevens; *Zin! Zin! Zin! A Violin,* illustrated by Marjorie
        Priceman, text by Lloyd Moss
1997   *Golem* by David Wisniewski, Clarion
        Honor Books: *Hush! A Thai Lullaby,* illustrated by Holly Meade, text by
        Minfong Ho, Melanie Kroupa, Orchard; *The Graphic Alphabet* by David
        Pelletier, edited by Neal Porter, Orchard; *The Paperboy* by Dav Pilkey,
        Richard Jackson, Orchard; *Starry Messenger* by Peter Sis, Francis Foster
        Books, Farrar, Straus & Giroux

The Canadian Library Awards

This award has been given each year (since 1947) by the Canadian Library
Association to a distinguished children's book authored by a citizen of Canada. A
similar medal has been given annually (since 1954) to a significant children's book
published in French.

1947   *Starbuck Valley Winter* by Roderick Haig-Brown, Collins
1948   *Kristli's Trees* by Mabel Dunham, Hale
1950   *Franklin of the Arctic* by Richard S. Lambert, McClelland & Stewart
1952   *The Sun Horse* by Catherine Anthony Clark, Macmillan of Canada
1954   *Mgr. de Laval* by Emile S. J. Gervais, Comité des Fondateurs de l'Eglise
        Canadienne
1956   *Train for Tiger Lily* by Louise Riley, Macmillan of Canada
1957   *Glooskap's Country* by Cyrus Macmillan, Oxford
1958   *Lost in the Barrens* by Farley Mowat, Little
        Le Chevalier du Roi by Béatrice Clément, Les Editions de l'Atelier
1959   *The Dangerous Cove* by John F. Hayes, Copp Clark
        Un Drôle de Petit Cheval by Hélène Flamme, Editions Lémèac
1960   *The Golden Phoenix* by Marius Barbeau and Michael Hornyansky, Walck
        L'Eté Enchanté by Paule Daveluy, Les Editions de l'Atelier
1961   *The St. Lawrence* by William Toye, Oxford
        Plantes Vagabondes by Marcelle Gauvreau, Centre de Psychologie et de
        Pédagogie
1962   *Les Iles du Roi Maha Maha II* by Claude Aubry, Les Editions du Pélican
1963   *The Incredible Journey* by Sheila Burnford, Little, Brown

Drôle d'Automne by Paule Daveluy, Les Editions du Pélican

1964   *The Whale People* by Roderick Haig-Brown, William Collins of Canada

Feerie by Cécile Chabot, Librairie Beauchemin Ltée.

1965   *Tales of Nanabozho* by Dorothy Reid, Oxford

Le Loup de Noël by Claude Aubry, Centre de Psychologie de Montréal

1966   *Tikta 'Liktak* by James Houston, Kestrel

Le Chêne des Tempêtes by Andrée Mallet-Hobden, Fides; *The Double Knights* by James McNeal, Walck; *Le Wapiti* by Monique Corriveau, Jeunesse

1967   *Raven's Cry* by Christie Harris, McClelland & Stewart

1968   *The White Archer* by James Houston, Kestrel

Légendes Indiennes du Canada by Claude Mélançon, Editions du Jour

1969   *And Tomorrow the Stars* by Kay Hill, Dodd

1970   *Sally Go Round the Sun* by Edith Fowke, McClelland & Stewart

Le Merveilleuse Histoire de la Naissance by Lionel Gendron, Les Editions de l'Homme

1971   *Cartier Discovers the St. Lawrence* by William Toye, Oxford University

La Surprise de Dame Chenille by Henriette Major, Centre de Psychologie de Montréal

1972   *Mary of Mile 18* by Ann Blades, Tundra

1973   *The Marrow of the World* by Ruth Nichols, Macmillan of Canada

Le Petit Sapin Qui A Poussé sur une Étoile by Simone Bussières, Presses Laurentiennes

1974   *The Miraculous Hind* by Elizabeth Cleaver, Holt of Canada

1975   *Alligator Pie* by Dennis Lee, Macmillan of Canada

1976   *Jacob Two-Two Meets the Hooded Fang* by Mordecai Richler, Knopf

1977   *Mouse Woman and the Vanished Princesses* by Christie Harris, McClelland & Stewart

1978   *Garbage Delight* by Dennis Lee, Macmillan

1979   *Hold Fast* by Kevin Major, Clarke, Irwin

1980   *River Runners: A Tale of Hardship and Bravery* by James Houston, McClelland & Stewart

1981   *The Violin Maker's Gift* by Donn Kushner, Macmillan of Canada

1982   *The Root Cellar* by Janet Lunn, Lester & Orpen Dennys

1983   *Up to Low* by Brian Doyle, Groundwood

1984   *Sweetgrass* by Jan Hudson, Tree Frog Press

1985   *Mama's Going to Buy a Mockingbird* by Jean Little, Penguin

1986   *Julie* by Cora Taylor, Western

1987   *Shadow in Hawthorn Bay* by Janet Lunn, Scribner

1988   *A Handful of Time* by Kit Pearson, Viking

1989   *Easy Avenue* by Brian Doyle, Groundwood Bks.

1990   *Sky Is Falling* by Kit Pearson, Viking Penguin

1991   *Redwork* by Bedard Michael, Lester & Orpen Dennys

1992   *Eating Between the Lines* by Kevin Major, Doubleday Canada

1993   *Ticket to Curlew* by Celia Barker Lottridge

1994   *Some of the Kinder Planets* by Tim Wynne-Jones

1995   *Summer of the Mad Monk* by Cora Taylor

1996   *The Tiny Kite of Eddie Wing* by Maxine Trottier; Honour Books: *In Flanders Fields: The Story of the Poem by John McCrae* by Linda

Granfield, illustrated by Janet Wilson; *There Goes the Neighborhood* by Valerie Lupini; *Big Boy* by Tololwa Marti Mollel; *The Only House* by Teresa Toten

1997   *Uncle Ronald* by Brian Doyle, Groundwood; Honour Book, *The Wagner Whacker*, Vanwell

The Carnegie Medal

The British Library Association gives this medal each year to the author of a distinguished children's book written in English and first published in the United Kingdom. The award was established in 1937.

1936   *Pigeon Post* by Arthur Ransome, Cape
1937   *The Family from One End Street* by Eve Garnett, Muller
1938   *The Circus Is Coming* by Noel Streatfield, Dent
1939   *Radium Woman* by Eleanor Doorly, Heinemann
1940   *Visitors from London* by Kitty Barne, Dent
1941   *We Couldn't Leave Dinah* by Mary Treadgold, Penguin
1944   *The Wind on the Moon* by Eric Linklater, Macmillan
1946   *The Little White Horse* by Elizabeth Goudge, Brockhampton Press
1947   *Collected Stories for Children* by Walter de la Mare, Faber
1948   *Sea Change* by Richard Armstrong, Dent
1949   *The Story of Your Home* by Agnes Allen, Transatlantic
1950   *The Lark on the Wing* by Elfrida Vipont Foulds, Oxford
1951   *The Wool-Pack* by Cynthia Harnett, Methuen
1952   *The Borrowers* by Mary Norton, Dent
1953   *A Valley Grows Up* by Edward Osmond, Oxford
1954   *Knight Crusader* by Ronald Welch, Oxford
1955   *The Little Bookroom* by Eleanor Farjeon, Oxford
1956   *The Last Battle* by C. S. Lewis, Bodley Head
1957   *A Grass Rope* by William Mayne, Oxford
1958   *Tom's Midnight Garden* by Philippa Pearce, Oxford
1959   *The Lantern Bearers* by Rosemary Sutcliff, Oxford
1960   *The Making of Man* by I. W. Cornwall, Phoenix
1961   *A Stranger at Green Knowe* by Lucy Boston, Faber
1962   *The Twelve and the Genii* by Pauline Clarke, Faber
1963   *Time of Trial* by Hester Burton, Oxford
1964   *Nordy Banks* by Sheena Porter, Oxford
1965   *The Grange at High Force* by Philip Turner, Oxford
1967   *The Owl Service* by Alan Garner, Collins
1968   *The Moon in the Cloud* by Rosemary Harris, Faber
1969   *The Edge of the Cloud* by K. M. Peyton, Oxford
1970   *The God Beneath the Sea* by Leon Garfield and Edward Blishen, Kestrel
1971   *Josh* by Ivan Southall, Angus & Robertson
1972   *Watership Down* by Richard Adams, Rex Collings

1973   *The Ghost of Thomas Kempe* by Penelope Lively, Heinemann
1974   *The Stronghold* by Mollie Hunter, Hamilton
1975   *The Machine-Gunners* by Robert Westall, Macmillan
1976   *Thunder and Lightnings* by Jan Mark, Kestrel
1977   *The Turbulent Term of Tyke Tiler* by Gene Kemp, Faber
1978   *The Exeter Blitz* by David Rees, Hamish Hamilton
1979   *Tulku* by Peter Dickinson, Dutton
1980   *City of Gold* by Peter Dickinson, Gollancz
1981   *The Scarecrows* by Robert Westall, Chatto & Windus
1982   *The Haunting* by Margaret Mahy, Dent
1983   *Handles* by Jan Mark, Kestrel
1984   *The Changeover* by Margaret Mahy, Dent
1985   *Storm* by Kevin Crossley-Holland, Heinemann
1986   *Granny Was a Buffer Girl* by Berlie Doherty, Methuen
1987   *The Ghost Drum* by Susan Price, Faber
1988   *Pack of Lies* by Geraldine McCaughrean
1989   *My War with Goggle Eyes* by Anne Fine
1990   *Wolf* by Gillian Cross, Oxford
1991   *Dear Nobody* by Berlie Doherty, Orchard
1992   *The Flour Babies* by Anne Fine, Little
1993   *Stone Cold* by Robert Swindells
1994   *Whispers in the Graveyard* by Theresa Breslin; Recommended: *MapHead* by Lesley Howarth; *Willa and Old Miss Annie* by Berlie Doherty
1995   *Northern Lights* by Philip Pullman (U.S. title: *The Golden Compass*)
1996   *Junk,* Melvin Burgess, Anderson

Coretta Scott King Award

Established in 1969, this award commemorates the life and work of Martin Luther King, Jr., and honors Mrs. King "for her courage and determination to continue the work for peace and world brotherhood." It is presented annually at the American Library Association to an African-American author (A) and illustrator (I) whose works "encourage and promote" world unity and peace, and serve as an inspiration to young people in the achievement of their goals. A plaque, honorarium and an encyclopedia are presented as gifts.

1971   *Black Troubador: Langston Hughes* by Charlemae H. Rollins
1972   *Seventeen Black Artists* by Elton C. Fax
1973   *I Never Had It Made, The Autobiography of Jackie Robinson* by Jackie Robinson, as told to Alfred Duckett
1974   *Ray Charles* by Sharon Bell Mathis (A) and George Ford (I)
1975   *The Legend of Africania* by Eloise Greenfield (A) and Herbert Temple (I)
1976   *Duey's Tale* by Pearl Bailey
1977   *The Story of Stevie Wonder* by James Haskins
1978   *Africa Dream* by Eloise Greenfield (A) and Carole Byard (I)

1979   *Escape to Freedom: A Play About Young Frederick Douglass* by Ossie Davis; (A) *Something on My Mind* by Tom Feelings (I)

1980   *The Young Landlords* by Walter Dean Myers (A)
Cornrows by Carole Byard, (I)

1981   *This Life* by Sidney Poitier (A)
Beat the Story Drum, Pum-Pum by Ashley Bryan (I)

1982   *Let the Circle Be Unbroken* by Mildred D. Taylor, Dial (A)
My Mama Needs Me by Mildred P. Walter (A) and Pat Cummings (I), Lothrop

1983   *Black Child* by Peter Magubane (I), Knopf
Sweet Whispers, Brother Rush by Virginia Hamilton, Philomel

1984   *Everett Anderson's Goodbye* by Lucille Clifton et al. (A) and Ann Grifalconi (I), Henry Holt

1985   *Motown and Didi: A Love Story* by Walter D. Myers, Viking

1986   *Patchwork Quilt* by Valerie Flournoy (A) and Jerry Pinkey (I), Dial
People Could Fly by Virginia Hamilton (A) and Leo and Diane Dillon (I), Knopf

1987   *Half a Moon and One Whole Star* by Crescent Dragonwagon (A) and Jerry Pinkney (I), Macmillan
Justin and the Best Biscuits in the World by Mildred P. Walter (A) and Catherine Stock (I), Lothrop

1988   *Friendship* by Mildred D. Taylor (A) and Max Ginsburg (I), Dial
Mufaro's Beautiful Daughters: An African Tale, edited and illustrated by John Steptoe, Lothrop

1989   *Fallen Angels* by Walter D. Myers, Scholastic
Mirandy and Brother Wind by Patricia C. Mckissack (A) and Jerry Pinkney (I), Knopf

1990   *Long Hard Journey* by Patricia McKissack and Frederick McKissack (A), Walker
Nathaniel Talking by Eloise Greenfield and Jan S. Gilchrist (I)
Black Butterfly, Children's Press

1991   *Aida* by Leontyne Price (A) and Leo and Diane Dillon (I), Harcourt
The Road to Memphis by Mildred D. Taylor (A)

1992   *Now Is Your Time: The African American Struggle for Freedom,* Walter D. Myers (A), HarperCollins
Tar Beach by Faith Ringgold, Crown

1993   *The Dark Thirty: Southern Tales of the Supernatural* by Patricia McKissack (A)
The Origin of Life on Earth: An African Creation Myth by Kathleen Atkins Wilson (I); text by David A. Anderson

1994   *Toning the Sweep* by Angela Johnson (A)
Soul Looks Back in Wonder by Tom Feelings (I); text by Maya Angelou et al.

1995   *Christmas in the Big House, Christmas in the Quarters* by Patricia and Frederick McKissack (A)
The Creation, James Ransome (I); text by James Weldon Johnson

1996   *Her Stories* by Virginia Hamilton (A) and Leo and Diane Dillon (I)
The Middle Passage: White Ships, Black Cargo by Tom Feelings (I) (introduction by John Henry Clark)

1997   *Slam!* by Walter Dean Myers (A), Scholastic
        Minty: A Story of Young Harriet Tubman by Jerry Pinkney (I); text by
        Alan Schroeder

The Eva L. Gordon Award

Established by the American Nature Study Society to recognize an author of children's science literature.

1964	Millicent Selsam
1965	Edwin Way Teale
1966	Robert M. McClung
1970	Jean Craighead George
1971	Veme Rockcastle
1974	Phyllis Busch
1976	Jeanne Bendick
1977	Nina Schneider and Herman Schneider
1978	George F. Mason; Dorothy Shuttleworth
1979	Ross Hutchins
1980	Glenn O. Blough
1981	Herbert Zim
1982	Peter Pamell
1983	Lawrence Pringle
1984	Seymour Simon
1985	Vicki Cobb
1986	Dorothy Hinshaw Patent
1987	Patricia Lauber
1988	Franklyn Branley
1989	Ada Graham and Frank Graham
1990	Joanna Cole
1991	Jim Arnosky
1992	Byrd Baylor
1993	Augusta Goldin
1994	Eric Carle
1995	Joanna Ryder
1996	David Macaulay
1997	Gail Gibbon

Hans Christian Andersen Award

1956	Author: Eleanor Farjeon (Great Britain)
1958	Author: Astrid Lindgren (Sweden)
1960	Author: Erich Klastner (West Germany)
1962	Author: Meindert DeJong (USA)
1964	Author: Rene Guillot (France)

1966 Author: Tove Jansson (Finland)
Illustrator: Alois Carigiet (Switzerland)
1970 Author: Gianni Rodari (Italy)
Illustrator: Maurice Sendak (USA)
1972 Author: Scott O'Dell (USA)
Illustrator: Ib Spang Olsen (Denmark)
1974 Author: Maria Gripe (Sweden)
Illustrator: Faarshid Mesghali (Iran)
1976 Author: Cecil Bodker (Denmark)
Illustrator: Tatjana Mawrina (USSR)
1978 Author: Paula Fox (USA)
Illustrator: Otto S. Svend (Denmark)
1980 Author: Bohumil Riha (Czechoslovakia)
Illustrator: Suekichi Akaba (Japan)
1982 Author: Lygia Bojunga Nunes (Brazil)
Illustrator: Zbigniew Rychilicki (Poland)
1984 Author: Christine Nostlinger (Austria)
Illustrator: Mitsumasa Anno (Japan)
1986 Author: Patricia Wrightson (Australia)
Illustrator: Robert Ingpen (Australia)
1988 Author: Annie M. G. Schmidt (Netherlands)
Illustrator: Dusan Kallay (Czechoslovakia)
1990 Author: Tormmmod Haugen (Norway)
Illustrator: Lisbeth Zwerger (Austria)
1992 Author: Virginia Hamilton (USA)
Illustrator: Kveta Pacovska (Czechoslovakia)
1994 Author: Michio Mado (Japan)
Illustrator: Jorg Muller (Switzerland)
1996 Author: Uri Orlev (Israel)
Illustrator: Klaus Ensikat (Germany)
1998 Author: Katherine Paterson (USA)
Illustrator: Tomi Ungerer (France)

International Reading Association Children's Book Award

Given for the first time in 1975, this award is presented annually for a book published in the preceding year and written by an author "who shows unusual promise in the children's book field." Sponsored by the Institute for Reading Research, the award is administered by the International Reading Association.

1975 *Transport 7-41-R* by T. Degens, Viking
1976 *Dragonwings* by Laurence Yep, Harper
1977 *A String in the Harp* by Nancy Bond, McElderry/Atheneum

1978   *A Summer to Die* by Lois Lowry, Houghton
1979   *Reserved for Mark Anthony Crowder* by Alison Smith, Dutton
1980   *Words by Heart* by Ouida Sebestyen, Atlantic/Little
1981   *My Own Private Sky* by Delores Beckman, Dutton
1982   *Good Night, Mr. Tom* by Michelle Magorian, Kestrel/Penguin (Great Britain); Harper (U.S.A.)
1983   *The Darkangel* by Meredith Ann Pierce, Atlantic/Little
1984   *Ratha's Creature* by Clare Bell, Atheneum
1985   *Badger on the Barge* by Janni Howker, Greenwillow
1986   *Prairie Songs* by Pam Conrad, illustrated by Daryl S. Zudeck, Harper
1987   *The Line Up Book* by Marisabina Russo, Greenwillow
1988   *Third Story Cat* by Leslie Baker, Little, Brown
1989   *Probably Still Nick Swansen* by Virginia E. Wolff, Henry Holt (Older)
       Rechenka's Eggs by Patricia Polacco, illustrated by Patricia Polacco, Philomel (Younger).
1990   *Children of the River* by Linda Crew, Delacorte (Older)
       No Star Nights by Anna E. Smucker, illustrated by Steve Johnson, Knopf (Younger)
1991   *Is This a House for Hermit Crab?* by Megan McDonald, illustrated by F. D. Schindler, Orchard (Younger)
       Under the Hawthorn Tree by Marita Conlon-McKenna, illustrated by Donald Teskey, Holiday (Older)
1992   *Five Words* by Pnina Kass, Cricket Magazine
       Rescue Josh McGuire by Ben Mikaelsen, Hyperion
       Ten Little Rabbits by Virginia Grossman, illustrated by Sylvia Long, Chronicle
1993   *Old Turtle,* by Douglas Wood and Cheng-Khee Chee, Pfeifer-Hamilton (Younger)
       Letters from Rifka by Karen Hesse, Henry Holt (Older)
1994   *Sweet Clara and the Freedom Quilt* by Deborah Hopkinson, Henry Holt (Younger)
       Behind the Secret Window by Nelly S. Toll, Dutton (Older)
1995   *The Ledger Book of Thomas Blue Eagle* by Gay Matthaei, Jewel Grutman, and Adam Cvijanovic, Thomasson-Grant (Younger)
       Spite Fences by Trudy Krisher, Bantam (Older)
       Stranded at Plimouth Plantation, 1626 by Gary Bowen, HarperCollins (Informational Reader)
1996   *More About Anything Else* by Marie Bradby and Chris K. Soentpiet, Orchard (Younger)
       The King's Shadow by Elizabeth Alder, Farrar, Straus & Giroux (Older)
       The Case of the Mummified Pigs and Other Mysteries in Nature by Susan E. Quinlan, Boyds Mill (Informational Book)
1997   *The Fabulous Flying Fandinis* by Ingrid Slyder, Penguin USA (Younger)
       Don't You Dare Read This, Mrs. Dunphrey by Margaret Peterson Haddix, Simon & Schuster (Older); *The Brooklyn Bridge,* by Elizabeth Mann, Mikaya (Informational Book)

The Kate Greenaway Medal

The Kate Greenaway Medal, given annually by the British Library Association, recognizes the outstanding illustration of a children's book first published in the United Kingdom in the preceding year.

1956   *Tim All Alone,* written and illustrated by Edward Ardizzone, Oxford

1957   *Mrs. Easter and the Storks,* written and illustrated by V. H. Drummond, Faber

1958   No award

1959   *Kashtanka and a Bundle of Ballads,* written and illustrated by William Stobbs, Oxford

1960   *Old Winkle and the Seagulls* by Elizabeth Rose, illustrated by Gerald Rose, Faber

1961   *Mrs. Cockle's Cat* by Philippa Pearce, illustrated by Anthony Maitland, Kestrel

1962   *Brian Wildsmith's ABC,* written and illustrated by Brian Wildsmith, Oxford

1963   *Borka,* written and illustrated by John Burningham. Jonathan Cape

1964   *Shakespeare's Theatre,* written and illustrated by C. W. Hodges, Oxford

1965   *Three Poor Tailors,* written and illustrated by Victor Ambrus, Hamilton

1966   *Mother Goose Treasury,* written and illustrated by Raymond Briggs, Hamilton

1967   *Charlie, Charlotte and the Golden Canary,* written and illustrated by Charles Keeping, Oxford

1968   *Dictionary of Chivalry* by Grant Uden, illustrated by Pauline Baynes, Kestrel

1969   *The Quangle-Wangle's Hat* by Edward Lear, illustrated by Helen Oxenbury, Heinemann; *Dragon of an Ordinary Family* by Margaret Mahy, illustrated by Helen Oxenbury, Heinemann

1970   *Mr. Gumpy's Outing* written and illustrated by John Burningham, Jonathan Cape

1971   *The Kingdom Under the Sea,* written and illustrated by Jan Piénkowski, Jonathan Cape

1972   *The Woodcutter's Duck,* written and illustrated by Krystyna Turska, Hamilton

1973   *Father Christmas,* written and illustrated by Raymond Briggs, Hamilton

1974   *The Wind Blew,* written and illustrated by Pat Hutchins, Bodley Head

1975   *Horses in Battle,* written and illustrated by Victor Ambrus, Oxford; *Mishka,* written and illustrated by Victor Ambrus, Oxford

1976   *The Post Office Cat,* written and illustrated by Gail E. Haley, Bodley Head

1977   *Dogger,* written and illustrated by Shirley Hughes, Bodley Head

1978   *Each Peach Pear Plum,* written and illustrated by Janet and Allan Ahlberg, Kestrel

1979   *Haunted House,* written and illustrated by Jan Piénkowski, Dutton

1980   *Mr. Magnolia* by Quentin Blake, Jonathan Cape

1981   *The Highwayman* by Alfred Noyes, illustrated by Charles Keeping, Oxford

1982   *Long Neck and Thunder Foot* (Kestrel) and *Sleeping Beauty and Other Favorite Fairy Tales* (Gollancz), both illustrated by Michael Foreman

1983   *Gorilla* by Anthony Browne, Julia McRae Books

1984 *Hiawatha's Childhood* by Errol LeCain, Faber
1985 *Sir Gawain and the Loathly Lady* by Selina Hastings, illustrated by Juan Wijngaard, Walker
1986 *Snow White in New York* by Fiona French, Oxford
1987 *Shadow in Hawthorn Bay* by Janet Lunn, Scribner
1988 *Crafty Chameleon* by Mwenye Hadithi, illustrated by Adrienne Kennaway, Hodder & Stoughton
1989 *Can't You Sleep, Little Bear?* by Martin Waddell and Barbara Firth, Walker Bks
1990 *War Boy: A Country Childhood* by Michael Foreman, Pavilion Books
1991 *Whales' Song* by Dyan Sheldon, illustrated by Gary Blythe, Hutchinson
1992 *Jolly Postman* by Janet Ahlberg, illustrated by Janet Ahlberg, Little
1993 *Zoo* by Anthony Browne, Knopf
1994 *The Way Home* by Gregory Rogers; text by Libby Hathorn
1995 *The Christmas Miracle of Jonathan Toomey,* illustrated by P. J. Lynch; text by Susan Wojciechowski

The Laura Ingalls Wilder Award

This award was first given in 1954 and was presented every five years from 1960 to 1980. Since 1980, it has been given every three years. The medal is administered by the Association of Library Service to Children of the American Library Association. The award recognizes an author or illustrator whose books, published in the United States, have over a period of years made a substantial contribution to literature for children.

1954 Laura Ingalls Wilder
1960 Clara Ingram Judson
1965 Ruth Sawyer
1970 E. B. White
1975 Beverly Cleary
1980 Theodore Geisel (Dr. Seuss)
1983 Maurice Sendak
1986 Jean Fritz
1989 Elizabeth George Speare
1992 Marcia Brown
1995 Virginia Hamilton

The Mildred L. Batchelder Award

This award is given by the American Library Association for the best translation of a work published in a language other than English.

1968 *The Little Man* by Erich Kastner, translated by James Kirkup, illustrated by Rick Schreiter, Knopf

1969   *Don't Take Teddy* by Babbis Friis-Baastad, translated by Lise Somme McKinnon, Scribner's

1970   *Wildcat Under Glass* by Alki Zei, translated by Edward Fenton, Holt

1971   *In the Land of Ur: The Discovery of Ancient Mesopotamia* by Hans Baumann, translated by Stella Humphries, illustrated by Hans Peter Renner, Pantheon

1972   *Friedrich* by Hans Peter Richter, translated by Edite Kroll, Holt

1973   *Pulga* by Siny Rose Van Iterson, translated by Alexander Gode and Alison Gode, Morrow

1974   *Petros' War* by Alki Zei, translated by Edward Fenton, Dutton

1975   *An Old Tale Carved Out of Stone* by Aleksandr M. Linevski, translated by Maria Polushkin, Crown

1976   *The Cat and Mouse Who Shared a House,* written and illustrated by Ruth Hurlimann, translated by Anthea Bell, Walck

1977   *The Leopard* by Cecil Bodker, translated by Gunnar Poulsen, Atheneum

1978   No award

1979   *Konrad* by Christine Nostlinger, translated by Anthea Bell, illustrated by Carol Nicklaus, Watts
        Rabbit Island by Jorg Steiner, translated by Ann Conrad Lammers, illustrated by Jorg Muller, Harcourt

1980   *The Sound of Dragon's Feet* by Alki Zei, translated by Edward Fenton, Dutton

1981   *The Winter When Time Was Frozen* by Els Pelgrom, translated by Raphael Rudnils and Maryka Rudnik, Morrow

1982   *The Battle Horse* by Harry Kullman, translated by George Blecher and Lone Thygesen-Blecher, Bradbury

1983   *Hiroshima no Pika,* written and illustrated by Toshi Maruki, translated by Komine Shoten, Lothrop, Lee & Shepard

1984   *Ronia, the Robber's Daughter* by Astrid Lindgren, translated by Patricia Crampton, Viking

1985   *The Island on Bird Street* by Uri Orlev, translated by Hillel Halkin, Houghton Mifflin

1986   *Rose Blanche* by Christophe Gallaz and Roberto Innocenti, translated by Martha Coventry and Richard Graglia, illustrated by Roberto Innocenti, Creative Education

1987   *No Hero for the Kaiser* by Rudolf Frank, translated by Patricia Crampton, illustrated by Klaus Steffans, Lothrop, Lee & Shepard

1988   *If You Didn't Have Me* by Ulf Nilsson, illustrated by Eva Eriksson, translated by Lone Thygesen-Blecher and George Blecher, McElderry

1989   *Crutches* by Peter Härtling, translated by Elizabeth D. Crawford, Lothrop, Lee & Shepard

1990   *Buster's World* by Bjarne Reuter, translated by Anthea Bell, Dutton

1991   *A Hand Full of Stars* by Rafik Schami, translated by Rika Lesser, Dutton
        Honor Book: *Two Shorts and One Long* written and translated by Nina Ring Aamundsen, Houghton

1992   *Man from the Other Side* by Uri Orlev, translated by Hillel Halkin, Houghton

1993   No award

1994   *The Apprentice,* by Pilar Molina Llorente, translated by Robin Longshaw
        Honor Books: *Anne Frank: Beyond the Diary* by Ruud van der Rol and
        Rian Verhoeven, illustrated by Vedat Valokay, translated by Tony
        Langham and Plym Peters, Viking; *The Princess in the Kitchen Garden* by
        Annemie Heymans and Margriet Heymans, translated by Johanna H.
        Prins and Johanna W. Prins
1995   *The Boys from St. Petri* by Bjarne Reuter, translated by Anthea Bell
        Honor Book: *Sister Shako and Kolo the Goat* by Vedat Dalokay, translated
        by Guener Ener
1996   *The Lady with the Hat* by Uri Orlev, translated by Hillel Halkin,
        Houghton
        Honor Book: *Star of Fear, Star of Hope* by Jo Hoestland, translated by
        Mark Polizzotti, Walker
1997   *The Friends* by Kazumi Yumoto, translated by Cathy Hirano, Farrar

National Council of Teachers of English Award for Excellence in Poetry for Children

This award is presented by the National Council of Teachers of English to a living
American poet in recognition of the poet's aggregate body of work in children's literature. It was given annually until 1982, and now is presented every three years.

1977   David McCord
1978   Aileen Fisher
1979   Karla Kuskin
1980   Myra Cohn Livingston
1981   Eve Merriam
1982   John Ciardi
1985   Lilian Moore
1988   Arnold Adoff
1991   Valerie Worth
1994   Barbara Juster Esbensen
1997   Eloise Greenfield

The Newbery Medal

Named in honor of John Newbery (1713–1767), the first English publisher of children's books, this medal has been given annually (since 1922) by the American
Library Association's Association for Library Service to Children. The recipient is
recognized as author of the most distinguished book in children's literature published in the United States in the preceding year. The award is limited to citizens or
residents of the United States.

1922   *The Story of Mankind* by Hendrik Willem van Loon, Liveright
       Honor Books: *The Great Quest* by Charles Hawes, Little; *Cedric the Forester* by Bernard Marshall, Appleton; *The Old Tobacco Shop* by William Bowen, Macmillan; *The Golden Fleece and the Heroes Who Lived Before Achilles* by Padraic Colum, Macmillan; *Windy Hill* by Cornelia Meigs, Macmillan

1923   *The Voyages of Doctor Dolittle* by Hugh Lofting, Lippincott

1924   *The Dark Frigate* by Charles Hawes, Atlantic/Little, Brown

1925   *Tales from Silver Lands* by Charles Finger, Doubleday
       Honor Books: *Nicholas* by Anne Carroll Moore, Putnam; *Dream Coach* by Anne Parrish, Macmillan

1926   *Shen of the Sea* by Arthur Bowie Chrisman, Dutton
       Honor Book: *Voyagers* by Padraic Colum, Macmillan

1927   *Smoky, the Cowhorse* by Will James, Scribner's

1928   *Gayneck, The Story of a Pigeon* by Dhan Gopal Mukerji, Dutton
       Honor Books: *The Wonder Smith and His Son* by Ella Young, Longmans; *Downright Dencey* by Caroline Snedeker, Doubleday

1929   *The Trumpeter of Krakow* by Eric P. Kelly, Macmillan
       Honor Books: *Pigtail of Ah Lee Ben Loo* by John Bennett, Longmans; *Millions of Cats* by Wanda Gág, Coward; *The Boy Who Was* by Grace Hallock, Dutton; *Clearing Weather* by Cornelia Meigs, Little; *Runaway Papoose* by Grace Moon, Doubleday; *Tod of the Fens* by Elinor Whitney, Macmillan

1930   *Hitty, Her First Hundred Years* by Rachel Field, Macmillan
       Honor Books: *Daughter of the Seine* by Jeanette Eaton, Harper; *Pran of Albania* by Elizabeth Miller, Doubleday; *Jumping-Off Place* by Marian Hurd McNeely, Longmans; *Tangle-Coated Horse and Other Tales* by Ella Young, Longmans; *Vaino* by Julia Davis Adams, Dutton; *Little Blacknose* by Hildegarde Swift, Harcourt

1931   *The Cat Who Went to Heaven* by Elizabeth Coatsworth, Macmillan
       Honor Books: *Floating Island* by Anne Parish, Harper; *The Dark Star of Itza* by Alida Malkus, Harcourt; *Queer Person* by Ralph Hubbard, Doubleday; *Mountains Are Free* by Julia Davis Adams, Dutton; *Spice and the Devil's Cave* by Agnes Hewes, Knopf; *Meggy Macintosh* by Elizabeth Janet Gray, Doubleday; *Garram the Hunter* by Herbert Best, Doubleday; *Ood-Le-Uk the Wanderer* by Alice Lide and Margaret Johansen, Little

1932   *Waterless Mountain* by Laura Adams Armer, Longmans
       Honor Books: *The Fairy Circus* by Dorothy P. Lathrop, Macmillan; *Calico Bush* by Rachel Field, Macmillan; *Boy of the South Seas* by Eunice Tietjens, Coward; *Out of the Flame* by Eloise Lownsbery, Longmans; *Jane's Island* by Marjorie Allee, Houghton; *Truce of the Wolf and Other Tales of Old Italy* by Mary Gould Davis, Harcourt

1933   *Young Fu of the Upper Yangtze* by Elizabeth Foreman Lewis, Winston
       Honor Books: *Swift Rivers* by Cornelia Meigs, Little; *The Railroad to Freedom* by Hildegarde Swift, Harcourt; *Children of the Soil* by Nora Burglon, Doubleday

1934   *Invincible Louisa* by Cornelia Meigs, Little

Honor Books: *The Forgotten Daughter* by Caroline Snedeker, Doubleday; *Swords of Steel* by Elsie Singmaster, Houghton; *ABC Bunny* by Wanda Gág, Coward; *Winged Girl of Knossos* by Erik Berry, Appleton; *New Land* by Sarah Schmidt, McBride; *Big Tree of Bunlahy* by Padraic Colum, Macmillan; *Glory of the Seas* by Agnes Hewes, Knopf; *Apprentice of Florence* by Anne Kyle, Houghton

1935   *Dobry* by Monica Shannon, Viking
Honor Books: *Pageant of Chinese History* by Elizabeth Seeger, Longmans; *Davy Crockett* by Constance Rourke, Harcourt; *Day on Skates* by Hilda Van Stockum, Harper

1936   *Caddie Woodlawn* by Carol Brink, Macmillan
Honor Books: *Honk, The Moose* by Phil Strong, Dodd; *The Good Master* by Kate Seredy, Viking; *Young Walter Scott* by Elizabeth Janet Gray, Viking; *All Sail Set* by Armstrong Sperry, Winston

1937   *Roller Skates* by Ruth Sawyer, Viking
Honor Books: *Phoebe Fairchild: Her Book* by Lois Lenski, Stokes; *Whistler's Van* by Idwal Jones, Viking; *Golden Basket* by Ludwig Bemelmans, Viking; *Winterbound* by Margery Bianco, Viking; *Audubon* by Constance Rourke, Harcourt; *The Codfish Musket* by Agnes Hewes, Doubleday

1938   *The White Stag* by Kate Seredy, Viking
Honor Books: *Pecos Bill* by James Cloyd Bowman, Little; *Bright Island* by Mabel Robinson, Random; *On the Banks of Plum Creek* by Laura Ingalls Wilder, Harper

1939   *Thimble Summer* by Elizabeth Enright, Rinehart
Honor Books: *Nino by* Valenti Angelo, Viking; *Mr. Popper's Penguins* by Richard and Florence Atwater, Little; *"Hello the Boat!"* by Phyllis Crawford, Holt; *Leader by Destiny: George Washington, Man and Patriot* by Jeanette Eaton, Harcourt; *Penn* by Elizabeth Janet Gray, Viking

1940   *Daniel Boone* by James Daugherty, Viking
Honor Books: *The Singing Tree* by Kate Seredy, Viking; *Runner of the Mountain Tops* by Mabel Robinson, Random; *By the Shores of Silver Lake* by Laura Ingalls Wilder, Harper; *Boy with a Pack* by Stephen W. Meader, Harcourt

1941   *Call It Courage* by Armstrong Sperry, Macmillan
Honor Books: *Blue Willow* by Doris Gates, Viking; *Young Mac of Fort Vancouver* by Mary Jane Carr, Crowell; *The Long Winter* by Laura Ingalls Wilder, Harper; *Nansen* by Anna Gertrude Hall, Viking

1942   *The Matchlock Gun* by Walter D. Edmonds, Dodd
Honor Books: *Little Town on the Prairie* by Laura Ingalls Wilder, Harper; *George Washington's World* by Genevieve Foster, Scribner's; *Indian Captive: The Story of Mary Jemison* by Lois Lenski, Lippincott; *Down Ryton Water* by Eva Roe Gaggin, Viking

1943   *Adam of the Road* by Elizabeth Janet Gray, Viking
Honor Books: *The Middle Moffat* by Eleanor Estes, Harcourt; *Have You Seen Tom Thumb?* by Mabel Leigh Hunt, Lippincott

1944   *Johnny Tremain* by Esther Forbes, Houghton
Honor Books: *These Happy Golden Years* by Laura Ingalls Wilder, Harper;

Fog Magic by Julia Sauer, Viking; *Rufus M.* by Eleanor Estes, Harcourt; *Mountain Born* by Elizabeth Yates, Coward

1945   *Rabbit Hill* by Robert Lawson, Viking
Honor Books: *The Hundred Dresses* by Eleanor Estes, Harcourt; *The Silver Pencil* by Alice Dalgliesh, Scribner's; *Abraham Lincoln's World* by Genevieve Foster, Scribner's; *Lone Journey: The Life of Roger Williams* by Jeanette Eaton, Harcourt

1946   *Strawberry Girl* by Lois Lenski, Lippincott
Honor Books: *Justin Morgan Had a Horse* by Marguerite Henry, Rand; *The Moved-Outers* by Florence Crannell Means, Houghton; *Bhimsa, The Dancing Bear* by Christine Weston, Scribner's; *New Found World* by Katherine Shippen, Viking

1947   *Miss Hickory* by Carolyn Sherwin Bailey, Viking
Honor Books: *Wonderful Year* by Nancy Barnes, Messner; *Big Tree* by Mary Buff and Conrad Buff, Viking; *The Heavenly Tenants* by William Maxwell, Harper; *The Avion My Uncle Flew* by Cyrus Fisher, Appleton; *The Hidden Treasure of Glaston* by Eleanore Jewett, Viking

1948   *The Twenty-one Balloons* by William Pène du Bois, Lothrop
Honor Books: *Pancakes-Paris* by Claire Huchet Bishop, Viking; *Li Lun, Lad of Courage* by Carolyn Treffinger, Abingdon; *The Quaint and Curious Quest of Johnny Longfoot* by Catherine Besterman, Bobbs; *The Cow-Tail Switch, and Other West African Stories* by Harold Courlander, Holt; *Misty of Chincoteague* by Marguerite Henry, Rand

1949   *King of the Wind* by Marguerite Henry, Rand
Honor Books: *Seabird by* by Holling C. Holling, Houghton; *Daughter of the Mountains* by Louise Rankin, Viking; *My Father's Dragon* by Ruth S. Gannett, Random; *Story of the Negro* by Arna Bontemps, Knopf

1950   *The Door in the Wall* by Marguerite de Angeli, Doubleday
Honor Books: *Tree of Freedom* by Rebecca Caudill, Viking; *The Blue Cat of Castle Town* by Catherine Coblentz, Longmans; *Kildee House* by Rutherford Montgomery, Doubleday; *George Washington* by Genevieve Foster, Scribner's; *Song of the Pines* by Walter and Marion Havighurst, Winston

1951   *Amos Fortune, Free Man* by Elizabeth Yates, Aladdin
Honor Books: *Better Known as Johnny Appleseed* by Mabel Leigh Hunt, Lippincott; *Gandhi, Fighter Without a Sword* by Jeanette Eaton, Morrow; *Abraham Lincoln, Friend of the People* by Clara Ingram Judson, Follett; *The Story of Appleby Capple* by Anne Parrish, Harper

1952   *Ginger Pye* by Eleanor Estes, Harcourt
Honor Books: *Americans Before Columbus* by Elizabeth Baity, Viking; *Minn of the Mississippi* by Holling C. Holling, Houghton; *The Defender* by Nicholas Kalashnikoff, Scribner's; *The Light at Tern Rock* by Julia Sauer, Viking; *The Apple and the Arrow* by Mary Buff and Conrad Buff, Houghton

1953   *Secret of the Andes* by Ann Nolan Clark, Viking
Honor Books: *Charlotte's Web* by E. B. White, Harper; *Moccasin Trail* by Eloise McGraw, Coward; *Red Sails to Capri* by Ann Weil, Viking;

The Bears of Hemlock Mountain by Alice Dalgliesh, Scribner's; *Birthdays of Freedom*, Vol. 1, by Genevieve Foster, Scribner's

1954 . . . And *Now Miguel* by Joseph Krumgold, Crowell
Honor Books: *All Alone* by Claire Huchet Bishop, Viking; *Shadrach* by Meindert DeJong, Harper; *Hurry Home Candy* by Meindert DeJong, Harper; *Theodore Roosevelt, Fighting Patriot* by Clara Ingram Judson, Follett; *Magic Maize* by Mary and Conrad Buff, Houghton

1955 *The Wheel on the School* by Meindert DeJong, Harper
Honor Books: *The Courage of Sarah Noble* by Alice Dalgliesh, Scribner's; *Banner in the Sky* by James Ullman, Lippincott

1956 *Carry On, Mr. Bowditch* by Jean Lee Latham, Houghton
Honor Books: *The Secret River* by Marjorie Kinnan Rawlings, Scribner's; *The Golden Name Day* by Jennie Lindquist, Harper, *Men, Microscopes, and Living Things* by Katherine Shippen, Viking

1957 *Miracles on Maple Hill* by Virginia Sorensen, Harcourt
Honor Books: *Old Yeller* by Fred Gipson, Harper; *The House of Sixty Fathers* by Meindert DeJong, Harper; *Mr. Justice Holmes* by Clara Ingram Judson, Follett; *The Corn Grows Ripe* by Dorothy Rhoads, Viking; *Black Fox of Lorne* by Marguerite de Angeli, Doubleday

1958 *Rifles for Watie* by Harold Keith, Crowell
Honor Books: *The Horsecatcher* by Mari Sandoz, Westminster, *Gone-Away Lake* by Elizabeth Enright, Harcourt; *The Great Wheel* by Robert Lawson, Viking; *Tom Paine, Freedom's Apostle* by Leo Gurko, Crowell

1959 *The Witch of Blackbird Pond* by Elizabeth George Speare, Houghton
Honor Books: *The Family Under the Bridge* by Natalie S. Carlson, Harper; *Along Came a Dog* by Meindert DeJong, Harper; *Chucaro: Wild Pony of the Pampa* by Francis Kalnay, Harcourt; *The Perilous Road* by William O. Steele, Harcourt

1960 *Onion John* by Joseph Krumgold, Crowell
Honor Books: *My Side of the Mountain* by Jean George, Dutton; *America Is Born* by Gerald W. Johnson, Morrow; *The Gammage Cup* by Carol Kendall, Harcourt

1961 *Island of the Blue Dolphins* by Scott O'Dell, Houghton
Honor Books: *America Moves Forward* by Gerald W. Johnson, Morrow; *Old Ramon* by Jack Schaefer, Houghton; *The Cricket in Times Square* by George Selden, Farrar

1962 *The Bronze Bow* by Elizabeth George Speare, Houghton
Honor Books: *Frontier Living* by Edwin Tunis, World; *The Golden Goblet* by Eloise McGraw, Coward; *Belling the Tiger* by Mary Stolz, Harper

1963 *A Wrinkle in Time* by Madeleine L'Engle, Farrar
Honor Books: *Thistle and Thyme* by Sorche Nic Leodhas, Holt; *Men of Athens* by Olivia Coolidge, Houghton

1964 *It's Like This, Cat* by Emily Cheney Neville, Harper
Honor Books: *Rascal* by Sterling North, Dutton; *The Loner* by Esther Wier, McKay

1965 *Shadow of a Bull* by Maia Wojciechowska, Atheneum
Honor Book: *Across Five Aprils* by Irene Hunt, Follett

1966   *I, Juan de Pareja* by Elizabeth Borten de Trevino, Farrar
Honor Books: *The Black Cauldron* by Lloyd Alexander, Holt; *The Animal Family* by Randall Jarrell, Pantheon; *The Noonday Friends* by Mary Stolz, Harper

1967   *Up a Road Slowly* by Irene Hunt, Follett
Honor Books: *The King's Fifth* by Scott O'Dell, Houghton; *Zlateh the Goat and Other Stories* by Isaac Bashevis Singer, Harper, *The Jazz Man* by Mary H. Weik, Atheneum

1968   *From the Mixed-Up Files of Mrs. Basil E. Frankweiler* by E. L. Konigsburg, Atheneum
Honor Books: *Jennifer, Hecate, Macbeth, William McKinley, and Me, Elizabeth* by E. L. Konigsburg, Atheneum; *The Black Pearl* by Scott O'Dell, Houghton; *The Fearsome Inn* by Isaac Bashevis Singer, Scribner's; *The Egypt Game* by Zilpha Keatley Snyder, Atheneum

1969   *The High King* by Lloyd Alexander, Holt
Honor Books: *To Be a Slave* by Julius Lester, Dial; *When Shlemiel Went to Warsaw and Other Stories* by Isaac Bashevis Singer, Farrar

1970   *Sounder* by William H. Armstrong, Harper
Honor Books: *Our Eddie* by Sulamith Ish-Kishor Pantheon; *The Many Ways of Seeing: An Introduction to the Pleasures of Art* by Janet Gaylord Moore, World; *Journey Outside* by Mary Q. Steele, Viking

1971   *Summer of the Swans* by Betsy Byars, Viking
Honor Books: *Kneeknock Rise* by Natalie Babbitt, Farrar; *Enchantress from the Stars* by Sylvia Louise Engdahl, Atheneum; *Sing Down the Moon* by Scott O'Dell, Houghton

1972   *Mrs. Frisby and the Rats of NIMH* by Robert C. O'Brien, Atheneum
Honor Books: *Incident at Hawk's Hill* by Allan W. Eckert, Little; *The Planet of Junior Brown* by Virginia Hamilton, Macmillan; *The Tombs of Atuan* by Ursula K. Le Guin, Atheneum; *Annie and the Old One* by Miska Miles, Atlantic/Little; *The Headless Cupid* by Zilpha Keatley Snyder, Atheneum

1973   *Julie of the Wolves* by Jean George, Harper
Honor Books: *Frog and Toad Together* by Arnold Lobel, Harper, *The Upstairs Room* by Johanna Reiss, Crowell; *The Witches of Worm* by Zilpha Keatley Snyder, Atheneum

1974   *The Slave Dancer* by Paula Fox, Bradbury
Honor Book: *The Dark Is Rising* by Susan Cooper, Atheneum/McElderry

1975   *M. C. Higgins, the Great* by Virginia Hamilton, Macmillan
Honor Books: *Figgs & Phantoms* by Ellen Raskin, Dutton; *My Brother Sam Is Dead* by James Lincoln Collier and Christopher Collier, Four Winds; *The Perilous Guard* by Elizabeth Marie Pope, Houghton; *Philip Hall Likes Me, I Reckon Maybe* by Bette Greene, Dial

1976   *The Grey King* by Susan Cooper, Atheneum/McElderry
Honor Books: *The Hundred Penny Box* by Sharon Bell Mathis, Viking; *Dragonwings* by Lawrence Yep, Harper

1977   *Roll of Thunder, Hear My Cry* by Mildred D. Taylor, Dial

Honor Books: *Abel's Island* by William Steig, Farrar, *A String in the Harp* by Nancy Bond, Atheneum/McElderry

1978　*Bridge to Terabithia* by Katherine Paterson, Crowell
Honor Books: *Anpao: An American Indian Odyssey* by Jamake Highwater, Lippincott; *Ramona and Her Father* by Beverly Cleary, Morrow

1979　*The Westing Game* by Ellen Raskin, Dutton
Honor Book: *The Great Gilly Hopkins* by Katherine Paterson, Crowell

1980　*A Gathering of Days: A New England Girl's Journal, 1830–32* by Joan Blos, Scribner's
Honor Book: *The Road from Home: The Story of an Armenian Girl* by David Kherdian, Greenwillow

1981　*Jacob Have I Loved* by Katherine Paterson, Crowell
Honor Books: *The Fledging* by Jane Langton, Harper; *A Ring of Endless Light* by Madeleine L'Engle, Farrar

1982　*A Visit to William Blake's Inn: Poems for Innocent and Experienced Travelers* by Nancy Willard, Harcourt
Honor Books: *Ramona Quimby, Age 8* by Beverly Cleary, Morrow; *Upon the Head of a Goat* by Aranka Siegal, Farrar

1983　*Dicey's Song* by Cynthia Voigt, Atheneum
Honor Books: *The Blue Sword* by Robin McKinley, Greenwillow; *Dr. De Soto* by William Steig, Farrar; *Graven Images* by Paul Fleischman, Harper; *Homesick: My Own Story* by Jean Fritz, Putnam; *Sweet Whispers, Brother Rush* by Virginia Hamilton, Philomel

1984　*Dear Mr. Henshaw* by Beverly Cleary, Morrow
Honor Books: *The Sign of the Beaver* by Elizabeth George Speare, Houghton; *A Solitary Blue* by Cynthia Voigt, Atheneum; *Sugaring Time* by Kathryn Lasky, Macmillan; *The Wish Giver* by Bill Brittain, Harper

1985　*The Hero and the Crown* by Robin McKinley, Greenwillow
Honor Books: *Like Jake and Me* by Mavis Jukes, Knopf; *The Moves Make the Man* by Bruce Brooks, Harper; *One-Eyed Cat* by Paula Fox, Bradbury

1986　*Sarah, Plain and Tall* by Patricia MacLachlan, Harper
Honor Books: *Commodore Perry in the Land of the Shogun* by Rhoda Blumberg, Lothrop; *Dogsong* by Gary Paulsen, Bradbury

1987　*The Whipping Boy* by Sid Fleischman, Greenwillow
Honor Books: *On My Honor* by Marion Dane Bauer, Clarion; *Volcano: The Eruption and Healing of Mount St. Helens* by Patricia Lauber, Bradbury; *A Fine White Dust* by Cynthia Rylant, Bradbury

1988　*Lincoln: A Photobiography* by Russell Freedman, Clarion/Houghton
Honor Books: *After the Rain* by Norma Fox Mazer, Morrow; *Hatchet* by Gary Paulsen, Bradbury

1989　*Joyful Noise: Poems for Two Voices* by Paul Fleischman, Harper
Honor Books: *In the Beginning: Creation Stories from Around the World* by Virginia Hamilton, Harcourt; *Scorpions* by Walter Dean Myers, Harper

1990　*Number the Stars* by Lois Lowry, Houghton
Honor Books: *Afternoon of the Elves* by Janet Lisle, Orchard Books; *Shabanu, Daughter of the Wind* by Suzanne Staples, Knopf; *Winter Room* by Gary Paulsen, Orchard Books

1991   *Maniac Magee* by Jerry Spinelli, Little
        True Confessions of Charlotte Doyle by Avi, Orchard Books

1992   *Shiloh* by Phyllis Reynolds, (Atheneum) Macmillan
        Honor Books: *Nothing But the Truth* by Avi, Orchard Books; *The Wright Brothers* by Russell Freedman, Holiday House Press

1993   *Missing May* by Cynthia Rylant, Orchard Books
        Honor Books: *What Hearts* by Bruce Brooks, HarperCollins; *The Dark-Thirty: Southern Tales of the Supernatural* by Patricia McKissack, Knopf; *Somewhere in Darkness* by William Dean Myers, Scholastic

1994   *The Giver* by Lois Lowry, Houghton Mifflin
        Honor Books: *Crazy Lady!* by Jane Leslie Conly, HarperCollins; *Dragon's Gate* by Laurence Yep, Harper Trophy; *Eleanor Roosevelt* by Russell Freedman, Clarion Books

1995   *Walk Two Moons* by Sharon Creech, HarperCollins
        Honor Books: *Catherine, Called Birdy* by Karen Cushman, Clarion Books; *The Ear, the Eye, and the Arm* by Nancy Farmer, Orchard Books

1996   *The Midwife's Apprentice* by Karen Cushman, Clarion Books
        Honor Books: *What Jamie Saw* by Carolyn Coman, Front Street; *The Watsons Go to Birmingham–1963* by Christopher Paul Curtis, Delacorte Press

1997   *The View from Saturday* by E. L. Konigsburg, Atheneum
        Honor Books: *A Girl Named Disaster* by Nancy Farmer, Orchard Books; *Moorchild* by Eloise McGraw, Margaret K. McElderry Books; *The Thief* by Megan Whalen Turner, Green Willow; *Belle Prater's Boy* by Ruth White, Farrar, Straus & Giroux

The Phoenix Award

The Phoenix Award is given by the Children's Literature Association to a book published twenty years earlier that did not receive any major award.

1985   *Mark of the Horse Lord* by Rosemary Sutcliff, Walck
1986   *Queenie Peavy* by Robert Burch, Viking
1987   *Smith* by Leon Garfield, Constable
1988   *The Rider and His Horse* by Eric Christian Haugaard, Houghton
1989   *The Night Watchman* by Helen Cresswell, Macmillan
1990   *Enchantress from the Stars* by Sylvia Louise Engdahl, Atheneum
1991   *A Long Way from Verona* by Jane Gardam, Macmillan
1992   *A Sound of Chariots* by Mollie Hunter, Harper
1993   *Carrie's War* by Nina Bawden, Harper; Honor Book: *A Proud Taste for Scarlet and Miniver* by E. L. Konigsberg, Atheneum
1994   *Of Nightingales That Weep* by Katherine Paterson, Crowell; Honor Books: *My Brother Sam Is Dead* by James Lincoln Collier and Christopher Collier, Four Winds; *Listen for the Fig Tree* by Sharon Bell Mathis, Viking
1995   *Dragonwings* by Laurence Yep, Harper & Row; Honor Book: *Tuck Everlasting* by Natalie Babbit, Farrar

1996   *The Stone Book* by Alan Garner, Collins; Honor Book: *Abel's Island* by William Steig, Farrar
1997   *I Am the Cheese* by Robert Cormier, Pantheon
1998   *A Chance Child* by Jill Paton Walsh, Macmillan
        Honor Books: *Devil in Vienna* by Doris Orgel, Dial; *Beauty* by Robin McKinley, Harper & Row

The Scott O'Dell Award for Historical Fiction

The award was established in 1981 by Mr. O'Dell and is administered by the Advisory Committee of the Bulletin of the Center for Children's Books. The book must be historical fiction, have unusual literary merit, be written by a citizen of the United States, and be set in the New World. It must have been published in the previous year by a U.S. publisher and must be written for children or young adults. There may be years when no award is given.

1984   *The Sign of the Beaver* by Elizabeth George Speare, Houghton
1985   *The Fighting Ground* by Avi [Wortis], Harper & Row
1986   *Sarah, Plain and Tall* by Patricia MacLachlan, Harper & Row
1987   *Streams to the River* by Scott O'Dell, Houghton
1988   *Charlie Skedaddle* by Patricia Beatty, Morrow
1989   *Honorable Prison* by Lyll B. De Jenkins, Lodestar
1990   *Shades of Gray* by Carolyn Reeder, Macmillan
1991   *Time of Troubles* by Pieter Van Raven, (Scribner's) Macmillan
1992   *Stepping on the Cracks* by Mary D. Hahn, (Clarion Books) Macmillan
1994   *Bull Run* by Paul Fleischman
1995   *Under the Blood Red Sun* by Graham Salisbury
1996   *The Bomb* by Theodore Taylor
1997   *Jip: His Story* by Katherine Paterson

The Orbis Pictus Award for Outstanding Nonfiction

Established in 1990 by the National Council of Teachers of English (NCTE) to recognize excellence in nonfiction writing, the name commemorates *Orbis Pictus* (1657), considered the first informational book written for children.

1990   *The Great Little Madison* by Jean Fritz; Honor Books: *The Great American Gold Rush* by Rhoda Blumberg; *The News About Dinosaurs* by Patricia Lauber
1991   *Franklin Delano Roosevelt* by Russell Freedman; Honor Books: *Seeing Earth from Space* by Patricia Lauber; *Arctic Memories* by Normee Ekoomiak

1992   *Flight: The Journey of Charles Lindbergh* by Robert Burleigh; Honor Books: *Now Is Your Time! The African-American Struggle for Freedom* by Walter Dean Myers; *Prairie Vision: The Life and Times of Solomon Butcher* by Pam Conrad

1993   *Children of the Dust Bowl: The True Story of the School at Weedpatch Camp* by Jerry Stanley; Honor Books: *Talking to Artists* by Pat Cummings; *Come Back, Salmon* by Molly Cone

1994   *Across America on an Emigrant Train* by Jim Murphy; Honor Books: *To the Top of the World: Adventures with Arctic Wolves* by Jim Brandenburg; *Making Sense: Animal Perception and Communication* by Bruce Brooks

1995   *Safari Beneath the Sea: The Wonder World of the North Pacific Coast* by Diane Swanson; Honor Book: *Wildlife Rescue: The Work of Dr. Kathleen Ramsay* by Jennifer Owings Dewey

1996   *The Great Fire* by Jim Murphy; Honor Books: *Dolphin Man: Exploring the World of Dolphins* by Laurence Pringle; *Rosie the Riveter: Women Working on the Home Front in World War II* by Penny Colman

1997   *Leonardi da Vinci* by Diane Stanley; Honor Books: *Full Steam Ahead: The Race to Build a Transcontinental Railroad* by Rhoda Blumberg; *The Life and Death of Crazy Horse* by Russell Freedman; *One World, Many Religions: The Ways We Worship* by Mary Pope Osborne

B

Selected Magazines for Children

American Girl. Pleasant Company, Box 998, Middleton, WI 53562

Boy's Life (boys 8 to 15). Boy Scouts of America, P. O. Box 15279, Irving, TX 75015

Calliope (world history). Cobblestone Publications, Inc., 30 Grove Street, Peterborough, NH 46206

Chickadee (preschoolers). Young Naturalist Foundation, P. O. Box 11314, Des Moines, IA 50340

Cobblestone (history). Cobblestone Publishing, Inc., 30 Grove Street, Peterborough, NH 46206

Cricket. Carus Corporation, P. O. Box 300, Peru, IL 61354

Dolphin Log (underwater life). Cousteau Society, Inc., 8440 Santa Monica Blvd., Los Angeles, CA 90069

Dragon Fly. National Science Teachers Association, American Association for the Advancement of Science, 1840 Wilson Boulevard, Arlington, VA 22201

Ebony, Jr. 820 South Michigan Avenue, Chicago, IL 60605

Faces (anthropology and natural history). Cobblestone Publishing, Inc., 30 Grove Street, Peterborough, NH 46206

Highlights for Children. P. O. Box 269, Columbus, OH 43272

Hopscotch (girls 6 to 12) P. O. Box 1292, Saratoga Springs, NY 12866

Kid City. Children's Television Workshop, 1 Lincoln Plaza, New York, NY 10023

Ladybug. Carus Corporation, P. O. Box 51145, Boulder, CO 80323

McGuffey Writer. McGuffey Foundation School, Route 27, Oxford, OH 45056

National Geographic World. National Geographic Society, P. O. Box 2330, Washington, DC 20077

New Moon. New Moon Publishing Company, P.O. Box 3587, Duluth, MN 55803

Odyssey (astronomy). Kalmbach Publishing Co., 21027 Crossroads Circle, Box 1612, Waukesha, WI 53187

Owl (science and nature). Young Naturalist Foundation, P. O. Box 11314, Des Moines, IA 50340

Ranger Rick (animals and environment). National Wildlife Federation, 8925 Leesburg Pike, Vienna, VA 22184

Seedling Stories. Short Story International. International Cultural Exchange, 6 Sheffield Road, Great Neck, NY 11021

Spider. Carus Publishing Company, Cricket Magazine Group, 315 Fifth Street, Peru, IL 61354

Sports Illustrated for Kids. P.O.Box 830609, Birmingham, AL 35283

3-2-1/Contact (Science, natural history, technology). Children's Television Workshop, 1 Lincoln Plaza, New York, NY 10023

Wonder Science. American Chemical Society, 1155 Sixteenth Street NW, Washington, DC 20036

Your Big Backyard (nature). National Wildlife Federation, 8925 Leesburg Pike, Vienna, VA 22184

Zillions. Consumer Union, 101 Truman Avenue, Yonkers, NY 10703

Selected Reviewing Media for Children's Books

Appraisal (science books)
ALA (American Library Association)
Booklist
The ALAN Review
Bulletin of the Center for Children's Books
Children's Catalog
Children's Literature Assembly Bulletin (NCTE)
The Horn Book Magazine
Kirkus Reviews
Language Arts
Library Journal
Library Talk
The New Advocate
Parents' Choice
Publishers Weekly
Reading Teacher
School Library Journal
Science Books and Films
VOYA—Voice of Youth Advocates
Wilson Library Journal

Glossary of Literary Terms

Allegory   A literary work in which characters and actions represent abstractions.

Alliteration   Repetition of initial consonant sound.

Allusion   Indirect reference to something or someone outside the literary work.

Antagonist   Force in conflict with protagonist: usually designated as self, another person, society, nature.

Anthropomorphism   The giving of human qualities to nonhumans—animals or objects.

Assonance   Repetition of vowel sound in phrase.

Backdrop setting   Generalized or relatively unimportant setting.

Ballad   Verse narrative of love, courage, the supernatural. May be of folk origin.

Biography   The history of the life of an individual.

Cadence   Rhythmic flow in prose.

Character   Human being, real or personified animal or object taking a role in literature.

Character development   Filling out a variety of character traits to provide the complexity of a human being.

Chronological order   Events related in the order of their happening.

Classic   Literary work that lives to be read and reread.

Cliché   Overused term that has lost meaning.

Cliff-hanger   Unresolved suspense that concludes a chapter.

Climax   Action that precipitates resolution of conflict.

Closed ending   Conclusion leaving no plot questions unanswered.

Coincidence   Chance concurrence of events.

Complication   Early action; part of rising plot.

Concept   An idea around which a work may be written.

Condescension   An attitude or tone that underestimates the reader.

Conflict   Struggle between protagonist and opposing force.

Connotation   Associative or emotional meaning of a word.

Consonance   Repetition of consonant sound in phrase.

Cumulative tale   A story, often folk in origin, that continually repeats a series, then adds a new item.

Denotation   Explicit or dictionary meaning.

Denouement   Final or closing action following climax.

Diction   Choice of words or wording.

Didacticism   In literature, an instructive or moralistic lesson often at the expense of entertainment.

Distanced tone   An attitude of objectivity through which a story is told.

Dramatic point of view   *See* objective or dramatic point of view.

Dynamic character   One who changes in the course of the story.

Echo   Words repeated in familiar pattern.

End rhyme   Rhyming words at the ends of poetic lines.

Epic   Long narrative poem about a heroic figure whose actions reveal the values of the culture.

Episodic plot   Plot with independent, short-story-like chapters linked by characters or theme more than by action.

Explicit theme   Theme stated clearly in the story.

Exposition   Presentation of essential information needed for understanding of the action.

Fable   Brief story, usually with animal characters, that states a didactic theme or moral.

Falling action   Final or closing action following climax; denouement.

Fantasy   Story about the nonexistent or unreal in which action may depend on magic or the supernatural.

Figurative language   Devices making comparisons, saying one thing in terms of another.

First-person point of view   "I" narration in which a person's experiences, thoughts, and feelings are told by himself or herself.

Flashback   Return to event that occurred before present scene; retrospect.

Flat character   One that is little developed.

Foil   A character whose contrasting traits point up those of a central character.

Folk epic   Long narrative poem passed down by word of mouth; often about a hero.

Folk rhyme   Rhymes passed down by word of mouth.

Folktale   Story passed down by word of mouth.

Foreshadowing   Hints of what is to come.

Formula fiction   Fiction with a hackneyed sequence of events.

Frame   Framework in which a story is set, frequently noted at beginning and end.

Genre   A kind or type of literature that has a common set of characteristics.

High fantasy   A type of fantasy characterized by conflict between good and evil.

Hyperbole   Exaggeration or overstatement.

Imagery   Verbal appeals to the senses.

Implicit theme   Theme implied from the story's context.

Inevitability   Sense that it had to happen; in literature a sense that the outcome was necessary and inescapable.

Integral setting   Essential and specific setting that influences character, plot, and theme.

Internal rhymes   Rhymes in a line that are after first and before last words.

Irony   Recognition of reality different from what it truly is.

Legend   A traditional narrative of a people, often with some basis in historical truth.

Limerick   Five-line humorous verse with traditional rhythm and rhyme pattern.

Limited omniscient point of view   Third-person narration in which story is seen through the mind(s) of one or a few characters.

Lyric poem   Songlike poem; compact expression of feeling.

Metaphor   Implied comparison.

Meter   Somewhat regular rhythm pattern of stressed and unstressed syllables in a line of poetry.

Motif   Recurring element in literary work, often found in traditional literature.

Myth   Story originating in folk beliefs and showing supernatural forces operating.

Narrative order   Sequence in which events are recounted.

Narrative poem   Poem that tells a story.

Objective or dramatic point of view   Third-person narration in which actions and speeches are recorded without interpretation.

Omniscient point of view   An all-knowing writer tells the story in third person.

Onomatopoeia   Words that sound like their meanings, such as *meow, moo*.

Open ending   Final outcome of conflict unknown.

Parody   Imitation of known form for comic effect.

Personification   Giving human traits to nonhuman beings or objects.

Phonetic intensive   Use of sound to enhance meaning.

Picture book   A book that relies on pictures to enlarge or illuminate the text; the pictures may even provide a correlative story of their own.

Plot   Sequence of events involving character in conflict.

Poetry   Distilled and imaginative expression of feeling.

Point of view   The mind(s) through which the reader sees the story.

Pourquoi   Tales that respond to the question "why?"

Primary theme   Major underlying and unifying truth of a story.

Progressive plot   Plot with central climax.

Protagonist   Central character in the conflict.

Pun   Humorous use of a word with several meanings.

Realism   Story based on the possible, though not necessarily probable.

Resolution   Falling action following climax.

Rhyme   Repetition of identical or similar stressed sound or sounds.

Rhythm   Recurring flow of strong and weak beats.

Rising action   Exposition and complications that lead to the climax.

Romance   Story with scenes and incidents remote from ordinary life.

Romantic novel   Story focuses on boy-girl relationships.

Round character   A fully developed or three-dimensional character.

Science fiction   Story that relies on invention or extension of nature's laws, not on the supernatural or magical.

Secondary theme   Less important or minor theme of a story.

Sensationalism   Focus on the thrilling or startling.

Sentiment   Emotion or feeling.

Sentimentality   Overuse of sentiment; false arousal of feelings.

Setting   The time and place in which the action occurs.

Simile   Stated comparison, usually using *like* or *as*.

Sound effect   Any device of sound that affects meaning.

Static character   One who does not change in the course of the story.

Stereotype   Character possessing expected traits of a group rather than being an individual.

Stock character   Flat character with very little development; found in numerous stories, such as folktales.

Style   Mode of expression.

Suspense   State of uncertainty that keeps the reader reading.

Symbol   Person, object, situation, or action operating on two levels of meaning—literal and figurative or suggestive.

Synesthia   Simultaneous appeal to several senses.

Theme   Statement giving the underlying truth about people, society, or the human condition, either explicitly or implicitly.

Tone   Writer's attitude toward his or her subject and readers.

Touchstone   Example of excellence referred to for comparison.

Understatement   Reverse exaggeration or playing down.

Verse   Here used to denote rhyming metrical structure with less emotional intensity than poetry.

Vicarious experience   Experience available to readers through reading about it rather than living it.

Wordless picture book   A book that has no written narrative but tells a story with pictures alone.

Acknowledgments

Art Acknowledgments

p. 2: Illustration from *Charlotte's Web* by E. B. White, illustrated by Garth Williams. Copyright © 1952, renewed 1980 by E. B. White. Illustrations copyright © 1952, renewed 1980 by Garth Williams. Reprinted by permission of HarperCollins Publishers.

p. 12: Illustration from *Where the Buffaloes Begin* by Olaf Baker, drawings by Stephen Gammell. Copyright © 1981 by Stephen Gammell, illustrations. Used by permission of Frederick Warne Books, a division of Penguin Books USA, Inc.

p. 40: Illustration from *The Girl Who Loved Wild Horses* by Paul Goble. Reprinted with the permission of Simon & Schuster Books for Young Readers, an imprint of Simon & Schuster Children's Publishing Division. Copyright © 1978 by Paul Goble.

p. 78: Illustration from *The Boy of the Three-Year Nap* by Dianne Snyder. Illustration © 1988 by Allen Say. Reprinted by permission of Houghton Mifflin Company. All rights reserved.

p. 102: Illustration from *The Trees of the Dancing Goats* by Patricia Polacco. Reprinted with the permission of Simon & Schuster Books for Young Readers, an imprint of Simon & Schuster Children's Publishing Division. Copyright © 1996 by Patricia Polacco.

p. 134: Illustration from *Uncle Jed's Barber Shop* by Margaree King Mitchell, illustrated by James Ransome. Reprinted with the permission of Simon & Schuster Children's Publishing Division. Illustrations copyright © 1993 by James Ransome.

p. 152: Illustration from *At the Crossroads* by Rachel Isadora, illustrated by Rachel Isadora. Copyright © 1991 by Rachel Isadora Turner. Reprinted by permission of Greenwillow Books, a division of William Morrow & Company, Inc.

p. 174: Illustration from *Do You Know Me?* by Nancy Farmer, illustrated by Shelley Jackson. Illustration copyright © 1993 by Shelley Jackson. Reprinted by permission of Orchard Books, New York.

p. 194: Illustration from *Hiawatha* by Henry Wadsworth Longfellow, pictures by Susan Jeffers. Copyright © 1983 by Susan Jeffers for pictures. Used by permission of Dial Books for Young Readers, a division of Penguin Books USA, Inc.

p. 216: Illustration from *Alice's Adventures in Wonderland* by Lewis Carroll (1865), illustrated by John Tenniel.

p. 246: Illustration from *Madeline's Rescue* by Ludwig Bemelmans. Copyright © 1951, 1953 by Ludwig Bemelmans. Copyright renewed © 1979, 1981 by Madeleine Bemelmans and Barbara B. Marciano. All rights reserved. Used by permission of Viking Penguin, a division of Penguin Books USA, Inc.

p. 280: Illustration from *My Dream of Martin Luther King* by Faith Ringgold. Copyright © 1995 by Faith Ringgold. Reprinted by permission of Crown Publishers.

p. 296: Illustration from *The Way Things Work* by David Macaulay. "The Can Opener" from *The Way Things Work* by David Macaulay. Compilation copyright © 1988 by Dorling Kindersley, Ltd. Text copyright © 1988 by David Macaulay and Neil Ardley. Illustrations copyright © 1988 by David Macaulay. Reprinted by permission of Houghton Mifflin Company. All rights reserved.

Literary Acknowledgments

Arnold Adoff. "Let the Biter Beware," from *Chocolate Dreams* by Arnold Adoff. Copyright © 1989 by Arnold Adoff. By permission of Lothrop, Lee & Shepard Books, a division of William Morrow & Company, Inc.

Dorothy Aldis. "Fourth of July Night," from *Hop, Skip and Jump* by Dorothy Aldis. Copyright © 1934, 1961 by Dorothy Aldis. Reprinted by permission of G. P. Putnam's Sons.

Anonymous. "Falling Snow," from *A Book of Children's Literature,* ed. Lillian Hollowell. New York: Rinehart & Co., 1939.

Harry Behn. "Circles," from *The Little Hill: Poems & Pictures* by Harry Behn. Copyright © 1949 by Harry Behn. Copyright renewed 1977 by Alice L. Behn. Used by permission of Marian Reiner.

Emily Dickinson. "The moon was but a chin of gold" and "There is no frigate like a book," from *The Complete Poems of Emily Dickinson*. Reprinted by permission of the publishers and the Trustees of Amherst College from *The Poems of Emily Dickinson*, Thomas H. Johnson, ed. Cambridge, Mass: The Belknap Press of Harvard University Press. Copyright © 1951, 1955, 1979, 1983 by the President and Fellows of Harvard College.

Aileen Fisher. "At Night," from *Out in Dark and Daylight* by Aileen Fisher. Copyright © 1980 by Aileen Fisher. Reprinted by permission of author.

Robert Francis. "The Base Stealer," from *The Orb Weaver* by Robert Francis. Copyright © 1960 by Robert Francis, Wesleyan University Press by permission of University Press of New England.

Nikki Giovanni. "The Drum," from *Spin a Soft Black Song* by Nikki Giovanni, illustrated by George Martins. Copyright © 1971, 1985 by Nikki Giovanni. Illustration copyright © 1985 by George Martins. Reprinted by permission of Hill and Wang, a division of Farrar, Straus & Giroux, Inc.

Jim Hall. "White Trash," from *False Statements* by Jim Hall. Copyright © 1986 by Jim Hall. Reprinted by permission of Carnegie Mellon University Press.

Langston Hughes. "Dream Deferred," from *Collected Poems* by Langston Hughes. Copyright © 1994 by the Estate of Langston Hughes. Reprinted by permission of Alfred A. Knopf, Inc.; "I Loved My Friend," from *Collected Poems* by Langston Hughes. Copyright © 1994 by the Estate of Langston Hughes. Reprinted by permission of Alfred A. Knopf, Inc.

Evelyn Tooley Hunt. "Mama Is a Sunrise," from *The Lyric* by Evelyn Tooley Hunt. Copyright © 1972 and reprinted by permission of the author.

X. J. Kennedy. "A Choosy Wolf," from *The Phantom Ice Cream Man*. Copyright © 1975 by X. J. Kennedy. Reprinted by permission of Curtis Brown, Ltd.

Vachel Lindsay. From "The Moon's the North Wind's Cooky," from *Collected Poems of Vachel Lindsay*. Copyright © 1925 by Macmillan Publishing Company, renewed 1953 by Elizabeth C. Lindsay. Reprinted with the permission of Simon & Schuster.

Myra Cohn Livingston. "74th Street," from *The Malibu and Other Poems* by Myra Cohn Livingston. Copyright © 1972 by Myra Cohn Livingston. Reprinted by permission of Marian Reiner.

Eve Merriam. Excerpted from "Inside a Poem," from *It Doesn't Always Have to Rhyme* by Eve Merriam. Copyright © 1964. Copyright renewed © 1992 by Eve Merriam. Reprinted by permission of Marian Reiner.

Lillian Moore. "Bike Ride," from *Think of Shadows* by Lillian Moore. Copyright © 1975, 1980 by Lillian Moore. Used by permission of Marian Reiner for the author.

Lillian Morrison. "Forms of Praise," from *The Sidewalk Racer and Other Poems of Sports and Motion* by Lillian Morrison. Copyright © 1965, 1968, 1977 by Lillian Morrison. Reprinted by permission of Marian Reiner for the author.

Elizabeth Madox Roberts. "The Worm," from *Under the Tree* by Elizabeth Madox Roberts. Copyright © 1922 by B. W. Huebsch, Inc., renewed 1950 by Ivor S. Roberts. Copyright © 1930 by Viking Penguin, Inc., renewed © 1958 by Ivor S. Roberts. Used by permission of Viking Penguin, a division of Penguin Books USA, Inc.

Carl Sandberg. "Lost," from *Chicago Poems* by Carl Sandberg, copyright © 1916 by Holt, Rinehart and Winston and renewed 1944 by Carl Sandberg. Reprinted by permission of Harcourt Brace & Company.

Alice Schertle. "Iguana," from *Advice for a Frog* by Alice Schertle. Copyright © 1995 by Alice Schertle. By permission of Lothrop, Lee & Shepard Books, a division of William Morrow & Company, Inc.

Kaye Starbird. "That Morning in June," from *The Covered Bridge House and Other Poems* by Kaye Starbird. Copyright © 1979 by Kaye Starbird Jennison. Used by permission of Marian Reiner.

John Updike. "October," from *A Child's Calendar* by John Updike. Copyright © 1965 by John Updike and Nancy Burkert. Reprinted by permission of Alfred A. Knopf, Inc.

E. B. White. Excerpts from *Charlotte's Web* by E. B. White, illustrated by Garth Williams. Copyright © 1952 by E. B. White. Renewed © 1980 by E. B. White. Illustrations copyright © 1952, renewed 1980 by Garth Williams. Reprinted by permission of HarperCollins Publishers, Inc.

Janet S. Wong. "Asians Are Supposed to Be Good at Math," from *Good Luck Gold and Other Poems* by Janet S. Wong. Copyright © 1994 Janet S. Wong. Reprinted with permission of Margaret K. McElderry Books, an imprint of Simon & Schuster Children's Publishing Division.

Annette Wynne. Reuse of "I Keep Three Wishes Ready," from *All Through the Year: Three Hundred and Sixty-five New Poems for Holidays and Every Day* by Annette Wynne (J.B. Lippincott). Copyright © 1932, 1960 by Annette Wynne. Reprinted with permission of HarperCollins Publishers, Inc.

Index